Urban Politics

D0514491

Sociology editor
Howard Newby

Senior Lecturer in Sociology
University of Essex

Urban Politics
A Sociological Interpretation

Peter Saunders

Lecturer in Sociology
School of Cultural and Community Studies
University of Sussex

Hutchinson

London Melbourne Sydney Auckland Johannesburg

Hutchinson & Co. (Publishers) Ltd
An imprint of the Hutchinson Publishing Group
17 – 21 Conway Street, London W1P 6JD

Hutchinson Group (Australia) Pty Ltd
30 – 32 Cremorne Street, Richmond South, Victoria 3121
PO Box 151, Broadway, New South Wales 2007

Hutchinson Group (NZ) Ltd
32 – 34 View Road, PO Box 40 – 086, Glenfield, Auckland 10

Hutchinson Group (SA) (Pty) Ltd
PO Box 337, Bergvlei 2012, South Africa

First published in hardback 1979
First published in paperback by Penguin 1980
This edition 1983

Printed in Great Britain by The Anchor Press Ltd
and bound by Wm Brendon & Son Ltd
both of Tiptree, Essex

British Library Cataloguing in Publication Data

Saunders, Peter, 1950-
  Urban politics.
  1. Metropolitan government – Great Britain 2. Great
  Britain – Politics and government – 1964-
  I. Title
  306'.2'0941   JS3091

ISBN 0 09 153111 X

Contents

Part 2 Empirical applications

Preface

This book is the culmination of a project which started in 1971 and which has occupied my attention, on and off, for the best part of a decade. The project began when I decided to conduct a case study of power and influence at the local level of British politics. The case study itself, which was based in the London Borough of Croydon, took just two years to complete, and in that period I managed to develop a number of insights into the relationship between a local authority and groups such as big business, council tenants and suburban owner-occupiers. Like all case studies, however, this research encountered two related problems. First, it was unclear how far the conclusions that were drawn from it could be generalized to other comparable towns and cities in Britain. Indeed, many of the central findings received little support from existing case study material. Secondly, there was a problem of how the empirical findings related to specific theoretical questions concerning the nature of political power; the relationship between the state and social classes, between class interests and political action and so on. Clearly, taken by itself, the Croydon research was interesting but inadequate.

In the years which followed this research, however, a number of stimulating theoretical developments took place in British urban studies, largely in response to the discovery of French Marxist urban theory. The more I read of this material, the more convinced I became that it not only had direct relevance to the Croydon study, but also that it could usefully be evaluated in the context of this study. So it was that, after a number of false starts, the present book began to take shape, the intention being to provide a critical analysis of certain key issues concerning British urban politics on the basis of both theoretical and empirical argument.

The book itself is organized into two sections. In Part 1 I consider some of the theoretical problems which are now at the centre of debate in urban sociology in Britain, and in Part 2 I attempt to situate these in the context of empirical material taken from the Croydon case study. These two sections could conceivably be read in isolation from each other, and given that a book like this is addressed both to the academic community with its (not always consistent) criteria of adequacy, and to the informed public with its (not unreasonable) expectations that it should provide some firm and intelligible conclusions, there is an obvious danger that the former may gravitate to Part 1 while the latter turn straight to Part 2. Such selectivity on the part of the reader would be unfortunate, however, for I have written the book in the belief that theoretical and empirical work must necessarily complement each other. Just as empirical case studies are of limited value unless they address key theoretical questions, so too theoretical debate tends to become sterile unless it is informed by empirical research. The two sections of the book are thus closely interrelated.

Inevitably, given the relatively long gestation period of this book, I have incurred many personal and intellectual debts since the project first began, and a preface provides a formal opportunity for acknowledging at least some of these. In particular I must express my thanks to John MacDonald, who supervised the initial research during my two years at Chelsea College, and to Ray Pahl, who has provided me with consistent help and guidance. After leaving Chelsea, I spent three fruitful years at the University of Essex where I benefited enormously from the suggestions and encouragement of Howard Newby and (before he left for the Antipodes) Colin Bell, and since 1976 I have similarly gained much from discussions with colleagues in the urban studies and sociology subject groups at the University of Sussex, and particularly from fellow members of the urban studies 'Monday Club'. In addition, a number of people have contributed directly to my work on this book, either by commenting on earlier drafts, or by helping with specific problems, and these include Jenny Backwell, Ray Barrell, Steve Chibnall, Mary Farmer, Michael Filby, Rob Flynn, David Harrison, Ray Holland, Nelson Polsby, Damaris Rose, David Rose, Sue Saunders, Martin Weegman and Barry Wood, as well as the students on my Cities and Society course at Sussex in 1977.

Some of the chapters in Part 1 have benefited from earlier exposure at seminars and conferences, and I should like to acknowledge the helpful comments and criticisms made on these occasions by participants at the SSRC stratification seminar at Cambridge, the sociology and urban and regional studies seminars at Sussex, the urban and regional research seminar at Kent, and the 1978 Institute of Local Government Studies conference on central–local relations at Birmingham. From 1971 to 1973 my research was funded by Chelsea College, London, and I was and remain most grateful for this support. Finally, I should also express my sincere gratitude to all those in Croydon who gave up their time to help me in my research. To these, and to other friends and colleagues, many thanks.

Part 1
Theoretical perspectives

Introduction

For a number of years after the Second World War, urban sociology in Britain appeared to be declining gently into its dotage. Useful empirical work was still being produced, not least the various studies during the 1950s of working class community life, but urban social theory was stagnant and had failed in most cases to go beyond the parameters formulated in the 1920s by the Chicago school of human ecologists. In the last few years, however, the discipline has been experiencing something of a revival due first to the increased emphasis on political factors in the work of Rex, Pahl and others in the 1960s, and more recently to the infusion of Continental Marxist urban theories which have raised fundamental questions about the relationship between the city and capitalist political economy. Urban sociology today is thus witnessing a resurgence of intense and challenging theoretical debate, and at the centre of this are a number of crucial questions concerning urban politics.

The purpose of this book is critically to examine some of the major and contentious issues which are now at the forefront of debate. Each of the four chapters in Part 1 focuses on a specific theoretical or conceptual problem raised in recent work, while the chapters in Part 2 attempt to consider these arguments in the light of an empirical study conducted in the early 1970s in a London borough. Taken as a whole, the book thus represents an attempt to review and assess the contribution of recent theoretical and empirical work to the sociology of urban politics. This appears a particularly important task at this time if we are to avoid replacing the somewhat sterile empiricism which characterized British urban sociology until a few years ago with the straitjacket of a new theoretical orthodoxy applied uniformly to the explanation of a wide range of problems. In gratefully making good our escape from the devil of 'abstracted empiricism', we must beware the deep blue sea of 'grand theory' (see Mills 1959). In the chapters that follow, I hope to indicate some of the areas where the new urban sociology has itself to be questioned if the revival of the discipline is not to degenerate into a series of doctrinal assertions and bland solutions.

The belief which underlies these chapters is that no single body of theory and no one paradigm can be expected to provide all the answers to the questions currently being posed in urban sociology, and that a degree of theoretical pluralism and epistemological tolerance is thus an essential precondition for the future development of the discipline. This is not to accept uncritically the Popperian view of science as an 'open society', nor is it to suggest that the different approaches can or should be reconciled and integrated (such questions of methodology are considered in Chapter 9). It is, however, to suggest that, while the new Marxist approaches may be useful and applicable in some areas, they are less so in others, and that dogmatic assertions of the scientificity of historical materialism and of the ideological basis of all alternative approaches can only stifle debate under the blanket of a new orthodoxy. It is particularly important that British urban sociology retain its critical faculties in the face of these new developments, for there are good reasons for arguing that a theory developed in the rather special circumstances of contemporary France and Italy may be less than entirely appropriate in the British context, irrespective of the question of its internal validity. This point can usefully be illustrated with reference to two of the key themes developed in the Marxist approaches to urban politics: the problem of the local state (discussed in Chapter 4), and the question of urban social movements (discussed in Chapter 3).

The problem of analysing the role of the state in advanced capitalist societies involves a host of complex issues which are currently the subject of an intense and often fruitful debate, both within Marxist theory itself, and between it and various non-Marxist approaches. This debate has been of particular significance for the study of urban politics, for its implications as regards the reasons and functions of state intervention through planning and the provision of services such as housing, roads and education are clearly relevant for any analysis of the 'local state'. Although the flavour of this debate has often been somewhat abstract and rarefied, it is possible to discern three principal positions within it, two of them Marxist and one broadly Weberian.

The position which has found considerable favour among many British writers (as well as their counterparts in western Europe and the United States) has been what I term in Chapter 4 the 'structuralist' perspective. This derives out of the attempt by Nicos Poulantzas to explain how the state in advanced capitalist societies necessarily performs a dual role, safeguarding the long-term interests of big monopoly capital on the one hand while buying off the working class through a reformist strategy on the other. This approach has been developed in the context of urban administration by Manuel Castells, who suggests that the role of the state in regulating land use through planning or in providing collective urban facilities can only be explained by means of a theory of the state which recognizes both its relative autonomy from any one class and its necessary long-term function in supporting the profitability of monopoly capital. The role of the local state is thus explained with reference to the necessary structural relationship between the various economic class interests, the political forces which represent these class interests, and the state which constitutes the expression of these political forces.

The two principal alternatives to this theory have both been developed as much in Britain as on the Continent. One, the instrumentalist perspective, while associated with various European Communist parties and their theories of state monopoly capitalism, has also been developed by Ralph Miliband in his study of the capitalist state in Britain; the other, the managerialist approach, represents a development of Weber's ideas by writers such as John Rex and Ray Pahl whose chief concerns have been with British local government processes. Both of these approaches, unlike the various 'representational' theories of liberal democracy, recognize the partiality of state policies, but they differ markedly from each other (and from structuralist theories) in the way in which such bias is conceptualized and explained. For Miliband, the state represents an instrument by means of which class domination is achieved politically; it is largely controlled by members of the bourgeoisie, it is influenced most strongly by members of the bourgeoisie and its policies are evolved in the context of an economic system whose perpetuation favours the bourgeoisie. For the managerialists, on the other hand, the state is an instrument controlled by officials, and the goals and values of these officials are thus crucial in determining policy outcomes. Poulantzas and Castells, however, dismiss both of these approaches as invalid, the former because it underemphasizes the autonomy of the state from the dominant classes, the latter because it overemphasizes it. Furthermore, both perspectives are seen as basically ideological rather than scientific since they focus on the actions of individuals rather than on classes and class forces which are considered to be the only correct theoretical tools for political analysis. For the structuralists, the state is not a 'thing' to be controlled by the whims of businessmen or bureaucrats, but is a relation which necessarily expresses the relative power of different classes and class fractions.

In surveying this debate, one can only agree with Pickvance and others who have suggested that empirical evidence on governmental policy-making is necessary if the different perspectives are to be assessed. There are problems, of course, concerning the relation between theoretical and empirical work, and some of these are discussed in Chapter 9, but it should be clear that a one-sided theoreticism is likely to prove as sterile as a one-sided empiricism, and that structuralist perspectives in particular are often characterized by the development of elaborate theories whose complexity varies in inverse proportion to their empirical applicability. The growth in the popularity of the structuralist approach in British urban studies has led to the rejection of any attempt to explain state policies in terms of the actions of politically powerful individuals, on the grounds that such explanations are naive and rest on metaphysical speculations about free will. Yet, as I argue in Chapter 4, the instrumentalist and managerialist perspectives have too readily been dismissed as simplistic, and have been replaced by theories which are inherently immune to empirical test. Furthermore, there are strong grounds for arguing that, in the British context at least, the insights developed by writers such as Miliband and Pahl can contribute to a very fruitful theory of the relation between the state and various economic interests – a theory which readily lends itself to empirical application.

The impact of the new Marxist urban theory has been apparent, not only in discussions of urban management and the local state, but also in the development of interest in urban class struggles; this is discussed in Chapter 3. Britain, of course, can boast no equivalent to the May events in Paris in 1968, nor to the outbreaks of popular unrest in Italian cities through the 1970s, but ever since Castells produced his theory of 'urban social movements', sporadic examples in Britain of squatting movements, rent strikes, anti-redevelopment protests and so on have assumed a new significance for some observers. The traditional concerns of British urban sociology with community pressure groups and voluntary associations have thus been supplanted by the analysis of potentially revolutionary urban social movements. But, as with the discussion of the local state, the question which all this raises is how far the new Marxist theory is appropriate for analysing such urban protests as do develop in this country.

The argument developed by Castells is basically that crises in the provision by the state of various facilities such as housing, schools, hospitals, etc., give the opportunity for new sources of class struggle to emerge around issues of consumption. These struggles facilitate the development of popular alliances (e.g. between tenants and shopkeepers) against monopoly capital and the state, and thus serve to broaden and strengthen the class struggle in society as a whole. This and similar arguments have found a receptive audience in British urban studies, yet there are at least three reasons for doubting their relevance to the analysis of urban protest in this country.

The first is that the class structure in Britain is very different from that of France or Italy. There are a number of reasons for this, but the important point which follows from it is that working class radicalism appears much stronger on the Continent than in Britain. The second point, which is related to this, is that France and Italy have effective and highly organized Communist parties which are capable of directing sporadic urban protests and integrating them into the broader working class movement. Castells himself has warned that, in the absence of such party organizations, urban protests are unlikely to achieve any significant degree of success since they occur around issues of consumption rather than production. This is a warning which should not be ignored by Marxists in Britain. The third point is that the growth of owner-occupation in Britain has had a highly significant effect in generating greater class fission in the urban context, and this directly contradicts a theory premised on the view that urban struggles broaden class alliances.

This question of the political significance of the spread of home ownership must clearly be central to any analysis of urban politics, for housing is the most significant element of consumption in the urban system. Most of the struggles which occur outside the factory gate are related directly to questions of housing, and in Britain, with some 50 per cent of families in the owner-occupied sector, such conflicts often occur between political groups expressing tenure divisions (tenants' associations, residents' associations and so on). The problem of how to analyse the political significance of tenure divisions is thus fundamental, and Chapter 2 is devoted to this question.

To the extent that Marxists have considered the problem of the spread of home ownership among the British working class, they have generally argued that the divisions it creates are ideological rather than economic. Put simply, the argument is that owner-occupation may serve to obscure class divisions, but it does not change them. This conclusion runs directly counter to the Weberian approach developed by John Rex in his concept of 'housing classes', for Rex sees tenure as an analytically separate basis for class formations. In Chapter 2, I consider both of these perspectives and argue that, while tenure categories cannot be conceived as classes, nor can the political divisions to which they give rise be dismissed as ideological since owner-occupation entails a potential source of wealth accumulation which can result in a conflict of economic interests between owners and non-owners. The conclusion derived from this is that political struggles over housing (or, indeed, over any other urban resources) cannot be directly related to economic class struggles as contemporary Marxist theory suggests. Furthermore, it also follows that such struggles, far from laying the foundation for a popular class alliance will necessarily generate new political divisions, the battle lines being drawn in different ways in different issues. It may be that in countries such as France and Italy, where rates of owner-occupancy are much lower and do not generally cross-cut economic class divisions, housing struggles do open up the possibility for broader alliances; but this is not the case in Britain, and the theory of urban social movements does not therefore appear very useful in this context.

The applicability of this theory to the situation in Britain can also be assessed empirically, and Chapter 3 includes a brief review of recent evidence on urban protest in this country. The conclusion drawn from this is that such protests have rarely transcended the limits of what Castells terms 'consumer trade unionism', i.e. the pursuit of short-term economic advantages within the existing political framework. Indeed, the picture which emerges quite strongly from the available evidence is that subordinate groups have generally experienced a fundamental dilemma of political activism which they have failed to resolve: whether to act within the system but thereby fail to pose an effective challenge, or to mobilize from outside the system (i.e. through 'direct action') but thereby run the risk of failing to articulate with it. In other words, some groups play by the rules of the game, achieve a voice in the policy-making process, but find there is little they are allowed to say, while others shout out their demands but find that nobody is listening. In some of the countries of Europe, and indeed in the United States, this dilemma has sometimes been resolved by taking grievances into the streets and confronting the state directly by physical force, but violent confrontation remains relatively uncommon in Britain (Northern Ireland apart), and the fundamental dilemma remains.

An appreciation of this dilemma is in many ways central to the sociological analysis of urban politics, and it is this which provides the basis for the discussion in Chapter 1. Not only does such an appreciation help to explain why some groups adopt conciliatory or 'reformist' strategies while others engage in more coercive action, but it can also provide valuable insights into why such a large section of the population comes to do nothing at all. The point here is that the characteristic political inactivity of so many people in the British political system can be explained in one of two ways. On the one hand, there are those whose interests are generally safeguarded by the policy-making process and who therefore do not need to act; on the other, there are those whose interests are routinely neglected or sacrificed by government but who feel they can do little about it. Political inaction may therefore be the result of the prior satisfaction of people's interests, or of their inability to make their interests heard, and it is an important task for any empirical study to be able to distinguish between these two explanations.

There is now a large literature on precisely this problem, and debate has centred around two key issues. First, how can people's interests be identified? One argument holds that interests can only be equated with people's expressed preferences – what people say they want must be taken as indicating where their interests lie – but this ignores the possibility that powerful groups may be able to distort people's perceptions of their true interests. The alternative view is that interests must be defined 'objectively', but this only raises the problem of the criteria according to which such objective assessments are to be made. The second question concerns how, even if the problem of defining interests can be resolved, inaction can be shown to have been caused by those in positions of power. The basic issue here concerns the relationship between action and structure, for it is necessary to determine whether the exclusion of a particular group's interests from the political system is a result of the actions of those who control the system, or of certain features of the system itself.

Both of these problems are discussed at some length in Chapter 1, and the tentative answers suggested there underlie many of the arguments in subsequent chapters. The conceptualization of interests, for example, is applied in Chapter 2 in distinguishing the interests of owner-occupiers from those of non-owners. Similarly, the discussion of the relationship between action and structure lies at the heart of the analysis of the state in Chapter 4. Thus Chapter 1 lays much of the groundwork for the subsequent chapters in Part 1 and, indeed, for the empirical analysis in Part 2.

The rationale behind the four chapters in Part 1 may therefore be summarized as follows. In Chapter 1 the central questions concerning the identification of objective interests and the relation between power and system constraints are explored in some detail. The concept of objective interests is then drawn upon in Chapter 2 for the analysis of the political significance of house ownership as a basis for social organization in housing struggles. Chapter 3 then develops this argument into a broader discussion of the potential and limitations of urban political protest in Britain, while Chapter 4 examines the role of the local state, paying particular attention to the nature of the relationship between the state and dominant economic classes.

1 Power, interests and causality

The upturned soap-box at Hyde Park Corner is a highly significant symbol in British political life. It provides us with familiar and reassuring evidence of the continued existence of the abstract rights and freedoms to which democratic citizenship entitles us – the freedom of speech, freedom of assembly and so on. Of course, we all recognize that to some extent our freedoms are fettered and our rights are restricted. We enjoy freedom of speech only insofar as what we say cannot be construed as seditious, treacherous, blasphemous or inflammatory, and our rights to free assembly may be waived by chief constables or stunted by the increasing use of nebulous and ill-defined laws of conspiracy. Nevertheless, the recurring Sunday spectacle at Hyde Park Corner serves to demonstrate that, despite the restrictions, our basic liberties remain intact.

But what of the orators? The impassioned street-corner speaker who fails to attract an audience is a familiar sight in Britain. Fired by the conviction of his own beliefs and frustrated by what he sees as the misguidedness of those around him, he becomes little more than a quaint extra on the tourists' itineraries, snapped at by their cameras, derided by a few scattered sceptics, but otherwise ignored by those hurrying by. This image of the tub-thumping militant delivering his message to a few bored onlookers is for many of us a comforting one. Not only does his presence, though slightly irritating, provide us with the opportunity to congratulate ourselves and our country on our tolerance, but his conspicuous lack of success also serves to confirm that it is our beliefs which are 'normal' (and by implication 'correct'), and his which are out of line. Similarly, the bedraggled demonstration in the High Street, the lost deposits at elections, and the unsold copies of left-wing papers on the news-stands all help remind us of the fringe status of the 'militants'. If most of us think alike, how can we all be wrong?

It would appear, therefore, that the rights and freedoms accorded the soap-box orator are in many ways more comforting and valuable for us than they are for him. Yet they are only valuable for most of us at a symbolic level, for very few people make active use of them. For example, although we all enjoy the right to voice our opinions, many of us do not even consider it worth our while to make the periodic pilgrimage to the polling booth, still less to become more actively involved in political affairs through membership of party organizations, pressure group campaigns or whatever. This has led Lukes (1977a) to suggest that many of our democratic rights may best be understood as elements of an elaborate political ritual which supports an unequal political system by endowing it with a spurious legitimacy. Because we all have the right to participate, the system is seen as fair. In this sense, the ideological significance of the right to vote is considerably greater than the political significance of the act of voting.

All this raises the question of why it is that so few of us take active advantage of our abstract political freedoms. There are two possible answers. The first is that we have no need to. This may clearly be the case for those powerful groups in society which government is careful not to offend. Miliband (1969), for example, has argued that, in a capitalist society, the interests of private capital will invariably and necessarily be taken into account in the development of national policy. If this is the case, then we should not expect to see business leaders standing on a soap-box. Or as Worsley puts it, 'Those with the ear of government do not need to organize mass lobbies of the House of Commons' (1964, p. 20). The alternative explanation is that in one way or another we may be prevented from engaging in effective political action. We may, in other words, be duped, hoodwinked, coerced, cajoled or manipulated into political inactivity. Thus in explaining why it is that inactivity seems to be the norm rather than the exception in Britain and in many other liberal-democratic societies, we face the problem of distinguishing the complacency which stems from a position of strength from the fatalism which stems from a position of weakness. The puzzle to which this chapter is addressed is that of dogs which fail to bark in the night.

Two models of political inactivity

The starting point for any explanation of political action or inaction lies in a consideration of the distribution of crucial political resources in society. In order to be effective it is first necessary to achieve control of a basic minimum of such resources – a protest campaign will fail unless it can mobilize numerical support and call upon a certain level of organizational capacity, just as an informal and private attempt at achieving influence will not get very far without the existence of various interpersonal contacts. Yet beyond the vote, which constitutes the minimal and virtually universal political resource in liberal-democratic societies, such resources tend to be very unevenly distributed, and these inequalities are often cumulative. The main reason for this is that the relationship between economic and political power is generally a close one, for as Newton has observed, money is 'the most flexible and convertible political resource of all' (1976, p. 227). Thus those who control the scarce and crucial material resources in society are also often those who enjoy the closest and most effective contacts with government, who can gain access to useful sources of information or restrict and bias the flow of information to others, who can through their investment decisions determine whether there shall be employment in one area or another (or no employment at all), or whether houses, offices or factories will be developed, and so on. This is not to argue that those who enjoy material wealth are necessarily also those who enjoy political power, although in a situation such as that described by the Lynds (1937) in 'Middletown', where virtually all key urban resources were controlled by a single family, this certainly seems more than plausible. What I am arguing, however, is that material wealth constitutes one of a number of key *potential* political resources, and that access to such resources is unequal and frequently cumulative. The possibilities for effective political action are thus unevenly distributed at the outset.

It is important to emphasize that the control of such resources in itself only constitutes a potential for exercising power, a capacity for political action. As Martin (1971) has shown, it is necessary to distinguish between having power and exercising it. Thus it is one thing to be in a position that affords the opportunity for effective political action, but quite another to use that position to engage in such action.

It is possible (though not common) for the politically weak to triumph over more powerful opponents; as March points out, 'The more powerful members of the community are not necessarily activated to use their power, while less powerful members may be hyper-activated' (1966, p. 46). Such David and Goliath situations are usually widely reported when they occur (e.g. the small man's victory against an impersonal bureaucracy), and they generally serve to reinforce the image of liberal democracy as a system of political equality in which anybody can stand up for their rights and win, but in such cases we often may be justified in suspecting that the issue itself is not of the greatest political significance as regards its ramifications for the status quo. Nevertheless, March's argument is a valid one. Power is a dynamic phenomenon which cannot adequately be analysed in any study that stops when it has demonstrated which positions are filled by which people. It is all the more unfortunate then that so much research into power in Britain has failed to transcend this static positional perspective. Although a number of studies of nominal elite groups in Britain have generated interesting evidence on the impeccably bourgeois lineages of top civil servants and military leaders, or on the deprivations of fagging, flogging and the Eton wall game suffered in common by so many company directors and Cabinet ministers during their formative years, they have rarely gone on to consider the way in which these and similar groups actually use their privileged positions. As Giddens notes, 'We are surely not justified in making direct inferences from the social background, or even the educational experience, of elite groups to the way in which they employ whatever power they possess once they attain positions of eminence. Because a man emanates from a specific type of class background, it does not inevitably follow that he will later adopt policies which are designed to promote class interests corresponding to that background' (1974, p. xii).

Once we pose the question of whether and how political resources come to be mobilized, we are obliged to take account of the process whereby the will to engage in political action becomes manifest. In other words, if the objective possibility for such action is present (i.e. through access to the necessary resources), yet inactivity results, then we need to explain why the will to act has apparently failed to develop. For Dahl (1963), the question appears unproblematical since he argues that for much of the time there will be no need to act in order to defend or assert our interests. There may be occasions, of course, when we feel that it is necessary to do something – when our garden lies in the path of a proposed motorway, or when the local authority rate demand doubles, for example – but for the most part we remain content to allow things to go on as they are and to delegate the responsibility for managing political affairs to those whom we elect. In a representative democracy, in other words, when dogs do not bark it is most likely because nothing has happened to provoke them. This is a model of democracy which owes much to the nineteenth-century elite theorists such as Mosca, who argued that the guarantee of political freedom lay in the competition of elites for mass loyalty, while the masses themselves remained generally apathetic and uninvolved. Thus, in his study of politics in New Haven, Dahl (1961) argued that although a very small proportion of the population was ever involved directly in city decision-making processes, the system was nevertheless democratic and pluralistic; this small group was obliged at every step to take account of the political preferences of the remainder of the population which at any time could mount an objection, and which enjoyed effective political sovereignty by virtue of its electoral control over the selection of political leaders. Dahl recognizes that mass political inactivity may reflect fatalism as much as satisfaction (1963, p. 61), but he also argues that those with intense preferences and political concerns will be motivated to voice them. This argument is discussed in more detail in Chapter 4, but for the moment we need only note that it rests on the assumption that people will always squeal when politicians tread on their toes. The fact that there was very little squealing in New Haven is thus taken as evidence that those in positions of power were careful about where they were putting their feet.

Dahl is not alone in developing this argument. Parsons (1966a), for example, argues that power is a system property, and that while different structurally defined positions within the political system necessarily afford differential access to it, the occupants of such positions nevertheless use power in the interests of the system as a whole, i.e. for the collective good. The relatively powerless members of society, he suggests, enter into a voluntary but binding relationship with the relatively powerful through the operation of the electoral system. As a result, the latter are obliged to use their positions for the pursuit of common interests while the former are obliged to obey the commands they issue. In this way, Parsons defines power as a 'means of effectively mobilizing obligations in the interests of collective goals' (p. 85), and he dismisses what he terms the 'zero-sum' conception of power which holds that for one party to a power relationship to gain, the other must necessarily lose. Thus he develops an analogy between the political and the economic systems to show that, just as a bank may use the funds deposited with it to create credit by lending more than it can actually repay at any one time, so too politicians may draw upon the trust vested in them by the electorate to create more power which can then be used for the collective good. If they become dissatisfied with the returns they are being paid, then electors may withdraw their deposits of trust at elections, just as bank depositors may withdraw their money balances in an attempt to seek a higher return elsewhere. And just as a bank must retain a certain level of gold reserves against the eventuality of any future loss of confidence on the part of investors, so too governments have reserves of force in the form of the police and the military which may be used in the event of their power being challenged (see Parsons 1967).

There are a number of problems with this analogy which point to the key issue raised by such work – namely, the problem of consensus. For example, far from being the reserve of last resort, it is quite evident that force has often been used to achieve power as much as to maintain it, and that the state's monopoly over the use of legitimate coercion may be used to prop up a vastly unpopular regime as much as to maintain a popular one against minority challenge. Furthermore, it can be argued that even in liberal democracies, force (or at least the implicit threat of it) lies at the very foundation of social stability (see, for example, Goode 1972 and Heydebrand 1972). Parsons assumes but does not demonstrate a moral basis for political life. Nor does he deal with the problem raised by his analogy that if governments, like banks, routinely owe obligations to their depositors which they cannot fully discharge, then some sections of the population seem likely to fail to receive the full benefits of citizenship to which they are entitled (see Gouldner 1970).

What all this amounts to is that theorists such as Dahl and Parsons appear to overemphasize the degree of consensus between the powerful and the powerless while also failing to recognize how power may come to be used to further private interests that may be totally incompatible with the 'collective good', no matter how defined. It is difficult to apply Parsons's ideas to an analysis of the Watergate affair, still less to the May events in Paris in 1968 or to the fall of Allende in Chile. As Giddens observes, 'However much it is true that power can rest upon agreement to cede authority which can be used for collective aims, it is also true that the interests of power holders and those subject to that power often clash' (1968, p. 264). Clearly, both Dahl and Parsons are concerned in their work with a particular type of power relationship in which the power of one party is seen by the other as legitimate. They are concerned, that is, not with power as the ability to achieve given ends (Weber's concept of *Macht*), but with power as the ability to issue commands with a high likelihood that they will be obeyed (Weber's concept of *legitime Herrschaft*). In other words, their view of power as involving consent and legitimacy corresponds closely to what Weber (1947) terms authority, such that their definition excludes by fiat coercion, inducement and, most significantly, manipulation.

These are critical omissions, for they do not allow for the basis of legitimacy to be questioned. For Dahl and Parsons, power relations in liberal democratic societies are legitimated by virtue of the voluntary consent of subordinates and the pursuit of common benefits by superordinates, yet the way in which such consent is achieved is taken as unproblematic. For example, their theories fail to take account of the possibility that if legitimacy begets power, power may also beget legitimacy. As Gouldner puts it, 'The judgement that something is legitimate can be coerced and rewarded situationally. . . . The powerful can enforce their moral claims and conventionalize their moral defaults' (1970, pp. 293 and 297). Nor does their theory allow for the possibility that the attribution of legitimacy consequent upon the pursuit of 'common goals' by those in power may only reflect the ability of the powerful to define what these common goals are. There seems no way in which Parsons's theory, for example, could take account of Marcuse's argument that political stability in capitalist societies reflects a process in which 'false' needs are constantly imposed upon people, and that these 'needs' are then met: 'The productive apparatus and the goods and services which it produces sell or impose the social system as a whole. . . . The products indoctrinate and manipulate; they promote a false consciousness which is immune against its falsehood' (Marcuse 1964, p. 24). And, following on from this, their emphasis on the voluntary and spontaneous basis of compliance totally neglects the possibility that an apparent consensus may be the product of what Schaar (1970) terms 'conditioning and symbolic bedazzlement', or of what Gramsci refers to as 'ideological hegemony' (see Boggs 1976). Theirs is a theory of the isolated individual conferring and withdrawing his deposits of political trust in a political and ideological vaccuum.

Once we recognize that the attribution of legitimacy within a power relationship may reflect the prior exercise of inducement, coercion or manipulation, then it becomes clear that we need to distinguish between distorted and undistorted forms. We need, that is, to distinguish between an authoritative relationship in which legitimacy is voluntarily ceded from below, and various forms of manipulative relationships in which legitimacy is in some way imposed from above. The problem here is that, empirically, both types of power relationships are likely to appear the same. In neither case are sanctions likely to be necessary in order to enforce or reward compliance, for the genuinely authoritative relationship does not depend upon stick or carrot while the manipulative relationship is based upon attributed legitimacy which may rarely be thrown open to question. And it is because these two conceptually opposite yet empirically indistinct types of power relationships cannot seemingly be assessed that two opposing epistemological positions are to be found in the various attempts to explain political inaction. Thus, while Dahl and Parsons can maintain that passivity and apathy on the part of large sections of the population is wholly explained by the genuine authority enjoyed and exercised by those they elect to political office, other writers can equally argue that such inaction is only indicative of the fact that the population has had the wool pulled over its eyes, or has in some other way been prevented from voicing or even recognizing its 'real' interests. The problem is how we determine which explanation to accept.

Take, for example, the work of Bachrach and Baratz (1970). By developing the concept of 'non-decision-making', they attempted to refute the view of Dahl and others that political inaction was necessarily indicative of a genuine consensus. They criticized the New Haven study on the grounds that it analysed only public and controversial issues and thus ignored those areas of policy-making where the sensitivity of potentially powerful local interests may have been sufficient to have prevented any open and critical debate from taking place. Power could be used, they argued, to stop any potentially disruptive opposition from emerging. It followed from this that any analysis of urban politics should take account of at least three ways in which opposition may be stifled. These may be set out diagrammatically as follows:

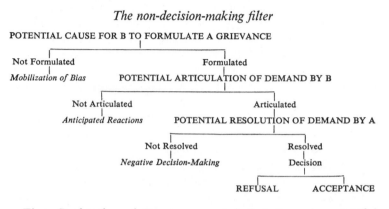

The non-decision-making filter

First, Bachrach and Baratz suggested that those in powerful positions may simply fail to respond in any way to the articulation of political demands by less powerful groups so that no decision is ever taken. In this way, the status quo may be maintained to the detriment of those who are currently disadvantaged by it while avoiding the difficulties of actually being seen to have taken what may be an unpopular decision. Some of the tactics by which this may be accomplished are obvious. The powerful may put their telescopes to their blind eye and refuse to acknowledge the existence of politically awkward demands. If pushed, they may establish committees or inquiries which fail to report until years later, or they may attempt to co-opt the leaders of a protest movement into positions within the power structure itself where they may more easily be controlled. But whatever the tactic, the strategy remains the same: to avoid the difficulty of making any decision, for or against. Following Parry and Morriss (1974), I term this strategy negative decision-making. It refers to those situations where dogs may bark themselves hoarse in the night but nobody listens.

The second level of non-decision-making identified by Bachrach and Baratz relates to those cases where disgruntled groups fail to press their demands. This may be because they believe that it would do no good if they did (they may anticipate either a polite refusal or no response at all), or because they fear for what could happen if they did speak out (they anticipate a retaliatory response). A useful illustration of how such anticipated reactions may result in non-decision-making can be found in the study of 'Springdale' by Vidich and Bensman (1958). There was in Springdale a widespread belief that a particular individual could invariably get his way in the politics of the town, and in consequence nobody organized against him, for everybody recognized the likelihood that he would defeat them. Indeed, Vidich and Bensman found that people came to anticipate his wishes before he even expressed them, thereby effectively adding to his power over them. Clearly, individuals may come to be powerful by virtue of others defining them as such (see Bierstedt 1950 and Van Doorn 1962). To the extent that this occurs, people may fail to act purely as a result of their perceptions of what Lehman (1969) calls 'symbolic power'. Non-decision-making deriving out of anticipated reactions therefore refers to those situations where dogs do not bark because they are 'muzzled', or because they believe they are muzzled.

The will to act is of course present, both in cases of negative decision-making and anticipated reactions, but this may not be the case with the third level of non-decision-making discussed by Bachrach and Baratz. The concept of mobilization of bias refers to those situations where dominant interests may exert such a degree of control over the way in which a political system operates, and over the values, beliefs and opinions of less powerful groups within it, that they can effectively determine not only whether certain demands come to be expressed and heeded, but also whether such demands will even cross people's minds. In a situation such as this, the demands which are formulated and expressed by subordinate groups will generally be of little consequence as regards any threat which they pose to the status quo. As Hacker lucidly argues, 'The elite is content to let the public blow off steam on certain questions. This is acknowledged to be necessary, for democracy must have issues to squabble about. If attention is focused on fluoride in the water and progressivism in the schools, then eyes will be deflected from more important matters' (1965, p. 135). Crucial issues thus never emerge for public debate, and to study the course of contentious issues (as Dahl did in New Haven) is merely to study what happens to the political crumbs strewn carelessly about by an elite with its hands clasped firmly around the cake. Or, to revert to the previous metaphor, dogs may fail to bark because they have either been doped, or at best fobbed off with a very inferior bone.

The concept of non-decision-making constitutes a strong challenge to Dahl's model of democratic pluralism, but to what extent can it be said to refute it? Bachrach and Baratz have themselves been widely criticized, not least because of the problems encountered from a positivist perspective in observing what is essentially a negative phenomenon. It is difficult enough observing decision-making without having to consider the possibility of non-decisions. There is, after all, an infinite variety of things that have not happened from which one may choose. It is with respect to this sort of problem that Parry and Morriss (1974) have suggested that the concept of non-decision-making should be abandoned, for to the extent that non-decision-making practices are observable, they may be understood as specific types of decisions, and to the extent that they are not, they cannot be studied. For example, Parry and Morriss argue that in the case of negative decision-making, the tactics adopted by dominant groups to delay or bypass awkward political decisions can themselves be seen as decisions and studied as such. The subcommittee that never reports can be analysed as easily and in the same way as that which reaches a speedy conclusion. Similarly, even where dominant groups actually do nothing that can be observed, the fact that the issue has been raised by less powerful sections of the population is sufficient to alert the observer to the possibility that a tacit decision not to decide has been taken. Parry and Morriss also suggest that at least some cases of inaction following anticipated reactions may be observable. Their argument here is that where inaction follows an attempt to 'fly a kite' (i.e. where a group makes a visible attempt to assess which way the political wind is blowing and then hastily withdraws), then this exploratory activity can be studied, and the group can later be contacted in order to establish why no subsequent action was forthcoming. This raises rather more problems, however.

The main difficulty with their prescription for the study of anticipated reactions is that few lower-class groups are likely to need to 'fly a kite' in order to assess the prevailing political climate. It seems clear that power relations are generally routinized and that in the course of everyday life, political constraints on our action are ordinarily taken for granted. Most of us 'know' in most situations what we can and cannot get away with, what we may or may not achieve. Our views of the world and of our place within it are rarely explicitly conscious, with the result that existing social relations come to be understood as almost natural. As the magazine *Ink* put it in its November 1971 issue, 'The system we live under usually seems as natural as woods and fields. Things are like they are because they are like that, that's life, and that's the way it goes. . . . We seem powerless to do anything about it because everything seems to be the result of huge impersonal forces which we can't understand, let alone control.' Or as Horkheimer and Adorno observe, 'Because reality, due to the lack of any other convincing ideology, becomes its own ideology, it requires only a small effort of mind to throw off this all powerful and at the same time empty illusion; but to make this effort seems to be the most difficult thing of all' (1973, p. 203). It is therefore only when power relations are in a state of flux (e.g. during a period of revolutionary upheaval), or when we are confronted with an entirely new situation for which we have no existing recipes for action, that we may need to test out our political efficacy. As Durkheim (1933) recognized, under 'normal' conditions our aspirations are limited to what we 'know' it is in our power to achieve. The very possibility of doing some things or of not doing others may never ordinarily cross our minds. Indeed, the very exercise of power may not even be consciously recognized by those who are subject to it. It is precisely this point which has caused so much difficulty for positivist power research. As we shall see in Chapter 9, the fundamental problem with so-called 'reputational' techniques for studying the distribution of power is not that people may see power 'wrongly' in the way that Polsby (1959), Rose (1967), Wolfinger (1960 and 1962) and others suggest, but rather that perceptions of power can only reflect people's conscious awareness of the political relationships in which they are situated, and thus cannot provide an adequate picture of these relations.

The cases where anticipated reactions actually may be observed are therefore likely to be limited. This is even more true, however, of the third level of non-decision-making, for it seems doubtful whether positivist criteria of adequacy could ever be met in analysis of the imposition of beliefs and manipulation of values. Merelman (1968),

for example, argues that it is impossible to devise any research programme that could provide evidence for the existence of a mobilization of bias. He also suggests that the concept is itself tautologous
since it depends on an initial assumption that a group does in fact
exist which has the power to stifle political activity that it finds
distasteful. He therefore concludes that Bachrach and Baratz have
ruled out even the possibility of a genuine consensus. In this he is
supported by Wolfinger who dismisses the concept of false consciousness as a 'label for popular opinion that does not follow leftist
prescriptions and a shorthand way of saying that the people don't
know what's good for them' (1971, p. 1066). Even Bachrach and
Baratz appear to defer to these and other critical attacks and to
question the validity of the concept. They write, 'The observer may
find that no one is aggrieved in the community. In that event, he
would be ill-advised to search for evidence of non-decision-making.
If there is no conflict, overt or covert, then the presumption must be
that there is consensus on the prevailing allocation of values, in
which case non-decision-making is impossible' (1970, p. 49).

This ultimate retreat into subjectivism is disturbing. It is also un-
warranted, for in its assumption that people are always conscious
of the objective political situation in which they find themselves, it
leads to the uncritical acceptance of the arguments of Dahl and
Parsons. I have argued that they fail to take account of the possible
significance of ideology as a source of political stability. To assume
genuine consensus in a situation where there is no apparent conflict
(that is, to give the system – and the powerful – the benefit of the
doubt) appears no more justifiable on theoretical grounds than to
assume that such a situation necessarily indicates the existence of
widespread false consciousness. The question raised by all this is
whether these two explanatory models can be assessed against any
theoretically neutral criteria of adequacy, or whether they constitute
arguments representing two distinct and incommensurable paradigms
within political theory.

The problem of relativism

Let us first return briefly to Parsons's work on power. We have seen
that, for Parsons, power is legitimated in the eyes of those subject
to it 'with reference to its bearing on collective goals' (1967, p. 308).

He therefore identifies two essential features of the exercise of power in liberal democratic systems: first, that it is based upon the voluntary consent of subordinates; and second, that it is used for the good of the social collectivity as a whole. Although this conception has been criticized earlier as a definition of *power*, both because the legitimacy enjoyed by ruling groups cannot simply be assumed and because these groups may at times use public office for narrow sectional advantage, we have nevertheless seen that these twin criteria may usefully be taken as the key elements in defining an ideal typical relationship of *authority*. In other words, legitimacy and communal benefit may be taken as the two essential and necessary features of a genuinely authoritative relationship.

It follows from this that if we wish to understand and explain the political inactivity of any given section of the population, then we must go beyond the merely subjective level of members' perceptions and attributions of legitimacy to those in positions of power. In addition to the analysis of attributed legitimacy, it is necessary to show whether the interests of such a group have *objectively* been met by the actions or inaction of those exercising power 'on their behalf'. Bachrach and Baratz fail to take this step, and for this reason they are forced to rely on perceptions of legitimacy as the sole criterion for assessing the existence of a genuine consensus. Against this position, I am suggesting that any analysis must take account of both the subjective and the objective situation – whether or not power is seen as legitimate, and whether or not it does contribute in fact to the common good. This approach necessarily rests on the central premise that it is possible to identify the real interests of a given individual or group independently of the way in which such interests may be subjectively conceived by those concerned. This, however, is problematic.

There appear to be three distinct approaches to the analysis of interests, each deriving out of a different epistemological tradition. Following Keat and Urry (1975), these may be termed the positivist, conventionalist and realist perspectives. The principal assumptions embedded in a positivist approach are that, first, an external world exists independently of our perceptions of it; secondly, that there are regular relationships between different elements of that world which may be expressed in the form of hypotheses and scientific laws; and thirdly, that such scientific explanations of real world events must be tested through observation or the collection of other direct sensory data. The conventionalist perspective, on the other hand, holds that observation is itself determined by theory, that different theoretical frameworks cannot therefore be assessed through recourse to empirical evidence, and (in some versions at least) that there is no external reality independent of our perceptions of it. Finally, realism shares with positivism the view that an external reality exists and that the task of science is to generate theories which can explain features of this reality, but argues against positivism that this reality is not necessarily observable. The realist is thus concerned to develop causal explanations of what we see through the generation of theories about underlying and unobservable structures and forces.

The clearest example of the application of a positivist perspective to the analysis of interests is provided by Dahl. He argues that any conception of interests must have an empirical referent, and that this can only be provided by the individuals concerned. In other words, a concept of objective interests which is not consistent with people's own perceptions of their interests is unacceptable. He therefore concludes that if an individual believes that a given exercise of power is in his interests, then to all intents and purposes it is in his interests, 'even though from the point of view of observers his belief is false or ethically wrong' (1961, p. 52*n*). Similarly, we have seen that Bachrach and Baratz feel obliged to deny the validity of any attempt by outside observers to transcend subjects' conceptions of their own interests. For these and other similar writers, a concept of objective interests appears almost metaphysical since it cannot be tested against observable data. Subjective preferences are seen as real while objective interests are not.

The problem with this argument is, as Parry (1969) and others have pointed out, that it rules out any consideration of ideology as a source of social control and political stability. It is, furthermore, logically inconsistent, in that it defines *a priori* the synonymity of interests and wants. Runciman, for example, argues that interests and wants are distinct concepts and that the relationship between them cannot simply be defined by fiat: 'Only when interest is so defined that it is possible for a man not to want his interests will the answer to the question whether his interests do influence his views be something to be demonstrated and not assumed' (1970, p. 216). Even if we were to follow Dahl in his argument that our identification of our own interests cannot be mistaken, it would still be necessary to distinguish between interests and wants since it would still be possible for an individual to want something that he himself recognized was not in his interests (a cancer-inducing cigarette, for example).

This distinction between interests and wants can be reconciled, however, to some extent within a positivist perspective. Barry (1967), for example, suggests that a 'policy, law or institution is in someone's interest if it increases his opportunities to get what he wants – whatever that may be' (p. 115). According to this argument, it is quite possible for people to mistake their interests – for example, by supporting a policy which will not offer them what they want. This argument represents a step forward in that it implicitly recognizes the possibility that an outside observer may come to an objective assessment of the consequences of a given policy with no reference to the subjective perceptions of it held by those affected. Nevertheless, it remains a concept of interests which still rests ultimately on such subjective criteria since it takes wants as unproblematic. Barry does not question where our wants come from, and he therefore comes nowhere near answering the argument of, say, Marcuse (see page 27). Nor does he take account of the distinction discussed by Giddens (1976) between conscious and unconscious wants. Thus, citing Freudian theory as his example, Giddens suggests that although we should see interests as referring to 'any outcomes or events that facilitate the fulfilment of agents' wants' (p. 85), nevertheless, 'since men are not necessarily aware of their motives for acting in a particular way, they are not necessarily aware of what in any given situation their interests are either' (p. 86).

Giddens's argument takes us some way towards a realist position on interests, for by suggesting the existence of unconscious wants and motives, he is effectively denying the positivist postulate that interests may be observable in some way. This is an argument which also figures strongly in the work of the Frankfurt school, and particularly in the writings of Marcuse and Habermas. Thus Marcuse (1964) distinguishes true and false needs, arguing that the latter are 'superimposed upon the individual by particular social interests in his repression', and that 'the only needs that have an unqualified claim for satisfaction are the vital ones – nourishment, clothing, lodging at the attainable level of culture' (p. 19). It follows from this that, although the individual remains *in the last instance* the final and sole arbiter of his own interests (for Marcuse denies that any external agency can or should determine this for him), he cannot recognize these interests while he remains subject to dominant ideologies which serve to distort them. For as long as individuals 'are kept incapable of being autonomous, as long as they are indoctrinated and manipulated (down to their very instincts), their answer to this question cannot be taken as their own' (p. 20).

The implication here is obvious, and it is an implication which has been drawn by a number of writers within and outside the Frankfurt school (and, indeed, within and outside the Marxist tradition). Interests, it seems, must ultimately be determined by the individual himself operating within a context of ideological neutrality and political equality. One prominent exponent of this argument is Habermas (1976). He develops the concept of discursive will-formation, by which he means the process whereby people reach a rationally based consensus through free, undistorted and unrestricted argument between equals. He also recognizes, of course, that normative or ideological constraints will ordinarily operate to prevent such undistorted discourse from taking place. The empirically existing world is not, therefore, the place to look in order to ascertain what people's interests are, or what a rational consensus may look like. Rather, Habermas suggests that interests can only be ascertained through hypothetical construction, 'by counter-factually imagining the limit case of a conflict between the involved parties in which they would be forced to consciously perceive their interests and strategically assert them. ... The social scientist can only hypothetically project this ascription of interests; indeed a direct confirmation of this hypothesis would be possible only in the form of a practical discourse among the very individuals or groups involved' (p. 114). For Habermas, then, interests are real but are ordinarily unobservable, and in order to understand what these interests are, it will usually be necessary to engage in some hypothetical exercise akin to Weber's use of the 'mental experiment' (Weber 1949). Such an exercise, under normal conditions, will not be capable of empirical confirmation or falsification, and does not therefore meet positivist criteria of adequacy.

Habermas's attempt to reconcile an ultimately subjectivist view of interests with a recognition of the existence of ideological constraint is reflected in the work of a number of other writers. Connolly (1972), for example, suggests that interests may be assessed in terms of the choice which an individual would make between various alternatives if he could first experience the consequences of each choice open to him. Similarly, Lukes (1974) argues that interests reflect the choices which individuals would make if they were acting under conditions of relative autonomy (by which he means a situation where the normative and coercive power exercised by others over their choice is relatively weak). This latter argument is in principle capable of empirical application since it requires, not an absolute independence from prevailing ideologies as Marcuse and Habermas suggest, but rather only a relative autonomy. But such an empirical application could only be achieved at the expense of theoretical rigour, for as Bradshaw (1976) points out, the concept of relative autonomy is suspect. For example, how can we know that A's influence over B's choices has been reduced to relatively insignificant proportions, or that B is not still subject to the influence of some third party? How, indeed, are we to judge the point at which B's autonomy is sufficiently well established for him to be seen as exercising choice in terms of his real interests (especially bearing in mind Marcuse's argument that our wants are manipulated 'down to our very instincts')? Given that Lukes (1976) admits that absolute autonomy is empirically impossible, it seems that, like Habermas and Connolly, his argument rests upon hypothetical conditions.

The problem with these attempts to retain the individual as the final arbiter of his own interests, apart from the fact that they lead to hypothetical analysis which can rarely be assessed empirically, is that they also lead to some extraordinary conclusions. To take an example discussed by Wall (1975), Connolly's position would oblige him to accept that heroin addiction is in the interests of an addict if that individual maintains that, knowing what he now knows, he would still have started on the habit. This is an argument which seems to make little sense, for although we may recognize the addict's reasons for wanting to be addicted, we can hardly accept that addiction is under any conceivable circumstances in his interest. As Wall puts it, 'It is not only that we know what the effects of taking heroin are, but also that we know that these effects are not compatible with anyone's interest – i.e. we know that they are *bad*' (p. 503). Similarly, Lukes, in his argument on relative autonomy, is obliged to accept that if the inhabitants of the steel towns studied by Crenson (1971) actually opted for their air to be polluted, then provided they made this choice in a situation of relative autonomy and with full access to all relevant information, then poisoned air would be in their interests: 'If, implausibly, under such acknowledged conditions, they actually preferred continued pollution, I would abandon the claim that air pollution was against their real interests' (1976, p. 129).

Although I have considered Marcuse, Habermas, Connolly and Lukes together, on the grounds that they all wish to retain an ultimate subjective referent for their conceptions of interests, there does appear to be one significant difference which separates them. For Marcuse and Habermas, it seems that real interests exist, and the problem lies in illustrating what these interests are in a context of political and ideological repression. For Connolly and Lukes, on the other hand, the concept of real interests appears to be more of a heuristic device which is a necessary tool for analysing such contexts. For example, as we shall see below, Lukes's position is essentially that of the conventionalist rather than the realist, but this is not the case with writers such as Marcuse and Habermas who are concerned with how individuals may come to recognize their existing real interests. For Lukes, real interests need to be demonstrated, empirically if possible; for Habermas, they need only to be recognized. Thus, while all these writers share an ultimately subjectivist and individualist conception of interests – and to this extent their arguments share the common weaknesses which I have outlined – they nevertheless differ in the epistemological status which they are prepared to accord the concept of objective interests.

An alternative perspective within realism, which seeks to avoid these weaknesses of ultimate subjectivism while retaining the argument that objective interests are real, is provided by contemporary theories in Marxist structuralism. The arguments of Poulantzas (1973) are a case in point. Poulantzas rejects any individualistic conception of power or interests. He defines power as the 'capacity of a social class to realize its specific objective interests' (p. 104), thus locating it, and the concept of interests, in the framework of class struggles. The interests of a class are determined in the field of class practices by what it can achieve as a social force in conflict with other classes. In the short-term, class interests are limited by what it is possible for a class to achieve within the context of a given structure, while in the long-term, they are limited only to what can be achieved through the weakening of other classes with which it is in conflict. Poulantzas recognizes that the members of a given class will not always be aware of the extent of their class interests: 'It is obvious that, in the field of practices, owing to the functioning of ideology in this respect, these interests *qua* limits can differ from the *representation* that agents or even classes make of them' (p. 112). Nevertheless, he does not accept that such subjective limitations constitute real limitations on class interests, since interests are limited only by what can be objectively achieved: 'Power, as capacity to realize interests, refers not to imaginary interests, in a situation where, on account of ideology, they are dislocated from interests-limits, but to those latter themselves' (p. 113). Thus he is careful to avoid the intrusion of any individualistic or subjectivistic element into his conception of interests. In contrast to writers such as Habermas and Marcuse, he writes, 'The concept of interests can and must be stripped of all psychological connotations' (p. 112).

Poulantzas's argument seems to be acceptable within the context of historical materialism. The problem with it is that it rests upon a prior acceptance of certain key aspects of Marxist philosophy; notably on the identification of two antagonistic classes within the pure capitalist mode of production. This has two consequences. First, it denies the possibility of a genuine consensus between the two principal classes, wage labourers and capitalists, since their relationship is necessarily one of antagonism and conflict and the long-term interests of the former can only be achieved through the defeat of the latter. This would seem to lead, for example, to the denial of the possibility that policies may be developed in the collective interest, and to a view of the role of the state which, while opposite to that of Parsons, nevertheless may be criticized on the same grounds of *a priori* theorizing (see pages 184–5). Thus, while for Parsons, those in positions of power are constrained to use their power for the collective good, for Poulantzas they are relegated to the status of 'relatively autonomous' supports of the long-term interests of the capitalist class. The second consequence of his position is a tautological argument, treating effects as causes. For example, if we start off from the position that the long-term interests of the proletariat lie in the future revolutionary transcendence of capitalism, and that the state in capitalist society necessarily functions in the long-term interests of the capitalist class, then it follows that the apparent victories of the working class under capitalism (e.g. the establishment of a welfare state) are at the same time defeats since they function in aiding the reproduction of labour-power and in defusing radical activism. Such an argument not only leads to some rather curious conclusions regarding the role of a revolutionary party (e.g. the implication would seem to be that Marxists should support rather than attack cuts in welfare services – see Corrigan 1977), but it explains the function of the welfare state as being the reason why it was established in the first place. As Pahl has shown, the argument is circular, all-embracing and impossible to falsify within its own core assumptions:

A theory which claims that the state ultimately serves the interests of the dominant classes is very hard to falsify. . . . This is largely because the position is based on certain assumptions about capital's need to accumulate, or about the fundamental contradictions inherent in the capitalist mode of production, which together form the paradigm. Criticisms which do not accept the basic premises of such a paradigm are considered to be invalid. One either has to attack the position according to the rules established by that position, or turn to other positions and play a different game [1977b, pp. 9–10].

The problem with Poulantzas's conception of interests as class interests specifically defined is that we need to believe it before we can accept it.

This problem leads us to consider the conventionalist perspective as it is applied to the assessment of objective interests. Conventionalism, it will be recalled, rejects the distinction found in both positivism and realism between theory and external reality, and argues that there are no objective criteria by means of which competing theoretical frameworks can be assessed. Taken to its logical conclusion (e.g. Winch 1958), it holds that any explanation is as good as any other since all explanations are embedded in particular scientific or common-sense theories which derive from specific forms of life. As applied to the problem of defining objective interests, it leads to the conclusion that the pluralist approach which equates interests with preferences is no more nor less valid than the Marxist one, for both derive out of paradigms which are themselves inherently untestable. Thus, from a conventionalist position, we are obliged to recognize that there exist two competing paradigms, and that the different conceptions of interests in each of them 'make sense' in terms of their own assumptions, but not in terms of those of the other. The two paradigms thus appear 'incommensurable' (Kuhn 1970a), and the concept of objective interests is seen as 'essentially contestable' (Gray 1975). Lukes himself adopts a conventionalist position when he writes, 'The notion of interests is an irreducibly evaluative notion. . . . So it is not surprising that different conceptions of what interests *are* are associated with different moral and political positions. . . . I would maintain that any view of power rests on some normatively specific conception of interests' (1974, pp. 34–5).

It is important to note at this point that a conventionalist perspective may either lead to the argument that objective interests may exist but that it is impossible to assess what they are (since any assessment is theory-dependent), or to the position that there are no objective interests, and that any conception of interests is therefore as valid as any other. The first position would lead us to suggest that all conceptions are not equally valid but that their relative validity can never be finally established. The second position, by contrast, would oblige us to accept Phillips's argument (1973) that sociology is about opinion rather than truth, and that the sociological enterprise consists entirely in providing arguments which are accepted or rejected according to personal preference since no objective evidence can be brought to bear on their confirmation or falsification.

Taking this second position first, we may advance both negative and positive criticisms of it which suggest that it is untenable. On the negative side, there are clearly logical difficulties with such an extreme argument for cognitive relativism. It leads, for example, to the acceptance of two mutually incompatible perspectives (the liberal view that interests are equivalent to preferences and the radical view that they are independent of preferences) as equally valid, but to accept either one as valid is necessarily to reject the other as invalid. Furthermore, the argument that real interests do not exist independently of our concepts about them is to make an absolute statement which is clearly inadmissible in terms of a relativistic epistemology. On the positive side, it does seem that criteria for assessing the different conceptions of interests which we have been considering may well exist independently of any particular theory. As Lukes puts it,

'The influence, however deep, of theories, systems, paradigms, per-spectives and so on upon men's perceptions and understanding is one thing; the relativist claim that there are no theory-independent objects of perception and understanding is another' (1977b, p. 157). Thus, we shall see below that it is possible to provide objective criteria for assessing whether or not interests have been met in any given situation once we define the relationship between interests and benefit. Our observation of whether a given group has gained or lost as a result of a particular policy does not depend on any particular theory of interests.

The less extreme conventionalist position bears some approxima-tion to the position reached by Kuhn (1970b) in his later work, where he denies that he is a relativist in the broadest sense of that term. Kuhn suggests that although we should beware the attribution of 'truth' to any argument, and although empirical observations remain dependent upon the prior acceptance of a particular paradigm (in the sense that no weight of empirical evidence can ever be sufficient to force agreement on the part of those who share a different paradigm), nevertheless, 'One scientific theory is not as good as another for doing what scientists normally do' (p. 264). It is difficult to see how this argument can be interpreted other than as suggesting that different theories are not equally useful for explaining real world events. It would seem to follow from this (although Kuhn is not entirely consistent here) that some degree of communication between adherents of different paradigms is possible, and that common criteria of adequacy may be found among them.

On the basis of this argument, it is possible to develop two proposi-tions regarding the use of a concept of objective interests. The first is that both of the major paradigms we have considered above consider that it is necessary for any theory to be able to explain both political action and inaction. Thus, although they disagree on how inaction is to be explained, they agree that no theory is adequate which does not provide such an explanation. This being the case, it is possible to argue that the liberal conception of interests as equivalent to pref-erences is inadequate according to criteria which its adherents themselves accept. The starting point for such an argument is the conventionalist position that our views of the world are necessarily refracted through theories about the world, whether they be common sense or scientific theories. Our understanding of the world is thus dependent upon the conceptual framework by means of which we interpret our everyday experiences and observations. It follows from this that our interpretations may be influenced by others who are in a position to restrict the range of available alternative interpretations, or to structure the flow of information and experiences reaching us. Parsons himself has recognized as much in his work on child socialization, for it is clear that the socialization process refers precisely to the transmission of particular conceptual frameworks which are to be used to make sense of later real world experiences. As Keat and Urry observe, 'Although no one set of concepts determines a single set of beliefs, it is equally true that not all beliefs can be expressed in a given set of concepts. As a simple example: we can believe either that a table is red, or that it is not red, while using the same concepts; but we cannot believe that it is square without an additional concept' (1975, p. 218). During both primary and secondary socialization, conceptual frameworks are provided to us by others, and while these do not determine our beliefs, the pattern of such frameworks nevertheless sets limits on our beliefs. The liberal conception of interests cannot deal with this, however, unless its adherents are prepared to argue that when A restricts the range of preferences available to B, then B's preferences still nevertheless represent his real interests. This could, of course, be argued, but the writers discussed earlier do not seem prepared to support such an argument. Indeed, the very basis of Wolfinger's attack on Bachrach and Baratz is precisely that no outsider can define our true interests for us. It follows from this that, since our preferences and our view of our position in the world is limited by others from the very moment of our birth, we cannot take these preferences as indicating our real interests, and the liberal position must therefore be rejected as inadequate.

The second proposition is that the concept of objective interests, although it cannot refer to subjective preferences, is nevertheless essentially contestable. It is one thing to argue that interests may not correspond to conscious wants and preferences, but quite another to stipulate that to which they do correspond. It is useful here to draw upon Lukes's distinction between cognitive relativism and moral relativism (1977b). As we have seen, Lukes does not accept that there are no universal criteria of logic and truth. He does, nevertheless, accept that there are no universal criteria of morality, although he feels uneasy about this. From this position, he then accepts that the identification of real interests is necessarily a moral question – a question about what is good for people and what therefore constitutes the 'correct' policy in any context – and is, in consequence, necessarily evaluative. In this, he follows Weber in suggesting that the value-basis of science precludes the possibility of drawing scientifically based assessments between competing value positions. (See Weber's essay, *Science as a vocation*, in Gerth and Mills 1948; also the excellent essay on Weber in Dawe 1971.)

It follows from Lukes's argument that, unless we are prepared to make absolutist moral claims – or alternatively accept the Marxian notion of 'objective social inevitability' (see Bradshaw 1976) – any conception of objective interests is based ultimately on personal moral and political values. Any analysis of power and of political inaction will therefore be essentially contestable. But can we say any more than this? The answer is that we can, but only if we are prepared to accept a definition of interests which, while necessarily ultimately contestable, nevertheless rests on the assumption that real interests refer to the achievement of benefits and the avoidance of costs in any particular situation. Such an argument, of course, has much in common with the ethical and political philosophy of the English utilitarians, and with Bentham's two principles of pleasure and pain, except that it breaks fundamentally with the conservatism of that philosophy by rejecting the view that individuals 'are the best judges of their own interests' (Bentham 1894, p. 63). In other words, the assessment of benefits and costs cannot be left to the individuals concerned, but is rather to be determined independently of their desires and preferences. (See Plamenatz 1958 who develops a similar argument in his criticism of the utilitarian tradition.)

There are, however, three potential criticisms which could be developed against my definition of interests. The first is that the very identification of benefit and cost is, like the definition of interests on which it is based, unavoidably evaluative. It may be suggested, therefore, that even if we accept that interests refer to the achievement of benefit and avoidance of cost, nevertheless there are no objective criteria by means of which benefit and cost can be assessed. On what grounds, for example, are we to argue that air pollution does not benefit those subject to it? But to put the question in this way is almost to answer it. The point is that benefits and costs are determined by the observer with reference to the context in which they are distributed. The context in which polluted air is distributed is one of health and longevity of life, and given this context, we know *objectively* that the higher the level of pollution, the greater is the cost to those affected. Put another way, and bearing in mind Lukes's rejection of cognitive relativism, it is possible to assess costs and benefits in any empirical context, once we have identified the nature of that context.

The argument here is consistent with that advanced by Runciman who suggests that an individual's interests relate to his position as regards the distribution of wealth, prestige and political power: 'To say, therefore, that something is in a man's interest is to say that it will result in an improvement in his position with respect to one or more of these three; and this is a matter which will be established quite independently of his wants and tastes' (1970, p. 218). Where my argument differs from Runciman's is that I would not wish to limit the context to that of wealth, prestige and power, but would extend the argument to cover any context. As regards the analysis of urban politics, for example, where the context is that of policy-making by institutions which function to allocate scarce public resources among different members of a defined population (see Williams 1975), it follows from my position that the interests of the different members of that population lie in securing the maximum benefits which can accrue to them through this allocative process (e.g. in terms of the quality of schooling made available to them, or the environmental and locational advantages of the area in which they live), and in avoiding as far as possible the costs which are thereby generated (e.g. in terms of local taxation, the location of public resources with negative external effects, and so on). It also follows that the pattern of these benefits and costs can be determined through empirical analysis. Such an analysis need not be limited to the level of material advantage and disadvantage, for although it is not possible to express all values in quantifiable terms, it is possible to specify the overall pattern of gains and losses without necessarily affixing standardized measures (e.g. see the social accounting method of Lichfield and Chapman 1968). Such an exercise will need to encompass both direct and indirect benefits as well as direct and 'opportunity' costs (see Tabb 1972). The point about it is that such an analysis can be accomplished *objectively*. We can, therefore, demonstrate which groups benefit from local authority density provisions and zoning policies, from cutbacks in welfare expenditure resulting in cuts in local taxation, or whatever. And by the same token, we can identify which groups have lost out as a result, irrespective of whether they recognize or accept the fact.

The second possible criticism of my definition of interests in terms of objective cost/benefit distribution is that it necessarily leads to a conservative position, taking as it does the existing context as the basis for attributing interests. By focusing, for example, on what could be achieved by any one group in the existing context of local authority policy-making, it ignores what could be achieved through the revolutionary rejection of that context. The analysis is therefore limited to what Poulantzas sees as short-term interests. This argument has to be accepted, but with two provisos. The first is that, like Poulantzas, I would not accept that subjective aspirations constitute limitations on what can be achieved. In other words, interests lie in the pursuit of the maximum (objectively defined) benefit possible within any given context and, as we shall see in Chapter 4, the horizons of what can be achieved may often be much broader than members themselves may think. The argument need certainly not be a conservative one. Secondly, it is apparent that any conception of long-term interests cannot be grounded empirically. Following Barry (1967), it is clear that the attribution of interests is at least implicitly comparative: 'Comparison enters into any evaluation in terms of interests. To say that a policy would be in someone's interests is implicitly to compare it with some other policy – often simply the continuance of the status quo' (p. 117). The problem with a conception of long-term interests is that there is no immediate comparative reference – the comparison is with something that has not yet occurred and which is not yet possible. It is for precisely this reason that Marxist structuralist analysis encounters the problems identified above. The identification of long-term interests would therefore seem to depend on ontological assumptions about human nature which can have no empirical reference. The argument outlined here is therefore necessarily limited to the identification of short-term interests.

The third potential criticism concerns the rationality of altruistic behaviour. A model of interests based upon the pursuit of maximum benefit may be criticized as not taking account of those situations where people deliberately act in a way which is not intended to bring about maximum benefit to themselves. The question raised by such situations is whether such action may be construed as rational. To the extent that it involves the pursuit of a particular goal or value, then it seems that it is (as we have seen, we are not in a position to evaluate such goals or values objectively). But because such altruistic behaviour is rational, it does not follow that a model of objective interests that advances an alternative mode of behaviour – namely that of maximizing benefits – is therefore invalid. It is quite possible to act rationally but against one's own interests as they are defined in any given context. Empirically, it may well be the case that in most situations, those who do not pursue their own advantage have no conscious reasons for their inaction, but this is by the way. The main point is that the subjective rationality or irrationality of any given action or inaction should not be confused with the question of whether that action or inaction is in the objective interests of those concerned. The socialist millionaire may quite rationally subscribe to the values of socialism, but his interests remain those of a millionaire.

The argument that I have developed is that, although objective interests cannot be said to exist independently of different conceptual frameworks, nevertheless costs and benefits do exist objectively and may be analysed empirically in any specified context of action. It follows that if the two are seen to be related through theory, then the former may be analysed in terms of the latter, thereby going some way towards avoiding the necessarily conservative model of Dahl, the methodologically inoperable model of Lukes and Habermas, the epistemological imperialism of Poulantzas, and the hopeless and impotent relativism of the more extreme versions of conventionalism.

Causality and constraint

Let us suppose that we encounter a situation where policies have been adopted by a local authority which have worked to the detriment of the objective interests of a particular section of the population. It may be, for example, that the public housing construction programme has been cut back, thereby disadvantaging local homeless families who are obliged to wait longer for accommodation. Such a policy, that is, may be understood as working against the objective interests of homeless families in relation to local housing policies.

Let us further suppose that these families have all remained silent and have not responded in any way to the new policy. If (as I suggested earlier) genuine authority is exercised both with the consent of those subject to it and in their interests, then the inaction of these families clearly cannot be explained as following the exercise of authority. The question is whether it can be explained as the result of some form of non-decision-making (either anticipated reactions or the mobilization of bias). In order to answer this, it is necessary to take a second step in the analysis and to show, not only that the interests of these families as regards the provision of housing have not been met, but also how their inactivity has been brought about or maintained. Have their political leaders been co-opted, and if so how? Have they failed to act out of fear or a sense of fatalism? Has their definition of their own needs and wants been distorted in some way? The question is thus one of establishing causality. As Lukes puts it, 'In brief, we need to justify our expectation that B would have thought or acted differently; and we also need to specify the means or mechanism by which A has prevented, or else acted (or abstained from acting) in a manner sufficient to prevent, B from doing so' (1974, pp. 41–2). Power, in other words, involves *causality* – it is the causal element in social relationships.

The attempt to establish whether and how a given action or in-action has been brought about causally inevitably encounters two problems. The first is whether social relationships can be analysed in causal terms – whether power can be said to exist independently of the perceptions and definitions of those subject to it. We saw earlier that where an individual defines another as having power over him, then the other gains such power as a result – the Springdale study provides a vivid illustration of this. But this raises the question of whether, when an individual believes that another does *not* have power over him, the other does not enjoy power as a result. The first problem concerning causality therefore relates to the relevance of subordinates' definitions of their situation. The second problem, by contrast, relates to the situation of superordinates. The question here is how far those in positions of power can be held causally responsible for the effects of their actions, given that these effects may not have been intended and that the individuals concerned may at least believe that they had no choice but to act in the way they did. This in turn raises the further question of how far those in power may be said to be constrained in their actions by forces outside their control, or indeed, the degree to which their actions may be understood as having been determined objectively by such forces. This section of this chapter is concerned with the issues raised by these two problems.

The argument that power relations do not involve social causality is based on the position, common to symbolic interactionism and phenomenological sociology alike, that individuals do not merely react (as physical objects do) to external stimuli, but rather actively interpret such stimuli, and act in accordance with the interpretations which they draw. It follows from this that, although the social sciences may draw upon concepts such as power and force which have been developed in the physical sciences, the application of such concepts in the explanation of physical and social behaviour is not analogous. Billiard balls may rebound off each other in a speed and direction which can be explained and predicted in accordance with physical laws, but individuals simply do not respond in this way to the external objects of their environment or to each other. As Weber pointed out, social action is subjectively meaningful and cannot adequately be explained without reference to the meanings which individuals bring to bear on any situation.

With one exception (that of object degradation where subordinates are simply not defined as human), every power relationship is to some extent reciprocal. As Simmel showed, when A exerts power over B, he does so in order to produce some result, and B's reaction will therefore in its turn influence A's subsequent action (see Wolff 1964). Any power relationship, with the one exception of object degradation, is therefore an example of social *inter*action; two parties are involved, each orienting his behaviour in terms of the other, and each thereby constructing a definition of the situation in the course of their ongoing relationship. The point is, then, that in neither the case of A's action in relation to B, nor of B's subsequent action in relation to A, can such actions be seen as causally determining the actions of the other, for these actions only become meaningful, and thereby take on the appearance of, say, objective constraints or forces, through the process of subjective interpretation. The implication of this argument seems clear enough; power involves the ability of one actor in a social relationship to convince the other that he does 'in fact' have power over him. Thus Silverman (1970), for example, suggests that the analysis of power in formal organizations involves not the examination of the distribution and use of objective power resources among different members of the organization, but rather the analysis of 'meaning-structures' within the organization (i.e. of how different members perceive the hierarchy and their own position within it), and of the processes whereby certain definitions of the situation come to be imposed in the organization through the control of 'symbolic sticks' (i.e. perceived power resources).

There are two problems with this argument, however. The first is that it begs the question of how definitions of the situation come to be imposed in the first place. Berger and Luckmann, for example, have suggested that the ability to impose one's view of the world on others rests ultimately on the control of objective power resources rather than simply 'symbolic sticks': 'The success of particular conceptual machineries is related to the power possessed by those who operate them. . . . He who has the bigger stick has the better chance of imposing his definitions of reality' (1966, pp. 126–7). Thus even if we accept (as surely we must) that A cannot directly cause B to engage in a given course of action in the way in which one billiard ball causes another to rebound at a certain angle, this does not mean that A cannot indirectly cause such action through his control of the means available to B to interpret his situation. As Giddens (1976) has noted, phenomenological sociology has too often assumed that the process whereby reality comes to be constructed through the everyday accounting procedures of members interacting in the social world is a democratic process, a 'collaborative endeavour of *peers*, each contributing equally to the production of interaction, whose only interests are in sustaining an appearance of "ontological security" whereby meaningfulness is constituted' (p. 113). In contrast to this view, Giddens suggests that

The creation of frames of meaning occurs *as the mediation of practical activities*, and in terms of differentials of power which actors are able to bring to bear. . . . *The reflexive elaboration of frames of meaning is characteristically imbalanced in relation to the possession of power*, whether this be a result of the superior linguistic or dialectical skills of one person in conversation with another; the possession of relevant types of 'technical knowledge'; the mobilization of authority or 'force', etc. 'What passes for social reality' stands in immediate relation to the distribution of power [p. 113].

Although Giddens's argument here itself raises further difficulties which I shall consider below (e.g. the question of how far those in power constitute objectively autonomous agents imposing 'their' definitions on others), it nevertheless demonstrates the important point that social reality is not constructed in a political vaccuum.

This in turn raises a further point of central importance, for it is not only the case that different actors bring different resources to bear in the process of jointly constructing a shared reality, but also that they accomplish this on the basis of certain core hegemonic principles and values which are generally taken for granted. Social reality, in other words, is constructed within a hegemonic framework which is itself rarely questioned. Thus while it is undoubtedly the case that ideologies (in the sense of relatively formalized systems of belief and explanation) are transmitted (or even imposed) in the course of interaction between more powerful and less powerful individuals or groups, the more important point is that these ideologies, together with the less explicit images of social reality which emerge through interaction, are underpinned by 'an entire system of values, attitudes, beliefs, morality etc.' (Boggs 1976, p. 39) which is taken as given by both the powerful and the relatively powerless groups in society. I have developed this argument in some detail elsewhere (Newby *et al.* 1978, Chapter 7), and here I need only draw attention to the fact, first, that individuals may be subject to causal influences on their actions of which they remain ignorant, and secondly, that certain aspects of such influences may lie outside the immediate social relationships in which they are engaged. It is not simply that members may therefore be mistaken about the nature of the power to which they are subject, but also that this power in large part transcends individual relationships. The implications of this for an analysis of causal responsibility in power relationships are discussed below.

The second problem concerning an exclusively interpretative approach to the analysis of power is that, as Burns (1972) points out in his review of Silverman's book, there are many occasions when the meaning attributed to a situation by subordinate parties seems largely irrelevant. Certainly, there seems no way in which we can hold to the view that power is only real to the extent that it is defined as such by others, if we consider cases such as the power of the employer to dismiss his employee, the power of a policeman to arrest a felon, or the power of a local authority housing manager to deny a family a house. In all three examples, something is done or not done to one party in the relationship, irrespective of how he defines his situation. That is, they all involve the application of sanctions. Now it may well be that these sanctions do not achieve the intended or desired effect as regards the subsequent actions of the other party, but this is to raise the issue of how the sanctions are interpreted, not whether they are applied. Furthermore, the *right* of one party to impose such sanctions may not be recognized by the other (e.g. as in the case of 'terrorists' who refuse to recognize the court which tries them), but this raises the question of legitimacy (see pages 27–8), not the question of power. As Ryan points out, 'People's beliefs are not only beliefs about their own states of minds, they are also beliefs about the factual consequences of each other's behaviour, and about the factual results of people playing the roles their society allots them. In other words, their beliefs go beyond the merely subjective, and can be falsified by the way the world turns out' (1970, p. 240). The fact that individuals may not recognize the existence of the power to which they are subject does not render that power any less real.

Let us now turn to the second problem raised by a definition of power in terms of social causality – namely the question of whether those whom we identify as exercising power can be deemed to have been responsible for the outcomes of their actions. In approaching this issue we need to distinguish at the outset between *causality* (which I take to be an essential component of power relationships) and *intention* or motive (which I do not). The view that power necessarily involves the deliberate and conscious intention to bring about a given effect is central to many established definitions. Weber, for example, defines power (*Macht*) as 'the probability that one actor within a social relationship will be in a position *to carry out his own will* despite resistance, regardless of the basis on which this probability rests' (1947, p. 152, my italics). Similarly, Bertrand Russell (1940) defines power as the production of intended effects, while Wrong (1968) argues that power cannot be said to have been exercised in cases where the effects of a given action are unintended. Lukes seeks to modify such definitions by introducing a concept of 'remediable ignorance'. His argument is that we may identify an exercise of power where one party does not know, but could find out, the effects of his actions on the other, but like these other writers, he too argues that where such ignorance is unavoidable, 'then talk of an exercise of power appears to lose all its point' (1974, p. 51).

Two questions appear to have become confused in these arguments. On the one hand, there is the question of whether one party to a power relationship can be held causally responsible for the effects of his action or inaction on others; on the other, there is the question of whether we wish to hold him morally accountable for these effects. The point I am making here is that, provided a causal element can be traced in a given relationship, then there seems no reason to insist that intention must also have been present in order to understand it in terms of an exercise of power. Indeed, notwithstanding his concept of remediable ignorance (which in any case seems to raise insuperable problems as regards its application to empirical research situations), Lukes himself seems to agree with this argument when he writes in reply to Bradshaw, 'I altogether fail to see why the actions involved in exercising power might not be unconsidered, routine, or performed in ignorance of alternatives . . . there are plenty of cases, such as those of negligence, where we hold people responsible for actions they did not decide upon' (1976, p. 130). This is a crucial point (although Lukes again here confuses causal and moral responsibility), for as we saw earlier, power relations are most often routinized or even institutionalized, and in such cases the intention to generate bias may rarely be in evidence, while knowledge of the full effects of one's actions (including both the primary and multiplier effects) may be unavoidably scanty. Thus I follow Clegg, who argues, 'If power were confined only to those instances where intended effects were achieved (then quite apart from knowing just what these would look like, or how they could possibly operate), important and everyday instances of power would be beyond our theoretical grasp' (1975, p. 69). It may be that we would wish to reserve our attribution of moral responsibility for those cases where intention is in evidence, but there seems no reason to do this as regards the analysis of causal responsibility.

There is, however, a more difficult problem relating to the attribution of causal responsibility which is thrown up by the work of Parry and Morriss (1974). They distinguish between three types of power. The first is the power to initiate routine political procedures; this will generally take the form of key and often contentious decision-making (they cite the partition of Ireland as an example). The second is the power to maintain routines once they are established; this will usually take the form of mundane decision-making practices within a context of precedent and custom. In both cases, there seems little inherent difficulty in attributing causal responsibility for observable outcomes (although, as we shall see, there are grounds for argument over this). The third type of power is more problematic, however. They identify this as consequential power – 'the distribution of power which is consequential upon the performance of the routine' (p. 332) – and they give as an example the power enjoyed since the partition by the Orange Order in Ulster. This is the power which is derived from the ongoing implementation of political routines with which those concerned may have had no part in implementing or perpetuating. This leads Parry and Morriss to conclude: 'It can thus be difficult for certain demands to penetrate the system and be fully recognized as issues. But this does not necessarily mean that the powerful have to be, or can be seen to be, consciously acting to thwart such demands. They may be the unconscious beneficiaries of the bias which does not have to be consciously mobilized by the system' (p. 332).

This argument recognizes that intention may not be a necessary component of power relationships, but it also suggests that those in positions of power may not even cause the bias which operates in their favour. If this is the case, then talk of an exercise of power in any causal sense does indeed seem to lose all point. In order to consider this problem, it is useful to distinguish two components of this 'unconscious' mobilization of bias – the ideological and the political.

One way in which the interests of dominant groups may unconsciously be served is through the operation of ideology. In other words, groups whose interests lie in challenging the status quo may effectively be prevented from doing so by virtue of their acceptance of what Parkin (1971) has identified as the dominant value system. The question which this raises is whether dominant groups can be held causally responsible for the dominant value system.

The answer to this question has to be no. As I argued earlier, the ruling ideas and values in society cannot be explained simply as the property and the product of the dominant groups or classes, for as Poulantzas (1973) correctly points out, if this were the case, then such ideas would presumably be so transparently biased that no subordinate class would accept them as their own. The point is that dominant ideologies reflect (to some extent) the life experiences of all classes, and they 'make sense' only because they are grounded in the form of life of the society as a whole.

What this means is that the politician and the industrialist are as much the captives of the prevailing hegemonic form of life as the homeless family or the worker. True, as Giddens (1976) points out, the former are likely to enjoy a greater propensity for renegotiating aspects of their reality than are the latter, but the point is that such negotiation takes place, in the ordinary course of events, within the boundaries of the paramount reality. As Clegg argues in his study of power relations on a building site, all members submit unthinkingly to the 'iconic domination' of the capitalistic form of life with its central emphasis on profitability and market relationships, and power only comes to be exercised within this context: 'Issues are constructed by the submission of the powerful to that which gives them their power – the iconic domination of their, in this instance, capitalistic form of life' (1975, p. 151). This is not to deny that the powerful may succeed in imposing their definitions of reality on others, but the definitions they impose are necessarily confined within the context of the dominant form of life or hegemonic principle. This context is never questioned because it makes no sense to question it (see Clegg, pp. 82–4, and Williams 1977, pp. 109–10). It is therefore only when this context is disrupted in some way that the power relationships founded upon it may themselves be thrown open to conscious examination (e.g. as can be seen in the case of company bankruptcies resulting in the establishment of workers' cooperatives). Indeed, it can be argued that it is only in such situations that dominant groups may need to resort to the use of relatively formal ideologies in an attempt to maintain the status quo (Newby *et al.* 1978, Chapter 7). In the ordinary course of events, they are the beneficiaries of a hegemonic form of life which is not consciously 'mobilized', and for which they cannot be held causally responsible.

When Parry and Morriss talk of an unconscious mobilization of bias, however, they appear to be referring, not to the effects of ideological hegemony, but to the effects of political systems. In other words, dominant groups are said to benefit from the operation of political systems without themselves being responsible for them. The argument seems to be that some groups get heard while others do not, and that some get what they want while others get nothing, all as a result of a bias inherent in the routines of ruling. A simple example would be the electoral system, for as minority parties never cease to point out, the first-past-the-post method of election has a built-in bias in favour of the largest parties; a bias which is never consciously mobilized or manipulated. As we have seen, Parry and Morriss make a similar point in relation to the political constitution of Ulster.

The idea that political systems contain and generate an inherent political bias implies a certain impotence on the part of those individuals and groups who run or attempt to influence them. But is it the case, for example, that those who benefit from a first-past-the-post system of election, or from an in-built Protestant majority in the six counties, cannot be held responsible for the continuation of the bias which operates in their favour? Clearly not, for electoral systems can be changed and (as the recent history of Ulster testifies) safeguards for minority groups could be established given the political will. The question which this raises is how far those who operate political systems are objectively constrained in their actions by external constraints over which they have no control.

At this point it is useful to draw a distinction made by Lukes (1977c) between rational and structural constraints. Structural constraints objectively prevent individuals from following certain courses of action. As Lukes puts it, 'Structural constraints limit the agent's freedom or power to act otherwise by precluding (rather than putting a price tag on) such a possibility' (p. 13). To argue that a given constraint is structural is therefore to argue that a particular course of action is simply not possible.

The clearest example of such an argument is provided by Poulantzas (1973) in his discussion of the role of the capitalist state. As we saw earlier, he rejects the individualistic conception of power, arguing that interpersonal relations should be analysed in terms of the concept of might (*puissance*), and that power refers rather to the field of class practices. Furthermore, in his critique of Miliband (Poulantzas 1969), he makes it clear that the motives and values of decision-makers are irrelevant to an understanding of state policies and interventions since such individuals are merely the bearers of objective structural relations between the state and the various classes in the social formation. In other words, the actions of politicians and administrators are simply the surface manifestation of underlying structural relationships, and the question of who occupies the various positions in the state apparatus, and of what their backgrounds, aims and values may be, is therefore of little significance given the objective role of the state in regulating the class struggle and maintaining the conditions for capitalist accumulation.

We shall consider Poulantzas's ideas in more detail in Chapter 4, but from this short review it is apparent that he rejects any attribution of causal responsibility for state policies to those who enact them. The argument is reminiscent of Marx's comments in the preface to the first German edition of *Capital* (vol. 1): 'Individuals are dealt with only in so far as they are the personifications of economic categories, embodiments of particular class relations and class interests. My standpoint, from which the evolution of the economic formation of society is viewed as a process of natural history, can less than any other make the individual responsible for relations whose creature he solely remains' (1976, p. 92). Such an argument, of course, renders the sort of work discussed in this chapter pointless, for it leads to the conclusion that, to understand political action, we should not launch into empirical studies of what individuals do, but should rather theorize the objective relations whose 'creatures' they are. For Poulantzas, it is not so much that individuals are subject to structural constraints on their actions, but that their actions are structurally determined.

A developed critique of this position must wait until Chapter 4, but to anticipate the argument, I would suggest that the relation between action and structure cannot be resolved adequately through *a priori* theorizing, but is in the last analysis an empirical question to be resolved through comparative analysis. The problem is to identify the scope of structural constraints on political action, and this can only be achieved by comparing similar situations where different individuals have acted differently (e.g. where two local authorities, faced with a similar problem and similar circumstances, develop opposing policies). As Lukes puts it, 'One can, in particular, point to evidence of the same agent acting differently under relevantly similar circumstances, or of relevantly similar agents so acting. . . . Such appeal to evidence and argument concerning counterfactuals is quite central to the explanatory enterprise' (1977c, p. 24). It is, quite simply, not good enough to argue, as Poulantzas does, that such divergences in political action reflect different historical conjunctures, for this can only lead into a hopeless tautology (see pages 184–5).

The second category of constraint identified by Lukes is rational rather than structural. Rational constraints are those which, from the point of view of the actor, provide sufficient reasons for action or inaction given the existence of certain values or beliefs: 'I retain the freedom or power to act otherwise, though given that I have the wants or beliefs that I have, my actions have been determined' (ibid., p. 13). Rational constraints thus constitute a cost on specific options which individuals are not prepared to pay. Given the argument already developed in this chapter, this does not mean that rational constraints relieve individuals of the causal responsibility for the effects of their actions. It is one thing, for example, to say that a given local authority could not provide adequate housing facilities because there was no way in which it could raise sufficient funds, but it is quite another to deny its responsibility on the grounds that additional housing would necessitate an increase in rates which its members were not prepared to countenance. Thus, notwithstanding Lukes's argument that rational constraints are subjectively real, it is apparent that objectively they do not constitute grounds for denying causal responsibility. Indeed, Lukes himself recognizes that 'powerful politicians characteristically appeal to structural constraints: they claim that what others count as possible courses of action are in fact precluded by external circumstances' (ibid., p. 24). Such justifications should clearly not be accepted at their face value.

Probably the most significant rational constraints on political action are the rules which govern it. It is not just that members are not structurally constrained to follow certain rules – i.e. that they can exercise choice – but more importantly that the rules themselves are open to interpretation. This, as we shall see, can be of crucial importance in the generation of bias in political systems, and it is to this that I now turn.

Competent rule use and the generation of bias

In the previous section we saw that any explanation of non-decision-making must rest first on the identification of objective interests independently of members' subjective preferences, and secondly on the attribution of causality regarding the production of inaction by the action or inaction of others. Although such inaction may be explained in part with reference to the dominant ideology in the society as a whole (e.g. where subordinate groups fail to recognize the contradiction between government policies and their own material interests owing to the effects of the core ideology of the state as representing the fusion of individual interests – see Poulantzas 1973, p. 214, and Clarke *et al.* 1977), it is also the case that one very important source of inaction and bias lies in the operation of political routines themselves. While the effects of ideology cannot be causally related to the actions of any identifiable individuals or groups (except where ideologies are found to be specific to particular social relationships – see Newby *et al.* 1978), this is not the case with the bias which is generated by routine political practices. Put simply, the rules (both formal and informal) governing differential access to political power generate a bias in favour of some sections of the population and against others, and the causal responsibility for this bias can be traced to those who operate the rules. Rules of access are thus rational constraints which are amenable to the interpretations of those who apply them.

In order to develop this argument it is useful to return to Clegg's work where the concept of rule is related to those of power and the structure of domination. Following Wittgenstein, he argues that behaviour is largely rule-governed. The argument that a policeman causes traffic to stop when he raises his arm, for example, only makes sense with reference to a set of explicit and implicit rules with which there is a broad and general familiarity within a given form of life. He also recognizes that rules are not absolute in that they are open to diverse interpretation, and that different individuals may enjoy a different degree of scope in interpreting them. Nevertheless, he establishes the basis of power in rules. Drawing an analogy with the game of chess, for example, he writes, 'Obviously, in an ongoing game, then a piece like the queen would start in a more privileged position than a pawn, simply because the extant rules, which are now open to interpretation, enable her to begin the sequence with more potential moves to make' (1975, p. 49). Of course, if power derives out of rules, then the basis of the rules themselves has to be established. To revert to his metaphor, we have to ask why chess came to be established as the game to be played. The answer provided by Clegg is, as we have seen, that the rules, and hence power, are founded in a form of life.

It follows from Clegg's analysis that, although rules regulate the behaviour of the powerful (necessarily since their power derives from a prior acceptance of the rules) as well as the powerless, the queen as well as the pawn, the ability of each to interpret the rules is asymmetrical. This, in fact, is where Clegg's chess analogy breaks down, for it is not simply that powerful actors have greater scope in their permissible actions, but also that they can authoritatively reinterpret (within limits) what the rules mean. In everyday life, queens may begin to move as knights. Rules, in other words, are not inherently meaningful; they have to be interpreted before they can be applied and, as we saw earlier, some people's interpretations are likely to carry more weight than others. As Hall observes, 'The fact is that rules are not extensive, clearly stated or clearly binding. They ... require interpretation and definition as they apply to specific situations' (1972, p. 44). Even in the most bureaucratic and apparently rigid of formal organizations, members invariably exercise some discretion in the way the rules come to be applied, and in the process they effectively redefine or reassert what the rules 'mean' (see, for example, Goffman 1961; Silverman 1970). Such ongoing interpretation and reinterpretation, furthermore, is accomplished through the routine interaction of members in their problem-solving activities. Although the effects may sometimes be traumatic (see, for example, Chibnall and Saunders 1977), the origins of such active reinterpretation lie in mundane interaction.

The meaning of rules is therefore revealed only through their operation: 'The issue of what rules, policies and goals mean for the bureaucratic actor upon the concrete occasion of their use (for example, to guide, to account for or to justify action) must be treated as problematic' (Zimmerman 1973, p. 253). And in their operation, rules will generally come to reflect the values and practical purposes of those who apply them and who are in a position to make their interpretations the authoritative ones. As Hall puts it, 'Rules are used and misused according to the interests of the participants, and even authority may find it to its advantage to ignore certain rules' (1972, p. 44). In a very real sense, therefore, those who make the decisions also make the rules according to which their decisions are taken. The rules to which they are obliged to address their actions do not so much govern and regulate what they do as provide the criteria of acceptability according to which they must reconcile their actions. This leads Zimmerman to develop the concept of 'competent rule use' – the process whereby individuals manage to satisfy themselves and others that their actions are 'reasonable' in any given context.

The point here, of course, is that such competence is differentially distributed. As Mills suggested in his classic study of power in America, 'If most men and women take whatever roles are permitted to them and enact them as they are expected to by virtue of their position, this is precisely what the elite need not do, and often do not do. They may call into question the structure, their position within it, or the way in which they are to enact that position' (1956, p. 24).

Thus we arrive at the conclusion that if power is founded on rules, then the rules are themselves dependent upon the exercise of power. The relationship is dialectical. This is clearly not to argue that any rule can be interpreted in any way to suit any powerful individual's interest as he chooses, for interpretations have to be shared with others. The argument, then, is that common-sense wisdoms may be expected to evolve among decision-makers serving to inform them of what the rules 'really' mean in any given situation, and how they should 'obviously' be applied in any given case. Whether consciously or otherwise, rules therefore come to mean what those in positions of power understand them to mean, and thus invariably to reflect their interests and values. Decision-makers are in this sense institutional innovators, irrespective of whether they deliberately amend or change the rules or merely 'carry them out'. If, as Parry and Morriss suggest, the everyday routines of ruling generate a consistent bias, then clearly this can only be explained with reference to the interpretive practices of those who discharge the routines.

It is in this context that we need to assess the various work conducted in Britain on public participation, community politics and so on. I discuss these questions in some detail in Chapters 5 and 7, but here we should note that the problems facing subordinate groups in their relations with agencies of the state are not simply the problems in overcoming 'bourgeois ideology' (cf. Cowley *et al.* 1977, p. 13). Nor, indeed, are they the problems of 'improving communications' (cf. Ferres 1977). Rather, the crucial problem is that of negotiating the rules of access as operated by local authority 'gatekeepers'. And the point here is that such rules are not neutral.

There is evidence available from a number of different case studies to suggest that the means of influencing local policy-making are governed by rules of access operated by local authorities. In his study of Kensington and Chelsea, for example, Dearlove shows that 'the rules of the game are the rules of access: they allow some groups to be involved and to be influential in the policy process gaining public policies which they favour, while denying others a part' (1973, p. 58). He then goes on to demonstrate how the rules of access place a premium on what we may term 'conciliatory' behaviour while penalizing more direct or 'coercive' influence attempts. Thus the councillors in Kensington and Chelsea reacted to various approaches from different groups in the borough according to their assessment of the relative 'respectability' of the groups, their strategies, and their demands. As Miller found in his study of Bristol, those in power come to condemn certain types of 'pressure tactics' as being 'in bad taste' (1970, p. 42). As we shall see in Chapter 5, I found similar evidence in my study in Croydon.

The significance of such evidence for an understanding of non-decision-making is twofold. First, the modes of political behaviour prescribed and endorsed by local authority rules of access are often not available to certain groups. Of course, we may all be in a position to vote in local elections (or as Marx rather acidly puts it, to decide 'once in three or six years which member of the ruling class was to misrepresent the people in Parliament' – 1968a, p. 289), and we can all write letters of complaint to our elected representatives or contribute to periodic (and arguably ritualistic) exercises in public participation. But the least advantaged groups in the population can take little advantage of the less formal and less public channels of influence endorsed by those in positions of power, and an emphasis on informality (see pages 232–6) will certainly operate to exclude those who do not enjoy the necessary personal contacts. Secondly, the rules of access are not themselves absolute, and qualitatively similar patterns of political activity may be defined as responsible in one case, while in another they are dismissed as disruptive. Given that competent rule use reflects the interests and practical purposes of those in positions of power, it follows that the definition of acceptable behaviour will often reflect not so much the inherent qualities of the behaviour in question, but more the assessment by those in power of the desirability of the demands being made. As Dearlove points out, if a group's demands are found broadly acceptable, then its tactics are also likely to be accepted as a legitimate means of advancing them. If, on the other hand, the demands are unacceptable, then the group itself may easily come to be defined as 'irresponsible' and therefore unworthy of consideration. In short, there is a close inter-relationship between the interests and demands of a given group, the way in which it comes to express these demands (since 'acceptable' demands are likely to lead to the provision by those in power of the 'acceptable' means of articulating them), and the success which it achieves.

Once we recognize the nature of this relationship between interests, strategies and political power it becomes possible to account for political inaction in terms, not of ideology (although this may well be significant), but of the rules of access. Those whose interests coincide with those of policy-makers will clearly rarely need to act at all in order to further or safeguard their position, and to the extent that they do act, they will generally do so in accordance with the rules of access. Those whose interests are opposed to the policies of powerful groups, on the other hand, find themselves in a dilemma. If they play by the rules of the game, there is no guarantee that their action will be deemed legitimate, and even if it is, they are likely to achieve little. If they flaunt the rules of access, on the other hand, their actions will undoubtedly be deemed illegitimate, and they will find themselves engaged in a battle which they are almost certainly doomed to lose (see pages 290–3). The third, and perhaps most common alternative, is to do nothing.

None of this is to argue that there need be a deliberate intention on the part of those in power to 'exclude' (Parkin 1974) subordinate groups. Parry and Morriss are correct in identifying the mechanisms of exclusion in the routines of ruling, the point being that these routines are the ongoing product of interpretive practices by those who implement them. Nor does this argument imply that those who are excluded as a result are necessarily aware of the contradictions with which they are faced. Where deprivation is an established feature of people's lives and political impotence is the norm, we should not expect to find any coherent political awareness. The fatalistic shrug of the shoulders is the characteristic response to routine exclusion practices. What this argument does suggest, however, is that different patterns of political inactivity can be distinguished through an analysis of objective interests and rules of access.

I noted at the start of this chapter that the upturned soap-box vividly symbolizes our right to free speech, but provides no guarantee of any right to be heard. As Ricci puts it, 'A realist might validly conclude that our rights permit us to speak, but they do not oblige our leaders to pay attention' (1971, p. 187). To secure a hearing, we may be obliged to follow as closely as possible the shifting and ambiguous rules of access, yet these rules are themselves loaded. For those who gain – whose voices are heard and whose interests are routinely taken into account – the liberal pluralist model of urban politics advanced by Dahl and others is clearly appropriate. But for those who lose, those who cannot make their demands heard and whose interests are routinely ignored or overruled, the right to a soap-box represents little more than the right to whistle in the wind.

2 Housing, class interests and political action

The relationship between property ownership and class structure lies at the heart of most theories of social stratification. In both the Marxist and the Weberian traditions, for example, ownership and non-ownership of property is identified as the key to understanding class inequalities and class conflicts. The concept of property, however, is used in a very specific sense in both of these theoretical traditions. For Marx, it represents expended labour-power or capital; and classes therefore arise according to their relationship to capital – whether they are buyers or sellers of labour-power. For Weber, on the other hand, property refers to the command over resources which can realize a return in the market, and classes therefore arise (at least in part) according to the differential degree of market power enjoyed by different groups with different degrees of access to profitable material resources.

Clearly, despite their many differences, both Marx and Weber were mainly concerned in their writings on class with the ownership of property in the form of capital, whether it be land, factories, banking and commercial capital or whatever. In this sense, the property-owning bourgeoisie appears today to be a small and somewhat select class; indeed, it can be argued that capital now refers more to an abstract category than to an identifiable class of people. Property ownership in a broader sense is, however, more widely dispersed than ever, and although this in part reflects the diffusion of capital ownership through shareholdings in joint stock companies and, more significantly, through insurance-linked property bonds, pension fund investments and the like, it also reflects the remarkable spread of house ownership among all classes in Britain. The owner-occupied sector today accounts for over 50 per cent of all households, and there is little doubt that for most families, house ownership constitutes the single largest investment of their entire lives. Furthermore, owner-occupation is no longer the sole prerogative of business and professional groups, for around 40 per cent of manual workers now own, either outright or through mortgage, the houses in which they live.

The continuing spread of house ownership as the dominant form of tenure in Britain raises the question of how, if at all, owner-occupation has affected class relations. The question needs to be broken down into the three main aspects of class relations and class practices, namely, the economic, the political and the ideological. As regards its ideological significance, for example, there seems little doubt that the diffusion of house ownership has had a significant effect on class relations in Britain, for while conservatives seek to extend it in order to secure and strengthen the foundations of a 'property-owning democracy', radicals identify its effects in the growing privatization of certain sections of the working class and in the blunting of the already dull edge of proletarian class consciousness. The question, however, is whether house ownership, particularly among the working class, has generated any significant consequences beyond its ideological effects. The primary concerns of this chapter, therefore, are to consider the economic importance of owner-occupation as a source of wealth and revenue, and to analyse the implications of this for political struggles which develop around housing issues.

The neo-Weberian approach and the concept of housing classes

For Max Weber, classes constituted aggregates of individuals who shared a common life situation by virtue of their economic power in commodity and labour markets. Although he followed Marx in arguing that classes were objectively-defined categories with a material base, Weber differed from Marx in arguing that classes could arise in any market situation, and were therefore not confined to the two major categories of political economy, wage-labour and capital. Indeed, he drew a somewhat confusing distinction between property classes, whose members shared common life-chances by virtue of their command over resources which could realize income, and acquisition classes, identified in terms of the degree of marketable skills enjoyed by different social groups in the population. Each of these analytical categories was then divided into positively privileged,

negatively privileged and middle strata, although the criteria according to which different individuals come to be allocated to one stratum
or another are never made clear, and Weber's examples are often
ambiguous.

What is clear about Weber's approach is that it is pluralistic,
descriptive and ideal-typical. Basically, it identifies many different
classes in society according to the size and source of their economic
rewards. The analysis is therefore grounded in the sphere of economic
activity concerned with distribution (rather than production as is the
case with Marx), and it leads logically to the conclusion that the
number of classes is almost infinite since there are as many differences
in market situation as there are individuals in the population. Weber
himself appears to recognize this when he writes, 'Only persons who
are completely unskilled, without property and dependent on
employment without regular occupation, are in a strictly identical
class status' (1947, p. 425). It was in response to this problem that he
introduced into his later work a third category – social class – which
referred to the cluster of different class positions between which an
interchange of individuals is readily possible. Utilizing the concept of
social class, it is possible (as Giddens 1971, suggests) to identify in
Weber's work a basic distinction between an upper social class of
highly-educated property-owners, a lower class consisting of those
with few marketable skills and little property, and a middle class
comprising on the one hand the petty bourgeoisie (i.e. those with
property but few skills), and on the other the intelligentsia (i.e. those,
such as technicians, administrators and professional employees, who
live by selling their skills rather than by exploiting their property). But
even after tidying up the taxonomy in this way, Weber's approach
begs a number of questions, not least of which is how, if at all, these
different social classes relate to each other. This, as we shall see later,
is a problem which returns to confront any class analysis grounded in
the Weberian perspective.

The implications of Weber's approach for an analysis of housing
struggles were first recognized by Rex and Moore (1967) in their study
of the housing market in an inner area of Birmingham. By attempting
to explain the housing situation of immigrant groups in Birmingham
through the adoption of a Weberian class approach together with an
analysis of the ecological and political forces which gave rise to the
'zone of transition', Rex and Moore were able to identify a process of

competition which took place over the allocation of scarce and desired housing resources. This competition they saw in terms of a struggle between different housing classes: 'We follow Max Weber who saw that class struggle was apt to emerge wherever people in a market situation enjoyed differential access to property, and that such class struggles may therefore arise not merely around the use of the means of industrial production, but around the control of domestic property' (pp. 273–4). While recognizing that power in the housing market was itself in large part a reflection of power in the labour market, since income from working and the security of employment are clearly key factors in determining access to credit for house purchase, they nevertheless argued that it was possible to occupy one class situation in relation to the means of production, and another with relation to the distribution of domestic property. Put another way, an individual's acquisition class membership would not necessarily correspond with his property class membership in the urban system.

One immediate problem confronting Rex and Moore's attempt to develop a Weberian model of housing classes was that it was by no means clear how many classes should be distinguished. As we have seen, an emphasis on market situation can lead to the identification of an infinite number of classes, and this problem is reflected in their work where they variously identify five (Rex and Moore, p. 36), six (ibid., p. 274) and seven (Rex 1968, p. 215) housing classes in the area of Birmingham they studied. Nor need the analysis have stopped there, for Moore (1977, p. 106) has recently argued that at least two more classes should have been added while Rex (1977, p. 221) has suggested that groups as diverse as blacks and fatherless families could equally be termed housing classes. The hierarchy of housing classes which they did identify, however, covered a range from the outright owners of whole houses in desirable areas to lodging house tenants in single rooms, each class being distinguished from those 'above' and 'below' it according to its power to achieve access to scarce and desired housing resources. Two key criteria were isolated as governing such access. The first was size and security of income, for this was crucial for gaining access to mortgage funding; the second was the ability to meet the need and length of residence qualifications laid down by the local authority as a prerequisite for gaining access to the public rented housing sector. Those groups (e.g.

relatively poor immigrants) who enjoyed neither high incomes and secure employment nor could fulfil the bureaucratic criteria of allocation were therefore obliged to seek shelter in the declining and decaying private rented sector located in the inner city zone of transition. There, they found themselves in conflict, not only with their landlords, but also with members of other housing classes – owner-occupiers and council tenants both saw the inner city private rented sector as an 'illegitimate' form of tenure and sought to limit its growth through the implementation by the local council of health and safety regulations, zoning decisions and the like.

Three major criticisms have been advanced against Rex and Moore's model of housing classes. The first, raised by Haddon (1970), is that it involves a confusion between a conceptual model of class which defines it in terms of potential power in the housing market and in the system of bureaucratic allocation, and the empirical application of the concept which rests upon the identification of housing classes in terms of their current housing tenure. Thus Haddon observes, 'They equate this typology of housing with "housing classes" assuming that, analytically at least, people who are *at the present moment* in the same type of housing accommodation constitute a housing class' (p. 128). The problem here is obvious; it does not follow that those who at any one time share a common pattern of tenure also share a common capacity to gain access to a more favoured type, now or in the future. As Gans (1968) has shown, it in necessary to distinguish, in the inner city in particular, between those who are trapped in a given form of tenure and cannot move out, those who choose to live in that area and in a particular form of tenure but who could move out if they wished, and those who, in the process of time, will move out and 'up' the housing ladder when they have accumulated sufficient funds for a deposit, or points for a council house. It would seem to follow from this that, 'The emphasis of the analysis ought to be on the *means and criteria of access* to desirable housing, and the ability of different people to negotiate the rules of eligibility' (Haddon, p. 129). Or to put it another way, the focus should fall on the policies, ideologies and activities of the managers and gatekeepers of the urban system (see pages 166–80).

Haddon's criticisms here seem very damaging, for Weber clearly saw class as referring to the potential power of any group in a market situation. However, Haddon's analysis is itself somewhat confused at this point, for we need to distinguish current and future potential. The fact that those occupying a given form of tenure may have the *future* potential to improve their class situation need not invalidate a model of housing classes based upon current tenure, for to recognize this is only to recognize the possibility of social mobility within the housing class system. The inner city is, of course, somewhat unique in this respect anyway, for its instability leads to a much greater degree of movement between different types of tenure than is the case with most residential areas. Taking the city as a whole, for example, it is apparent that such movements generally take the form of a transition from the private rented sector to one of the two other major tenurial sectors (owner-occupation and council tenancy): 'The two categories of owner-occupiers and council renters provide distinct end points to the various moves between tenure types: flows move into them, but once a household lives in either type it rarely moves out, instead it makes moves within its own tenure' (Robson 1975, p. 41).

It follows, therefore, that although mobility between tenure types will be relatively rare in most areas of the city, it will be more common in inner areas where the bulk of private lower-cost rented accommodation is concentrated. But even in the inner city, the fact that a significant proportion of the population will at a future date be in a position to secure access to one or other of the two major forms of tenure does not invalidate a model of class based on current tenurial situation, since class power in the market refers to *current* potential, not future potential. To draw an analogy with the occupational hierarchy, we should be sceptical of any analysis which limited itself to the study of movement over time between shop-floor and management while dismissing as insignificant the relationship between management and workers. It follows from this that Haddon's criticism is relevant only in those cases where individuals occupy a 'lower' form of tenure (in terms of the hierarchy identified by Rex and Moore) yet could, if they wished, occupy a more favoured type. Such individuals do, of course, exist – for example, the intellectuals and artists of whom Gans writes. But even this need not invalidate the housing class model, any more than the existence of graduate dustmen invalidates models based upon occupational hierarchies. The numbers involved in both cases are small, and although any theory must take account of them, this does not mean that such theories must be reconstituted around them. For the great majority of people, therefore, current housing tenure and power in the housing market coincide at any one point in time, and Rex and Moore's emphasis on current housing situation is, consequently, justifiable.

The existence of individuals and families who choose to live in a less favoured form of tenure does, however, raise a second and possibly more pertinent criticism of the housing class model; namely, its assumption of a unitary value system regarding the desirability of different forms of tenure. Central to Rex and Moore's analysis of conflict between different housing classes is their assertion that competition takes place over the allocation and distribution of scarce *and desired* forms of housing in the city. The problem here is that different groups appear to have different ideas about what constitutes a desirable housing resource, and that these ideas often conflict with the hierarchy of housing types identified by Rex and Moore. They argued that owner-occupation and council tenancy could be seen as the two most desirable and 'legitimate' forms of tenure, the first because it was in accord with the values of property-ownership, the second because it was seen as legitimate with reference to welfare state values. Other forms of tenure were therefore less desirable. Yet in a study conducted in an inner area of Newcastle, Davies and Taylor (1970) show that landlordship of lodging houses is positively desired by certain immigrant groups as a means of accumulating wealth in a situation where other channels (notably the occupational hierarchy) are blocked. Similarly, research in Bath (Couper and Brindley 1975) has demonstrated that many people seem to prefer renting to owning, and that among those who prefer renting, council accommodation is by no means always preferred to a private tenancy. Indeed, one quarter of the tenants interviewed in this survey were in private accommodation and reported that they would not consider applying for a council house. The implication of these and other studies of housing values (see also Lambert and Filkin 1971 for a review of this research) is that there is no generalized desire for the two forms of tenure which Rex and Moore see as desirable, and that the central process of competition identified in their theory is therefore invalid.

Two points need to be made about this line of criticism. The first is that research such as that conducted in Bath cannot determine whether people really do not want a particular form of tenure such as owner-occupation, or (very different) whether they fail to aspire to it. It may be, for example, that for certain sections of the population, owner-occupation is so much out of reach that it is dismissed as inconceivable, and aspirations are levelled down accordingly. Couper and Brindley themselves recognize this problem: 'Preferences depend on people's knowledge about available alternatives and their perception of what is possible for themselves, both now and in the future, as well as on their basic values and ideologies' (1975, p. 567). What people say in answer to a questionnaire survey is by no means an accurate indication of what their values actually are. However, Rex (1971) has himself 'conceded that multiple value systems do exist', so there is no need to labour this point. More important is the point that research into subjective values and preferences cannot invalidate a theory of housing classes which is based upon the objective identification of class interests (see pages 43–8). In other words, if housing classes are defined in terms of the objective material situation of different tenure groups, then the key question concerns not which forms of tenure are seen as desirable (a question about ideology), but rather which forms give rise to which benefits and costs. Both Marx and Weber argued that classes are identified objectively, and there is no reason to suppose that those sharing a common class situation should also share a common recognition of their situation, or a common set of values about it. The problem as far as Rex and Moore's work is concerned is that, although they argued that housing classes did not necessarily share a common class consciousness, they nevertheless situated their analysis in the process of *competition* (which necessarily takes place on the basis of subjective preferences) rather than *conflict* (which can be identified in terms of conflicts between different objective class interests, and which need not, therefore, depend upon subjective preferences). Their focus on values, preferences and competition, rather than ideologies, interests and conflict, inevitably leads us to question whether their model of housing classes was in fact a class model at all.

This is precisely the issue raised by the third and most significant criticism of their work, and for this we must again turn to Haddon (1970). He argues that Rex and Moore have misinterpreted Weber and that their use of the concept of class is invalid. To understand this criticism, it is necessary to consider the distinction drawn by Weber between classes and status groups as two separate phenomena of the distribution of power. Weber argues that individuals may act collectively as classes or as status groups (or, indeed, as parties based on one, both or neither of these affiliations). This does not mean that status is necessarily a dimension of inequality independent of material class inequality, for Weber stresses that economic class power can be used to bring about the recognition of status inequalities, just as status groups may draw upon their prestige to develop and consolidate a privileged economic position. Thus, he recognizes that empirically, status groupings may correspond closely to social and property class groupings, but adds, 'Stratificatory status may be based on class status directly or related to it in complex ways. It is not, however, determined by this alone' (1947, p. 428). Similarly, 'status honour need not necessarily be linked with a "class situation". On the contrary, it normally stands in sharp opposition to the pretensions of sheer property. Both propertied and propertyless people can belong to the same status group, and frequently they do with very tangible consequences' (Gerth and Mills 1948, p. 187). Status groups and classes are therefore analytically (and often empirically) distinct. Status groups are based upon the distribution of prestige or social honour rather than on material economic inequalities. They are, furthermore, subjectively recognized by members and outsiders, unlike classes which arise objectively out of differential market situations. As Weber summarizes the differences between them, 'Classes are stratified according to their relations to the production and acquisition of goods; whereas status groups are stratified according to the principles of their *consumption* of goods as represented by special styles of life' (Gerth and Mills, p. 193).

It is the essence of Haddon's critique of Rex and Moore that what they have identified as housing classes are in fact housing status groups. The concept of class, he suggests, is used by Weber to refer to the power to realize income through the disposal of property (or skills) in the market. Housing cannot therefore form the basis for class formations since it is an element of consumption, which Weber clearly locates in his definition of status groups. The housing to which an individual achieves access thus *reflects* rather than *constitutes* his class situation: 'Use of housing is an index of achieved life chances, not primarily a cause' (1970, p. 132). It therefore follows that when one tenure group mobilizes in political action against what it sees as a threat from another (e.g. as in Birmingham when pressure was exerted politically to limit the spread of the lodging house zone, or – more dramatically – in the Oxford housing estate studied by Collison 1963, where a wall was erected to separate owner-occupied from council housing), this constitutes action based upon status which may therefore obscure and cross-cut underlying class similarities or differences. Haddon then goes on to suggest that a distinction should be drawn between the housing market – which gives rise to different patterns of consumption, and hence to differences of housing status – and the domestic property market – which gives rise to genuine class divisions (in the Weberian sense) according to the capacity of different groups to realize financial returns from the sale of land and developments. From this perspective, housing *classes* (as opposed to housing status groups) consist of those who realize income from the sale of domestic property against those who are 'negatively privileged' in this respect. As we shall see below, this is a model which has much in common with the neo-Marxist approach to housing and the class structure.

Haddon's analysis must be taken as a convincing refutation of Rex and Moore's neo-Weberian housing class thesis. It does, however, raise two problems, both of which may lead us to reject the Rex and Moore model, but nevertheless to retain the Weberian concept of class in the analysis of the housing market. The first relates to Weber's concept of property classes as referring to the ownership of types of property which are usable for returns. In his discussion of the types of property ownership which differentiate the class situations of the propertied, Weber includes the 'ownership of domestic buildings' along with the ownership of various productive resources, agricultural land, mines, money and so on (Gerth and Mills, p. 182). Now, although he does not draw out the implications of his list, it is apparent that Weber means by 'domestic buildings' those forms of housing which may be let out for rent or sold for profit, and in this sense, Haddon's argument is consistent with Weber's analysis. Nevertheless, it is also clear that Weber's conception of class as referring to market situation leads him to discuss these various forms of property as significant because they are *usable* for returns (not, that is, necessarily *used* for this purpose). Thus, one individual may own a large house and rent it to another, a second individual may own a similar house and let out one or two rooms while living in the rest of the house himself, and a third may own a comparable house and not use it to generate any rental return at all. In Weber's terms, all three are in the same class situation since their market power with respect to their property is equivalent, while for Haddon, they occupy different class situations because they use their property differently. But on what grounds can the sole occupier of a big house be seen as occupying a different class situation from that of his neighbour who let out a room? The first problem with Haddon's analysis of classes as referring to the suppliers and consumers of housing is therefore that it focuses on the actual use, rather than the potential usability, of domestic property resources, and the only way in which this problem can be overcome is by retaining tenure as a key element in housing class situations. Put simply, the owner-occupier enjoys the right and the ability to use his property to generate returns, while the tenant in a council house cannot do this.

The second problem with Haddon's analysis is that it ignores the question of whether housing is in fact entirely an element of consumption. This is an issue which I shall explore later in this chapter, but for the moment we need only note that if any particular form of housing has an accumulative potential, then action taken in defence of it cannot simply be dismissed as action based on status differentiation. As we shall see, it is quite clearly the case that owner-occupied housing does have such a potential, and that large capital gains can be realized through owner-occupation which cannot be realized through other forms of tenure. It follows that, from a Weberian perspective, owner-occupation may be seen as the basis for property class formation. I shall consider the problems which this argument raises later in the chapter.

Marxist approaches: owner-occupation as ideology

From the perspective of Marxist political economy, patterns of home ownership are irrelevant to the determination of economic class relations. There are a number of confusions and ambiguities in Marx's work on class, but what is clear throughout his writings is that, in capitalist societies (or at least in the pure capitalist mode of production), class relations are objectively determined by the contradictory relationship between capital and wage-labour. The two classes of capitalists and proletarians are in a contradictory relationship, not simply because one owns property and the other does not, but because they enter into relations of production in which capital grows through the appropriation of the surplus value created by labour. As Marx explained in one of his earlier works, 'The antithesis between lack of property and property, so long as it is not comprehended as the antithesis of labour and capital, still remains an indifferent antithesis, not grasped in its active connection with its internal relation – an antithesis not yet grasped as a contradiction' (1964, p. 132). Unlike Weber, therefore, Marx was insistent that classes could only be analysed through their relationship with one another, a relationship which necessarily came to express the contradictory relationship generated within the process of production. As he notes in the *Grundrisse*, 'The relation is realized only in the act of production itself, where capital really consumes the alien labour' (1973, p. 307).

It follows from this that the only market exchange in which classes develop is that involving the sale of labour-power for wages, and the only source of new value lies in the subsequent use of that labour-power by capital. Thus the return of rent to the landlord or interest to the investor represents only a redistribution of value which has already been created in the process of production of commodities. As Marx observes,

> Rent, interest and industrial profit are only different names for different parts of the surplus value of the commodity, or the unpaid labour enclosed in it, and they are equally derived from this source and from this source alone. They are not derived from land as such or from capital as such, but land and capital enable their owners to get their respective shares out of the surplus value extracted by the employing capitalist from the labourer (1969a, p. 61).

Clearly, then, when the worker enters into exchange relationships with other sections of capital in order to purchase commodities such as housing, food or whatever, this does not constitute a class relationship since no further surplus value is extracted. As Engels writes of the landlord–tenant relationship,

> The tenant, even if he is a worker, appears as a man with money; he must already have sold his commodity, a commodity peculiarly his own, his labour power, to be able to appear with the proceeds as the buyer of the use of a dwelling. ... No matter how much the landlord may overreach the tenant, it is still only a transfer of already existing previously produced value (1969a, pp. 307–8).

In short, the consumption of commodities such as housing, no matter whether it is achieved through purchase or renting, and no matter how much it costs, cannot in any way change the objective class relations which arise out of the process of production.

Having said this, it is apparent that Engels at least is not entirely consistent in following this argument through. His inconsistency is revealed most clearly in his attack on Emil Sax and his 'bourgeois' approach to the housing problem. Sax had argued (in common with many politicians and ideologues of our own time) that the solution to the housing problem lay in extending house ownership to the working class, thereby elevating them from the ranks of the property-less to the status of the propertied and thus transforming them into capitalists. Engels correctly identified the fallacy in this argument as deriving from Sax's confusion of different types of property:

Capital is the command over the unpaid labour of others. The little house of the worker can therefore become capital only if he rents it to a third person and appropriates a part of the labour product of this third person in the form of rent. But the house is prevented from becoming capital precisely by the fact that the worker lives in it himself, just as a coat ceases to be capital the moment I buy it from the tailor and put it on (1969a, pp. 330–1).

The worker's house thus constitutes property in the form of individual means of consumption (rather than means of accumulation), and the fact that both types of property are expressed through the same concept does not imply that they amount to the same thing (see Rose *et al.* 1976). Clearly, house ownership cannot transform a wage-labourer into a capitalist. However, Engels then goes on to say, 'The worker who owns a little house to the value of a thousand talers is, true enough, *no longer a proletarian*, but it takes Herr Sax to call him a capitalist' (1969a, p. 331, my italics). The implication of this would appear to be that, although house ownership does not constitute ownership of capital, it is nevertheless sufficient to differentiate the class position of the worker who owns his house from that of the worker who does not.

A number of possible arguments follow from this, although none is entirely convincing. First, it could be suggested that workers who own their own houses constitute a distinct 'fraction' within the working class as a whole, but this appears little more than a semantic 'solution' to the problem, for it is difficult to see how house ownership could be said to affect class interests as regards the objective relations of production into which both owners and tenants are obliged to enter as sellers of labour-power. Secondly, it could be argued that, although house ownership does nothing to change the economic situation of the working class, it does affect their political and ideological class practices. In his discussion of the middle class, for example, Poulantzas (1975) suggests that it should be distinguished from the working class, not only in terms of its economic function (i.e. the working class creates value directly and thus constitutes productive labour, whereas the middle class constitutes unproductive labour), but also politically and ideologically (e.g. through the ideological division between mental and manual labour). It could therefore be suggested that house ownership, like mental labour, functions on an ideological level to distinguish between different groups of workers, but this argument is not very satisfactory given the problems which attach to Poulantzas's formulation (e.g. see Hunt 1977). Thirdly, it could be argued that house ownership is pertinent at the economic level in providing access to revenue, and that it therefore constitutes one criterion of membership of the middle class. This is a possibility which I shall consider in more detail later in the context of Carchedi's recent work on the middle class. Here I need only note that, were such an argument accepted, it would lead out of a Marxist analysis and back into a distributional model of class with all the problems which that entails.

Few Marxists writing on housing today would accept any of these three possibilities. Rather, they argue in one of two ways. First, writers such as Castells follow the orthodox Marxist position and appear to ignore the quotation from Engels given above. Thus Castells describes the landlord–tenant relationship, for example, as, 'A relation between supply and demand, and therefore a market situation, not a relation of production. Indeed, we know that any assimilation of the tenant–landlord relation to the worker–capitalist relation is meaningless' (1977a, p. 146). He then goes on to suggest that a housing crisis is a crisis in the distribution of a particular commodity, and that it therefore may transcend class divisions arising out of the process of production and come to affect a range of different classes (see pp. 112–13). Other Marxists, on the other hand, suggest that relations to housing as a commodity themselves constitute one aspect of a generalized class struggle in society between capitalists and workers. Clarke and Ginsburg, for example, argue that, 'The immediate struggle between tenant and landlord over an item of consumption cannot be divorced from other conflicts in society, and particularly the dominant struggle between capitalist and worker. Just as in a particular wages struggle a worker is engaged as a specific type of worker engaged with a specific capital, so in a housing struggle the worker is engaged as a specific type of working class tenant confronting a specific capital. . . . The housing struggle analysed objectively is a struggle between capital and labour over the provision of housing, even if it is a struggle which is diffused both by the fragmentation of capital and by the fragmentation of the working class' (1975, p. 4).

This evident disagreement over whether relations to housing mirror class relations in the society as a whole is a fundamental one, but both sets of writers are agreed on the broader point that tenure divisions do not themselves constitute criteria of objective class formations. Indeed, in their discussions of owner-occupation, both argue that house ownership is important only at the ideological level in fragmenting the working class movement. Castells (1975), for example, suggests that the increasing homogeneity of workers at the point of production may be offset by increasing differentiation of residential status which atomizes relationships and leads to 'the ideological integration of the working class in the dominant ideology' (p. 185). Similarly, Clarke and Ginsburg suggest that 'the fragmentation of tenure categories raises the possibility of an ideological fragmentation of the class struggle' (1975, p. 5).

It is clear, therefore, that whatever their differences, those whom I have identified as contributing to the neo-Marxist approach agree that tenure divisions and residential status can have nothing to do with class formations, but rather that conflicts generated around the housing issue will take the form of the consumers of housing as a single category mobilizing against the suppliers (including landlords, developers and the state). Their analysis therefore has much in common with Haddon's critique of Rex and Moore in that it dismisses tenure divisions as irrelevant (except in so far as these divisions serve to obscure fundamental economic interests), and sees the basic conflict as a dichotomous one. From this perspective, owner-occupiers and tenants are in the same situation, are subject to the same contradictions and crises, and face the same adversaries. The argument is summed up by the slogan which appears on the back cover of a recent Community Development Project report: 'I rent, you buy, we lose, they profit' (1976a). Any analysis of housing struggles must therefore be based on this conflict between suppliers and consumers. As Ambrose and Colenutt put it, 'One is acting in accordance with an economic imperative and wants the highest possible financial return. The other needs housing or some other socially important facility at the lowest possible cost. Wants against needs, owners against users; the conflict can be stated in a number of ways' (1975, p. 15).

It does not go unnoticed by the advocates of this position that many owner-occupiers fail to recognize any common purpose which they may be said to share with tenants, and that for the most part they actively endorse any attempt to distance them spatially and socially from lower-income non-property owning groups. However, given that tenure divisions are more symbolic than real, and that objectively the two tenure groups are divided in terms of status rather than according to any significant conflict of material interests, then it follows that their tenacious attempts to maintain an identity distinct from that of other housing consumers can only be explained in terms of false consciousness. As Fletcher writes, 'Housing classes are not economic classes and . . . domestic property is politically significant by virtue of its contribution to a false consciousness. This is a consciousness that fails to recognize that those who are ensnared by the precariousness of their domestic security are really in a remarkably similar situation' (1976, p. 464).

This argument is a common theme in much of the literature. Owner-occupation is seen as an important means whereby capitalist interests, aided and abetted by the state, have divided the working class and strengthened their control. Boddy, for example, notes that, in contrast with working class tenants, 'The position of mortgaged owner-occupiers has never formed a focus or provoked political activity of a radical nature. On the contrary, the rise of working class owner-occupation tends to fragment class consciousness arising from the common position of the labour force in relation to the production process by overlaying groupings arising from differentiated tenure categories' (1976, p. 34). Like Emil Sax, owner-occupiers are led to believe that ownership of a few square yards of freehold gives them a vested interest in the capitalist system of private property. They are, furthermore, constrained to follow a pattern of life which renders them passive workers and ideal consumers. To gain access to the owner-occupied sector they are obliged to secure steady employment and to subscribe to bourgeois values of privatism and thrift (Castells 1975, p. 182, CDP 1976a, p. 42), and once having been granted a mortgage, they remain resolutely conservative. As Gray puts it, 'Owner-occupation, through its associated emphasis on the value of private property, self-reliance and gain, consumerism and so on, and the practical and very effective ties imposed by the need to make regular mortgage repayments effectively acts as a mechanism of social control' (1976, p. 84).

Thus, although house ownership is dismissed as unimportant economically, its political and ideological consequences for class relations are emphasized. Indeed, some writers suggest that the state has deliberately fostered the growth of owner-occupation for precisely this reason. Castells, for example, discusses the ideology of French politicians who 'wished to bring the class struggle to an end by making each worker an owner – outside his work, of course' (1977a, p. 161); Cockburn suggests that in Britain, 'Successive governments have used owner-occupation purposively as an inducement to workers to identify with bourgeois values' (1977, p. 45n); and Clarke and Ginsburg have little doubt that 'the capitalist class as a whole has a clear commitment to owner-occupation on ideological grounds, and it was this ideological commitment which ... was fundamental in determining the emphasis on owner-occupation from the fifties onwards. .... Owner-occupation has been seen as fundamentally important both in fragmenting the working class and in giving the worker a "stake in the system" ' (1975, p. 25).

We have already seen that there can be no arguing with the view, common to all these writers, that house ownership is not capital ownership, and that working class house owners are not capitalists. Where these writers can be criticized, however, is first, in the implicit theory of ideology which they are using, and secondly, in their denial of the economic relevance of domestic property ownership.

The theory of ideology which lies behind most of these arguments is crudely instrumentalist. The owner-occupier is seen as the unreflexive receptacle of ruling class ideology, an individual whose horizons are limited to the defence of his own little patch and who cannot see that in reality he has nothing to defend. He has been bought off by a mere trifle, and the extension of house ownership since the war has been one of a variety of ways in which he and others like him have been hoodwinked, divided, repressed and moulded for continuing exploitation. Not only do such arguments ignore historical evidence to the effect that the values of independence and thrift which are seen as the consequence of increasing rates of owner-occupancy were common among sections of the working class in England in the nineteenth century, and that the sponsorship of owner-occupation by the state since the 1930s may therefore have reflected as much as generated these values (see Rose 1978), but they are also founded on the view that such values were in some way imposed onto a passive proletariat in order to ensure its continuing compliance to the capitalist system. Such a view must surely be rejected, both because it fails to recognize the role of subordinate classes in constituting dominant ideologies (see pages 55–6), and because it grants to the state a degree of canniness, intentionality and foresight which is totally unrealistic. Certainly the state since the 1930s has deliberately fostered house ownership, but this can better be explained as the result of pragmatism and a long tradition in British social policy of relying, wherever possible, on the private sector, than as evidence of a deliberate attempt at ideological mystification (e.g. see Gilbert 1970, Chapters 3 and 5).

More important from our present perspective, however, is the view, expressed by these writers, that owner-occupation has been of little or no significance as regards the economic situation of individual owners. This is in direct contrast with Pahl's suggestion that, 'A family may gain more from the housing market in a few years than would be possible in savings from a lifetime of earnings' (1975, p. 291), for *if* this is the case, there is surely little reason to dismiss the spread of house ownership as of merely ideological significance. If house ownership provides access to a means of accumulating wealth which is not available to non-owners, then it presumably makes little sense to dismiss as 'false consciousness' the desire to own a house and to protect its market value. The question, therefore, is whether owner-occupation can generate real material gains.

The economic significance of house ownership

There are certain beneficial aspects of owning a house which are indisputable. Ownership of any commodity in a system of private property relations normally entails rights of control, beneficial use and disposal which are exclusively defined in law (see Rose *et al.* 1976), and housing is no exception. Unlike the tenant, the owner of a house enjoys the capacity to control the property (subject, of course, to planning and other restrictions imposed by the state) and to dispose of it when and to whom he sees fit. Because he is in a market situation rather than a bureaucratic system of allocation, an owner enjoys a choice over where to live (which can be crucial given the spatial inequalities found between different areas in terms of schooling, environment, proximity to cultural and employment centres, and so on) and the form of accommodation in which to live. He thus enjoys a degree of choice, limited by his power to pay, which is nevertheless denied to the council tenant. His rights of beneficial use are also much wider than those of the tenant (e.g. he is not subject to controls on keeping pets or the colour of his front door), and he also enjoys crucial rights of disposal through sale and inheritance. But although all of this is of undoubted significance in affecting both the life style and the life chances of the owner-occupier as compared with the tenant, none of it warrants the identification of house ownership as a basis for class formations in either the Weberian or Marxist sense of that term. It is therefore necessary to go beyond factors such as these and to consider in more detail what is entailed in the right of beneficial use. In other words, it is important to analyse whether the benefits enjoyed by the owner-occupier also extend to financial gain and wealth accumulation.

Those writers from within the neo-Marxist perspective who have addressed themselves to the question of whether house ownership entails a direct and real material accumulative potential have generally argued in one of two ways. On the one hand they have argued that the apparent gains in property values which accrue to owner-occupiers at times of inflation are in fact illusory (i.e. owner-occupiers are led to believe that they have gained when in fact they have not, and therefore become even more strongly committed to an ideology of private property ownership which actually misrepresents the realities of capitalist property relations); or, on the other hand, they have suggested that if individual house owners do gain, this is only possible at the expense of future buyers (i.e. owner-occupiers as a category or a sector of housing consumers merely exploit each other while making no gains from any other category – capital or non-owners). Both of these arguments need to be carefully examined for, as we shall see, although they both contain an element of truth, they are also both premised on some confused thinking about a question which is in some ways more complex than it has often been given credit for.

As regards the first argument – that apparent gains are illusory – this can indeed be shown to be the case, but only if certain assumptions are made about the nature of house price inflation which bear no relation to the historical experience in Britain, and which are in any case not made explicit by those who advance this argument. In order to demonstrate this, it will be useful to construct a hypothetical example. Let us assume that an individual buys a house for £5000 using £500 from his own resources and a mortgage for £4500. Let us also assume that there is an annual rate of inflation of 10 per cent which is evenly reflected in house prices, interest rates, rents, wages and so on. It follows from this that, if this annual inflation rate continues, this individual will find that in just over seven years his house will have increased in price to £10,000, thereby realizing a notional untaxed money gain of £5000. However, those who argue that owner-occupation does not generate wealth immediately point out that, while the price of this individual's house has doubled, so too has the price of all other houses, and assuming that he wishes to buy an equivalent house to the one he has sold (given that he has to live somewhere), he has therefore gained nothing. The only people who have gained are those involved in the supply of housing re-sources – landowners sitting on sites ripe for development, owners of more than one house, and so on.

A number of objections may be raised to this. For a start, it may be argued that not all individuals will wish to buy an equivalent house to the one they have sold; at a certain stage in the life-cycle, people may buy smaller and cheaper properties, or career changes may lead to moves to parts of the country where the average level of house prices is cheaper. In such cases, they will not need to reinvest the whole of the notional gain they have realized. What this demonstrates is that house price inflation leads to wealth accumulation, irrespective of whether this wealth is immediately realizable. This point is forcibly made by Ball who writes:

> It is often argued that such increases in property values are not gains to the owner as they are unrealizable given that another house of similar price has to be purchased. The argument is obviously fallacious; the correct comparison is between owning and not owning at one point in time. . . . Wealth is created for owners but not non-owners. Whether this wealth is ever realized is immaterial; it still exists, even if it is used only as an inheritance for future generations [1976, p. 25].

In fact, we may go further than this, for it does not follow from the neo-Marxist critique that such accumulation of wealth is not realizable in terms of income. Quite the reverse. In terms of our example, it is apparent that when the owner-occupier sells his house for £10,000, he is able to appropriate the entire increase in value even though he has only paid for a fraction of the house out of his own resources. Where he started out with a £500 deposit, he ends up, not with £1000 (representing the monetary value of his original deposit following a 100 per cent inflation), but with £5500 (representing the inflated value of his deposit plus the inflated value of that part of the house for which he has not yet paid). Expressed in real terms, his capital has grown by 450 per cent in just over seven years. He can, if he chooses, reinvest the whole of this accumulated wealth in the purchase of a new house, but if he does so, he will be able to buy much more than just an equivalent house – i.e. he can take out a mortgage for £9000 (which, in real terms, is equivalent to his original mortgage), add his deposit of £5500, and buy a house for £14,500. Alternatively, if he wishes, he can reinvest in an equivalent house costing £10,000, taking out a mortgage for £9000 (which costs him no more in real terms than his original mortgage of £4500 did), adding a deposit of £1000, and putting the remaining £4500 (which in fact has a real value of £2250) in his pocket. As this example shows, owner-occupation is a form of tenure which allows for realizable wealth accumulation which is not open to those who rent their accommodation (i.e. a tenant over the comparable period will simply find that he is paying twice the rent – in money terms – at the end than he was at the beginning).

The question necessarily raised by all this is, if owner-occupiers can accumulate wealth in real terms, where does it come from?

Clarke and Ginsburg appear in no doubt: 'The gain is achieved at the expense of another owner-occupier who purchases the house. . . . The important point is that from the point of view of the sector as a whole, capital gains do not represent a benefit' (1975, p. 19). Similarly, the CDP report cited earlier argues that it is those entering the housing market at a later date who 'are persuaded to pay the inflated house prices which ease the established owners' burden' (1976a, p. 43). It follows from this that, while owner-occupiers engage in mutually exploitative transactions with one another, developers and land-owners and money-lenders extract the benefits, and that the owner-occupied sector as a whole cannot be seen as providing the basis for class formations. The argument, however, is invalid, for as we shall see, gains are only made from other owner-occupiers or future buyers when house price inflation is increasing faster than the general rate of inflation, yet wealth is, as we have already seen, accumulated even when we assume a uniform rate of inflation. Thus, to return to our example, when the individual sells his house at £10,000, he sells it at the same real value as the price at which he bought it. The buyer, in other words, pays twice as much as he did in money terms, but the same amount as he did in real terms, since not only house prices but wages have doubled in the intervening period. The real gain cannot therefore be explained in terms of exploitation of the buyer. So where does it come from?

The answer is, quite simply, that the owner-occupier's gain represents (indirectly) his own enforced savings over this period. The point is, of course, that in order to protect the real value of its loan to the owner-occupier in a situation of 10 per cent annual inflation, the lending institution must have increased the interest charged to a level where repayments cover both the real rate of interest (say, 3 or 4 per cent) and the erosion of the value of the loan (10 per cent per annum). The real rate of interest represents the charge for the use of the loan and may therefore be seen as equivalent to the rent paid for the use-value of a dwelling by a tenant, while the additional interest is used to offset the falling value of the loan of £4500 and will therefore equal the inflated value (appropriated by the mortgagee) of that part of the house which the loan has been used to pay for. Under the conditions stipulated in the example (i.e. a uniform inflation rate), therefore, the borrower puts in his pocket at the end of the period the equivalent of what he has paid to the building society over and above the real rate of interest. It follows from this that he could equally have rented a house at an annual rent equal to the real value of this 3 or 4 per cent rate of interest, and invested his additional monthly payments in a finance institution paying 10 per cent interest to depositors. At the end of the period, he would then have accumulated in savings a capital sum equal to that which he realizes by selling his house. There is, in other words, a fallacy in Ball's argument, cited earlier, that the owner-occupier gains relative to the tenant, for the real comparison is that with the tenant who invests the same amount each month as the owner-occupier pays out in interest over and above the real interest rate.

This argument clearly lends support to the neo-Marxist position, for it demonstrates that the wealth accumulated through owner-occupation derives from the owner-occupier's own payments and that, although the tenant cannot accumulate wealth in this way, he can nevertheless accumulate the same amount by investing the difference between the rent he pays for the use-value of his house (assuming this is equivalent to the real rate of interest paid by the owner-occupier for the use value of his loan) and the total amount paid by the owner-occupier to the building society. Put simply, neither of them accumulates except through his own (forced or voluntary) savings, and both are obliged to pay a real sum (in real interest or in rent) to some fraction of capital for the use of their respective dwellings. Are they not, therefore, in identical class situations?

There are two reasons why this conclusion does not follow. The first is that the owner-occupier's investment is in the house in which he lives while the tenant's (assuming he chooses to save on the same scale) is in some financial institution. It follows, therefore, that the owner-occupier has a vested interest in the domestic property market, while the tenant who invests elsewhere has a vested interest in the rate of interest paid (or perhaps the dividends paid on share-holdings) in the finance market. Few tenants, of course, invest the substantial sums with which we are concerned in stocks and shares or bank accounts, but given that they must do this if they are to maintain comparability with the owner-occupier, let us assume that they do in fact do this. Two consequences follow. First, owner-occupiers as a group will have a vested interest in seeing the rate of house price inflation in the domestic property market increase faster than the rate of interest in the finance markets, while tenants with investments outside housing will have exactly the opposite interests. This is because rent levels will necessarily reflect current house prices. However, there is a paradox here, for the tenant who has investments outside housing will have an interest qua investor in seeing interest rates increase, but an interest qua tenant in seeing them decrease (since interest rates will themselves affect the cost of housing and thus average rents). Leaving this paradox aside, however, it remains the case that tenants and owner-occupiers have incompatible interests as regards the relative rate of inflation in the domestic property market, and they cannot therefore be subsumed under one category of consumers.

Secondly, it also follows that owner-occupiers as individuals have an interest in securing the value of their own house relative to that of others. The housing market is, of course, uneven, and houses in one area may increase faster than those in another. It is clearly economically rational for any one owner-occupier to ensure that the value of his house does not drop relative to that of others, and this in turn may lead him into a conflict with the interests of tenants – e.g. in cases where a proposal is made to build council housing on a plot adjacent to owner-occupied housing. As we shall see later, when owner-occupiers mobilize politically against such a proposal, they cannot be accused of suffering from a 'false consciousness' which prevents them from recognizing their common situation as consumers of housing. What both of these points indicate is that, even if tenants secure the same returns as owner-occupiers by investing comparable sums elsewhere (which is itself empirically highly unlikely), they nevertheless have different interests as consumers of housing, and these differences are based in their differing situations in relation to the domestic property market.

The second reason for rejecting the conclusion that all consumers of housing share common material interests is that the argument outlined above, to the effect that the wealth accumulated by owner-occupiers is merely the result of their own involuntary savings, is true of the abstract and formal model set up by way of illustration of the issue, but is not true of empirical and historical reality. In Britain, at least, the history of house price inflation simply does not accord with the key assumptions on which this model was based. These assumptions were (*a*) that the general level of house prices inflates at the same rate as the overall rate of inflation, including that of wages; (b) that interest rates charged on credit for house purchase are adjusted to take account of the true rate of inflation (i.e. so that the real rate of interest is maintained over time); and (c) that interest payments by owner-occupiers are met entirely out of their own resources. None of these assumptions is, in fact, empirically valid, and it follows that the fallacy in the neo-Marxist argument lies not so much in the logic of their analysis (although, as I have shown, the analysis is flawed) – which is the point which Ball attempts to establish – but more importantly in the premises on which their argument has to be based. Let us consider each of these assumptions in turn.

The assumption that house prices increase at the same rate as all other prices and wages is clearly false. The astronomical increase in house prices in Britain in the early 1970s should be sufficient to warn us against any such assumption, but even taking the longer term, it is apparent that there has been no prolonged period in this century when house prices have not increased faster than the general inflation rate. If we take the last ten years, for example, it has been shown that the market value of housing has increased faster than the return on any conventional form of investment (see the *Estates Gazette*, October 1976) – i.e. it would have been impossible for any non-owner to have achieved a return on investment comparable to that achieved by owner-occupiers. Housing, quite simply, has been getting more expensive in real terms. There appear to be a variety of reasons for this which we cannot go into here, but clearly the finite scarcity of development land is a key factor (especially since the introduction of comprehensive negative planning controls after the war effectively limited available building land still further without taking state control of development sites). The Community Land Act of 1975 may be seen as an attempt to rectify this, but as Ambrose (1976) has shown, the central aim of nationalizing development values very soon became emasculated. The long-term trend towards real increases in land and house prices thus shows no sign of being halted or reversed. Now it is true that in this situation, the gains made by owner-occupiers are achieved at the expense of new buyers, as the neo-Marxist position suggests. However, there seems little reason why this should prevent us from seeing owner-occupiers in terms of a model of property classes, since non-owners are by definition not members of that class, and the premium they pay to existing owners for entry into that class may be recouped with profit at a later date when they too come to sell. Furthermore, this is not the only source of real gain for house owners. Indeed, it is probably the least significant source.

The second assumption was that interest rates charged on housing loans are adjusted to take account of the overall rate of inflation. Again, the assumption is grossly misplaced. In the 1970s, for example, the rate of inflation in Britain has at times reached around 25 per cent, yet the mortgage rate has never exceeded half that amount. If the rate of interest charged to building society borrowers were to take account of the true rate of inflation, it would have had to have reached around 30 per cent in the mid 1970s – a rate which would have necessitated impossibly high repayments, and which would therefore have attracted virtually no borrowers. In times of inflation, it is therefore necessary for building societies to lend money at substantially negative real interest if they are to lend any money at all. This has two important consequences. The first is that owner-occupation becomes a very attractive form of investment – a mortgage is almost a licence to print money. This is undoubtedly one of the major factors which explains the house price explosion in the early 1970s, for the almost indiscriminate release of funds by the building societies at that time (which is generally seen as the cause of the subsequent rise in prices) was only a reflection of the high demand for credit on the part of potential buyers intent on purchasing relatively cheap property at negative rates of interest.

The second consequence is that building society investors lose heavily in real terms. The fact that, as Cullingworth puts it, 'When inflation is brought into account, an owner-occupier may find himself buying his house for nothing' (1972, p. 58), is thus a reflection of the losses sustained by those whose money is being borrowed. The vast majority of those who lose are small investors – they would certainly include our hypothetical tenant who is trying desperately to keep pace with the rate of accumulation of owner-occupiers – for they constitute the bulk of building society depositors. Indeed, it is apparent that the necessity to lend at negative real rates of interest to house buyers (and hence to pay negative real rates to investors) gives rise to a significant regressive redistribution of wealth in society, since most depositors will be less wealthy than most borrowers. The second and highly significant source of real wealth for the owner-occupier is therefore the small investor.

The third source of his wealth is the tax-payer. This is in part because in recent years the British government has felt it necessary to provide grants and loans to the building societies in order to keep interest rates down, and the source of these has, of course, been general taxation. More importantly, however, owner-occupiers receive tax allowance on the interest they pay on their housing loans – i.e. they receive a subsidy out of general taxation. Council rents, too, are subsidized, but the situation is not analogous, partly because the subsidy is in large part provided from within the local authority housing sector (through the system of pooled historic costs), and partly because the allowances made to owner-occupiers constitute subsidies on both the use-value and the future exchange value of their dwellings. Tax subsidies, in other words, operate to ensure that house owners gain more through increased house prices than they lose through increased interest payments. It may be, of course, that the advantages of tax relief could be abolished by some future parliament, but given the commitment of the three major political parties (including the Labour Party) to increasing home ownership, and the fact that over half of the electorate would stand to lose from such a measure, such a possibility seems unlikely. Precisely because owner-occupiers do collectively constitute a group with distinct material interests to defend, their significance is felt at both the local and the national levels of British politics, and this provides strong grounds for arguing that their tax subsidies could not be withdrawn without a prolonged political battle.

There is also a fourth source of wealth for owner-occupiers, although this applies not to the category as a whole, but rather to the individual home-owners who comprise it. Given that house owners have a material interest in ensuring that the value of their property at least remains comparable to that of similar houses, it is clear that real increases in value may be achieved through the expenditure of labour-power on improvements. Indeed, here too the government provides further financial assistance through improvement grants, so owner-occupiers (as well as private developers) can secure substantial gains in future exchange value both through the creation of value through labour, and through additional government subsidy. The candid advice offered by the *London Property Letter* to prospective builders and developers that, 'Properly done, conversions are the next best thing to counter-feiting for making money' (quoted by Merrett, 1976, p. 44), could apply equally to existing and prospective owner-occupiers. Again, of course, this possibility is not available to non-owners.

Owner-occupation is, therefore, an accumulative form of tenure. The wealth to which it gives rise is derived from enforced saving, from future buyers, from small and large investors alike, as well as from general taxation, and (potentially) from the ability to increase capital through the expenditure of labour-power. It is therefore achieved at the expense of a variety of different classes in society but mainly, it seems, from the poorer sections who do not themselves own domestic property. As Townsend (1976) notes in his discussion of the 1975 Royal Commission on income and wealth, the inequality of wealth distribution in Britain is much greater than that of incomes, and owner-occupation is a significant factor in this distribution. Thus, as Pahl argues, domestic property ownership provides half the population with access to an accumulative form of wealth which can prove almost as important as earned income in determining in- equalities of material life chances.

Some possible implications for Weberian and Marxist approaches

If we accept the analysis of the role of domestic property ownership in the previous section, then the argument has some significant implications for both the Weberian and Marxist approaches to the question of housing tenure. Nor are these implications merely 'abstract' or taxonomic, for the problem of housing classes is, in the final analysis, a problem of political strategy. In other words, the basic question to be answered is whether owner-occupiers and tenants are potentially allies or adversaries in political struggles over housing.

The answer which emerges from a reassessment of the Weberian approach is that they are potentially both. Owner-occupiers, that is, constitute a 'middle' property class whose interests may align with those of either the 'positively privileged' class of housing suppliers, or the 'negatively privileged' class of non-owners, according to the nature of the issue.

The Weberian view of owner-occupiers as a middle class in the property class system differs from the orthodox Marxist, the traditional Weberian, and the neo-Marxist approaches outlined earlier in a number of ways. It differs from the orthodox Marxist position in that it denies that direct expropriation of surplus value through the wage labour-capital relation is a necessary feature of class relations, and as a consequence of this, it argues that class structuration is not solely dependent on production relations, and that a basically dichotomous class model is inappropriate in both the acquisition and property class systems. It differs from Rex and Moore's Weberian perspective in that it denies the relevance of the ecological factor (i.e. spatial segregation), it rejects an arbitrary pluralism in favour of a trichotomous model of housing classes, it emphasizes the process of real wealth accumulation as a necessary criterion of analysis, it rests on an objective assessment of class interests rather than on any assumption of shared values, and it includes the suppliers of housing as one class in the property class system. Finally, as we have seen, it rejects the neo-Marxist position in that it recognizes a fundamental economic cleavage, and hence class division, within the category of housing consumers.

A Weberian approach to housing tenure will thus rest on the identification of three classes differentiated according to their varying relationships to the distribution of housing. Each of these may, of course, be further sub-divided into distinct strata. The first of these classes is private capital engaged in the supply of housing or in the provision of facilities and services necessary to its supply and distribution. The interests of this class lie in profit maximization, although this will be achieved in different ways by different strata within it. The major strata within this class may be identified as finance capital (engaged in lending money for house purchase, housing development and housing improvements), industrial capital (engaged in the construction of housing), commercial capital (the 'exchange professionals' such as estate agents, solicitors and surveyors engaged in the market distribution of housing) and landed capital (both landowners and rentiers such as private landlords). Sometimes these various strata will come into conflict with each other (e.g. the interest of finance capital in securing the maximum returns of money lent is clearly incompatible with the interest of industrial capital in raising cheap loans for investment), but what unites these different strata into a single class is their shared interest in the returns to housing as a commodity.

The middle class in this schema consists of owner-occupiers for whom housing represents both use value and exchange value. Again different strata could be identified, notably around the division noted by Rex and Moore between mortgagees and outright owners, for certain benefits which accrue to the former (e.g. tax relief on mortgages) will be of little material concern to the latter. Other divisions according to the size, value, location and age of the property may also become significant in certain cases. Dennis (1970), for example, argues that few of the customary benefits of owner-occupation were enjoyed by the owners of the small old houses in a redevelopment area of Sunderland which he studied. Owner-occupiers there found that the only major advantage they enjoyed over tenants related to rights of control (rather than benefit or disposal): 'The home cannot be valued as a tangible object to be handed down in the family, nor can owner-occupation be regarded as a means of obtaining security of tenure' (p. 236). However, even in such an extreme case as this, owner-occupiers can still be shown to share fundamental common interests against tenants, for their right of benefit has not entirely disappeared. This is illustrated by Silburn's study of a similar slum area in Nottingham where an attempt to bring owner-occupiers and tenants together into a single organization failed when tenants supported redevelopment as the means whereby they could gain access to a council tenancy, while owners fought for the area to be improved as the means whereby they could enhance their property values (Silburn 1975). Such conflicts between owner-occupiers and tenants are by no means unusual (e.g. see, for example, Repo 1977 on the fate of the Trefann Court residents' movement, and Cowley *et al.* 1977 on the 'Barnsbury scandal'), and cases like this only serve to underline the economic and political division between these two tenure groups.

The third housing class which can be identified from a Weberian perspective is thus the non-owners of domestic property – tenants who stand to gain nothing from increased exchange values. Again there are subdivisions to be drawn, principally between council tenants (the largest category which, following Rex and Moore, could be further subdivided into those in purpose-built property and those in short-life housing), private tenants (differentiated into those in the 'luxury' sector, those in older self-contained properties, and those in rented rooms) and homeless families. As with the other two classes, these strata within the class share a fundamental interest in common (namely low rents and a plentiful housing stock), although conflicts may also occur between them (e.g. the 1972 Housing Finance Act generally operated to the benefit of private tenants – and, indeed, their landlords – while increasing rents in the public sector).

This application of Weberian stratification theory to the question of housing tenure suffers from a number of weaknesses and may be criticized on at least five grounds. The first of these is probably the least significant – namely, that the model is not exhaustive, exclusive or complete. There are, for a start, some categories of housing suppliers and consumers (e.g. housing associations, tenants in co-ownership schemes and, most crucially, local authority housing departments) which do not clearly belong to any of the three classes outlined. It is, furthermore, possible for one individual to 'belong' to more than one class (e.g. the owner-occupier who lets out a room), while the inclusion of strata as diverse as the tenant of a luxury penthouse suite and the lodger in rented rooms as members of the same housing class is clearly absurd. However, such confusions and complications in the model may be said to reflect the fact that class divisions are never concise and clear-cut, and in its defence it may be argued that such detailed problems of classification do not undermine the main thrust of the argument.

A second criticism is that, like Rex and Moore's original formulation, the model elaborated here is essentially static. As Bell notes, 'Class ought to be treated as a *relational* concept. . . . However, with use of the concept of housing class it has not always been clear either who is exploiting whom, or what relational aspects are involved' (1977a, p. 38). This is a more serious problem than the first although it is clear from the analysis in the previous section that relations of exploitation can be established – i.e. that the sources of returns for owner-occupiers can be identified. The problem, however, is that owner-occupiers as a 'class' do not exploit tenants as a 'class', but rather derive their increasing wealth from highly specific sectors of the population (aspiring home owners and building society investors), or from virtually the entire population (through tax relief). That they have distinct interests from tenants does not place them in a necessarily antagonistic relationship with them.

Related to this is a third criticism, also made by Bell. that the model represents a distributional treatment of class 'regarding it as yet another commodity that is distributed more or less equally in society (like income, age and washing machines)' (ibid., p. 38). This cannot be taken directly as a criticism of the approach outlined here, for the three-fold distinction of housing classes is premissed on the view that housing is a unique commodity since it alone among consumption goods provides access to further wealth accumulation. The point about washing machines, cars and other consumer durables is that they function for *use* (see Rose *et al.* 1976), and they can therefore have no significance as regards class (as opposed to status) formation. Owner-occupied housing, on the other hand, has a dual function for use and accumulation and is therefore highly significant for the identification of property classes

This argument, however, raises the question of whether housing is unique in this respect, or whether there are other forms of property which share this dual function. One obvious example would be works of art, although it could (perhaps somewhat tenuously) be argued that their primary function lies in accumulation, unlike reproductions and prints whose primary function lies in their use value. More problematic is the case of insurance policies and annuities, for although they may be said to function for use (i.e. as a store to be used up during retirement – see Renner 1949, pp. 234–6), they are clearly, like house ownership, an important means of wealth accumulation. Presumably, therefore, the house-owner and the policy-holder must both be included as members of a middle property class, in which case the question arises as to how this property class system articulates with the acquisition class system. This leads into the fourth criticism, for it is by no means clear from a Weberian perspective how individuals such as the house-owning factory worker or the policy-holding coal miner can be classified in terms of the overall class system. It is one thing, therefore, to argue that house ownership objectively separates the economic and political interests of different tenure groups, but quite another to argue that this places them in different 'class situations'.

The fifth criticism is that the analysis is based upon certain crucial historical conditions – namely, a disproportionate rate of house price inflation, negative real rates of interest on house loans, and government tax subsidies. In each case, arguments can be adduced as to why these conditions should continue (e.g. land shortages, the

impossibility of recouping high rates of interest, the political un-
popularity of any attempt to dismantle the tax subsidy), but the
crucial point is that, if these conditions were to alter so as to prevent
continuing accumulation through house ownership, then the logic of
the Weberian position is that the different tenure categories would no
longer constitute distinct property classes, but could only be represented as specific political interest groups ('parties' in Weber's
terminology). This is perhaps the most serious weakness of this whole
approach – that in the final analysis it is empirical and descriptive,
dependent upon the continuation of specific conditions which are
external to the analysis itself.

What then can be salvaged from the Weberian approach to
housing stratification? Only this: that, despite its theoretical inadequacies, it does recognize that conflicts over housing, analysed
objectively, cannot be reduced to the classic class categories of
political economy. Whatever else is wrong with the argument, it
remains the case that a simple model of capitalist against non-
capitalist interests cannot validly be applied to an understanding of
political struggles over housing, and that any political strategy which
assumes that it can is unlikely to succeed (see pages 123–4).

The question which this raises is whether Marxist theory can be
developed in order to take account of the specificity of political
struggles over housing, and at this point it is necessary to refer back
to the first section of this chapter where three possibilities were
outlined. We need not dwell on the first two, for we saw that an
argument in terms of class 'fractions' provides only an ad-hoc and
untheorized solution, while an application of the Poulantzian position encounters the problem of whether and how ideological class
practices can be seen as constitutive of objective class relations. The
third approach, however, is worth considering a little more. This
involves a development of recent work by Carchedi (1975) on the
identification of the middle class in the conditions of advanced
capitalism.

Basically, Carchedi argues that advanced capitalist production
involves a complex labour process in which the concept of the productive worker must be expanded to include all those who play a
part in the labour process. Drawing upon Marx's notion of the
collective worker, he therefore argues, first, that while the capitalist
will always perform the traditional functions of capital (i.e. control

and surveillance of the workforce), he may also contribute to the function of the collective worker through his coordination of the work process (i.e. the management role), and secondly, that while all sections of the employed workforce will always contribute to the functions of the collective worker, certain sections may also carry out some of the 'global functions of capital'. Of particular significance here is the situation of the new middle class: 'This fact, that the new middle class performs the global function of capital even without owning the means of production, and that it performs this function in conjunction with the function of the collective worker, is the basic point for an understanding of the nature of this class' (ibid., p. 51). It follows that three classes can be theorized in the conditions of an advanced capitalist mode of production: a class of capitalists which carries out the functions of control and repression in the work place, a class of proletarians which carries out the functions of production of commodities, and a middle class which does both, part of its time being devoted to production, and part to control.

Carchedi uses this argument to explain income differentials between the working and middle classes, for while the former are paid a wage which expresses only the value of their labour-power, the latter are paid both in respect of the value of their labour-power, and out of revenue in respect of their contribution to the global functions of capital. Because they aid capital, in other words, the members of the new middle class are able to draw upon the revenue which accrues to capital. However, Carchedi then goes on to argue that the tendency within capitalism to reduce skilled labour to average labour may lead to a process of proletarianization of the new middle class in which its contributions to the global functions of capital, and hence its claim to revenue, are gradually eroded. Irrespective of its validity, this last point leads us to ask whether the middle class may be in a position to counter this decline in real income through access to other sources of revenue outside the work situation, and it is here that house ownership, together with ownership of other accumulative forms of property such as insurance policies and pension schemes, may be important.

It could be argued, then, that house ownership provides one criterion of middle class membership since it constitutes an important source of revenue over and above wage payments. The problem, however, is that such an argument breaks with the central Marxist

concern with production relations and leads us back into the Weberian problematic of distribution relations. Yet it is apparent that a
breach has to be made somewhere in the orthodox Marxist position if
a theory is to be developed which can explain the political struggles
involving owner-occupiers in terms other than ideological manipulation. When owner-occupiers mobilize politically (and as we shall
see in Chapter 6, they do so frequently and with considerable effect),
their actions reflect a concern with their own material situation and
cannot be dismissed as 'false consciousness'. This would appear to
leave Marxist analysis with two options; either house ownership
must in some way be included in an analysis of class position, or it
must be recognized that political struggles involve groups which
cannot be analysed in class terms. Both options involve some
concession to Weberian theory; the first because it takes into account
market relations other than the exchange of labour-power for wages,
the second because it breaks with the traditional base-superstructure
metaphor in recognizing a necessary non-correspondence between
economic class categories and political action. The second of these
alternatives appears the more fruitful, for the first only encounters
the sorts of problems already discussed in relation to any concept of
housing classes.

This second option is closely related to Hirst's recent critique of
economism and Poulantzian relative autonomy. As we shall see in
Chapter 4, Hirst argues that an economistic theory of politics is
invalid because it is clear that political practices are not merely
organized around class interests, and that political struggles cannot
be assumed to represent classes in action. He also criticizes the concept of relative autonomy between economics and politics, arguing
that this is a spurious solution to the problem of economism since it
still rests on the principle of economic determinacy. He concludes:

When we turn to confront the dominant political issues and struggles of
the day, classes, categories of economic agents, are not directly present in
them. . . . The issues, the ideologies, the classes specified within the political
arena are constituted there – one cannot read back beyond it to some
essential arena of class struggle beyond politics. This is what is meant by
non-correspondence [1977, pp. 125 and 131].

It would therefore follow from Hirst's argument that housing conflicts involving different tenure groups constitute one of a number of
political struggles in which individuals and groups from different

economic classes are engaged. There is, in other words, no reason to expect that such issues must be fought along class lines, for they are fought by groups which are constituted through the issue itself.

Once we recognize the necessary non-correspondence between class categories and political housing struggles, it is possible to analyse the way in which political groups are constituted around housing issues by drawing on Parkin's work on different modes of social closure. Thus Parkin argues that class analysis, rather than focusing on objective relationships to the means of production, may prove more fruitful if it considered political struggles in terms of whether specific groups operate a strategy of 'exclusion' – which he defines as 'the attempt by a given group to maintain or enhance its privileges by the process of subordination' (1974, p. 4) – or solidarism – 'collective responses of excluded groups which are themselves unable to maximize resources by exclusion practices' (ibid., p. 5). Exclusion, in other words, is the characteristic strategy of dominant groups set on defending their privileges, while solidarism is the characteristic response to this on the part of subordinate groups. Parkin also notes that solidarism is often much weaker than exclusion as a strategy of social closure since it imposes greater individual costs – an argument to which we shall have cause to return in later chapters.

Parkin's identification of these two strategies of closure provides a useful means whereby housing conflicts may be analysed, for despite his own preference for a dichotomous model of conflict between those who exclude and those who are excluded, it is apparent that different strategies may come to be adopted by different groups in different situations, and that the distinction drawn earlier between those who live off housing, those who live in it and those who do both can usefully be analysed in terms of modes of social closure. Thus, as we shall see in Chapter 6, the political situation of owner-occupiers may lead them to adopt both solidaristic strategies in their battles against a local authority or a private developer, and strategies of exclusion in their attempts to maintain their privileged situation vis-à-vis non-property-owning groups. Given their specific interests in relation to housing, therefore, they are engaged in a constant struggle to force concessions on the one hand, and to repel threats on the other. And according to the nature of the conflict, this may lead them to seek common ground with either the representatives of private capital or with non-property-owning groups.

Thus we arrive at the conclusion that the two major patterns of housing tenure – ownership and renting – are important determinants of the real political divisions which are constituted in housing struggles. This does not mean that tenure categories can be taken as synonymous with property class formations in the Weberian sense, but neither does it suggest that the political mobilization which takes place on the basis of these categories is merely a form of false class consciousness serving only to blur the real class interests and class antagonisms which lie behind them. While all consumers of housing can find common ground in some issues, they are objectively on opposing sides in others, and any attempt to dismiss the divisions between them as of only ideological significance is not only theoretically misplaced, but is likely to result, if taken seriously by community activists, in the attempt to reconcile the irreconcilable with disastrous consequences.

3 The new urban politics

There is a long tradition in western social and political thought which associates urbanism on the one hand with individual freedom and liberation from what Marx termed the 'idiocy of rural life', and on the other with increasing misery, social disorganization and political disruption. These twin strands of thought are found, of course, in the work of Marx and Engels, and especially in their emphasis on the significance of spatial concentration in aiding the development of a radical working class movement. But they are found also in varying liberal and conservative perspectives, and are reflected in various political movements from the nineteenth century onwards (e.g. the establishment of paternalistic company towns such as Bournville in England or Pullman in the United States, the development of the garden city movement in the early twentieth century, the growth of environmental movements in the last few years, and so on) which have aimed at averting the social and political consequences that are seen to develop out of an increasing concentration of a disadvantaged class in towns and cities. In the nineteenth century especially, the new industrial towns were seen by liberals and conservatives to represent 'a formidable threat to the established social order' (Glass 1968, p. 67), but even today, there is a strong ideological legacy of antiurbanism which may be explained with reference to the perceived threat to the status quo posed by urban concentration.

In this chapter, I wish to consider the extent to which the potential for urban political mobilization may still constitute a real treat to the established social and political order. More specifically, I shall consider how far political class struggles may be identified outside the factory gate in the societies of the advanced capitalist world – i.e. how far the basic contradiction identified by Marx between wage-labour and capital is being overlaid by or displaced into specifically urban struggles concerning the distribution of 'indirect wages' in the form of housing, educational facilities, and the like. We may note at the outset, of course, that in the case of Britain, the prospect of political upheaval in the towns and cities no longer appears as 'frightening' or as likely as it did one hundred years ago. With the notable exception of the urban guerilla war in Ulster (which cannot easily be explained as a 'revolutionary' situation as such), there appears to be little widespread urban political unrest in the United Kingdom. Elsewhere, however, explosions of unrest have developed – notably in the United States, where the black ghetto riots of the 1960s served to focus the attention of government and radicals alike upon the 'urban question', and in France, where the events of May 1968 vividly demonstrated that 'contemporary society, far from living up to its chosen image of a monolithic machine, subject to no more than short periodic breakdowns to be cured by legislation and government decrees, was extremely vulnerable where and when it least expected' (Posner 1970, p. 15).

These developments have led radicals in Europe and America to reconsider the political potential of urban 'class' conflict. David Harvey, for example, has suggested that the continued existence of regressive redistributive mechanisms in capitalist cities is producing greater inequality and injustice, and has said that 'unless this present trend can be reversed, I feel that almost certainly we are also headed for a period of intense conflict (which may be violent) within the urban system' (1973, pp. 94–5). He claims to find evidence for this in the open conflicts in United States cities, and argues further that 'in Britain, the same processes are at work' (p. 95). Similarly in Europe, and notably in France, a body of Marxist theory has begun to develop since 1968 which sees peculiarly urban issues as constituting a highly significant 'political stake for the bourgeoisie and for popular struggles' (Olives 1976, p. 175). In short, Marxist theory is coming more and more to recognize and to anticipate the growth of class struggles in the urban context in advanced capitalist societies – i.e. the development of a new urban politics based upon the mobilization of a broad section of the populace which is subject to class exploitation as much (and often more visibly) outside work as it is within it.

The question which is raised by all this is first, why in theoretical terms a new urban politics should be expected to develop (especially in a society such as Britain where ghetto riots have been few and far between, and where the Paris events of May 1968 have no comparable counterpart), and secondly, whether there is any evidence to suggest that a new urban politics in fact is developing as a new and significant challenge to capitalist hegemony. These two questions provide the key themes of this chapter. With reference to the latter, I shall draw upon evidence gathered in various studies of working class activism in relation to urban issues, and shall argue that, in Britain at least, such studies tend to reveal the existence of severe restraints on lower class mobilization in the urban context. With reference to the former, I shall consider the work of Manuel Castells (whose book, *The Urban Question*, is – despite his own protestations to the contrary – the single most influential work in the new Marxist theory) and of others, setting out first the principal arguments, and secondly the problems raised by them. Let us begin, then, with a consideration of the arguments developed in this new theoretical approach to the problem of urban politics.

Collective consumption, contradictions and the rise of urban social movements

For Castells, the conventional treatment of the urban in social science is fundamentally ideological insofar as it has been based upon a supposed connection between ecological and cultural factors: 'The urban ideology is that specific ideology that sees the modes and forms of social organization as characteristic of a phase of the evolution of society, closely linked to the technico-natural conditions of human existence and, ultimately, to its environment' (1977a, p. 73). It is ideological because it serves to mystify the nature of the process whereby particular spatial forms are produced and reproduced, and to lead to the conclusion that urbanism as it appears today is in some way a natural outcome of the adaption of human societies to their environment. In fact, argues Castells, cities and city life are a direct reflection of a logic inherent, not within nature, but within the capitalist mode of production as mediated by the historical conditions pertaining at any particular time in any given society (i.e. at a given historical conjuncture). Spatial forms, urban 'ways of life' and 'urban problems' can only be understood, therefore, in terms of the relationship between urbanism and capitalism. More specifically, just as the factory is the locus of production in the capitalist mode of production (i.e. production is the dominant element), so the city is the locus of the process whereby labour-power is reproduced: ' "The urban" seems to me to connote directly the processes relating to labour power other than its direct application to the production process' (1977a, p. 236). The urban unit is therefore the unit whereby labour-power is reproduced, just as the production unit is that in which the means of production are reproduced. Furthermore, the process which structures space is that concerned with the reproduction of labour-power.

Within a capitalist (as in any other) mode of production, labour-power is used up in the social process of production, and it must therefore be replaced on both a daily and a generational basis. This involves both the simple reproduction of labour-power (i.e. meeting basic needs at the material level – such as housing), and its extended reproduction (i.e. ensuring a continual supply through, for example, the provision of schools and other amenities which serve to produce labour-power as a commodity in the form in which it is needed by capital). The reproduction of labour-power is thus achieved through the provision of essential means of consumption: 'The consumption element expresses, at the level of the urban unit, the process of the reproduction of labour power' (Castells 1977a, p. 238). The means of consumption may, of course, be met individually (through the market) or collectively (i.e. they are socialized and administered by that state). What is crucial to Castells's argument is the fact that, in advanced capitalist societies, the means of consumption are increasingly socialized. Put another way, the reproduction of labour-power takes place increasingly through the provision of collective as opposed to individual means of consumption. The reasons for this are complex, but basically they lie in the contradictions which develop in the process of reproducing labour-power.

Following Althusser, Castells argues that the basic contradiction identified by Marx in the capitalist mode of production – that between wage labour and capital – is in itself insufficient to bring about a necessary political rupture. As Althusser puts it,

The whole Marxist revolutionary experience shows that, if the general contradiction (it has already been specified: the contradiction between the forces of production and the relations of production, essentially embodied in the contradiction between two antagonistic classes) is sufficient to define the situation when revolution is the 'task of the day', it cannot of its own simple direct power induce a 'revolutionary situation', nor *a fortiori* a situation of revolutionary rupture and the triumph of the revolution. If this contradiction is to become *'active'* in the strongest sense, to become a ruptural principle, there must be an accumulation of 'circumstances' and 'currents' so that whatever their origin and sense ... they *fuse* into a *ruptural unity*: when they produce the result of the immense majority of the popular masses *grouped* in an assault on a regime which its ruling classes are *unable to defend* [1969, p. 99].

For a revolutionary situation to develop, it is therefore necessary for the basic contradiction to be reinforced by others. These may develop within the economic system itself (i.e. within and between the processes of production, consumption and exchange), and between it and the other levels of social organization (i.e. the political and ideological levels). What Castells attempts to show is how such multiple contradictions do arise within the urban system (i.e. the process of reproducing labour-power) and therefore how the urban system may contribute significantly to the development of a revolutionary rupture in society as a whole (assuming, in particular, that these contradictions cannot be resolved, or that in the attempt at resolving them, other contradictions develop; in either case, the contradictions become 'overdetermined' – i.e. they come to exert their own ruptural influence in the social formation as a whole, and hence on other contradictions at other levels).

It seems that a number of contradictions may be identified (e.g. see Castells 1976, pp. 152–3). However, the major contradiction appears to be located within the economic 'instance' between the two key elements of production and consumption. As we have seen, the consumption element refers to the process of reproduction of labour-power, and this is vital for production. However, there is a tension between the allocation of resources to the (profitable) process of production, and their allocation to the (generally unprofitable but necessary) process of consumption (see also Gorz 1967). Given that in the capitalist mode of production, the production element will always be dominant, it follows that crises are likely to develop in the provision of the means of collective consumption. Thus Castells argues that, 'The urban problematic oscillates between two essential poles' (1977a, p. 270) – namely consumption (at the level of property relations) and production (at the level of productive forces, or the relation of real appropriation) – and that dislocation may occur either through favouring consumption at the cost of production, or (more usually) vice versa. This principal contradiction between production and consumption, the needs of capital and the need to reproduce labour-power, 'provokes lacunae in vast areas of consumption that are essential to individuals and to economic activity' (Castells 1975, p. 177), and it therefore lies at the heart of the crisis of the urban system. In the case of the housing crisis, for example, Castells shows how industrial development in any given area calls forth an increased need for housing for the new labour force, but that the private construction industry, left to itself, cannot provide the necessary housing resources. This is because private capital responds only to solvent demand which is limited by the fact that housing is a necessarily expensive resource, and because the level of private investment in the housing industry remains low due to the long rate of capital rotation, the unprofitability of building to rent, the constant possibility of state regulation (e.g. rent controls), and the low rate of profit due to the generally small scale of the industry. It follows that the only way in which the necessary resources can be provided is through massive state intervention, both in the direct provision of housing to rent, and in subsidizing private building funds. What is true of housing is true also of other means of collective consumption – public transport, education, health care and so on. In all of these cases, private capital alone cannot meet its own need to reproduce labour-power, and in the absence of massive state intervention, a crisis will result with significant effects at the political level. As Castells puts it, 'The intervention of the state becomes necessary to take charge of the sectors and services that are noncompetitive (from the point of view of capital) but necessary for the functioning of economic activity and/or the appeasement of social conflicts' (1975, p. 178).

It will now be clear why it is that the necessary means of consumption become progressively socialized in advanced capitalist societies. The state necessarily intervenes in the process of the reproduction of labour-power on behalf of the long-term interests of capital. This, of course, raises the question of the relation between the state and the various different classes, but we shall suspend our judgement on this issue until the next chapter. Suffice it to say here that for Castells (following Poulantzas), the state (the so-called 'administration element' at the political level) is in a structurally-defined relationship to the system of production such that its interventions at the economic level necessarily function to regulate system contradictions in the interests of monopoly capital. State intervention in the provision of the collective means of consumption is thus explained as an attempt to regulate the process of reproduction of labour-power, and/or to buy off working class political pressure (since it is easier to cede to working class demands on questions relating to distribution than on the question of production relations). Thus Castells writes:

> The state apparatus intervenes in a massive, systematic, permanent and structurally necessary way in the process of consumption. . . . Thus we shall witness a takeover by the state of vast sectors of the production of means essential to the reproduction of labour power: health, education, housing, collective amenities, etc. It is here that the 'urban problematic' sends down its roots. . . . The state becomes the veritable arranger of the process of consumption as a whole: this is at the root of so-called 'urban politics' [1977a, p. 459].

What is achieved by this massive level of state intervention? The element of production – the relation of real appropriation – remains dominant, and the logic of the system remains unchanged (i.e. the pursuit of profit maximization by capital). The basic contradiction between consumption and production therefore remains unchanged, but state intervention serves to politicize the issue of collective consumption: 'To the extent that these means of collective consumption are generally managed by public authorities (the state at its different levels – national, regional and local), the entire urban perspective becomes politicized, since the organization of hospitals, schools, housing and transportation are at the same time fundamental determinants of everyday life' (Castells 1977b, p. 64). The argument here is reminiscent of that of Habermas (1976) who suggests that state intervention leads to the emergence of a visible agent which may be held responsible for economic effects which people previously accepted as almost natural and inevitable. When the state intervenes in the provision of consumption facilities, it therefore politicizes an economic contradiction, and aids the emergence of a collective response: 'It globalizes and politicizes all the problems in making their collective treatment more necessary and visible but at the same time in making their confrontation by the individual more difficult' (Castells 1975, p. 190).

Now it is important to note at this point that Castells does not argue that this politicization of the urban contradictions necessarily results in increased working class agitation. The point is that the state attempts to regulate class relations through its interventions, and in this, it may be successful: 'The politicization thus established is not necessarily a source of conflict or change, for it may also be a mechanism of integration and participation: *everything depends on the articulation of the contradictions and practices* or, to put it another way, on the dialectic between the state apparatus and urban social movement' (1977a, p. 463, my italics). In other words, the political response of those subject to a crisis in the provision by the state of the means of collective consumption is not predetermined, but is rather dependent upon the level of their political practice. Castells is, of course, insistent that political practices (whether on the part of planners and administrators, or of lower class groups) cannot be explained except with reference to the structural contradictions which give rise to them, and that the study of urban politics must therefore take as its starting point, not political practices *per se*, but rather, the identification of system contradictions (this, it may be noted, is not inconsistent with my argument in Chapter 1 that analysis should begin with the identification of interests rather than actions in relation to any given policy question). Nevertheless, although political practices reflect structural contradictions, they are themselves the source of independent effects: 'Since the structures only exist in practices, the specific organization of these practices produces autonomous (though determined) effects that are not all contained simply in the deployment of structural laws' (1977a, p. 244). It follows that the response of lower class groups to urban crises is a crucial independent factor in determining political outcomes.

Such responses may differ widely according to the nature of the issue at stake and the way in which those involved are organized. For a response to be classified as an urban social movement, Castells argues that it must be aimed at producing a 'qualitatively new effect', by which he means that it is aimed at effecting a change in the dominance of capitalist property relations, or a modification of power relations by weakening the structure of political domination or by strengthening the development of working class organization. Clearly, not all responses fall into this category – indeed, as we shall see later, much of the available evidence on urban class struggles indicates rather more modest ambition on the part of those involved, even where radical organizers attempt to raise the level of the protest or to develop a broader class consciousness. In such cases, Castells suggests that we should talk, not of urban social movements, but rather of participation or protest movements which result, not in qualitatively new effects, but in reproduction of the existing system of social relations (i.e. reinforced control) and in reform respectively. An urban social movement, therefore, is defined as, 'A system of practices resulting from the articulation of a conjuncture of the system of urban agents and of other social practices in such a way that its development tends objectively towards the structural transformation of the urban system or towards a substantial modification of the power relations in the class struggle, that is to say, in the last resort, in the power of the state' (Castells 1977a, p. 263).

Throughout his work, Castells stresses the familiar Leninist argument that a social movement aimed at qualitative transformation cannot be expected to develop spontaneously, but is rather dependent upon organization from outside. This is partly because working class experience of deprivation and crisis has to be explained in terms of Marxist theory before it can provide a basis for radical and effective action. Organization, in other words, plays a crucial role in explaining and linking contradictions, and thus in channelling any spontaneous response into the 'correct' (i.e. party) line:

> The role of the organization (as a system of means specific to an objective) is fundamental, for, although the support-agents make possible the constitution of combinations between the structural elements, it is the organization that is the locus of fusion or articulation with the other social practices. When there is no organization, urban contradictions are expressed either in a refracted way, through other practices, or in a 'wild', way, a pure contradiction devoid of any structural horizon [1977a pp. 271-2].

Organization cannot, of course, achieve anything without there first being the existence of contradictions giving rise to some dissatisfaction on the part of those affected, and Castells recognizes that radicals have at times attempted to impose 'utopian' objectives onto quite parochial movements with disastrous results. Nevertheless, he also insists that no urban movement will proceed beyond a reformist stage without political organization from outside. This is not only because the contradictions need to be brought together, but because, in the case of urban protests, these contradictions are themselves secondary to the basic contradiction in capitalist society between wage-labour and capital. Any spontaneous protest, left to itself, will thus focus only on issues of consumption, and will be characterized by what Castells rather disparagingly refers to as 'consumer trade unionism', entirely neglecting the fundamental significance of capitalist production relations (which themselves, of course, account in the final analysis for the crisis in provision of collective consumption): 'It does seem that whatever the level and the content of the various "urban issues", they can all be characterized as secondary structural issues, that is to say, ones not directly challenging the production methods of a society, nor the political domination of the ruling classes' (1977a, p. 376). It follows from this that organization is essential in linking an urban social movement with the working class movement as a whole, without which it can never directly challenge the system of capitalist economic and political relations with which it is really in conflict (see also Mingione 1977). For Castells, then, effective urban conflicts must be linked into the overall class struggle: 'The new questions posed by the urban problematic are expressed in action that reopens the roads to revolution in our societies by linking other forms of conflict with those arising from the productive system and from political struggle' (1977a, p. 378). It follows from this that, where strong revolutionary parties are already in existence, urban struggles may play a decisive part in the class struggle as a whole. Where such organizations are weak, however, then urban issues remain secondary to conflicts arising directly out of the process of capitalist production.

Where the new sources of contradiction in the urban system may prove highly significant, however (even, one may suppose, in the absence of a strong revolutionary party), is that they affect more than just the working class: 'The urban social movements which result from this contradiction are a new factor which directly affects the dynamics of the transformation of the advanced societies to the extent that they affect those social strata (such as the middle class) which, until the moment, have not been involved in social conflicts' (1977b, p. 64). The argument here is that a crisis in the provision of the means of collective consumption will hit the working class and middle class alike; the middle class need hospitals, they use public transport such as rail commuter links, they send their children to state schools (or, at least, some of them do). It follows that new patterns of inequality arise in the urban system which do not correspond with those generated in the work situation: 'At the level of urban problems . . . one can see most easily how the combination of the logic of capital oppresses not only the working class but the ensemble of possibilities for human development' (1975, p. 192). There thus arises in the urban system an 'objective community of interests, this partial interclassism of contradictions at the level of collective consumption' (ibid., p. 192). Urban social movements may therefore develop based upon a broad alliance of anticapitalist classes, rather than on the proletariat alone, and these will 'incorporate the great majority of the people in the political battle against capitalism' (ibid., p. 193). The significance of urban social movements is therefore twofold: they open up new fronts in the class struggle, and they open up new alliances as well.

A critical evaluation of the Castells thesis

Three principal criticisms can be discerned in the reaction from Marxists and non-Marxists alike to Castells's work. The first concerns his definition of the urban system in terms of the process of reproduction of labour-power through consumption, the second relates to his discussion of the significance of urban social movements and the role of political organizations, and the third (and in my view most crucial) refers to the inadequacies of his concept of collective consumption.

The first line of criticism, concerning his definition of the urban system, need not delay us long, for not only does it not bear directly on the issue of urban social movements, but it is apparent that parts of this critique are based upon a misreading of Castells, while other parts have been incorporated by him into his work. The criticism, simply stated, is first, that collective consumption is significant beyond its role in the reproduction of labour-power, and secondly, that the urban system cannot be defined solely in terms of consumption processes. The first point is developed by Harvey (1977) who follows Baran and Sweezy (1966) in identifying the fundamental problem in advanced monopoly capitalism as being underconsumption. Baran and Sweezy argued in their book, *Monopoly Capital*, that the domination achieved by a handful of large corporations in modern capitalist economies is such that competition no longer regulates price levels. The corporations make their own prices (within limits), and far from the rate of profit falling (as Marx predicted), this means that surplus continues to grow. The problem, however, concerns how this surplus is to be absorbed, and thus how the growth in productive capacity is to be utilized so as to avoid economic stagnation. Baran and Sweezy themselves identify the great spread of suburbanization in the United States as one means whereby surplus has been absorbed, and Harvey, too, adopts this argument:

> In 1945 . . . the United States found itself with an enormously enhanced productive capacity. . . . The problem to be resolved at this point was to find ways to keep the productive capacity of the United States economy employed and to prevent widespread unemployment of labour . . . a variety of strategies emerged for stimulating consumption, not least of which were a set of fiscal and monetary policies designed to accelerate and enhance the suburbanization process . . . a process that embraced the construction of highways and utilities, housing and public facilities, shopping centres and commercial functions as well as a rising demand for automobiles, energy and the like [1977, pp. 123–4].

Provision of the means of collective consumption by the state is thus necessary, not simply to reproduce labour-power, but to absorb the growing surplus of monopoly capital.

At one level, this argument is entirely consistent with Castells's own analysis. He too, for example, argues that the suburban explosion in the United States can be understood in terms of 'the need to find massive new outlets' for investment of surplus capacity (1977a, p. 386), and that the role of the state was crucial in this process (e.g. in underwriting the mortgage system, providing highway links and so on). Indeed, in his afterword to the English edition of *The Urban Question*, he makes the point explicitly: 'Monopoly capital, in search of new investment outlets, occupies and transforms new sectors of the economy. . . . It is clear that this transformation results from the interest of capital invested rather than from social demand' (pp. 456–7). Furthermore, he also argues that state investment in the means of collective consumption is important in the struggle by capital to maintain profitability, partly because the state socializes unprofitable sectors, and partly because it regulates the level of demand and provides monopoly capital with guaranteed markets and profit levels (e.g. consider, in this respect, the relation between the

National Health Service in Britain and the major drug companies).

Two points need to be made, however. The first is that a recognition of the role of the state in sustaining demand does not imply an acceptance of Baran and Sweezy's underconsumption thesis. As Gamble and Walton (1976 pp. 108–10) point out, the major problem for capital lies, not in realizing surplus value, but in extracting it (e.g. by increasing productivity), and evidence (such as that cited by Baran and Sweezy) to the effect that there is a tendency for the mass of profits to increase does not in any way run counter to the assertion that there is also a tendency for the *rate* of profit to fall. The second point is that Castells does not deny that state intervention performs the important function of sustaining demand, but rather argues that the defining feature of collective consumption lies in the reproduction of labour-power. This thesis cannot be overthrown simply by citing the other functions which socialized consumption performs.

A more important line of criticism, therefore, is that which denies the definition of the urban system as primarily a system for the reproduction of labour-power. According to this line of argument, it is not just that the state performs a number of functions in its intervention in the urban system, but that the crucial function lies in its direct contribution to the process of production. Lojkine (1976), for example, argues that the provision of urban amenities is not simply a response on the part of the capitalist state to the problems encountered by capital in reproducing labour-power effectively, but it also constitutes an attempt to provide the facilities necessary for the process of production itself – i.e. for the economic reproduction of capitalist production relations – which cannot profitably be provided by private capital. He cites the provision of roads as one key example. Roads, he suggests, are a crucial urban element in the process of capital circulation, yet their construction is not profitable for private capital since they are not immediately productive. He writes: 'In the capitalist mode of production, the building of roads – necessary to the reproduction of the economic system as a whole, but scarcely profitable for a newly-born capitalism restricted to the immediate exploitation of productive labour – is the task of the *political* agent which is responsible not only for ideological cohesion but also for the *economic reproduction* of the relations of production, in other words: the State' (pp. 139–40). From the outset, then, the state in capitalist societies is engaged in the dual function of ensuring political order and of providing necessary elements for the process of production. It follows that the urban system must be defined so as to include, not only the function of reproducing labour-power, but also this productive function. As Harloe puts it,

The improvement of urban conditions via state provision is more importantly a reaction to the falling rate of profit of capital and hence its inability to provide wages sufficient to ensure the adequate reproduction of the labour force for the purposes of production and/or *its inability to finance the cost of other factors entering into production.* In other words, it is mainly a problem connected with the generation rather than the realization of surplus value ... the separation of consumption from production in Castells' analysis ... and the focus on collective consumption for the study of the role of state urban policies seems far too narrow a perspective and is misleading. 'Urban' processes and forms cannot be understood without reference to the production of capital *and* the reproduction of the labour force [1977, p. 22, my italics].

Castells has, in fact, dealt with this argument in his afterword to his book, and sees it as the result of confusion and misunderstanding. In the first place, he recognizes that of course any given city or urban area will include units of production – factories as well as roads. The point, however, is to identify theoretically what it is that constitutes an urban unit, and he argues that just as an urban unit cannot be defined in terms of institutional boundaries (because these by no means coincide with 'real' urban units), so too it cannot be defined in terms of any production unit, since production occurs on a much wider scale (regional, if not national or international). The specificity of the urban lies in its character as a residential unit – a unit of the labour force: 'An urban unit is not a unit in terms of production. On the other hand, it possesses a certain specificity in terms of residence, in terms of "everydayness". It is, in short, the everyday space of a delimited fraction of the labour force' (1977a, p. 445). This is not to deny that urban units perform functions other than the reproduction of labour-power, including functions in the process of capitalist production. Castells is, after all, quite explicit in identifying production and exchange as well as consumption elements at the economic level within the urban system, just as he also points out that the factory (a unit of reproduction of the means of production) contains elements of consumption and exchange (not to mention political domination) in addition to its key element of production.

The point, then, is that a definition of the urban system as a unit of consumption aiding the reproduction of labour-power does not deny that other practices and processes also occur, but it rather focuses on what is considered to be the defining process. As Castells recognizes, the test of such a definition lies in how useful it proves to be in helping us analyse and understand 'urban problems' such as population concentration, state intervention, the growth of urban struggles and attempts at urban reform. None of the critics has demonstrated the inadequacy of his approach in these terms.

All this brings us onto the second major line of criticism against the Castells thesis, and this concerns his arguments concerning the relationship between urban social movements and the class struggle in society as a whole. As we saw in Chapter 2, Castells does not see urban struggles as themselves constituting class struggles (this is essentially where he differs from Clarke and Ginsburg, for example). It follows from this that urban protests will remain at best reformist unless they are linked into the main working class movement by outside political organizations. Lojkine rejects this argument, however, for it only holds good (according to him) for as long as we continue to define the urban system as a system of consumption. If, on the other hand, we follow Lojkine in identifying urbanism as playing a key role in both consumption and production, then it follows that urban conflicts are necessarily class conflicts:

> If our hypothesis is correct, in other words if the new relations to urban space of the big industrial and financial groups shatter the ideological boundaries within which some have attempted to confine the urban (reproduction of labour power, consumption cut off from production), the new forms of struggle against the urban environment should result in a direct confrontation with the economic agents which shape it, namely the big firms, main beneficiaries of the spatial segregation of collective infrastructure [Lojkine 1977, p. 142].

Similarly, Mingione (1977) argues that where conflict erupts openly in the urban system (i.e. provided the working class has not been incorporated into the system or divided by it), then it occurs within the context of the working class movement as a whole, even in those cases where it remains limited to sectoral struggles.

The crucial question raised by this dispute takes us back to the problem discussed earlier of determining the relationship between economic classes and political struggles (see pages 100–2). As we saw there, Castells's argument is in some ways compatible with Hirst's thesis of a 'necessary non-correspondence', for he recognizes that conflicts arising around issues of consumption are not themselves class conflicts – hence the need for a party leadership to forge the link between the two. The view developed by Lojkine and Mingione (and, indeed, by writers such as Clarke and Ginsburg in Britain) that the principal economic classes are directly represented in such struggles – that tenants' movements, squatting movements and the like are the manifestation of the working class struggle on the urban plane – appears grossly unrealistic, for not only do those involved in such activities rarely see themselves as engaged in a broader class struggle, but the issues on which they mobilize are rarely related directly to class divisions at the economic level. Conflicts between tenants and owner-occupiers, sometimes drawn from the same class, are just one example of this. The implications of this are not only that the argument developed by Lojkine and Mingione must be rejected, but also that Castells's view cannot be accepted as it stands. This is because Castells seems to suggest that, given the correct leadership, those engaged in urban struggles can be led to 'discover' the contiguity of their particular quarrel with the lines of class conflict in the society as a whole, yet this is clearly problematic. Castells, like Lojkine, falls foul of what Pickvance (1977a) terms the 'urban fallacy' – i.e. the assumption that a common political situation in the urban system is sufficient to overcome traditional class divisions at the economic level. This is a common and significant weakness in much of the Marxist work in this field (especially since it lies at the heart of the argument that urban struggles can help forge a popular alliance of anti-monopoly capital forces) and it is a point to which I shall return later in this chapter.

  Closely related to this question of the definition of the 'social base' in urban politics is the problem of how a social base is transformed into a social or political force. How do urban social movements develop? For Castells, this appears a somewhat mechanistic process: wait for the structural contradictions to give rise to a particular issue in which definite 'stakes' can be identified, and then add an organizationally competent political leadership to prevent the movement from slipping into reformism. Yet the process is clearly more problematic than this, for as Pickvance (1977b) argues, Castells here ignores the important questions of subjective consciousness:

The issues at stake and social base affected are said to be determined by structural contradictions, and the social force appears from the social base at the wave of a magic wand of organization. This appears to me to ignore what is not only a major theoretical problem but also a major problem for political practice, namely how, in Marxian terms, does a class in itself become a class for itself? To answer by the implantation of a revolutionary political group simply moves the question one step further back: under what conditions is this possible? [ibid., p. 177].

Organization, in other words, may well prove fruitless in raising a protest to the level of an urban social movement, even where the 'stakes' are deemed high.

As we saw in Chapter 2, this classic problem of the relationship between a class in and for itself is generally avoided in neo-Marxist structuralism by means of the argument that classes only exist in and through their practices at the various levels of the social formation (cf. Poulantzas 1975). However, the theoretical ellision of practices with structural levels or 'instances' produces a recurring tension in this work (a tension which is evident in Castells's discussion of the emergence of urban social movements) between deterministic and voluntaristic explanations of political practice. As Clarke *et al.* suggest:

One of the central and recurring difficulties is the tension between the theoretical weight attached to the notion of structural causality and the important role that class struggle is accorded. . . . On the one hand, a particular characteristic is identified as the consequence of the function or role performed by a particular instance, while on the other hand, it is attributed to the specific balance of forces in the class struggle [1977, p. 114].

I shall consider this tension in more detail in Chapter 4, for it is revealed most clearly in recent Marxist contributions to the theory of the capitalist state.

Considerations like these lead Pickvance to suggest that Castells's analysis of the formation of urban social movements is inadequate, and that in order to understand how a social base becomes a social force, it is necessary to study, not only the issue and the organizational activity which surrounds it, but also the structure of social relations at the base (e.g. kinship, friendship and institutional links between individuals), the value orientations of individual members which affect their willingness to participate in political action and their mode of participation, the alternative sources of identification and consciousness which may exist (e.g. racial as opposed to class identification), and the costs imposed by participation in terms of time, money, personal loyalties and so on. Now it is true, as Harloe (1977) argues, that many of these factors can themselves be explained largely in terms of the class character of the social base in question; social network links, values, and time and money available all reflect social class differences. Nevertheless, Pickvance's criticisms do lead us out of a structuralist materialist analysis such as Castells clearly wishes to retain. In his afterword to *The Urban Question*, for example, Castells fully endorses Borja's criticism of any subjectivist approach to urban social movements, and reaffirms that such movements can only be explained as the expressions of structural contradictions. Clearly, there is no room in such an argument for any consideration of values as explanatory variables, yet Pickvance is surely right to question the validity of any explanatory account which ignores them. According to Harloe, the deficiency can be made good within the materialist problematic – presumably with reference to class practices at the ideological level (i.e. the familiar concept of false consciousness). But as I noted in Chapter 1, arguments about ideological manipulation must be used with great care, and must demonstrate both that interests are not being met and that ideological practices have caused the inaction of those who are disadvantaged. If these criteria are to be met, then it clearly is necessary, as Pickvance argues, to analyse alternative sources of identification (since class identification may not be the only social base which is relevant to political action), and the sources of people's values and beliefs in relation to any given issue.

Pickvance has also criticized the Castells thesis for devaluing or ignoring, first, the activities of organizations which achieve results through institutional means (although he accepts that these results will never be more than reformist – no revolution was ever made by going through the normal channels), and secondly, non-mass-based political action (e.g. the importance of personal approaches as opposed to mass demonstrations). His point here is that institutional and individual forms of activism can be highly significant: 'Mobilization of the social base is only one way in which urban effects are produced . . . both types of action are empirically important, and the neglect of either is unjustified' (1976, p. 211). Again, I would endorse this argument. We shall see in Chapter 6 that personal contacts and private negotiations are the principal means whereby suburban owner-occupiers achieve their political successes – owner-occupiers rarely engage in open and direct challenges to political authority, and when they do, we may often be justified in suspecting 'tactical protest' rather than any genuine political contradiction. Whether this is also the case with lower class groups is a question which we shall examine below, but we need only note at this point that they too may often have recourse to both types of strategy.

The third major criticism of Castells's argument refers to his concept of collective consumption. This is an important concept in his argument, for his entire thesis rests on the view that the provision of the facilities necessary for the reproduction of labour-power is made increasingly by the state (owing to the unprofitability of their production for private capital) and that crises affecting this provision (which are inevitable, given the contradiction between production and consumption as competing processes for resources) therefore become increasingly politicized and involve large sections of the population beyond the working class alone. Crises in state provision of the collective means of consumption therefore generate urban social movements based upon a broad alliance of noncapitalist classes. But what is collective consumption?

For Castells, the defining element of collective consumption is that it is provided by the state. It is this which distinguishes it from individual consumption, which refers to the consumption through the market of commodities produced for profit by private capital: 'This is the distinction between individual consumption and collective consumption, the second being consumption whose economic and social treatment, while remaining capitalist, takes place not through the market but through the state apparatus' (1977a, p. 460). It is collective because its production is socialized by the state. An alternative definition, however, is provided by Lojkine (1976) who sees as a key feature of collective consumption that fact that it is consumed collectively: 'The mode of consumption is collective and is thus by its nature opposed to individual privative appropriation. Parks or lessons cannot be consumed individually – at least, not in their current increasingly socialized form' (p. 122). Thus, while Castells defines collective consumption in terms of the nature of the *provision* of facilities, Lojkine defines it in terms of the nature of their *use*. Nor is

this a mere definitional quarrel, for it is apparent that the two approaches identify different types of facilities as 'collective', and therefore point to different bases for the formation of urban social movements. For example, schools or hospitals are elements of collective
consumption for Castells only in so far as they are provided by the
state, yet Lojkine's position leads to the conclusion that they are
collective even when privately owned and administered since they are
collectively consumed.

According to Pahl (1977a), neither definition is very useful. When
the concept is defined in terms of collective provision, it fails to take
account of those facilities which, though provided by private capital,
are consumed in the same way as those provided by the state:

> Are roads, parks, housing and leisure facilities *inherently* facilities which
> must be collectively controlled? Surely not: turnpike or toll roads were once
> common and could become more widespread again. Parks, zoos, beaches
> and mountains may be privately owned. . . . Clearly, the nationalization
> of privately-owned leisure facilities such as bingo halls or amusement parks
> would neither increase nor decrease the means of collective consumption
> [pp. 168-9].

Nor is Lojkine's definition any better, for facilities such as education
are not inherently collective in the way they are used. Why, for
example, should the process of learning from a book at home be
individual consumption while the same book read at school becomes
collective consumption? As Pahl points out, the concept of collective
consumption must refer to more than simply the aggregation of units
of individual consumption; collective consumption is *qualitatively
different* as a process. If it is not, then we are led into, say, distinguishing a car journey on one's own and a car journey with others as
inherently different types of activity with different political consequences. In this way, Pahl comes to reject the concept of collective
consumption as meaningless:

> What is the *precise* distinction between the personal and the collective
> consumption of any facility? It cannot be the cost of the facility, it cannot
> be the nature of the facility, it cannot be the ownership of the facility or the
> way it is used. If we cannot define a collective *mode* of consumption, how
> can we continue to use the term meaningfully? [ibid., pp. 169-70].

Similarly, Szelenyi (1977) suggests that the concept of collective
consumption be replaced by that of 'urban non-productive infrastructure' as a less inherently ambiguous term.

Although I would accept Pahl's criticism of Lojkine as entirely valid, his criticism of Castells does seem to be misplaced. This is because he appears to ignore the key role of the state in politicizing urban crises. There is nothing in Pahl's critique to suggest that Castells is wrong in arguing that increasing state intervention in the process of consumption may lead to a stronger reaction on the part of disadvantaged groups when facilities are not provided at a socially adequate level. As we saw earlier, when the state takes responsibility for providing consumption facilities, people have someone or something to point an accusing finger at when things go wrong, especially since the state presents itself as the democratic and neutral arbiter of competing interests and the responsive representative of all. It is entirely consistent, therefore, for Castells to argue that collective consumption, defined as those facilities provided by the state on account of their unprofitability, has qualitatively different political effects from individual consumption via the market. There is no reason, therefore, to abandon the concept (as Pahl suggests), nor to change its label (Szelenyi's concept of unproductive urban infrastructure is clearly no substitute since it does not contain the dynamic element of state intervention, crisis and political reaction which are defining features of Castells's approach).

The concept of collective means of consumption thus refers, as Castells suggests, to the collective provision of socially necessary facilities – facilities which aid the reproduction of labour-power. What is wrong, or at least confused, in the Castells thesis, however, is not the definition of the concept but the way in which it is used. This point can most usefully be illustrated with reference to the provision of the most crucial and significant element in the urban system of collective consumption – housing. The obvious point to be made here is that housing may be provided either collectively, by the state, or individually, through the market. In both cases, of course, it is consumed individually (i.e. if we follow Lojkine's definition, then housing is clearly not one of the means of collective consumption). But even following Castells's definition, over half of all housing in Britain cannot be included in the collective means of consumption. Castells himself recognizes as much: 'The same product (housing, for example) will be treated both by the market and by the state, and will therefore be alternately a product of individual or collective consumption, according to the criteria, which will change according to the historical situation' (1977a, p. 460). The consequence of this is that a crisis in the provision of housing should not be expected to lead to the development of urban social movements based upon a 'broad anticapitalist alliance'; only the propertyless dependent upon state provision will be affected. Yet Castells himself fails to recognize this. Indeed, he writes, 'If for housing the number of privileged people is larger, the crisis of housing largely transcends the frontiers of the popular classes' (1975, pp. 191–2), yet if he means by 'privileged' those owning their own homes, then that argument surely does not follow. A similar point may be made in relation to other facilities such as schools and hospitals, for a crisis in state schooling or in national health medicine, though affecting larger numbers than a crisis in public housing provision, will still fail to affect those whose children attend private schools or who seek health care in the private sector.

We may, in fact, go further than this. First, it is apparent that a crisis in the provision of collective means of consumption, far from bringing the different noncapitalist classes together, may serve to drive them even further apart. Again, housing is the obvious example, for a shortage of housing resulting in political agitation by the homeless may well be seen by owner-occupiers (and possibly by some secure council tenants) as a threat to their values and, more significantly, to their property. Political mobilization in response to a crisis in the provision of collective consumption may therefore be interpreted by many members of the middle and working classes alike, not as a crusade to be supported but as a threat to be resisted. Nor is a radical political leadership likely to convince them otherwise, for their assessment is clearly no mere ideological prejudice. As Cockburn correctly states in relation to the squatting movement (to take one obvious example): 'Squatting is not only a practical solution to individual housing need, it is a statement about property and ownership. As such it is a political movement' (1977, p. 80). The irony, of course, is that while property owners (including owner-occupiers) recognize this all too clearly, those involved in this and other forms of 'community action' often do not.

The second point is that even those sections of the urban population who are similarly subject to state provision (e.g council tenants) may fail to come together in the face of a crisis in the supply of housing by the state. As we shall see in Chapter 7, this was generally the case in Croydon, for example. In part, this directs our attention to those factors discussed by Pickvance as affecting the transformation of a social base into a social force, but it also leads us to consider why collective provision should necessarily lead to a collective response where the facilities in question are consumed at the level of the individual. This is not to advocate a return to Lojkine's definition of collective consumption in terms of collective use, but it is to recognize that a crisis in collective consumption individually consumed may have very different political consequences from a similar crisis in the collective provision of facilities which are consumed collectively.

There are two main reasons for this. The first is that, where facilities are consumed at the level of the individual or single family unit, there is less likely to be a collective awareness of shared deprivation than where they are consumed collectively. This will not always be the case, of course; tenants in a block scheduled for demolition, for example, are likely to be highly aware of the similar plight faced by their neighbours. Nevertheless, it remains the case that in many housing issues, deprivation will tend to be individualized because housing itself is individually consumed. This is precisely, of course, why many writers have commented on the political divisiveness of the waiting list system for council house allocation – the problem of producing low cost housing goes on, but it is generally seen as an individual problem by those affected. This brings me on to the second point which is that a crisis in the collective provision of facilities consumed by individuals will only affect those who have yet to acquire access to them. Again, housing is a case in point, for once a family has achieved access to a council house, the crisis in council house building is no longer a problem, at least as regards securing access to housing (hence the significance of Parkin's comments on the weaknesses of solidarism among subordinate groups, noted on page 101). A rent rise, of course, may still generate a collective response of some consequence (e.g. the battle against the 1972 Housing Finance Act), but such action is usually specific, short-lived and far from 'solid'.

What all this amounts to is not that Castells's concept of collective means of consumption is meaningless, but rather that he has applied it to inappropriate situations (i.e. to privately owned housing which does not fall into his definition of collective consumption) and to cases where individualized consumption of state facilities may well prevent a collective response from emerging (i.e. to public housing where the problem of provision remains unsolved but affects a constantly changing social base). It follows from this that a crisis in collective consumption may well generate movements based upon and around facilities such as public transport, public health and education, where the issue is politicized by virtue of the role of the state and collectivized by virtue of the nature of the facility, but that his argument may not apply to housing (which is, of course, the most significant of all urban resources). A crisis in the provision of housing will not provoke an anticapitalist class alliance (due to the existence of the private sector), nor will it necessarily lead to a solidaristic response on the part of those most affected (due to the individualistic mode of its consumption). Political conflicts around the housing question, therefore, are likely to take the form of issue-specific protests, they will not generally provide the potential base for the development of new political alliances, and they will often suffer from fragmentation owing to the strain between collective action and individual costs. Whether broadly based social movements could develop around other areas of collective consumption which do affect a wider population and which involve collective use (e.g. health, transport or education facilities) is an open question, although in Britain at least, the prospect seems unlikely. Such protests as have occurred in these areas (e.g. commuter groups or groups of parents concerned about their children's schooling – see Chapter 6) have remained specific, both in terms of the issues raised and the social base mobilized. The conclusion suggests itself that the new urban politics looks suspiciously like the familiar pressure group politics with the same limited horizons and potentials.

Ultimately, of course, the significance of urban-based conflicts can only be resolved through empirical research. Although in this section I have indicated a number of important theoretical and conceptual weaknesses in Castells's position – notably in his view of the relation between housing struggles and class struggles, and in the development of his concept of collective consumption – it is clear that this theory was developed, not in abstraction from real world events, but in large part as a response to them. The fundamental question thus concerns, not the theoretical weaknesses of the approach (although critical debate at this level remains obviously important), but the usefulness of the ideas for developing an understanding of empirical situations. Castells himself suggests that his approach is to be justified 'only by the fecundity of the research results acquired as a result of these new bases' (1977a, p. 450). Let us therefore leave the question of theoretical adequacy and turn to consider how far his thesis may prove applicable to the analysis of urban conflicts in Britain and elsewhere.

New politics, old dilemmas

Neighbourhoods in Britain tend to be relatively homogenous in terms of the socio-economic characteristics of their residents, and one of the more fruitful legacies of the Chicago school of urban sociology has been the recognition of a substantial contiguity between spatial and social structures. It is for precisely this reason, of course, that the fear among dominant groups of the consequences of the spatial concentration of the working class, noted at the start of this chapter, was so pronounced in the nineteenth century. As Glass notes,

> The more the towns were deserted by the upper and middle classes, the more plainly were they also the barracks of a vast working class whose lessons in the power of combination had already begun, and whose sporadic riots were already portents of latent insurrection. The industrial town was thus identified with the working class: it was feared so strongly because the working class was so frightening [1968, p. 67].

The question, however, is whether the 'community', the spatial unit of reproduction of labour-power, today represents a viable social base for significant political mobilization.

Pahl thinks not, for despite the relative class homogeneity of specific neighbourhood units (council estates, inner city areas suburbia etc.), he suggests that the operation of spatial inequalities rarely coincides with the traditional lines of class inequality:

> Since different groups benefit at different times in different parts of the same city, common city or nationwide situations of deprivation rarely occur. Those who claim they can see the development of 'urban social movements' leading to radical changes in the nature of urban society would find difficulty in getting empirical support from British evidence (1975, p. 273).

This is an interesting argument, for Pahl here recognizes the empirical validity of a fundamental argument in Castells's thesis – namely, that new patterns of inequality arise out of the process of collective consumption – but draws precisely the opposite conclusion – namely, that this leads to further class fragmentation rather than to any popular class alliance.

Pahl's conclusion is supported by Bell and Newby (1976) who deny the possibility of any 'common urban consciousness'. Community action, they suggest, is often premised on a consensual and harmonious view of community which ignores class differences by emphasizing common territorial interests (see also Cockburn 1977, pp. 160–1). This is not to deny that local protests around local issues can and do develop (although Bell and Newby suggest that these are often middle class in their membership and objectives – a point which I shall take up in Part 2 and which is supported by a number of empirical studies of urban protest in Britain, such as those by Batley 1972 and Mutch 1977). But precisely because these are *local* issues, they fail to mobilize any inter-class alliance, and they often result in a minor shift of collective resources from one local area to another (usually, it may be added, from a working class to a middle class area, as in various cases of the re-routing of proposed road developments or, to take an example from Chapter 7, in campaigns for the provision of children's nurseries). As Bell and Newby conclude, 'Only a nationwide or locality wide programme can be genuinely redistributive otherwise we will witness a succession of briefly spluttering popular local action groups that if successful will indeed direct resources to themselves but away from others who either have not or cannot mobilize' (1976, p. 204). What is essentially the problem, therefore, is the acceptance of the 'urban fallacy' identified by Pickvance – the emphasis on the 'community' as the social base to the virtual exclusion of existing class divisions.

This leads us to consider a second and related problem, for locally-based political action is not only likely to be highly specific in terms of its social base, but will also be strictly limited in its objectives. As Pahl puts it, 'Taking direct action may lead to a local authority amending its housing policy or providing more pre-school playgroups, but once the particular goal has been achieved, there seems little evidence that such groups continue aiming at broader political goals' (1975, p. 272–3). It is for this reason that Castells sees the political character of the leadership of such movements as a crucial factor in their development into urban social movements, but the potential for such leadership will often be limited by the nature of the issue. The point here is that urban protests are more often defensive than aggressive. People mobilize *against* rent increases, road schemes, urban renewal programmes and the like, but they do not often mobilize *for* increased social services expenditure, improved school facilities, an acceleration in the provision of council housing and so on. It is at least debatable whether a committed radical leadership can transform a defensive into an aggressive strategy; whether, to take one example, a squatting movement aimed at securing accommodation for homeless families can be developed into an attack on bourgeois property rights. It is important, therefore, to distinguish positive action from negative reaction, for urban protest generally falls into the latter category. In his analysis of various struggles against urban renewal schemes in Paris, for example, Olives found that the only effective protests were those which either sought to preserve the status quo or which were aimed at securing adequate rehousing for the families affected. In both cases, protest took place in reaction to policies which threatened to make their situation worse. By contrast Olives notes,

None of the other specific demands (such as rent reductions, lower fares, etc.) nor the global demands which accompanied some of the actions was satisfied. Their political and ideological relevance apart, it is obvious that the latter were out of step with the level of development of the struggles in progress (balance of forces) and the state of development of working class mass organizations (in this case tenants' committees for example) [1976, p. 183].

Or to put it another way, disadvantaged groups are more likely to mobilize in reaction to a threat (such as urban renewal) than in response to a situation of on-going deprivation.

One consequence of this is that it is in the character of much urban protest that it takes place within the parameters set by the system itself. Defensive strategies rarely give rise, even potentially, to revolutionary consequences. As one community activist has observed, 'Although community action campaigns may be successful in their own terms, the end result may only be small scale compensatory provision . . . which, while representing a positive improvement in the situation, does nothing to alter the crucial determinants of the lifestyles and life chances of the residents' (Young 1976, p. 117). Because they do not pose a fundamental political threat, because they are not aimed at securing 'revolutionary reforms' (Gorz 1967, Holland 1975), such movements are easily and often swiftly coopted or otherwise institutionalized by local authorities. Hain (1976), for example, notes that two London boroughs appointed 'participation officers' in response to the development of such movements, while the story of the London squatting movement is largely one of institutionalized conflict resulting in an agreement with local authorities over the temporary use of empty housing stock (see Bailey 1973a, Kay *et al.* 1977, p. 141, Cockburn 1977, pp. 76–80). This is not to deny that essentially defensive and institutionalized political strategies can produce positive results; Pickvance is clearly correct in criticizing Castells for dismissing the use of institutional means of influence as unimportant. But such strategies are accommodative and facilitative rather than oppositional. In Gorz's terms, they demand what can be rather than what should be (1967, p. 8). They thus provide infertile ground for the implantation of even the most revolutionary of political leaderships.

There appears a certain reluctance in much of the new Marxist urban theory to recognize the amazingly absorbent quality of liberal-democratic regimes. New forms of protest are recognized, but the new forms of accommodation which develop in response to them are ignored or dismissed as obstacles which can be overcome by a committed radical leadership. Yet as Habermas argues,

> The degree of tolerance has increased. The headlines already report on university strikes and citizens' initiatives, regretfully adding 'without incident'. The new techniques of demonstration have altered little but the level of expectation. Thus there arises a grey area in which the social system can live with the non- (or not yet-) institutionalized opposition it calls forth without having to solve the problems that are the occasion, ground or cause of the protests. Blows directed against stonewalls bounce off rubber screens [1976, p. 129].

In the case of Britain at least, there is little evidence to suggest that the new urban politics have succeeded in transcending this 'repressive tolerance' (Marcuse 1976). Community action has chalked up its successes without posing any fundamental threat to dominant economic and political interests. As Dickens concludes in his review of housing struggles in Britain, 'The general point is not that these victories did not occur, but rather that they appear to have occurred without the opposition losing' (1977, p. 4). At best, urban struggles have been a source of some inconvenience to dominant groups; at worst, they have actually aided the efficient management of the urban system by channelling opposition into manageable forms while providing a necessary feedback into the policy-making process (see Chapter 7).

Thus we arrive at the fundamental dilemma, noted in Chapter 1, which confronts all those engaged in urban protest: whether to pursue a limited strategy of reformism within the system, or to pose a direct challenge from outside it. As Darke and Walker put it:

> The radical pressure group finds itself in a classic political dilemma. To maintain views which are unpopular with power holders in local government ensures that members and officers will largely disregard the group, while a moderation of views to help bring the voluntary group's agenda forward for debate with the local authority may mean relinquishing some basic principles or beliefs [1977, p. 80].

As Darke and Walker go on to suggest, the immediacy of such protests, the need to achieve some pay-off for the investment of time, money and commitment which membership of campaigns like this involves, invariably results in the latter ameliorative strategy. Precisely because these groups are usually defensive, formed around a single issue, they lack the will and the ideology which would enable them to maintain a long-term campaign outside and in opposition to the formal political process.

Castells, of course, recognizes this dilemma. In particular, he recognizes that a strategy which takes the system as given and seeks to work within it will inevitably result in either the reproduction of the system (in the case of the participatory movement) or in piecemeal reform (in the case of the protest movement). But he also recognizes that any attempt to graft a radical leadership onto a limited movement is 'utopian' since an urban social movement must exist in embryonic form before it can be actualized through political intervention. This will be the case only in specific historical conjunctures where there occurs a fusion of contradictions between the various elements of the urban system. The conditions for the development of an urban social movement must exist before political leadership can bring forth such a movement.

It is my contention, however, that in Britain neither the necessary conditions nor the appropriate form of leadership have developed or are likely to develop in such a way as to generate urban social movements as defined by Castells. This is not so on the Continent. In Milan, for example, large-scale rent strikes have achieved some success even in the face of trade union and Communist Party opposition (Rising Free n.d.); in Copenhagen, working class neighbourhoods have organized to force the city authorities to increase facilities and initiate improvements (Gamst-Nielsen 1974); in Paris, lower class groups have mobilized against evictions and commercial redevelopment of their neighbourhoods (Olives 1976, Castells 1977a, Chapter 14); and in Spain, urban protests have proved particularly significant vehicles for working class action against a repressive political regime (Borja 1977). Whether or not examples such as these constitute 'urban social movements' (as opposed to protest movements) is open to question, but what is clear is that in countries like France and Italy, urban struggles are more widespread, more radical and more closely linked into the working class movement than is generally the case in Britain. In Britain, urban struggles such as the squatting movement (Bailey 1973a), campaigns against disruptive road schemes (Clark 1972) or even rent strikes (Moorhouse *et al.* 1972, Corrigan and Ginsburg 1975, Schifferes 1976) are generally sporadic and isolated both from each other and from the working class movement. Indeed, as we have seen, the most successful movements have often been those of the middle class which have resulted in a redistribution of resources away from more disadvantaged areas.

An explanation of the differences between Britain and countries such as France and Italy would require an exhaustive historical analysis which lies beyond the scope of this book, but three related factors may at least be indicated. These concern the different patterns of uneven development, the different impact of ideological hegemony, and the different history of working class organization. All three point to the significance of historical variations, and all three situate the specific problem of urban struggles in the wider questions of the character of social organization in the countries concerned.

The first factor concerns uneven development and regional imbalance. Both France and Italy are characterized by a stark division between highly industrialized areas and underdeveloped areas of peasant agriculture. Britain, too, of course, has its 'regional problem', but here the imbalance is between the new industrial and commercial sectors located in areas like the Midlands and the south-east, and declining industrial areas in the north-east, Scotland and so on. The vital difference is that Britain does not have an underdeveloped agricultural sector – the British peasantry effectively disappeared with the enclosures in the nineteenth century. There is, therefore, no large-scale migration of rural labour into the industrial centres such as has occurred, say, between the south and north of Italy, and there is no fundamental cleavage or contradiction in Britain between a capitalist and non-capitalist economic sector. There is little doubt that much of the radicalism of the workers in the north Italian towns can be related to their experience of moving from a backward peasant economy into an advanced capitalist-industrial economy – an experience without parallel in contemporary Britain (e.g. see Mann 1973).

The second factor concerns the problem of ideology. A common theme which emerges from many of the studies of urban protest in Britain concerns the widespread political disenchantment or 'alienation' which activists have encountered among disadvantaged groups. Damer (1974), for example, suggests as a result of his study in a Scottish housing estate that many families were reluctant to identify with the area at all, and that even the active trade unionist was apt to shed any notions of collectivism as he passed through his garden gate. Similarly, in his account of his experiences in the London squatting movement, Bailey feels obliged to admit that the movement was a failure in terms of its original political objectives: 'One of the chief aims of those who started the movement was to spark off large-scale direct action. . . . Unfortunately the hoped-for self-activity of hundreds and thousands of people just did not occur. Fear, alienation, conditioned acceptance of imposed values all prevented this' (1973a, p. 184). And Pahl (1975, p. 257) has identified 'a massive false consciousness' among disadvantaged groups in the urban system.

As I argued in Chapter 1, the problem of ideology must be analysed in terms of the social formation as a whole; it is impossible to understand the 'political alienation' of groups in an urban context without relating it to an analysis of the dominant ideology in the wider society. A number of factors are important here. Poulantzas (1973), for example, explains the persistent dangers of 'economism' in the British working class movement in terms of the historical pattern of the rise of the bourgeoisie which accomplished its 'revolution' under the political domination of the old landed aristocracy. Saville (1973), on the other hand, traces the economism and reformism of the British labour movement to the failure of Chartism in the 1840s, and the subsequent period of political collaboration with the interests of capital which effectively insulated the movement from the growth of Marxism on the continent. Anderson (1965) identifies a 'cumulative constellation' of fundamental moments in British history – the fact that Britain experienced the first and 'least pure' bourgeois revolution, that the proletariat emerged in the absence of socialist theory, that there was no antagonism between the new bourgeoisie and the old aristocracy, that the empire consolidated the aristocratic style of leadership and fostered an intense patriotism in all classes, that Britain emerged victorious from two world wars with its social structure intact. But whatever the explanation, there can be little disagreement with Anderson when he writes, 'The power structure of English society today can be most accurately described as an immensely elastic and all-embracing hegemonic order. . . . The hegemony of the dominant bloc in England is not articulated in any systematic major ideology, but is rather diffused in a miasma of commonplace prejudices and taboos' (p. 30–1). It is clear that the historical constitution of the British working class has been fundamentally different from that of its European counterparts with the result that its often intense class awareness has generally failed to develop into a transcendent class consciousness.

This leads us on to the third, and arguably most significant factor which distinguishes the British situation from that on the Continent; namely, the lack of a mass-based communist movement in Britain. The point here is that even if the preconditions for the emergence of urban social movements were to develop, the leadership deemed essential by Castells would be lacking. Most of the Marxist urban theorists whose work has been discussed in this chapter recognize the importance of leadership in linking urban struggles into the wider class struggle. Precisely because urban struggles are not themselves class struggles (because they occur around issues of consumption rather than production, and because classes are not directly engaged in them), it follows that their relevance for any revolutionary strategy is dependent upon their integration into the mainstream working class movement. As Mingione argues, 'An able and mature working class leadership is the key to the transcendence of the limited sectoral character of territorial conflict. Without this, the struggle for housing, better social services or a different urban structure will be a limited and partial one in which the real antagonisms are not identified and the root causes of the conflict unaffected' (1977, p. 36). In Britain, however, no such 'able and mature' leadership can be said to exist.

Clearly, if urban and industrial struggles are to be brought together then this can only be accomplished through the existing institutional framework of the labour movement. At the present time, however, the labour movement in Britain shows little sign of being able or willing to forge such an integration. Cockburn (1977, p. 168), for example, bemoans the fact that trade unions have rarely recognized the need to defend the 'social wage', while the conclusion reached by the various Community Development Project teams points to the fragmentation of the working class movement:

> Tenants' associations are usually concerned with specific issues and their demands are made upon the landlord who is often a Labour-controlled council. Labour councils find themselves defending their actions against the tenants and making marginal concessions to buy off the pressure. . . . Trade unions are a major source of labour movement strength in the industrial sector but they are still predominantly concerned with industrial issues despite increasing recognition of the need to defend the social wage. Trades councils provide a more community based forum for trade unionists in a particular area and are more likely to take a direct interest in housing and broader social problems. But their effectiveness may depend upon many other factors including their organizational strength and their ties back into the community. . . . Nationally and locally, the labour movement is divided [CDP 1976b, pp. 31–2].

The picture drawn in this report bears a striking similarity to that which emerges in Chapter 7.

Even if the labour movement could be cajoled into establishing firmer links between the industrial and urban contexts, however, this would still fail to provide the sort of leadership identified as necessary by Castells. The point is that the Labour movement in Britain is essentially and inherently reformist. It has never posed a direct challenge to the interests of capital, and the likelihood is that it never will (Miliband 1972). More radical parties seem for ever condemned to remain on the fringe of British politics, unlike the Communist parties in France and Italy which, for all their compromises and concessions, at least remain wedded to a theory of class struggle and which have managed to develop a strong electoral base. There is, it seems, no realistic alternative to the Labour Party, yet that party poses no alternative.

In his addendum to *The Urban Question*, Castells suggests that where strong revolutionary parties exist with a broad level of support within the working class, urban struggles can play a highly significant part in developing a popular challenge to monopoly capital. Where, on the other hand, such parties have failed to develop, 'then urban issues are relatively secondary in relation to the workers' struggle and to directly political conflicts' (1977a, p. 465). In such a situation, he suggests, radicals would do better to concentrate their efforts in building a revolutionary working class movement at the workplace where the principal contradiction between wage-labour and capital is directly represented. This is a conclusion which has too often been overlooked by those who seek to apply the theory of urban social movements to urban conflicts in Britain. Even if Castells is correct in suggesting that a revolutionary leadership can integrate urban struggles with the class struggle (and, as we have seen, even this is doubtful in the light of Hirst's argument about a necessary non-correspondence between economic classes and political issues – an argument which is underlined by Schifferes's conclusion that housing struggles 'involve conflict between sections of classes on both sides' (1976, p. 69)), it is clear that in Britain, such a leadership is absent. The most that can be expected of the 'new' urban politics in this country is that there should be a growth of what Castells terms 'consumer trade unionism': limited, piecemeal, reactive and localized expressions of solidarism and dissent with some consequences for the distribution of key urban facilities, but with little significance for any future transition to a qualitatively different mode of organization of society.

4 The question of the local state

The foundations of urban sociology as a distinct academic discipline were laid in the years following the First World War by Robert Park and his associates at the University of Chicago. Other observers of city life before them had noted many of the characteristics which they observed (e.g. the famous concentric ring pattern of residential growth and the social differentiation of various parts of the city had been noted by Engels in Manchester in the 1840s and by Booth in London at the turn of the century), but the importance of the Chicago school lay in its development of a coherent body of theory which purported to explain such patterns as the inevitable manifestation of underlying natural forces in human society. This theoretical perspective – human ecology – was based upon the argument that city growth and urban ways of life reflected a basic biotic struggle for existence among different members of a human population, and that the same processes that had been observed in relation to the ecology of the plant and animal worlds (e.g. invasion, dominance over a natural area, succession, and – most significantly – competition) thus had their counterparts in the organization of human existence. Although Park recognized that the cultural level of human society could and did mediate this process of biotic competition and could produce effects opposed to those determined by natural forces (e.g. through political regulation and planning of the human environment), and although subsequent developments in the theory of human ecology have generally come to lay greater emphasis on the role of this cultural dimension, it is nevertheless the case that Park's identification of natural ecological forces has cast a long shadow over the development of urban sociology in the western world. Without too much exaggeration, it can be said that much of the work which has followed in urban sociology and human geography constitutes either an extension of, or a debate with, this central idea produced by the Chicago school.

The reaction against ecological determinism and naturalistic explanation in urban sociology has taken a number of forms, but in most cases it has sought to assert the primacy of human action and individuals' values in shaping the human environment. In other words, there has been an increased emphasis on the independent significance of the cultural level of organization, and in particular, on the importance of the political system in influencing the pattern of urbanism. The question of power and decision-making has thus come to be seen as a key feature of any explanation of urban processes. In the United States, this can be seen in the explosion of academic interest in community power research following the publication of Hunter's *Community Power Structure* in 1953, although it is worth noting that some observers during this period remained highly sceptical of the validity of such work. Long (1958), for example, suggested that the frantic search for cabals of conspiring businessmen in a range of different American cities was misguided, and that 'decisions' were not so much consciously made by a small elite as unconsciously evolved out of an 'ecology of games' within the community.

Nevertheless, American interest in the question of community power remained strong well into the 1960s; one recent count suggests that around 500 different empirical case studies have been completed in addition to hundreds more articles and monographs discussing the theoretical and methodological questions raised by such work (see Chapter 9). In Britain, by contrast, academic interest in community power research remained muted for reasons which we shall consider below. Nevertheless, a number of case studies of local authority decision-making have been completed over the last twenty years or so. Furthermore, work by Pahl and Rex in the 1960s served to direct the attention of British urban sociologists towards the activities and values of those whom Pahl called the 'gatekeepers' of the urban system – individuals such as local authority managers and councillors, building society managers, estate agents, social workers and the like who determine the allocation and distribution of scarce urban resources such as housing, and who are therefore responsible for the perpetuation of patterns of privilege and deprivation. As Pahl put it, 'These managers of the urban system provide the independent variables of the subject' (1975, p. 206).

Both the American concern with community power and the

British interest in urban managerialism thus reflected a growing dissatisfaction with ecological theories which sought to portray as 'natural' what was clearly the result of human action and decision-making, and to dismiss the individual actor as insignificant when he was in fact central to the urban problematic. As Norman observes, 'The argument that unequal distribution of scarce resources was partly explicable as a consequence of "social" factors, particularly the decision-making of a range of local gatekeepers, was a direct attack on the ecological school of thought which dominated both urban sociology and the application of sociology in urban planning' (1975, p. 6). The emphasis thus shifted from the analysis of biotic struggles to the analysis of power and its distribution. Rex and Moore (1967), for example, showed in their classic study of housing in inner Birmingham that local authority policies on zoning and the allocation of council housing directly created and perpetuated a system of housing inequality to the disadvantage of immigrant groups, while Pahl (1970) developed the concept of a socio-ecological system, suggesting that, 'The built environment is a result of conflicts, taking place in the past and in the present, between those with different degrees of power in society' (p. 60). While this perspective was by no means an entirely voluntaristic one (since constraints on the actions of the powerful were recognized), it nevertheless represented a qualitative shift from a concern with underlying ecological forces to a concern with manifest political actions and ideologies.

In the 1970s, however, this perspective has itself come under attack, not from ecological theorists asserting the primacy of biotic forces, but from Marxist theorists asserting the ultimate determinacy of material ones. This new Marxist critique, while totally opposed to what it sees as the ideological basis of ecological theory, nevertheless shares with the ecological perspective a distrust of voluntaristic explanations and an emphasis on structure and constraint as opposed to action and social power. The challenge which it poses to community power and urban managerialist research has thus posed again the central problem which was expressed (though not resolved) in the biotic/cultural dichotomy developed by Park; namely, how far the organization of space and the perpetuation of urban inequalities can be explained without reference to the values and subjective orientations of actors (notably those occupying strategic positions in decision-making organizations) within the urban system. What is at issue here is not whether political intervention constitutes an important factor in the explanation of urban phenomena, for the crucial significance of the state is recognized by both managerialists and their critics. Rather, the issue is how the role of the state is to be explained. It is with this question that we shall be concerned in this chapter.

State policies: functions and causes

The starting point for any analysis of the role of the modern state in advanced capitalist societies lies in the recognition that the scope of its social and economic functions has expanded enormously since the mid nineteenth century. This is not to suggest that the state in Victorian Britain was as wedded to the minimal nightwatchman role as is sometimes assumed, for while the principle of *laissez-faire* undoubtedly governed economic policy, the growth of legislation in housing, health, education and so on indicates a considerable extension of state responsibility in social affairs during this period. Indeed, Fraser notes the paradox that 'the very age of individualism apparently saw the birth of the centralized administrative state' (1973, p. 102), and he reminds us that Herbert Spencer, a leading advocate of minimal government, had already written two books attacking the growth of state regulation and intervention by the time of the Great Exhibition of 1851.

The distinctiveness of the modern state, therefore, lies not in the fact that it is interventionist, but in the character and scope of its intervention. More specifically, its character has become increasingly positive and directive while its scope has broadened to encompass areas of economic activity which have traditionally been considered private and thus inviolable.

Running parallel to this progressive increase in the strength and scope of state intervention since the nineteenth century has been an equally significant tendency toward centralization. We shall examine some of the reasons for, and consequences of, this shift away from local and regional forms of administration later in this chapter. Here we need only indicate some of the evidence for it: the decline of the locally administered Poor Law and its replacement by a nationally organized system of social services during the first half of the twentieth century; the progressive imposition by central government of statutory duties on local authorities with respect to education, housing and so on; the increase in the significance of central government as a source of finance for local authorities; the reduction of local authority controls over the utilities (gas, water, electricity), public transport, land use planning, etc. Thus, while the importance of the state in managing the economy and its distributional effects has been increasing, the relative significance of the 'local state' has apparently been declining.

What these introductory remarks indicate is the need to identify the areas in which the state is now actively involved, and to assess the degree to which the local state is significant in each area.

We may begin by indicating four sets of problems to which the nation-state in capitalist society has always had to address itself. The first two reflect Bentham's utilitarian principles of legislation: the state has guaranteed the security of property rights, and has attempted to provide a minimum level of sustenance for the poor. Without some guarantee of the rights of property (involving both civil and criminal law), production would cease. As Bentham put it, 'Property and law are born together and die together. Before laws were made there was no property; take away laws and property ceases' (1894, p. 113). Thus, while it may be fruitful to ask, *pace* Hirsch (1978), why the domination of property should come to be expressed through the state rather than within the economic class relation itself, the point remains that it has historically been a primary function of the state in capitalist societies to provide such an 'external' political guarantee of property relations.

The problem of providing subsistence has, of course, consistently generated difficulties for the state. On the one hand, the conditions of the propertyless classes cannot be allowed to deteriorate beyond a certain level at which the quality of labour declines, the political compliance of the labour force is threatened, or liberal humanitarian values are grossly affronted. On the other hand, public support of those in need cannot be allowed to increase to a point where it weakens the work ethic or imposes too great a burden on those who accumulate. Put simply, the growth of collective social support poses at least a potential threat to the system of private property which the state attempts to guarantee. Thus the concern has always been to maintain support at a minimum necessary level and to provide support, as far as possible, on the basis of individual insurance contributions, thereby avoiding 'taxing industry for the support of idleness' (Bentham 1894, p. 133).

The remaining two problems traditionally confronted by the state concern the need to regulate relations with other nation-states on the one hand, and relations within the boundaries of the state on the other. In other words, there has always been a need for foreign policy and for a domestic system of control or repression. Both of these areas of state activity may in large part be related to the problem of maintaining the security of private property, for foreign policy (whether waged through war or through treaty) has often been concerned with the defence or expansion of markets and sources of supply, while domestic 'law and order' can be used to regulate class antagonisms (e.g. through anti-trade union legislation) and to defend the rights of private property.

All four traditional areas of state activity have undergone significant changes and extension in the last one hundred years. The subsistence function, for example, has developed into a system of welfare support founded on a principle of citizenship (i.e. of right) rather than supplication (although elements of the latter still remain in the modern welfare system), and this reflects the extension of state provision ('collective consumption') into areas such as housing which were previously left to the market or to private charity. The foreign policy function has assumed a new importance with the internationalization of capital and the growing threat to British capital posed by competition from abroad, and this is reflected in the growth of competitive cooperation between individual nation-states aimed at stabilizing the international economy (e.g. through the IMF) and broadening international markets (e.g. through the EEC). The internal control function has also expanded, both in respect of increased state involvement in maintaining social cohesion, and through the growth of corporate planning involving capital, organized labour and the state. But most significant of all, the role of the state in guaranteeing property rights has expanded. The historic concern with regulating detention (Renner 1949) – i.e. with ensuring the rights of those with property to use it, dispose of it and benefit from it as they choose – has developed into a concern with maintaining the economic conditions necessary for profitability to be maintained. To some extent the state always did ensure these conditions (e.g. by providing and backing a standardized medium of exchange – Holland 1975), but the unique characteristic of the modern state is that, in order to sustain private economic activity, it has itself intervened more and more within the private sector and has thus become a key agency within the system of production. Thus we see the paradox of the modern state: in safeguarding private property, it has itself intervened massively within the private sector, both directly (e.g. through nationalization of key industries) and less directly (e.g. through the provision of subsidies, the development of planning agreements and so on).

What is important from our present perspective is that this enlarged significance of the state has been mirrored at the local level. In other words, although local government in Britain has progressively been losing its functions to Whitehall and Westminster over the last hundred years, it has at the same time been gaining in significance with respect to those functions which it continues to administer (particularly in its controls over land use planning and in its provision of social facilities such as housing, education, welfare services and roads). These functions cover three of the four areas of state activity outlined above; the 'local state' is important in the provision of collective consumption, in the regulation of class relations, and in sustaining the conditions for capital accumulation. The only area in which it does not play a part is in foreign policy, although the equivalent function here may be its role as mediator between the central state and the local population (see the discussion of the urban managerialism thesis below).

These key functions can usefully be examined in relation to O'Connor's distinction between three types of state expenditure: social investment, social consumption and social expenses (O'Connor 1973). Social investment and social consumption are described by O'Connor as two components of 'social capital' – i.e. expenditures which are necessary if private accumulation is to continue and to remain profitable. The former takes the form of 'constant capital' which, like private investment in machinery, is necessary in order to improve the productivity of labour, while the latter constitutes 'variable capital' which, like the payment of wages, serves to reproduce labour-power on a daily or generational basis. Both social investment and social consumption are thus indirectly productive forms of investment which, if not undertaken by the state, would have to be undertaken by capital itself in order to increase the rate of profit. Social expenses on the other hand are not productive, but rather reflect the state's social control function in that they aid the legitimation of the system. While social expenses are a necessary form of expenditure, they therefore nevertheless represent a drain on profits rather than a support of them.

In his discussion of social investment, O'Connor draws a further distinction between physical and human capital. Both are indirectly productive and both, he suggests, are mainly the responsibility of local or regional rather than national levels of government. Thus investment in physical capital takes the form of state provision of economic infrastructure such as roads, utilities and the preparation of sites for industry and commerce through planned urban renewal. His argument is that such resources are permanently necessary for production to take place, yet are prohibitively expensive or risky for private producers to provide for themselves. He recognizes, of course, that state provision of, say, roads or other communication links does not function only in the interests of private capital since they are used to some extent by all classes, but he does argue that its major function nevertheless lies in aiding the process of capital accumulation. Similarly with respect to social investment in human capital (by which he means mainly state education and state sponsorship or support of research and development), no single producer can afford to meet the necessary costs, so the state is again obliged to shoulder the responsibility. Given the argument that social investment functions mainly in the interests of capital rather than the society as a whole (an argument which is open to debate as we shall see), O'Connor then goes on to show that the socialization of these costs inevitably generates a fiscal crisis in the state itself since, while footing the bill, it collects none of the revenue from its investment. And given that social investment is a key feature of local government expenditure, it is therefore possible to explain the crises of local government finance which have occurred in Britain, the United States and elsewhere.

Like social investment expenditures, state spending on social consumption is also divided into two categories. The first consists of those goods and services which are provided by the state to be consumed by the workforce – i.e. those facilities referred to by Castells in his concept of collective consumption (see pages 106–9). Again these are provided mainly at the local level, the key resource being housing. According to O'Connor, collective consumption not only serves to reproduce labour-power and to improve its quality, but it also helps to depress money wages since part of the cost of producing the worker is borne by the state rather than by the individual and his family, with the result that the value (in Marxist terms) of labour-power is reduced and the rate of profit is thus increased. The second category of social consumption is social insurance against unemployment, sickness and so on, and here again, O'Connor suggests that state policy functions more in the interests of capital (since it reduces economic insecurity and thereby fosters social harmony between employer and employee) than it does for the workforce. With the erosion of the Poor Law during this century in Britain, however, this second category of social consumption has ceased to be a principal function of local government, and it need not therefore concern us here.

If social investment corresponds to the role of the state in sustaining production, and social consumption corresponds to its role in ensuring subsistence, O'Connor's third category of expenditure – social expenses – corresponds to its role in maintaining social cohesion and control. Social expenses are thus those unproductive outlays undertaken by the state in respect of the need to ensure order or (in Marxist terms) to reproduce the relations of production. Expenditure on the police, courts and other agencies of 'law and order' provide an obvious example as we saw earlier, but O'Connor's concern is mainly with the problem of legitimation rather than coercion, and in this his work reflects, not only traditional functionalist orientations to the question of social consensus, but also the growing awareness among Marxist theorists from Gramsci onwards that the state performs a crucial legitimating function in advanced capitalist societies which serves to mask or even pre-empt its more traditional coercive character.

Like many contemporary Marxist writers, O'Connor sees legitimation as increasingly problematic in the conditions of advanced capitalism. His argument is that the growth of the monopoly capital sector has generated both a surplus productive capacity and a pool of surplus labour. State expenditure on social expenses can be seen as an attempt to overcome both problems. The problem of underconsumption results in increased military expenditure (due to the need to expand foreign markets) which, as Baran and Sweezy 1966 suggest, in turn helps to soak up surplus capacity. The problem of surplus labour stimulates the growth of welfare spending (due to the need to defuse potential class conflict) and this too helps to generate new demand within the economy. The problem of legitimation thus involves increased state spending on unproductive welfare provisions, and this too contributes to the growing fiscal crisis of the state. The point is, then, that social expenses in respect of legitimation are necessary yet pose a fundamental contradiction to the state's other principal function of ensuring continued accumulation, since expenditure on welfare or coercion is an increasing drain on revenue which is needed for social investment and consumption.

O'Connor's argument here can usefully be taken in conjunction with that of Habermas who arrives at a similar conclusion from a rather different direction. Habermas (1976) suggests that in a system of *laissez-faire* capitalism, no single individual or institution can be held responsible for the vagaries of the market, and the market system generates its own legitimacy by virtue of the ideology of equivalent exchange. In advanced capitalism, however, the state is seen as a key agent of economic management by virtue of its involvement in social investment and social consumption, and economic relations thus become politicized within the state itself. The rationale of the free market therefore no longer serves to justify economic inequalities since the market is itself seen to be subject to political manipulation. What emerges from this analysis, therefore, is that the state itself undermines traditional sources of legitimacy, and faces the double problem of establishing a new legitimacy for its own role as well as maintaining legitimacy in the face of the growth of a surplus population. Social expenses are thus forced to rise, yet as we have seen, this directly conflicts with the need to devote ever greater amounts of revenue to the support of accumulation.

O'Connor recognizes that his three categories of state expenditures are not exclusive categories, and that any one area of expenditure is likely to perform more than one function. The provision of housing by a local authority, for example, can be seen as both social consumption (since it aids the reproduction of labour power) and social expenses (since it aids social consensus by ensuring the supply of a crucial resource which the market cannot provide at an adequate level). Ball (1978), for example, argues that the direct involvement of the state in the provision of working class housing from 1919 onwards was fundamentally a response to the inability of the private sector to ensure an adequate supply – a deficiency with immense implications for the continued reproduction of labour-power needed by industry. But he also recognizes that the form and timing of this intervention were in part a response to the problem of maintaining legitimacy at a time when working class militancy was pronounced and when there was a genuine fear of the possibility of revolutionary action. This example again illustrates the point I made earlier that state policies are likely to be the result of several factors and are likely to perform more than one function. Indeed, as O'Connor notes, state expenditure on welfare not only serves a legitimating function, but also indirectly aids capital by generating new demand for its surplus capacity. As we shall see in Chapter 8, local authority housing contracts can be highly significant in aiding the realization of profits in the private sector, and it follows that state expenditure on an item like housing may therefore be important in sustaining production as well as in reproducing labour-power and maintaining social cohesion.

While bearing in mind this overlapping of functions, O'Connor's typology provides a useful framework for analysing the role of the 'local state' in Britain today. If we combine his analysis with the more specific study of the local state provided by Cockburn (1977), we can construct a taxonomy of the key functions as follows:

Sustenance of private production and capital accumulation
a) through the provision of necessary non-productive urban infra-structure (e.g. road developments)
b) by aiding the reorganization and restructuring of production in space (e.g. planning and urban renewal)
c) through the provision of investment in 'human capital' (e.g. education in general and technical college education in particular)
d) through 'demand orchestration' (Holland 1975) (e.g. local authority public works contracts)

Reproduction of labour-power through collective consumption
a) by means of the material conditions of existence (e.g. low rent local authority housing)
b) by means of the cultural conditions of existence (e.g. libraries, museums, recreation parks)

Maintenance of order and social cohesion

a) through the means of coercion (e.g. police)
b) through the support of the 'surplus population' (e.g. social services and other welfare support services such as temporary accommodation)
c) through support of the agencies of legitimation (e.g. schools, social work, 'public participation')

Many of the functions identified in this taxonomy are of course performed in conjunction with other levels of government and administration, and many are financed mainly through central government. Nevertheless, as we shall see in the final section of this chapter, local authorities in Britain retain a considerable degree of autonomy in respect of most of these functions. A more important point to note is that this taxonomy does not imply any necessary correspondence between the functions of state policy and the interests of any particular class, nor does it rest on any assumptions about the necessary causes of state action. Let us consider these two points in more detail.

This analysis of the functions of the local state has drawn heavily upon current Marxist analyses, but the taxonomy does not imply an acceptance of any Marxist theory of the state. Few observers would doubt the importance of the state today in the areas of production, consumption and social control, although conservatives may well see it as too heavily engaged in production and insufficiently committed to its control function. In other words, conservatives may wish to identify dysfunctions as well as functions – e.g. the high tax burden on profits, the inefficiency of bureaucratic centralized economic management, the erosion of the will to work by the extension of welfare services and so on – but such 'dysfunctions' (or contradictions) are also identified in Marxist approaches, and their existence does not deny the fact that the state is involved in the areas identified. Neither conservatives nor Marxists see the relation of the state to civil society as an entirely harmonious one. Where they differ, therefore, is not in the identification of the state's functions, but in their assessment of these functions. The point is that I have thus far discussed the 'functions' of the state without indicating for whom or for what the functions operate. A key division between Marxist and liberal or conservative approaches is that the former see these functions as tied to the interests of a specific class – capital, or particular fractions of capital. Liberal and conservative thinkers, on the other hand, generally identify the state as in some way the embodiment of the collective national interest, sometimes favouring one group, sometimes another, but all the time acting in the long-term interests of the social collectivity as a whole. To identify the chief functions of the state (as in the taxonomy) is not therefore to say anything about the necessary neutrality or partiality of the state, for this is a problem to be considered through further theoretical analysis and cannot be resolved by means of a descriptive taxonomy.

The second point is that it is crucially important to retain the distinction between cause and function. In detailing the functions performed by the local state, I have deliberately left aside the question of why and how these functions came to be performed in the first place. As Yaffe argues in his analysis of the history of British social policies, 'Above all it is essential to distinguish their concrete historical *origins* from the ongoing *function* they play within that particular social formation' (1973, p. 76). Yaffe gives the example of reforms which are won through working class action but which later come to perform functions in the interests of the dominant class. In such a case, it would clearly be fallacious to attempt to explain such policies in terms of the functions they have come to perform. Again, therefore, we see that the argument so far in this chapter has been essentially descriptive – a mapping exercise identifying what the area of state activity is without attempting to explain why it is as it is. A discussion of the functions of the state can of itself say nothing about how the state operates or the nature of its relationship with different classes.

The question of functions and the question of causes each therefore generates theoretical disagreements – are the functions of the state necessarily class-biased?; to what extent do state policies reflect external political pressures? By taking these two problems together, it is possible to identify four distinct theoretical perspectives on the question of the relationship between the state and capital in advanced capitalist societies. Representational perspectives see the state as responsive to political pressures from all sections of society and suggest that the functions of state policies consequently represent a wide range of diverse interests. Managerialist theories, on the other hand, see the functions of the state as operating in the (bureaucratically defined) national interest, but suggest that external political pressures play virtually no part in the formulation of public policy. Instrumentalist theories hold that the state functions in the interests of the capitalist class or fractions thereof, and explain this bias with reference to the power exerted by this class over the decision-making process. Finally, structuralist theories also accept a fundamental and necessary bias in state policies, but attribute this to the form and structural location of the state within the social formation, rather than to any influence or control exerted by dominant classes confronting the state. These four perspectives are summarized in the following typology:

		Functional bias of state policy	
		Collective	*Specific*
Primary cause	*External*	representational	instrumentalist
of state policy	*Internal*	managerialist	structuralist

As with all typologies, we shall see that there are certain theoretical positions which do not fit unproblematically into any of these four categories. This is especially the case with the work of Claus Offe (which is considered in the discussion of managerialist perspectives) and the German 'state derivationist' school (discussed in the section on structuralist theories). Nevertheless, the two dimensions of cause and function do appear to constitute the principal parameters in the debate over the state, and as such the typology helps to indicate the basic divisions between the different perspectives. It is to an examination of these perspectives that I now turn.

Theoretical perspectives on the state

Representational perspectives

Representational perspectives on the state share in common the view that the state is neutral in its functions and independent of any particular class interests. The state itself is seen as a set of political institutions standing outside civil society, and it is this position of externality and superiority which enables it to regulate and mediate the conflicts within civil society, by the use of force if necessary. Thus, 'The Government is any government that successfully upholds a claim to the exclusive regulation of the legitimate use of physical force in enforcing its rules within a give territorial area. The political system made up of the residents of that territorial area and the Government of the area is a State' (Dahl 1963, p. 12).

The crucial implication which follows from this view of the neutrality and externality of the political apparatus is that the state is a pawn up for grabs between competing contenders for political power. It is omnipotent (in that it monopolizes the legitimate use of force) yet subservient (in that it responds to whatever pressures are exerted upon it). As Dahl observes,

> When an actor controls the state, he can enforce his decisions with the help of the state. . . . The state is, then, a pawn of key importance in struggles over power, for the relatively great resources of the state and its exclusive claim to regulate severe physical coercion mean that those who control the state inevitably enjoy great power [ibid., pp. 50–1].

Furthermore, Dahl recognizes that in the struggle for political power, some groups are better equipped than others. Indeed, he suggests that in the periods before elections, political resources (such as the power of propaganda) may be highly unequal, and in this he echoes Schumpeter's view that small groups may be in a position to 'fashion and, within very wide limits, even to create the will of the people' (Schumpeter 1954, p. 263).

There is much in all this which would meet with the approval of Marxist theorists such as Miliband (see pages 160–3). However, despite their emphasis on the malleability of the state and on the existence of political inequalities, representational theorists deny that the state necessarily generates any consistent class bias. This denial is premised on four arguments. First, they reject the view that economic class divisions constitute the major lines of cleavage in political conflicts. Dahl, for example, writes, 'In a pluralistic pattern conflicts tend to be non-cumulative. People who are in conflict over one issue are not necessarily in opposite camps when the next issue comes up' (1963, p. 78), and he developed this point in his study of New Haven (1961) where he showed that although a small number of people was involved in many political issues (the mayor being the prime example), many other people were involved in single issues. The picture is thus one of shifting alliances between different groups constituted around different political bases according to the issue at hand – a view which leads Dahl to reject the concept of majority rule in favour of that of 'minorities rule'. It is worth noting, however, that Dahl's theory is concerned with American democracy, and that the United States is one of the few advanced capitalist nations which has not developed a party system based more or less loosely around class divisions. As MacPherson (1973) points out, the 'extreme pluralist assumption' embodied in this theory may be more applicable to the conditions of expansion and prosperity (not to mention ethnic pluralism) which have in the past characterized the United States than to the established political systems of Western Europe where class divisions appear to outweigh all others.

Secondly, although these theorists recognize the existence of political inequalities, they also argue that policy outcomes will reflect, not differences in power, but differences in intensity of preferences. The argument here takes the form of a simple syllogism: (*a*) 'Political activity is to a significant extent a function of relative intensity [of preferences]' (Dahl 1956, p. 134); (*b*) 'The probable outcome of a policy decision is partly a function of the relative amount of political activity carried on for or against the alternatives' (ibid., p. 134); therefore (*c*) 'All other things being equal, the outcome of a policy decision will be determined by the relative intensity of preference among the members of a group' (ibid., p. 135). In other words, as we saw in Chapter 1, the argument rests on the assumption that people shout when they have a reason to, and the louder they shout, the better their reason, and the greater is the likelihood of their views being accepted.

Thirdly, the overall neutrality of the state and its freedom from any intrinsic class bias is guaranteed by the electoral process. It is not argued that elections lead to the implementation of the public will – for a start, the public rarely has a political will worth speaking of (Schumpeter), besides which there is no single public, nor even a single majority, but a collection of minorities, each with their own preferences which cannot be aggregated into any genuinely agreed collective policy. The importance of elections is not that they enable the public to determine policy, but that they are resolved on the basis of political equality (one adult, one vote) and, more important, that they provide a guarantee of political accountability. As Birch puts it, 'The fact that the next general election is never more than five years away is one of the more important factors that induce politicians to respect public opinion and adjust their policies to intimations of public need' (1964, p. 236). Or as Dahl (1956) argues, elections, taken together with the constant competition between aspiring leadership groups, provide the crucial means of popular control over those in positions of power in the state.

This argument is significant for it lies at the heart of the claim made by representational theorists that theirs is a realistic theory of politics. For a start, it denies that democracy must rest on anything other than self-interest, and self-interest itself is taken as given – a fact of human nature (see MacPherson 1977, pp. 84–6). In other words, both electors and leaders pursue their own narrow interests, but the interest of the latter in achieving power constrains them to act in accordance with the preferences of the former. As Schumpeter puts it, 'In order to understand how democratic politics serve this social end, we must start from the competitive struggle for power and office and realize that the social function is fulfilled, as it were, incidentally – in the same sense as production is incidental to the making of profits' (1954, p. 282). Furthermore, the theory is claimed to be realistic since it no longer defines democracy as rule by the people, but rather as rule by those the people have chosen. The level of political sophistication of the typical citizen, according to Schumpeter, is 'infantile', and it is therefore nonsense to suggest that the people raise or resolve political issues. Their role in a democracy is therefore limited to 'accepting or rejecting the men who are to rule them' (ibid., p. 285). And according to Birch, they are quite satisfied with this minimal role: 'The public themselves do not appear to object to this assumption that their leaders know best. . . . All the evidence suggests that the British people still like being governed' (1964, pp. 244–5).

The fourth factor which explains why the state is not the instrument of any one class is that the entire political system is grounded in a fundamental consensus which belies any notion of class domination or 'false consciousness'. The evidence for this is simply that any regime based on coercion rather than consent 'would be certain to fail for a coerced majority could simply vote against the incumbents at the next election and replace them with more responsive officials' (Dahl 1963, p. 76). Nor is this argument limited to the more pluralistic context of the United States, for in Britain too, class antagonisms are seen as of decreasing political importance:

To be sure, class rivalries still have their place in British politics, but the post-war growth in the prosperity of industrial workers has blurred the economic conflict between classes while the acceptance of the policies of the welfare state by all parties has blurred the political conflict. Few people now regard the Parliamentary system as a facade of which the main function is to disguise the real struggle between capitalists and proletariat [Birch 1964, p. 229].

The establishment of consensus is thus a function of the end of ideology. Political issues take place around superficial disagreements, for there is a broad agreement on all the basic questions:

Prior to politics, beneath it, enveloping it, restricting it, conditioning it, is the underlying consensus on policy that usually exists in the society among a predominant proportion of the politically active members. Without such a consensus no democratic system would long survive the endless irritations and frustrations of elections and party competition. With such a consensus, the disputes over policy alternatives are nearly always disputes over a set of alternatives that have already been winnowed down to those within the broad area of basic agreement [Dahl 1956, pp. 132–3].

Crucial in maintaining this political harmony are the political parties. It is not simply that the parties provide the organized means of expression of divergent interests within the system, but that they actually function to moderate conflict and to blunt the edge of political struggles. MacPherson, for example, argues that the creation of political stability out of economic conflict has been the primary function of the party system since the extension of the franchise to the working class – a function which has been 'remarkably successful' (1973, p. 191). Birch confirms this when he suggests that the system produces a convergence of the parties towards the centre – a process which he sees as one of the strengths of the British political system (1964, p. 125). The parties' search for the middle ground thus serves to create and sustain the very political consensus which Dahl sees as necessary for the system to work at all.

Despite the existence of political inequalities, therefore, the state retains its neutrality with respect to any one group. It is, quite simply, a political market place in which the 'supply' of decisions comes to balance and reflect the level of effective demand. Representational theories thus treat political institutions as 'mainly inert recipients of pressures from interest groups. When the output of laws and orders is treated as the result of the input of pressures, it matters little what persons are in office as the government. The government, as the mechanism through which decisions are made, becomes in effect as impersonal or anonymous as the market in the economic model' (MacPherson 1973, p. 188). Individual politicians are thus the instruments of political majorities (Dahl 1963, p. 90). In short, the causes of state action lie outside the state itself, and its functions serve the interests of the majority at any one time.

Representational theories have been widely criticized, and as we saw in Chapter 1, one of the major problems which they fail to address is that of ideology. Thus despite Schumpeter's warning that the political naivete of the majority of the population makes it relatively easy for a committed minority to 'create the will of the people' (1954, p. 263), and despite Dahl's recognition that the means of propaganda are very unequally distributed in society, representational theorists continue to assert that the consensus on which the entire system is founded is in some way spontaneous, and that the key concept is that of subjective preference rather than objective interest. Arguments about 'non-decision-making', and questions about how preferences come to be formulated in the first place, are thus rejected out of hand. Furthermore, the problem of 'effective demand' is almost totally ignored in these analyses. As MacPherson (1977, p. 87) points out, the market analogy which underpins representational theories of the state inevitably raises the question of how far political demands are backed by effective political 'purchasing power'. Just as economic demand in a market economy refers not to what people would ideally like, but to what they can afford to buy, so too political demands are only effective when they are backed up by the control of political resources. Dahl's argument that preferences are linked to action, and that the more intense the preference, the stronger the demand will be and the greater will be the likelihood of its success, must therefore be rejected, for it is quite possible (and arguably quite common) for a group to have an intense preference and yet be unable effectively to do anything about it.

The major weakness of this entire theoretical approach is thus the problem of political inaction discussed in Chapter 1. In contrast to nineteenth century democratic theorists such as John Stuart Mill, who saw liberal democracy as the means whereby all individuals could more fully develop their potential through political participation, these modern-day writers welcome mass apathy as both an indication of the health of the system and as a necessary condition for its continued existence. As Lukes observes, 'Electoral apathy, incompetence, and so on, which exist in most stable "modern democracies" are now considered to be conditions of their successful functioning and are therefore taken to be the new democratic norms' (1977, p. 42). People are not expected to show any great interest in the way in which their lives are governed, and any effective increase in the level of political participation is seen as pathological, a threat to the stability of the system and an indication that the system is not functioning properly.

This curious twist in the conceptualization of democracy reflects a shift in twentieth century democratic theory away from any normative theory of what democracy is or should be towards a new 'realism' which is founded on tautology. In other words, modern democratic theory takes as its starting point the *empirical* question of what it is that characterizes those political systems which we in the west choose to call 'democratic'. The elements thus identified are then developed into a theory of democracy 'warts and all', and this theory is then shown to fit the conditions found in advanced western capitalist societies. This procedure is outlined most clearly by Dahl (1956) who suggests that democratic theory can be developed only by merging analysis with description. Yet the inevitable consequence of this empiricism is that representational theories turn out, on closer inspection, not to be 'theories' at all. Rather, they are idealized descriptions of particular political systems, serving to elevate every element of those systems into virtues, and to justify what they find by ad hoc rationalization.

It is not therefore surprising to find that representational approaches have no theory of ideology since they are themselves ideological. They provide not an explanation of political processes but a description couched in terms set by the system itself – a description which necessarily justifies whatever processes they find. At a theoretical level, therefore, there is no way in which criticism can impinge upon them, for alternative theoretical perspectives will always be dismissed as utopian or metaphysical, as bearing no relation to the 'facts'. It follows that those critics of the representational approach must either ignore it and start from their own alternative premises (cf. Poulantzas), or must engage in debate at an empirical level (cf. Miliband) by seeking to show that the description which it offers is distorted. This latter strategy can make some headway (e.g. Miliband's description of the political process in Britain clearly reveals biases and inequalities which it is difficult to reconcile with even the new democratic 'theory'), but ultimately it encounters the limits set by the ideological boundaries drawn up by the position it seeks to attack. This is clearly demonstrated by the non-decision-making debate where any attempt to approach the fundamental question of political inaction from any starting point which questions the basis of individual preferences is swiftly ruled out of order. As Laclau observes, 'The "empirical validity" and the "theoretical validity" of a theory are not aspects which can be differentiated. . . . In so far as the object of knowledge is produced by theoretical practice itself, the methods of verification are part of the theoretical system itself' (1975, p. 94). Like all ideologies, representational theories are thus seen by their advocates as 'obviously true', and there is little that theoretical debate or empirical research can do to challenge this article of faith. When a key text on the British political system begins with the words, 'Everyone knows that the British constitution provides for a system of representative and responsible government' (Birch 1964, p. 13), there is clearly little point in attempting to question such a fundamental orthodoxy on its own terms.

Instrumentalist perspectives

The position most often contrasted with the representational approach to the state is instrumentalism. This can be seen, for example, in Miliband's critique of liberal pluralist theory (Miliband 1969), and, at the level of local political studies, in the long-running debate in American social science between the advocates of elitist and pluralist approaches to the question of community power (for a summary see Rose 1967 and Bell and Newby 1971). An instrumentalist perspective on the state thus characterizes writings in both the elitist and Marxist perspectives. In the former it can be seen in the work of Mosca and Michels through to the study by Mills (1956) of the relationship between economic, military and political elites in American society, and in the latter it has run as a common theme from the *Communist Manifesto* onwards. What both of these traditions share in common is a view of the state as the instrument whereby one group achieves political domination over another, although they differ in the way these groups are conceptualized, elite theorists distinguishing between the elites and the masses, Marxists distinguishing between the ruling class and the proletariat. Although these two perspectives occasionally fuse (as in Miliband's discussion of civil service and other elites), they are nevertheless distinct approaches, and it should be remembered that elite theory developed in the late nineteenth century largely as a response to and critique of Marxism. In this section I shall concentrate on Marxist instrumentalism, for this provides a clearer and more systematic theoretical position than do most elite theorists whose work, like that of the representational theorists, tends to be more descriptive than analytical.

Considerable support for an instrumentalist interpretation of the Marxist theory of politics can be generated through a reading of some of the key texts of Marxism. Perhaps the best-known quotation is from the *Communist Manifesto* where Marx and Engels wrote, 'The bourgeoisie has at last ... conquered for itself, in the modern representative state, exclusive political sway. The executive of the modern state is but a committee for managing the common affairs of the whole bourgeoisie' (1968, p. 37). The Manifesto, however, is often described by Marxists as a polemical tract of only limited theoretical significance, so it is as well to look elsewhere for support of this position. A similar argument can be found in *The German Ideology* where Marx and Engels suggest that the division between economic and political power which arises with the development of capitalism merely obscures rather than transforms the traditional class character of the state: 'Through the emancipation of private property from the community, the state has become a separate entity beside and outside civil society; but it is nothing more than the form of organization which the bourgeois necessarily adopt both for internal and external purposes for the mutual guarantee of their property and interests' (1974, p. 80). The argument here is that a state standing outside classes is a necessary means whereby the dominant economic class can regulate relationships both within itself (i.e. between different fractions of capital) and between it and the proletariat. *The German Ideology*, of course, has been termed one of the 'works of the break' between the 'young' and the 'mature' Marx (Althusser 1969, p. 34), yet support for an instrumentalist position can be found equally in the later works. In *The Civil War in France*, for example, Marx describes the state as 'an engine of class despotism' (1968, p. 285); in his 1891 introduction to the work, Engels reasserts that 'the state is nothing but a machine for the oppression of one class by another' (1968, p. 258); and in his *Family, Private Property and the State*, Engels argues that the modern representative state provides a new means of class exploitation by capital [Engels 1970, p. 328].

In all of these examples, the state in capitalist society is conceived as a political apparatus standing outside civil society, and the fact that it functions in the interests of capital is explained as due to the external relationship between it and the capitalist class. Yet there is another theme running through these works which at least modifies this picture. This concerns the argument, found notably in *The Eighteenth Brumaire*, but also in some of the texts already referred to, to the effect that, at least in certain historical periods, the state attains a considerable degree of autonomy from all classes. From the various historical works on France, for example, we can see that Marx distinguishes three periods in the first half of the nineteenth century. Under Napoleon, he suggests, the state bureaucracy represented the means whereby the political domination of the newly emergent bourgeoisie was prepared; under the Restoration, it duly became the instrument of bourgeois rule; and then under the second Bonaparte it became independent of the bourgeoisie in a situation where 'the bourgeoisie had already lost, and the working class had not yet acquired, the faculty of ruling the nation' (1968, pp. 286–7). In this third period, according to Marx, Bonaparte came to 'represent', not the bourgeoisie but the peasantry, although he adds that the former prospered enormously under his rule. The implication of this is spelt out by Engels: 'By way of exception ... periods occur in which the warring classes balance each other so nearly that the state power, as ostensible mediator, acquires, for the moment, a certain degree of independence of both' (1970, p. 328).

As we shall see when we discuss the structuralist perspective, there is considerable debate within Marxism as to whether this autonomy is exceptional or functionally necessary at all times. For the moment, however, we need only draw attention to the evident division in these texts between what Miliband (1965) terms the 'primary view' of the state as subordinate to the dominant economic class, and the 'secondary view' of the state as itself the dominant and superior force in society.

However we interpret the relation between these two views, it is apparent that for many later Marxists, the 'secondary' view was almost totally forgotten or ignored. Lenin, for example, is quite clear that the state represents 'the organization of violence for the purpose of holding down some class' (1960, p. 168), and he therefore rejects any suggestion that the capitalist state can be taken over by the working class by constitutional means. Laski (1935), while defending constitutionalism, nevertheless also identifies the state's primary function as safeguarding capitalist production and the class relations generated by it, and traces the class character of the state to the motives and values of those who control it and whose position is challenged by any socialist threat. And Baran and Sweezy (1966) reject outright any view which implies that the state can somehow be or become an independent social force. According to his critics, Miliband too fails to recognize any state autonomy, but as we shall now see, this does not appear to be the case.

Miliband (1969 and 1977) has provided perhaps the most sophisticated or detailed development of instrumentalist theory. In his earlier book, he presents evidence (which, as we have seen, he intends to serve as an empirical refutation of representational perspectives) to show that the social composition of state positions in government, the civil service, the judiciary, the military and police, legislative assemblies and local government is such as generally to ensure that the interests of capital will receive a sympathetic hearing. He also argues that big business is itself sufficiently powerful in advanced capitalist societies effectively to dictate public policy, and that although the capitalist class is to some extent divided into competing economic 'elites', its members nevertheless share 'common interests and common purposes which far transcend their specific differences and disagreements' (1969, p. 45). In all of this, he effectively follows Laski's argument about the significance of the class backgrounds of top decision-makers and the political might of big business, but he also goes beyond Laski in pointing to the structural constraints which limit and direct policy-making, even where those in positions of power are not drawn from the capitalist class and hold no brief for capitalist interests. Thus, although he suggests that social-democratic leaders have in general 'eagerly bent themselves to the administration of the capitalist state' (ibid., p. 244), he also recognizes that their scope for radical innovation is in any case strictly hemmed in by the imperatives of the economic system which they are obliged to administer (see also Westergaard and Resler 1975, p. 248, for a similar argument).

Basically, therefore, Miliband explains the bias in function of the state as the necessary consequence of three causes: the class backgrounds of those who administer it, the power exerted over them by business interests, and the dependence of the state upon continued capitalist accumulation which it is therefore constrained to support. The argument is summarized in the later book where he writes,

Taken together, as they need to be, these three modes of explanation of the nature of the state – the character of its leading personnel, the pressures exercised by the economically dominant class, and the structural constraints imposed by the mode of production – constitute the Marxist answer to the question why the state should be considered as the 'instrument' of the 'ruling class' [1977, pp. 73–4].

Two points need to be emphasized about Miliband's analysis. The first is that he identifies the state as a set of political institutions distinct from civil society which can be and are taken over by the representatives of dominant economic classes, or by the political representatives of other classes who nevertheless remain prepared to rule on behalf of capital. The point is, then, that he draws a clear distinction between state action and class action and refuses to conflate the two theoretically, even though they overlap closely in practice: 'In reality, there is the capitalist state on the one hand and "monopoly capital" on the other. The relation between them is close and getting ever closer, but there is nothing to be gained, and much by way of insight to be lost, by a reductionist oversimplification of that relation' (1977, p. 96). The state, therefore, is a means of class domination, but there is no necessary and automatic correspondence between class power and state power. This argument is significant as both a strength and a weakness of Miliband's position. As a strength, it clearly constitutes a recognition of the 'secondary' view of the state found in Marx's work and avoids the more obvious problems of a straight economic-determinist theory. As a weakness, however, it raises the question which necessarily confronts any Marxist analysis which denies a straightforward economic determinacy and which

Miliband makes no attempt to resolve – namely how the relation between economic classes and political forces is to be theorized. I shall return to this in a moment.

The second point, which follows directly from the first, is that Miliband is hesitant about describing the state as an 'instrument' of class domination since he recognizes that it does enjoy some autonomy from the capitalist class and its constituent fractions. The existence of conflicts between the different sectors of capital, even though they may be less significant than the interests which bind them together, nevertheless implies that the state, in mediating between them, must be in a position to distance itself from any one of them. Thus he suggests, 'While the state does act, in Marxist terms, *on behalf of* the "ruling class", it does not for the most part act *at its behest*' (ibid., p. 74). He explains this 'relative autonomy' (which should not be confused with Poulantzas's concept of 'relative autonomy' discussed below) as due to the degree of freedom enjoyed by those in positions of power for determining how best to serve the interests of the 'nation' (i.e. capital). We have already seen that he identifies the mode of production as a constraint, but not a determinant, of political action. It follows that there must be some residue of discretion left for political leaders to determine their responses in the context of these constraints, and that what they choose to do with their discretion will in large part reflect their own values and the intensity of political pressures exerted upon them. Miliband summarizes this point unambiguously:

> The question is not one of purpose or attitude but of 'structural constraints'; or rather that purposes and attitudes, which can make *some* difference, and in special circumstances a considerable difference, must nevertheless take careful account of the socio-economic system which forms the context of the political system and of state action [ibid., p. 93].

The gaping hole left in this analysis, however, concerns the problem of how this area of discretion is theorized – i.e. how the economic – political relation is theorized. If the state can act to some extent autonomously, then we need to know how to draw the line between determinism and autonomy, constraint and discretion, action and structure (see pages 57–9). This is a serious deficiency in Miliband's work, for it results in ad hoc attributions of causality to either those in power or to the structure without any apparent theoretical rationale.

For example, in his detailed study of the history of the British Labour Party, Miliband argues that the record of the 1964–70 Wilson administration was due, more than anything else, to the basically conservative ideology of leading cabinet members:

> What happened between 1964 and 1970 was not due to the unfavourable economic circumstances which the government inherited; or to the entrenched conservatism of top civil servants; or to the machinations of speculators and the hostility of capitalist interests at home or abroad. It was above all due to the particular ideological dispositions which the men who ran the government brought to their tasks [1972, p. 360].

Yet this argument, which is in any case difficult to reconcile with his emphasis on constraint in his other works, remains pure assertion. What is necessary but lacking is some way of assessing the limits on voluntarism, for in the absence of this there appears no reason why volition should not play the major part in determining state policies in which case it becomes almost impossible to hold to the sacred orthodoxy of Marxism that capital and the state are in some way necessarily related. From most of his work, there seems little doubt that Miliband seeks to emphasize the significance of constraint rather than will, yet he fails in a fundamental way to relate the former to the latter.

One attempt to get around this problem from within an instrumentalist perspective is provided by Lojkine (1977) who suggests that although the state functions as the instrument of dominant economic interests, its policies are mediated by the effect of class struggles. His position appears to differ from Miliband's in at least two respects. First, he does not accept Miliband's contention that all sections of capital share fundamentally common interests, but rather argues that the monopoly capital fraction has its own distinct interests (reflecting its privileged ability to manipulate the market) which necessarily conflict, not only with those of the working class, but also with those of other competitive sections of capital. The state, therefore, is the instrument of the monopoly capital fraction, and as a result will come to develop policies which operate to the advantage of this class and to the disadvantage of all other classes and class fractions. Secondly, because the control of the state by monopoly capital interests is nevertheless mediated by the balance of forces in the class struggle, it follows that the state will sometimes be obliged to respond to the interests of other classes, even against the interests of the monopoly fraction. The 'relative autonomy' of the state is therefore theorized, following Engels, not in terms of the discretion allowed to state personnel, but as the consequence of the balance of class forces in any historical conjuncture.

Lojkine illustrates his first argument with reference to his study of commercial redevelopment in Lyon and Rennes. He argues that the state attempts to maintain a political unity among the different sections of capital, but that this objective is constantly undermined by its commitment to the monopoly fraction which results in the growing exclusion of other capitalist interests from the benefits of its policies. Thus, in Lyon and Rennes he shows how the major part of local commercial capital has been excluded from the development schemes in favour of big companies moving in from outside. This, he suggests, has resulted in the accelerated growth of divisions within local capital itself (i.e. between the few firms which do manage to benefit and the majority which do not), and to increasing alienation of local capitalists from the local authority. Thus he concludes that, 'The state attempts to maintain the illusion that a consensus exists among all store owners. But this ideology is cut off nowadays from its former social roots due to the pauperization of a large number of small shopkeepers who are now displaying a defiant attitude towards the municipal councils they traditionally supported' (ibid., p. 149). The implication of this argument is that a broad alliance of small shopkeepers and the working class could come to be formed against monopoly capital and the local state, although as we saw in Chapter 2, this seems unlikely, at least in the British context. Nevertheless, Lojkine's analysis of the relation between the local state and monopoly capital may prove a very useful one for analysing commercial redevelopment in British towns and cities (see Chapter 8).

Less convincing, however, is Lojkine's analysis of the sources of state autonomy from monopoly capital. His argument here is that, although the state is an instrument of the monopoly interests, it may come to exercise some independence in one of two ways. Either, it may impose certain policies on the big companies against their will where it anticipates trouble from subordinate classes, or it may act in the interests of subordinate classes as a result of their successful mobilization in an urban protest movement or in municipal elections. The first case represents a strategy of making immediate concessions in order to buy off working class pressure; the second represents a genuine gain for the working class as a result of a successful protest or of electoral success.

The first case brings Lojkine's analysis close to that of the structuralists (discussed below) except that his explanation is in terms of the foresight of those in positions of power in anticipating trouble and acting to prevent it, rather than in terms of an automatic functional model such as is found in the work of Poulantzas. The second case, however, brings him closer to the theoretical position of the representationalists discussed above, since it rests on the argument that the state responds to political pressures from subordinate as well as dominant classes, and that it is possible to take over the state apparatus and to use it in the interests of the working class. Lojkine's analysis here is not, of course, a pluralist one since he retains a class-based analysis, but it does reflect his view that Communist Party victories in municipal elections in France represent a fundamental source of real political change (a view which Castells has also apparently come to accept recently – see Pickvance 1978, p. 175).

Clearly there is a tension in Lojkine's analysis: his argument appears to amount to little more than the view that the local state is the instrument of monopoly capital except in those cases where it is the instrument (via Communist control) of the working class! Nor can this tension be reconciled (as Pickvance 1977a suggests) since it reflects the same problem which attaches to Miliband's work; namely, how the relative autonomy of the state is to be theorized while retaining the argument that capital (or one fraction of it) remains in control of it. For Miliband, the answer is that state personnel enjoy some degree of discretion, but the limits of this discretion are unspecified. For Lojkine, the answer is partly in terms of discretion (since state personnel can act to thwart anticipated working class agitation even against the demands of monopoly capital), and partly in terms of the balance of class forces which can tilt the state in favour of the working class (through Communist control of municipal authorities), in which case the state is no longer the instrument of monopoly capital.

It follows from both Miliband's and Lojkine's work that, if the instrumentalist position is to be maintained (i.e. if one class is to be seen as dominant in relation to the state), then it is necessary to specify the limits on state discretion. Miliband does not even attempt this, while Lojkine's analysis in terms of the balance of class forces is

self-defeating since it leads ultimately to a rejection of the instrumentalist position wherever working class parties (including, presumably, the Labour Party in Britain) gain electoral victories. It is
in this context of the need to specify the scope of state discretion that
I turn now to consider managerialist theories, for while the instru-
mentalists start out from the fact of class domination and end up with
an awkward residuum of state discretion, the managerialists begin
from the assumption of state independence, and then develop an
analysis to take account of the factors which reduce this autonomy.
In the light of the problems discussed in this section, it may be suggested that this latter strategy is the more promising.

Managerialist perspectives

While the instrumentalist position has its origins in Marx, managerialist perspectives derive mainly out of Weber, and in particular they
reflect the two key principles in Weber's political sociology: that
there is no necessary relationship between economic classes and
politics, and that the mode of political domination in modern societies
is increasingly and necessarily bureaucratic. The first of these principles leads to the view that political forces or 'parties' may develop
around a wide variety of different social bases of which class membership is only one (albeit an important one), while the second leads to
the argument that the state is not necessarily class-biased since the
bureaucratic mode of domination is essentially independent and
neutral with respect to class interests. The increasing rationalization
of administration thus reduces the possibility of effective political
control over the state bureaucracy, for such control 'is possible only
in a very limited degree to persons who are not technical specialists.
Generally speaking, the trained permanent official is more likely to
get his way in the long run than his nominal superior' (Weber 1947,
p. 338). Furthermore, although Weber recognizes that bureaucratization has 'very frequently benefited the interests of capitalism' (Gerth
and Mills 1948, p. 230), and that these interests have sometimes been
able to exert considerable influence over policy, he traces the origins
of such policies to the internal workings of the state itself, rather than
to the effect of external political pressures.

Applied to the analysis of the local state, Weber's influence is most
obvious in the work on 'urban managerialism'. As it first developed

in the work of Rex, Dennis and the earlier Pahl, the urban managerialist thesis held simply that inequalities in the urban system could be
explained as the product of a 'socio-ecological system' in which
inevitable spatial inequalities were reinforced or mediated by the
actions of strategic urban gatekeepers. Pahl, for example, wrote:

> There are fundamental *spatial* constraints on access to scarce urban
> resources and facilities. Such constraints are generally expressed in time/
> cost distance. There are fundamental *social* constraints on access to scarce
> urban facilities. These reflect the distribution of power in society and are
> illustrated by: bureaucratic rules and procedures; social gatekeepers who
> help to control and distribute urban resources. . . . Populations limited in
> this access to scarce urban resources are the *dependent* variable; those con-
> trolling access, the *managers* of the system, would be the independent
> variable [1975, p. 201].

In other words, the explanation of economic and social inequalities
was to be accomplished through analysis of the values and actions of
those who managed the urban system – a category which included
not only local authority bureaucrats, but also council members,
social workers, building society managers, estate agents and any
other group which controlled access to urban facilities such as housing or social services. Pahl did not suggest that such people were
solely responsible for the prevailing pattern of urban inequalities, for
he argued that they were constrained by basic ecological forces
(principally competition for land and houses) which generated spatial
inequalities irrespective of the actions of urban managers. But he did
see the managers as a crucial factor in any explanation:

> The controllers, be they planners or social workers, architects or educa-
> tion officers, estate agents or property developers, representing the market
> or the plan, private enterprise or the state, all impose their goals and values
> on the lower participants in the urban system. . . . We need to know how
> the basic decisions affecting life chances in urban areas are made. . . . We
> agree that certain urban resources will always be scarce and that social and
> spatial constraints will mutually reinforce one another whatever the dis-
> tribution of power in society may be. However, given that certain managers
> are in a position to determine goals, what are these goals and on what
> values are they based? [ibid., pp. 207–8].

The contrast with the instrumentalist approach is immediately
apparent, for the emphasis here is firmly on the actions of the managers rather than the constraints of the structure. Empirically, this

emphasis proved very fruitful, since urban managers constituted a visible and relatively accessible target for research, and there followed a brief period of valuable work – notably, of course, Rex and Moore's study of inequalities in access to scarce housing resources in Birmingham, but also a number of other studies focusing on the strategic significance of groups such as planning officers (Dennis 1970, Davies 1972) and building society managers (Ford 1975). However, this earlier managerialist thesis failed to confront two major questions. First, as Norman (1975) points out, it did not and could not specify how the relative importance of different sets of urban managers could be assessed. In other words, it lacked a *theory* of power and in practice consisted of little more than descriptive data-gathering on those who were assumed, for one reason or another, to occupy important positions in the urban system. Secondly, because of this lack of a theoretical basis, it inevitably failed to take adequate account of the context of constraints in which urban management decisions were taken. Pahl recognized the importance of ecological factors, but he failed to explain how the two components of his 'socio-ecological system' articulated with one another, and he underemphasized the significance of other constraints such as the control exercised by central government and the limits imposed by the reliance of local government on continued capital accumulation. This latter point was a particularly serious omission, for as Gray points out, 'The managerial approach, in concentrating on studying the allocation and distribution of "scarce resources", fails to ask why resources are in scarce supply' (1976, p. 81). In its emphasis on political autonomy, therefore, the early managerialist thesis lost sight of the importance of economic factors in curtailing that autonomy. It was this need to relate managerialism to political economy which led Pahl to reject his earlier formulations and to develop a second, and more sophisticated, theory of urban management.

In this later version, Pahl maintains that it is still useful to study the ideologies and motives of those who control the allocation of resources in the urban system, but he suggests, first, that such an analysis should be grounded in a specific theory of the state, with the consequence that urban managers come to be defined as local state bureaucrats (rather than elected politicians or gatekeepers in the private sector), and secondly, that it should take explicit account of the internal structure of the state (i.e. the relation between central and local levels) and of its external relationship with the private sector. The argument, therefore, is that local state bureaucrats perform a crucial role in mediating between the private and public sectors (competitive capitalism and welfare statism), and between the central state and the local population (see also Darke and Walker 1977, p. 72 for a similar argument). Their role is thus qualitatively different from that of managers in the private sector: 'It seems to me that one set of urban managers and technical experts must play crucial *mediating roles* both between the state and the private sector and between central state authority and the local population. Another set of private managers control access to capital and other resources' (Pahl 1977c, p. 55). The importance of state bureaucrats at the local level, therefore, is that they determine how a given surplus (the size of which depends upon investment and other decisions in the private sector) will be distributed: 'The urban managers remain the allocators of this surplus; they must remain, therefore, as central to the urban problematic' (1975, p. 285). And given the fact that state intervention in the provision of various urban resources is increasing, it follows that, notwithstanding the constraints imposed by the market, local managers' allocation decisions are of increasing significance in mediating the effects of market inequalities (see also Rex 1977, p. 223).

This last point is crucial, and it reflects Pahl's view that the relationship between the state and the private sector is in the process of undergoing a qualitative transformation from state support of capitalist accumulation to state direction of this process. 'In general', he writes,

It could certainly be argued until fairly recently that the state was subordinating its intervention to the interests of private capital. However, there comes a point when the continuing and expanding role of the state reaches a level where its power to control investment, knowledge and the allocation of services and facilities gives it an autonomy which enables it to pass beyond its previous subservient and facilitative role. The state manages everyday life less for the support of private capital and more for the independent purposes of the state. . . . Basically the argument is that Britain can best be understood as a corporatist society [1977a, p. 161].

This argument, which closely follows that of Winkler (1976, 1977), thus serves to re-establish the autonomy of the state theoretically (rather than by assumption as in the case of the earlier managerialist formulation), and to demonstrate the crucial mediating role of state bureaucrats in the new corporate relationship between state and capital. Put simply, the dynamics of capital accumulation have given rise to problems in the private sector (industrial concentration, declining profitability, high technological development costs and growing international competition – Winkler 1976, p. 117) which the traditional supportive role of the state has proved incapable of resolving. The state has therefore moved from support to direction, or from allocation to production (Offe 1975), thereby bringing it closer to capital while at the same time enhancing its power over it. It is therefore increasingly important to discover the 'independent purposes of the state' – which at the local level means studying the decisions of the urban managers.

This emphasis on the autonomy of the state should not be confused with the representational perspective, however, for although the corporate state makes its decisions in the 'national interest' (as defined by those who manage it), its emphasis is on efficiency rather than equality or social justice, and access to the power of the state is strictly circumscribed. The relationship between the state and civil society is one of 'institutionalized pluralism' in which the key economic interests of big capital and organized labour are increasingly fused into a tripartite relationship with the state (i.e. they are directly represented in the state itself, and the state is represented in them through vertical integration by means of quasi-governmental organizations), while other interests are left out in the cold. As Cawson (1977) notes, this means that corporate means of representation may come to exist side-by-side with a pluralist system of pressure group politics, the former operating to determine policy in the sphere of production, the latter retaining its impact in the sphere of consumption.

If this is the case, then a number of important points follow. First, it is clear that corporatism does not imply egalitarianism, nor any redistribution of resources between different classes. Critics such as Westergaard (1977) who dismiss the corporatist thesis on the grounds that the corporate society is every bit as unequal as the capitalist one are therefore missing the point, for Winkler stresses that corporatism is inherently hierarchical and recognizes the necessity for a system of unequal rewards. Similarly, those like Hill (1977) who reject the thesis by arguing that capitalist production relations remain intact and that the state continues to support capitalist accumulation appear to forget that Winkler sees it as 'an elemental fact' (1976, p. 103) that any state will sustain the institutions of the dominant economic groups. There is nothing in the corporatist thesis, in other words, to suggest that the state is either egalitarian or neutral – what it is is independent and dominant. And if the thesis concerns mainly the state's role in production, then there is clearly no reason why it should have anything to say about questions of consumption such as those raised by Westergaard.

Secondly, if corporatism concerns the productive functions of the state rather than its role in providing for collective consumption or in ensuring order and legitimacy, then we should not expect to find much evidence of corporate representation at the local level, except with regard to planning (and possibly highway provisions) where the local state does play an important productive role. In other words, consumption policies at the local level may still reflect the differential power of different groups in the urban system to influence local authority allocation decisions, for it is only in the areas of local policy concerned with production and capital accumulation that corporatist strategies may be expected to develop.

This leads on to a third point which is that it is necessary when considering recent changes in the organization and structure of the local state to bear in mind Pahl's distinction between the role of urban managers as mediators between the central state and the local population and their role in mediating between the public and private sectors. Factors such as the 1974 reorganization of local government in England and Wales and the development of new 'corporate planning' techniques (see Cockburn 1977) have undoubtedly had implications for the first of these. Jessop (1978), for example, suggests that these changes have helped to insulate local power from popular control while tying it in more closely with centralized policy-making. Given the significance of local government as a source of state spending (and hence as a tool of state economic policies), it is obviously important that it be brought under central control if a rational economic strategy is to be followed by the central government. But the implication of this for a study of the local state is that the growing corporatism has reduced rather than increased the autonomy of urban managers who begin to look less like mediators and more like puppets on the end of Whitehall's strings. As regards their second role, however, the impact of recent changes is less clear. Indeed, we should not necessarily expect any increased corporate representation of private interests in the local state to be reflected in formal organizational changes, for Winkler suggests that corporatism should not be confused with increased bureaucratization. Corporate management involves flexibility and delegated powers, not rigid bureaucratic management styles. The role of urban managers in mediating between the private and public sectors is thus a question for empirical investigation rather than theoretical deduction.

It is, however, possible to speculate a little with respect to the key area of planning policy, for it is here if anywhere that we should expect to find the development of corporatist representation at the local level. The question here is not, of course, how far local planning policies restrict the free operation of capitalist production in space, for proscription of the rights of property has always been a feature of public policy under capitalism, and laws limiting the rights of property are by no means inconsistent with a capitalist system. As Dunham observes,

If property is the established expectations which the law gives an owner, then *as long as the owner is not commanded to use his property in a particular way* and is secured some freedom of choice as to its use, it cannot be said that government restriction on land use has in it any denial of private property [1972, p. 281, my italics].

The point about the development of corporatism is not, therefore, that it limits the freedom of capital, but that it denies it through the prescription of use, even to the extent that it removes from capital the 'legal right of sabotage' (Veblen 1964, p. 66) – i.e. the right of the producer to withhold his commodity from the market. As Winkler points out, corporatism thus represents a fundamental attack on the key capitalist principles of private property and the free market: it is 'an economic system of private ownership and state control' (1977, p. 48).

How far, then, does local authority planning prescribe land use? According to Ambrose, the failures of planning controls in Britain since the war have been precisely that they have been almost entirely negative. Local planning authorities have been unable to plan positively because they have been unable to control the supply through the market of development land, and have had to limit themselves to refusing permission for those developments which they do not care for, rather than sponsoring those developments which they would wish to see brought forward: 'Land use planning does not plan land use, nor could it so long as it has little or no power to command the use of, and determine the price of, the key inputs to the development process (land, capital, construction effort). Instead, it acts as an arm of bourgeois interests' (Ambrose 1977, p. 11). For Ambrose, in other words, the role of the local state in respect of capital accumulation remains facilitative rather than directive. Yet the 1975 Community Land Act was introduced precisely to increase the positive powers of local authorities by enabling them to gain control of all development land in their areas. In his discussion of this legislation (Ambrose 1976), Ambrose points to the substantial modifications made in this legislation in its passage through Parliament, and concludes that it is likely to change very little. Indeed, he points to the relative enthusiasm for the legislation expressed by the big development companies as evidence that the Act is a far cry from socialist planning. But this, of course, is just the point – the Act represents, not a victory for socialism, nor even an extension of capitalism, but a qualitatively new element in land use planning – corporatism. The Community Land Act, when fully operational, will retain private ownership in land while giving the local state control over its future development, and it therefore represents perhaps the most important move towards corporatism at the local level that we have yet seen.

The managerialist perspective is important, therefore, in that it provides an explicit theory of the autonomy of the state in advanced capitalism. Applied to the analysis of the local state, it goes some way to answering the question which Miliband and Lojkine fail to answer – i.e. how far the local state operates independently from the interests of capital – in that it focuses attention on the *internal* operation of the state apparatus, both as regards the constraints imposed by the central–local relation, and as regards the relationship between the local state and capital expressed in the form of 'institutionalized pluralism'. And yet the advantages of this approach are in some ways the disadvantages of instrumentalism, and vice versa, for in focusing on the internal features of the state, the question of its external relationship with the non-incorporated section of the local population is left relatively untheorized. It is here that recent work by Claus Offe becomes important, for he provides one means whereby the managerialist and instrumentalist perspectives can be reconciled.

Offe begins by drawing an important distinction between the state's role in allocation and in production. He defines allocation as, 'A mode of activity of the capitalist state that creates and maintains the conditions of accumulation in a purely authoritative way' (1975, p. 128), and he suggests that this corresponds to the state's traditional role in distributing resources (such as roads, police and compulsory education) over which it has always exercised control. He then argues that, in the conditions of advanced capitalism, this allocative role proves insufficient to maintain the conditions for capital accumulation, and that the state is therefore obliged to take on an additional productive function – i.e. itself to engage in the production of commodities and services which the private sector can no longer produce. Thus the state becomes involved in the supply of housing, health, energy, communications and so on.

With respect to the allocative function, Offe argues that state policy will reflect the political pressures exerted from outside it:

> Political power, or power in and over the state apparatus and its parts, is the sole criterion and determinant of allocation . . . directives as to what use is to be made of these state-owned resources can be directly derived from manifest interests and power relationships that become apparent in the process of politics and political conflicts [ibid., pp. 129 and 132].

Thus in the conditions of liberal capitalism, for example, the state was indeed largely the instrument of ruling class domination (Offe 1976, p. 394), and its allocative decisions today continue to reflect the power exercised over it by dominant economic classes.

In fact, Offe takes this instrumentalist analysis one step further by attempting to show how the internal organization of the state systematically generates a class bias by laying itself open to the demands of those groups whose interests coincide with a 'collective capitalist interest', while selectively operating against anti-capitalist interests (Offe 1974). Here he essentially attempts to develop a framework for analysing non-decision-making which rests, not on the conscious actions or inactions of individuals, but on features of the system itself, and he suggests that the theoretical problems involved in demonstrating a class bias in the organization and functioning of the state reflect the fact that, in addition to its coordinative and repressive functions, the state must also perform a legitimating function which serves to deny any such bias. Analysis should therefore be directed at the growing tension between the increasing support of capital and the increasing need to legitimate this partiality – an argument which has much in common with Habermas's thesis of legitimation crisis. As Offe puts it, 'The credibility gap opening up signifies the hour of truth' (1974, p. 50).

There is, therefore, in Offe's work a very strong instrumentalist strand. It is simply not the case, therefore, that his 'conception of autonomy and his primary focus on the consequences of state intervention as a crisis-solver leads him to ignore the extent to which different classes are differentially able to . . . voice specific demands for state action' as Esping-Anderson and his co-writers suggest (1976, p. 191). Far from it; he explicitly relates the allocative policies of the state to the influence of capitalist interests, and he devotes a long article to an analysis of how the internal organization of the state filters out non-capitalist demands. Having said this, however, it is also the case that there is a second strand in Offe's work which does emphasize the autonomy of the state, and this relates to his discussion of the state's productive function.

Central to Offe's position here is the argument that, while allocative decisions can safely be resolved in line with the political pressures which come to be exerted from outside, productive decisions cannot, for the demands of the most powerful groups will not necessarily be consistent with the sorts of policies which are necessary for ensuring continued accumulation. Nationalization of basic industries, to take one obvious example, has rarely been welcomed by capitalist interests, but it has arguably been necessary for their own long-term survival. But if it cannot simply follow the dominant political pressure in its productive decisions, the state clearly faces the problem of determining the criteria according to which it should act. In other words, the state must arrive at its own decisions, and it follows that under these conditions, it will not represent the instrument of any class: 'Under the conditions of late capitalism, any attempt to explain the political organization of power through the categories of political economy becomes implausible' (1976, pp. 395–6). The origins of state policies are thus internal to the organization of the state itself.

The problem here is that the organization of the state does not allow it to follow the policies which are necessary to support accumulation in late capitalism. Thus Offe (1975) examines three modes of organization by which the state attempts to reconcile its internal structure to its required activities, and finds all three wanting. The first involves increased bureaucratization, and is reflected in the current drift towards centralization. Bureaucracy, however, is entirely inappropriate since it is inflexible and inefficient; as a means of administering allocative decisions it is suitable since all that is required is some mechanism for translating political demands into policy outputs, but as a means of resolving problems of production it is too rigid and cumbersome. The second involves increased state planning, but Offe argues that effective planning is impossible 'because of the acts of retaliation that planning provokes on the part of capital as a whole or individual accumulating units' (ibid., p. 143). The third involves increased democratization as an attempt to monitor state policies through feed-back from the public. According to Cockburn (1977), this is the rationale for the move towards public participation in planning, for the development of corporate planning strategies at the local level has necessitated some form of cybernetic adjustment. But according to Offe, increased democratization only opens up channels for popular (i.e. anti-capitalist) demands which will run counter to the need to support capital accumulation, and this strategy is therefore unworkable (a point also made by Cockburn who suggests that public participation can back-fire in the sense that it can be used by the working class as an effective means of protest). Thus Offe concludes that none of these three strategies is workable: 'Whichever is pursued, it tends to violate rather than establish the balance of the state and the accumulation process' (1975, p. 144). Nor is it possible to combine all three, since this merely generates secondary contradictions: 'No agency can simultaneously open itself to directives that come from the top of the bureaucratic hierarchy, from the experts, and from its clientele' (ibid., p. 144).

The picture which emerges from this analysis is that of a state attempting to maintain its principal function of aiding capital accumulation while constantly being frustrated by its own inadequate mode of internal organization. It is this internal structure which prevents it from being either the source of rational long-term planning or the receptive instrument of dominant economic interests. Rather, the state acts pragmatically: 'The principal function . . . may be described as cautious crisis management and long-term avoidance strategy' (Offe 1976, p. 415). The result is that the politics of the modern capitalist state are technocratic rather than popular, and the paraphernalia of representative democracy – parliaments, parties and elections – serve only to legitimate policies which would have been developed anyway. The evolution of the welfare state, for example, is seen by Offe (1972) as the consequence of the state's intervention in response to immediate problems and emergent crises, rather than as the result of any political or ideological commitment to values of equality or social justice. Like Weber and his emphasis on the disenchantment of the modern rational world, and like Winkler with his identification of the new paramount value of efficiency of administration, Offe's technocratic politics are thus indicative of the growing gap between state policy and popular control. Where Offe differs from Weber and Winkler, however, is that he suggests that the new technocratic politics themselves give rise to new contradictions and fail to provide for rational planning of the economic system.

This conclusion follows from Offe's insistence that, in a capitalist system, the state cannot order the production process. In other words, those who own the means of production retain Veblen's right of sabotage – the right not to produce in unprofitable situations, as well as the right not to be prevented from producing in profitable ones. Because the private sector retains this initiative, it follows that the state will always be limited to a reactive rather than active role in relation to the economy, and the result of this is that economically less significant groups, and economically less significant areas of life (i.e. those not directly related to production), are increasingly ignored. The state, in other words, only reacts to problems and immanent crises in those areas where the stability of the system as a whole is most fundamentally threatened: 'Certain vital areas of society will have slight prospects of state intervention or state subvention when they find themselves in a crisis, simply because the consequences of such a crisis would have no important relevance for the stability of the system as a whole' (Offe 1976, p. 415). Although particular groups in the population (e.g. the surplus labour force – Offe 1972) can be identified as suffering more than others from this, it is a key feature of Offe's argument that the new inequalities which develop from the reactive interventions of the state are spread throughout all classes – i.e. they are horizontal rather than vertical.

Although he does not spell it out, it seems that Offe is referring here to the same phenomenon identified by Castells – i.e. the increasing tension between state support of production (capital accumulation), and state support of consumption. Roweis whose argument closely follows Offe's, makes this clear: 'The widening disparity between the attention given to problem areas with high crisis potential and those with low potential is reflected in the discrepancy between the most advanced production and military apparatus and the stagnating organization of housing, transportation, health, education, daycare etc.' (1975, p. 21). And as we saw in Chapter 3, state neglect of collective consumption affects virtually all classes (though by no means equally) and thus may generate the potential for new class alliances (although this is highly problematic).

While accepting his broad conclusions, one question mark must be placed against Offe's work, and this concerns his argument that the state is merely reactive and is incapable of evolving a form of internal organization which can adequately discharge the functions it is called upon to perform. As we have seen, Winkler suggests that a new corporate form of state organization is emerging in which the state does not merely react, but rather actively intervenes in the production decisions of big firms. This is a possibility not considered by Offe, for it does not involve increased bureaucratization or democratization, but rather represents an extension of rational planning to include major capitalist interests. This extension of planning does not encounter the resistance of entrenched economic interests (as Offe suggests) because these interests are vertically integrated into the state itself and they are themselves used as agents of the corporate state to implement agreed policies. Corporatism is precisely that form of state organization which Offe sees as necessary but impossible, for it combines central control and rational planning with flexibility and delegated responsibilities.

If we amend Offe's argument to take account of Winkler's corporatist thesis, then it is possible to develop a convincing theory of the state which takes account of both the managerialist and instrumentalist perspectives. This theory would rest on the distinction between the corporate and non-corporate (or pluralist) sectors of state policy-making. The corporate sector would be concerned with production. Here the state can be seen as taking an increasingly independent and directive role in close consultation with big business and organized labour, this independence being limited only by the need to maintain capital accumulation. The pluralist sector, on the other hand, would be concerned mainly with consumption. Here the state can be seen as external to the various different classes or political forces in civil society, and thus as open to influence by the most powerful of them. But given its prior commitments to supporting and directing production, consumption facilities will in any case be in short supply, with the result that inequalities of political power in society will come to be reflected in the distribution of social resources. This, of course, will militate against any inter-class alliance around issues of collective consumption, for a crisis in the provision of these resources will lead to an intensification of political struggles in the pluralist sector over the distribution of the little that is available.

The implications of this argument for the analysis of the local state are that, as regards its production functions (i.e. primarily planning and road provisions on the one hand, and its demands for capital goods – such as houses – from the private sector on the other), we should expect to find an increasingly close relationship between local authorities and private business enterprises with the former as the dominant partner. This will be reflected in, for example, regular quasi-official and informal meetings between the two (and possibly to an increase in 'corrupt' practices as one means of cementing the relationship – see page 315), and in a growing division within local authorities themselves between those in key positions of power (i.e. chief officers and possibly leading council members) and those who are excluded from corporate policy-making. As regards its consumption functions (i.e. education, housing, social services and so on), we should expect to find the local state responding to political pressures from the locality, although this process will be subject to certain important qualifications. First, external political pressures will be mediated by bureaucratic definitions of what is possible and by the political composition of local councils – as we shall see in Chapter 5, for example, there appears little basis for the representational theorists' argument that elected politicians feel constrained to respond to popular pressures. Secondly, the facilities which are available for distribution are limited by the local revenue base, by the need to support capital accumulation (e.g. through spending on road schemes), and by central government controls on local authority spending. Thirdly, the effects of local state distributive policies will be mediated by existing spatial inequalities and by the operation of 'ecological' forces. These constraints are discussed in more detail in the final section of this chapter.

A coherent analysis of the local state will thus need to take account both of the arguments of Pahl and Winkler on the one hand, and of Miliband and Lojkine on the other, and the way in which this is accomplished will reflect the ideas of Offe and others who have distinguished between those areas where the state is largely the instrument of dominant political forces, and those where these forces are subjected to, and incorporated within, attempts by the state to extend its control over the production process. The only major alternative to this approach is that provided by structuralist analysis, but as we shall now see, this suffers from an inherent logical problem which must lead to its rejection.

Structuralist perspectives

The structuralist approach to the state is premised on the argument that classes, not individuals, constitute the scientific categories of political analysis. This is because the production process, which is increasingly collectivized in advanced capitalism, generates objective relations between capital and wage-labour into which individuals enter as agents of one or other of these two classes. These agents of production only appear as individuals in the law (e.g. in legal contracts between 'individuals' or in individual rights of property ownership) and in the political system (i.e. in a system of representation based upon individual preferences expressed in elections). It follows from this that the individual is an ideological rather than a scientific category – the 'juridico-political ideology' is for Poulantzas (1973, p. 128) the dominant element of the ideology of the capitalist mode of production – and that scientific analysis must therefore penetrate the surface of this ideological representation of society in order to identify the 'real' categories of economic and political analysis (i.e. classes).

The consequence of this for the analysis of the state is that any approach which focuses on the individuals who appear to administer it (managerialism) or on the individuals who appear to influence or dominate it from outside (instrumentalism) has to be rejected as ideological. Thus Poulantzas argues that the capitalist state cannot be understood as a 'thing' set apart from classes, but can only be analysed as the 'condensate' of the political relations between classes. He is highly critical of both the instrumentalist and managerialist perspectives, suggesting that the former leads to a view of the state 'as a passive tool in the hands of a class or fraction, in which case the state is seen as having no autonomy whatsoever', while the latter errs in the opposite direction by seeing state power as 'incarnated in the power of the group that concretely represents this rationality/power (bureaucracy, elites)' (1976, p. 74). The state is therefore neither an instrument of class domination, nor a centre of power independent from classes, but is rather the representation of the balance of class forces in any particular society at any particular time. In the present era of monopoly capitalism, it follows that, in the long term, the state necessarily represents the interests of monopoly capital, since this is the dominant class and the dominant political force. Nevertheless, the working class is clearly not powerless, and the state will therefore generate policies in the short-term which favour its interests, even against the short-term interests of the dominant class. The consequence of this is that the state comes to perform a dual function. On the one hand it serves to unify the divergent fractions of capital under the hegemony of the monopoly fraction by safeguarding capitalist accumulation even against the immediate demands of different fractions pursuing their own short-term interests. On the other, it serves to fragment the unity of the working class by undermining its solidarity through short-run class compromises and reforms (cf. Poulantzas 1973, pp. 287–8). In short, the state is 'relatively autonomous' of any one class, although it necessarily functions in the long term in the interests of monopoly capital.

It is important to distinguish this concept of 'relative autonomy' from that employed by Miliband. For Miliband, the state is relatively autonomous in that the constraints imposed upon it are not total – those who control the state have a limited degree of discretion which enables them to decide how best to serve the interests of the capitalist class, and their decisions will not always coincide with the demands made upon them by members of that class. For Poulantzas, on the other hand, the relative autonomy of the state is structurally determined by the relationship between the economic and political instances in the social formation. Although the nature of this relationship

will ultimately be determined by the prevailing forces and relations of production (i.e. the economic determines which instance will
be dominant in the social formation), and in capitalism this ensures
that the economic will be the dominant instance, it does not follow
that the economic determines the political. Rather, each level in the
social formation is relatively autonomous from each other, and it
follows that the class practices which correspond to these levels will
also be relatively autonomous. The state does not therefore directly
represent the economic interests of any one class. Indeed, there are
times when the dominant political class is different from the dominant
economic class (e.g. in nineteenth-century England where the landed
aristocracy ruled despite the economic domination of the bourgeoisie), although even in situations such as this, the state must still
operate in the long-term interests of the capitalist class since it is
merely the expression of the balance of political class forces.

The implications of this theory for the analysis of urban politics
are explored in the work of Castells. The first obvious implication is
that any search for 'community power', or any analysis of the actions
of 'urban managers', is misconceived. Castells rejects those approaches which take individuals as their focus, seeing them as
doomed either to remain at the level of naive description (i.e. indicating who does what without being able to explain why), or to be
grounded in metaphysical assumptions of free will. For him, the
starting point must lie, not in the study of local state institutions and
policy-making procedures, but rather in the analysis of the class
struggle, for it is only in this way that the 'stakes' can be identified
and the actions of the local state explained. Urban management, in
other words, can only be explained in the context of class struggles
which reflect the growing contradictions within the social formation.
Like Poulantzas, therefore, Castells sees the state as performing the
function of regulating system contradictions and the struggles to
which they give rise through its response to the political strength of
non-capitalist classes – a function which operates in the long term in
the interests of monopoly capital:

> The state apparatus not only exercises class domination, but also strives,
> as far as possible, to regulate the crises of the system in order to preserve
> it. It is in this sense that it may, sometimes, become reformist. Although
> reforms are always imposed by the class struggle and, therefore, from
> outside the state apparatus, they are no less real for that: their aim is to

preserve and extend the existing context, thus consolidating the long term interests of the dominant classes, even if it involves infringing their privileges to some extent in a particular conjuncture [1977a, p. 208].

State intervention, therefore, will always be limited to reformism – i.e. to the long-term reproduction of the system. Poulantzas (1976), for example, makes it clear that the concessions won by virtue of the political power of the working class will inevitably be ineffectual as regards the strategic long-term interests of that class. State intervention is always regulatory in function. The same point is made by Castells:

If one accepts the idea of the political system as regulating the system (concrete social formation) as a whole *according to the structural laws on which it is based*, then urban planning is its intervention on a given reality in order to counteract the dislocations expressed. . . . Not every conceivable intervention by M [the management element] is possible because it must take place within the *limits* of the capitalist mode of production, otherwise the system would be *shaken* rather than regulated [1976, p. 166].

State intervention cannot change capitalist ownership relations, nor can it intervene directly to control capitalist accumulation. Its role is limited to that of responding to system crises as manifested in class struggles, and it may do this by intervening indirectly in the production process (e.g. with financial support), or directly in the processes of exchange and consumption. The actions of those individuals who administer the state are thus explained with reference to the structural relationship between the political and the economic, the state and capital. Thus Castells describes urban planning as political intervention in the different elements of the urban system (production, exchange and, most significantly, consumption) with the purpose of regulating contradictions and reproducing class relations within the existing capitalist mode of production. British post-war planning legislation, for example, is explained as the result of the need to respond to working class power without fundamentally changing the system of property relations.

One of the criticisms which has been made of this perspective is that it fails to explain why state intervention has taken different forms in different capitalist societies (cf. Pahl 1977b). But such criticism is misplaced, for Poulantzas stresses that state intervention is dependent upon particular historical conjunctures. The class struggle takes different forms in different places at different times, and patterns of state intervention will thus vary accordingly (see also Hill 1977). Poulantzas makes this point clearly in his response to Miliband: 'The (capitalist) state, in the long run, can only correspond to the political interests of the dominant class or classes ... Yet, within these limits, the degree, the extent, the forms, etc. (how relative, and how it is relative) of the relative autonomy of the state can only be examined ... with reference to a given capitalist state, and to the precise conjuncture of the corresponding class struggle' (1976, p. 72). The problem of international variations (as with the problem of variations between different local authorities within a single state) thus turns out to be no problem at all. Armed with their concepts of relative autonomy and historical conjunctures, the structuralist theorists can account for any conceivable situation.

This is, paradoxically, one of the problems with structuralist analysis: not that it fails to account for particular empirical situations, but that it claims to account for all situations. It is therefore impossible to envisage any conceivable empirical test of its key assumptions – as we saw in Chapter 1, it is effectively immune from falsification – and in any case, the Althusserian epistemology from which it derives rules out any resort to empirical disconfirmation as 'empiricist'. From this perspective, observable phenomena merely contribute to the raw materials of the thought process; scientific knowledge is the result of the application of the correct theoretical tools (derived from a particular reading of Marx) to these raw materials, and it follows that such knowledge cannot therefore be assessed for validity by resort back to observable phenomena. Two problems are raised by all this. First, how do we know that an explanation couched in terms of underlying structures is a valid explanation when those structures are only revealed in class practices? And secondly, how can we assess the explanatory power of these theories when the concept of relative autonomy rules out any counterfactual argument? While instrumentalist theories can to some extent be evaluated by searching for situations where the state does not appear to have acted in the interests of the dominant class, and managerialist theories can similarly be evaluated by analysing situations where it has, structuralist theories, with their emphasis on both class domination and the absence of class domination, exclude both possibilities. If the state acts to support monopoly capital, then this is due to the political domination of that class; if it does not, then this is due to its relative autonomy from that class. Clearly, as we have seen throughout this chapter, any coherent theory of the state must be able to take account both of the political power of capitalist interests and of the ability of the state to act independently of those interests, but this can only be achieved by stipulating those situations in which capital predominates, and those in which the state predominates, and not by developing a theory which can be moulded to fit any situation at will.

Pickvance has suggested that the question of how far the state may act independently of any class is one which can ultimately be resolved only through emprical investigation: 'Our aim is to argue that governmental institutions cannot be dismissed as sources of minor changes, and to this extent must be treated as sources of urban effects in the same way as social movements. In other words, that the role of authorities in initiating change is an empirical question, requiring analysis of policy-formation within governmental institutions' (1976, p. 204). To a large extent he is, of course, quite correct in this assertion, yet as we have seen, structuralist theory, like the representational theories discussed earlier, rests on self-fulfilling assumptions which do not lend themselves to empirical test. The one statement common to both Poulantzas and Castells which could, seemingly, provide the necessary empirical criteria – namely the argument that the state can never intervene directly to fundamentally alter the system of capitalist property relations – is in practice equally tautological since what would count as a fundamental alteration is nowhere specified. The apparent growth of corporatism in Britain, representing an attack on the sacred principles of the market, profit, and the freedom of property, can thus easily be dismissed through semantic argument even though it appears to represent just such a 'fundamental alteration'. Similarly, every reform introduced by the state, no matter how far reaching, must by a priori definition be an attempt to fragment the working class and thereby maintain long-term capital accumulation (see Corrigan 1977).

Not only is there a problem of tautology, however, there is also a problem of teleology. Despite its emphasis on contradiction rather than equilibrium, on conflict rather than consensus, and on the ultimate determinancy of the economic level rather than the equivalence of system elements, the structuralist theory of the state shares in common with conservative structural-functionalist theories of society the problem of how system regulation can be explained without reference to the purposive actions of individuals. How do system needs come to be fulfilled when nobody deliberately sets out to fulfil them?

Structural-functionalism has generally sought to overcome this problem of teleology by means of evolutionary theories and the principle of cybernetic feedback (see Mennell 1974, pp. 158–64). Poulantzas and Castells, on the other hand, attempt to resolve it by means of a theory of class struggle which stresses, first, that the state necessarily responds to the political power of all classes, and secondly, that this has the effect of fragmenting the working class and thus regulating the relations between it and the dominant classes. Even if we accept this argument, however, there is still the problem of demonstrating that this is the necessary function of all state interventions. It is one thing to argue that the *effect* of state policies is generally to consolidate the situation of monopoly capital, but it is quite another to suggest that this is their necessary *role* (Poulantzas 1973, p. 284). The point can be made even more clearly with relation to Castells's definition of urban planning as the intervention of the state with the *aim* or *intention* of assuring the extended reproduction of the system by regulating or repressing contradictions (1977a, pp. 263 and 432). How can the state have aims or intentions if it is merely the condensate of political class relations, and if it is not itself a 'thing'?

Structuralist theories thus encounter the familiar problem of functionalist sociology of explaining causes in terms of their effects. As we saw at the start of this chapter, it is of crucial importance that theories of the state distinguish between the causes of its interventions and the functions of its interventions. If this distinction is to be retained in structuralist theories, then there appears no necessary reason why state policies which are caused by political class forces should always function in the long-term interests of one of those classes. Where, apart from human volition, is the mechanism which ensures that this will invariably be the case? For Castells, it seems that the mechanism lies in the 'aims' or 'intentions' of the state, but this can only imply that the state is a 'thing' apart from classes, that the state is therefore subject to conscious human agency, and that the motivations of those who control it must therefore remain central to any analysis. Similarly, on closer inspection it appears that Poulantzas is unwilling to reduce practices to structures, for he argues that structures impose limits upon practices but do not determine them (see Hindess 1978, p. 92). Again, therefore, voluntarism creeps into the analysis; having abolished the individual, the individual is then brought back into the analysis as an indispensible adjunct to it, yet as Hindess points out, the relation between practices and structures is untheorized. Poulantzas's analysis thus comes to suffer the same fate as Miliband's, for it fails to specify how action and structure articulate. As Gold and others have observed, structuralist theories generally fail to 'explain the social mechanisms which actually generate a class policy that is compatible with the needs of the system' (1976, p. 36), and this would seem to reflect the simultaneous theoretical rejection and pragmatic acceptance of individual action as one factor in their explanations.

If structuralist theories of the state tend to suffer from tautology and teleology, there is still one more criticism which can be made of them, and this concerns the concept of relative autonomy. It is not simply that the use of this concept provides an insurance against any empirical disconfirmation, but also that the concept fails in the final analysis to escape the dangers of economistic determinism. As Walton and Gamble suggest, 'There is no other way the principle of determination by the economy in the last instance could be followed except by assuming that the economy is also determining in the first instance. . . . Otherwise the "economy" can have no causal impact at all, and the three levels must be treated as completely independent' (1972, p. 139). It is left to Hirst (1977) to draw out the implications of this; namely that, given the obvious problems with economism, there is no alternative but to recognize the necessary non-correspondence between economics and politics, classes and the state. And if classes do not correspond to political forces while the state does not necessarily function in the interests of any one class, then it follows that the state cannot be theorized as a condensate of class relations. Rather, the state is external to classes and independent of them: 'First and foremost the *state exists*, it is a definite apparatus to be confronted, and not a function. . . . Outside specific institutional forms state power does not exist: institutions represent the means of its existence and exercise' (ibid., pp. 152–3; see also Laclau 1975 and

Shaw 1974, both of whom similarly stress the separation of classes from the state).

It follows from Hirst's critique that although any state must clearly maintain the conditions under which production can take place, neither the form of the state, nor the content of its policies, can necessarily be explained with reference to the relations of production. The so-called 'state derivationist' theorists, who basically seek to derive the form and content of the state from a materialist analysis of capitalist production relations, must therefore be rejected along with the structuralists, for both end up in economic determinancy; the structuralists because of their assertion of the determinate role of the economic in organizing the relations between the levels of the social formation, the state derivationists because they explain the separation of the economic and the political as the reflection of the needs of capitalist social relations (see Holloway and Picciotto 1978). It is thus one thing to recognize that the state must necessarily maintain the conditions of existence for production to take place, but quite another to argue that particular relations of production give rise to specific forms of state (see Hindess 1978).

But if there is nothing in the way in which social production is organized which necessitates a particular form of political apparatus or a particular type of public policy, then it follows that a materialist analysis cannot provide a theory of the state. Rather, the assumption must be that of a 'necessary non-correspondence' between economic classes and politics; a principle which appears more Weberian than Marxist, even allowing for the argument that the state must secure the conditions of existence of economic life. The starting point, in other words, rests with the managerialist conception of the state as set apart from and regulating class relations. This does not imply a neutral state, for certain sectional interests will come to be reflected in its policies, either as a result of their direct corporate representation within it, or as a consequence of their ability to exert influence over it. Nor does it imply a totally autonomous state, for its independence will be restricted by a number of factors, including its reliance on private production. It is precisely the task of any study to analyse how the state comes to adopt policies favourable to some groups and not others, and how far its freedom of action is restricted by external factors over which it has no control. It is with a brief discussion of this latter question as it applies to the problem of the local state that we may bring this chapter to a close.

The local state and the problem of autonomy

When Pahl revised his urban managerialism thesis, it was largely in recognition of the fact that local managers, whether in the private or public sectors, were not autonomous agents determining through individual acts of volition which resources would be directed to which groups in the local population. Pahl's own earlier work served to remind him of the significance of ecological forces operating in the 'socio-ecological system'; his concern with the developing corporatism led him to place greater emphasis on the vertical constraints imposed by central government on local managers; and the new Marxist urban theory underlined the dependence of local managers on the process of capital accumulation. There were, in other words, three major sets of constraints operating to limit the autonomy of the managers of the local state, and these can be summarized as ecological, political and economic forces. The significance of these three should not be underestimated, for although they certainly do not determine policy outcomes, they do restrict the range of options available. As Pahl put it, 'It is clear that attacks at the level of urban management may be misdirected. It is rather like the workers stoning the house of the chief personnel manager when their industry faces widespread redundancies through the collapse of world markets' (1975, p. 284). The question, then, is how far these external structural constraints limit managerial autonomy.

The problem of ecological constraints raises two related questions: is there something inherent in the nature of spatial organization itself which leads to some pattern of inequality, and if so, is there any necessary reason why this pattern of inequality should come to reflect differences in economic power? Pahl's answer to the first question is that towns and cities are inherently unequal. Irrespective of the mode of economic and political organization, he argues that different locations will always give rise to advantages and disadvantages in terms both of externality effects (i.e. certain people will always live near positively-valued public resources such as parks or sources of employment, while others will live near to negatively valued resources such as gasworks or sewage farms) and time-cost distance (i.e. certain people will incur greater costs than others in travelling to work or to do their shopping). This argument has been disputed by some writers since it leads to the conclusion that the socialist city will necessarily be an unequal place in which to live. Harloe, for example, argues that spatial forms currently found in capitalist and state socialist societies 'are not an essential feature of any such society but are a consequence of a particular organization of economic life, i.e. social factors' (1977, p. 5), while Gray (1976) similarly accuses the managerialist approach of failing to ask why certain resources are in short supply in the first place. What lies behind such criticisms is the view that spatial inequalities are the physical consequence of the tendency within capitalism for resources to become centralized and for certain areas to develop while others are neglected. Socialist planning, it is argued, can direct resources according to need rather than the dictates of the market with the result that positive and negative facilities can be more evenly distributed in space. However, there are clearly limits to how far this can be accomplished, for while socialist planning may result in decentralization of key resources, it remains the case that some people will still be located in more favourable geographical situations than others. As Harvey (1973) points out, it is the peculiar feature of space that no two users can occupy the same site, and this would seem to affirm Pahl's conclusion that distribution in space can never be entirely egalitarian.

The second, and more immediate, question is therefore whether urban managers can effectively determine who is to benefit most from the pattern of locational advantages. In a socialist city such as Prague (Musil 1968) it appears that they can, for in the absence of the market it is left to those with political power to determine the criteria according to which different groups are allocated to different parts of the city. This does not seem to be the case in the capitalist countries, however. Harvey (1973), for example, suggests that the urban system in capitalist societies exhibits its own inherent logic corresponding not to the plan but to the market. While local politicians and administrators may attempt to bring about some redistribution of resources according to the criterion of 'social justice', the logic of the market consistently operates in the opposite direction, diverting funds and investment away from the areas of greatest social need into the areas of greatest economic return. Attempts to reduce urban inequalities thus constantly founder on the rocks of a market system whose very imperatives are the perpetuation of inequality and the maintenance of scarcity. When slums are cleared in one inner city area they merely reappear in another while all the time the most advantageous sites are monopolized (as the Chicago school demonstrated) by those who can best afford to pay for them. Inequalities in the place of work are thus reproduced and exacerbated in the place of residence. Attempts to fly in the face of market forces often end in financial disaster and political embarrassment. In the London Borough of Camden, for example, the Labour-controlled housing committee recently decided to develop much-needed council housing in the upper-class area of Hampstead. As the committee chairman explained in an interview with the *Guardian*, 'There was no reason why we should not be able to develop sites in the Hampstead area. It was unreasonable to expect us in the future to leave everybody up there living in a very underdeveloped site and at the same time having to maximise housing in areas which were already very overcrowded.' The result, however, was that the council had to pay an extraordinarily high market price for the land such that each house eventually cost £67,000, and rents, even after a council subsidy of £130 per house per week, amounted to £30 – far in excess of what most families on the waiting list could afford to pay.

Ecological constraints thus constitute a major limitation on the autonomy of the local state, but they are by no means total. Local authorities do have considerable negative planning powers which enable them to restrain the development of further spatial inequalities if not actually to reverse them. And as we saw earlier, the Community Land Act does potentially provide local planning authorities with the power positively to shape the future development of the urban environment. Furthermore, local councils enjoy a significant degree of control over certain key public resources – education and housing for example – and the way in which these are deployed may significantly affect the distribution of indirect incomes. It remains the case, of course, that it is much easier to swim with the tide than to struggle against it – the Camden experience shows that much – but if it is considerably easier to preserve the privileges of favoured areas rather than to undermine them, or to provide office blocks and roads rather than houses and school books, it does not follow that this is the only course open to those who control the local state. Ecological factors can represent considerable and sometimes formidable constraints on political action, but they never determine it.

The second type of constraint is political. This again takes two forms: first the limitations imposed on action by the internal organization of the local state apparatus, and secondly the limits imposed through vertical integration into central government. The first of these directs our attention to the familiar question of the relationship between elected politicians and the local state bureaucracy, and here it has generally been argued that the increasing complexity of local government and the growth of corporate planning strategies have served to insulate council officers from the political pressures exerted by the elected members. This argument was reflected in Pahl's reformulation of the urban managerialism thesis where he limited his definition of managers to local state bureaucrats, excluding council members from the analysis altogether. However, there is some evidence to suggest that leading members of majority party groups in local authorities may enjoy more power than is sometimes imagined, and that any analysis which totally excludes them may be found seriously wanting. As we shall see in Chapter 5, recent changes in the organization of local government may have strengthened rather than weakened the power of leading council members, the bureaucracy being experienced more as an ally than as a constraint.

The limitations imposed by central government are more serious, however. There has been a progressive erosion of the power of local government relative to Whitehall and Westminster since the late nineteenth century, and this has been particularly marked since the war with the loss of local control over gas and electricity, hospitals, trunk roads, water and sewage services and so on. Even more significant than this has been the corresponding increase of central regulation of those services which are still administered locally. Thus, local authorities are constrained in their policies by national legislation, by government circulars and planning programmes, and by the financial controls exercised by Whitehall, the most significant of which relate to the government rate support grant (the size of which can effectively limit the range of services which can be financed), the imposition of cost yardsticks (e.g. in housing construction), and the ability of central government to withhold loan sanction for capital expenditures (which can prevent a local authority from embarking on a capital programme). The result is that local authorities are often obliged to follow the national line; when they are ordered to cut back expenditure or to raise council house rents, few councils have the power or temerity to argue, and the fate of those who do (e.g. the celebrated case of the Clay Cross councillors in Derbyshire who refused to implement the government 'fair rents' legislation and who consequently were threatened with both dismissal from office and a surcharge for the subsequent arrears) is probably enough to encourage the others.

Yet the constraints imposed by central government are not as restrictive as is sometimes assumed. As regards the loss of functions, for example, it is necessary to bear in mind that although the range of local authority responsibilities has been reduced, the significance of the remaining services has been increasing, and this is reflected in the steady growth of local government spending as a proportion of GNP since the war (see Hambleton 1978). Nor is central control over these remaining services anything like total. As Cox observes, 'In recent years in the fields of planning and education alone, British city governments have revealed a vigour in pursuing individual policies which belies the argument that they are mere puppets on the central government string' (1976, pp. 35–6). The long and bitter battles over the reorganization of secondary education provide one obvious example of how local authorities may stand out against government circulars. Indeed, direct legislation will tend to be open to diverse interpretations at the local level, not simply because it is often permissive rather than mandatory, but also because, as Newton puts it, 'Some may abide by the spirit of the policy, some by the letter, some may bend the policy, others break it and others look for loopholes' (1975, p. 14). Nor is the financial control exercised by the central exchequer as stringent as is sometimes claimed (see Davies 1968), although expenditure cuts have been enforced strongly since 1976.

The overall picture which emerges is confused and contradictory. While it is clear that power has become increasingly centralized, it is also the case that local autonomy in some areas of policy remains marked. Thus a number of studies (e.g. Alt 1971, Boaden 1971) have revealed a strong correlation between political party control and patterns of expenditure which can only indicate that local politicians can and do leave their ideological imprint on patterns of local authority services, and consequently upon the distribution of indirect incomes. In policies such as housing, for example, there is a clear relationship (controlling for need) between Labour-controlled authorities and relatively high provision of council stock. Clearly urban managers (however defined) play an important part in determining patterns of inequality. Yet, as Flynn (1978) argues, the picture is fragmented, different functions being performed at different levels with differing degrees of central control.

What this confusion and fragmentation appears to indicate is the inherent ambivalence in the relation between the central and local state. On the one hand, increased intervention in economic management (manifest in the tendency towards corporatism) necessitates rational and centralized planning – local authority expenditures must clearly be strictly controlled if a successful economic strategy is to be followed (in 1974, local government spending accounted for over twelve per cent of GNP). On the other, responsiveness to local political pressures and social and economic needs remains equally important, both to ensure some degree of feedback into the planning process (see Offe 1975, Cockburn 1977), and to retain legitimacy. It is this tension between centralization and local accountability which lies at the heart of such recent developments as the 1974 reorganization of local government (e.g. with its split planning functions), current proposals for regional devolution, and the growth of public participation exercises. It is also this tension which ensures that local managers will continue to retain considerable, though uneven, autonomy from central control.

The third major constraint is the market, and here too there are two distinct questions to be posed. The first concerns the necessity of maintaining the conditions of existence for private production, and leads us to consider how far local authorities are obliged to devote valuable resources to the support of capital accumulation. The second concerns the size of the revenue base, and the ability of local authorities to generate additional funds to support spending on items not directly related to the support of production. Both questions are, of course, related, in that the greater the public support of private profitability, the greater will be the potential revenue base which may be drawn upon for other items of public expenditure, although (as we shall see in the case study reported in Part Two) it does not follow that this potential revenue base will in fact be tapped.

Perhaps the single most important item of local authority expenditure as regards the provision of necessary economic infra-structure for private production concerns roads and associated developments (e.g. car parks for town centre shops and offices). Related to this are local planning schemes (e.g. for urban renewal) and other areas of local policy (such as housing) which affect the supply of labour power for local industry. But in analysing local council policies in these areas, it is clearly necessary to bear in mind Miliband's argument that those who control the state apparatus enjoy some discretion in determining how best (and how far) to support capital accumulation. Expenditure on roads, as in other items, varies widely between different local authorities, and while some councils actively encourage private profitability through policies which appear almost totally subordinate to the demands of the local business sector, others remain notably less enthusiastic. The same is true of local taxation policies, some councils preferring to keep non-productive expenditures to a minimum in order to reduce the rate burden on local businesses (and other propertied interests), while others pursue a relatively high spending budgetry policy financed to a large extent out of taxation on local industry and commerce.

This, however, brings us on to the second and more pertinent aspect of the economic constraints on the local state – namely its reliance on the private sector for its revenue. The problem of a shrinking revenue base is particularly marked in the inner city (especially in the United States where local taxation provides a much greater proportion of local revenue than in Britain – in Britain the problem is to some extent mediated by the special needs component of the rate support grant) where the multiplication of social needs, and hence the escalating demands for social expenditure, proceeds in direct relation to the flight of high-income families and profitable monopoly sector industries. But the problem is not confined to the inner cities, for it is obviously the case that any local authority will be limited in its scope by the amount it can raise through local taxation. Beyond this, the only other sources of revenue are central government (discussed above) and the finance market. Resort to either of these two sources merely opens up additional constraints, however, for central government support is determined in Whitehall, not by local managers, while reliance on the finance market places local authorities at the mercy of finance capital. The fact that local councils

have increasingly been obliged to borrow in the City of London to
finance their capital expenditures (notably housing) has progressively
reduced their room to manoeuvre since future revenue has increasingly come to be committed to paying interest charges incurred on past
borrowing. In 1970/71, for example, the Greater London Council
was paying 90 per cent of its rent revenue in interest payments to
finance capital (Kay *et al.* 1977), while in 1974/75, over 60 per cent of
all local government housing costs was taken up in interest charges
(Ball 1978). Increasing loan debts thus impose constraints on policies
in areas like housing, both in terms of the rents which must be
charged, and in terms of the ability to finance new development. As
Bailey concludes,

> The councils themselves . . . often have little control over what they can
> and cannot do. . . . They put rents up when interest rates tell them they
> must. The types of houses or estates they can afford to build are governed
> more by the money they can borrow and the charges they must pay for this
> than by even their wishes, let alone their tenants' wishes [1973b, p. 93].

Of all the constraints operating on the local state, the inability to
finance social expenditure appears the most significant of all.

Yet despite all this, the fact remains that the ecological, political
and economic constraints on urban managers serve only to narrow
the scope of decision-making; they do not determine it. As Williams
observes, 'While the economic and technological realities may provide
constraints for the political order, there remain large discretionary
areas in which urban polity carries out its who-where decisions'
(1975, p. 117). The precise limitations on such discretion can only be
settled through empirical analysis, and especially through comparative work which takes account of those cases (such as Camden)
where attempts have been made to transcend them. As Offe argues,
'The class character of the state becomes evident analytically only
in an *ex post* perspective, namely when the limitations of its functions
becomes apparent in class conflict' (1974, p. 45). In other words, the
question of how far the local state necessarily comes to reflect in its
policies the interests of dominant groups can only be answered by
considering the limits which it encounters when it attempts to act in
accordance with the interests of opposing groups. The question of
discretion and constraint is thus ultimately an empirical rather than a
theoretical question. It follows from this that the study of community

power and the analysis of urban managers – the problems of where power resides, how it is used, how it is influenced, and how far it is restricted – must remain central to discussions of urban politics, and that empirical work will continue to play a fundamental role in the development of such discussions. It is this conclusion which provides the underlying rationale for the chapters which follow.

Part 2

Empirical applications

Introduction

There is a noticeable strain in much contemporary sociology between theoretical and empirical work. There is, indeed, something of a division of labour within the discipline, some sociologists devoting most of their time to the development of often highly sophisticated theoretical perspectives with little concern for their empirical applications, while others busy themselves with large-scale research projects which generate interesting case material but which sometimes appear to bear little relation to the dominant theoretical concerns of the day. Sometimes, of course, theoretical and empirical perspectives do come to complement each other, but such a happy coalescence is often difficult to achieve given the level of abstraction and generality of the former, and the concrete and specific character of the latter. Certainly, in the field of urban politics, there has been little empirical material published in Britain which can be related directly to the sorts of questions considered in the preceding chapters.

Most research conducted in this field in recent years has taken the form of case studies on individual local authorities (see, for example, Bealey *et al.* 1965, Jones 1969, Hampton 1970, Davies 1972, Newton 1976). These studies have considerably advanced our understanding of local policy-making processes. They have, for example, documented the ways in which local councils make their policy decisions, and in so doing they have pointed to the growing concentration of power in a diminishing number of hands. They have indicated the increased complexity of local government administration and the privileged position which the bureaucracy occupies in relation both to the elected members and to the consumers of local authority outputs in the areas of planning, housing and so on. They have focused on the role of the political parties in local government today and on how the development of the party caucus has changed traditional patterns of decision-making. Yet few of these studies have managed to transcend the limitations of a view of political power which locates it almost entirely in the formal organs of government – what Worsley (1964) terms 'Politics II'. As Worsley argues, such a restrictive perspective invariably fails to consider the broader questions of power – what he terms 'Politics I', or the exercise of restraint in any social relationship: 'Politics II illuminates very little except when studied in the context of Politics I, for power is never concentrated exclusively in governments or parties' (ibid., p. 30).

What is clear, therefore, is that although there is now a considerable literature on British local government, there have been precious few studies of what may be termed 'community power'. As one political scientist has noted, 'It is astonishing to have to record that with the exception of some unpublished doctoral theses, there exist no studies of community power in Britain' (Crewe, 1974, p. 35). There are two main reasons for this. The first is that such research as has been conducted into the broader questions of political power at the local level has generally concluded that power is indeed concentrated almost entirely in the formal institutions of government. This has been the conclusion drawn both from the various local government studies already cited (e.g. Newton found no evidence of business involvement in local politics in Birmingham, while Bealey and his colleagues failed to trace any connection between the local political and economic leadership groups in Newcastle-under-Lyme), and from British community power studies (discussed in Chapter 9). Indeed, in Bristol, Clements (1969) has devoted much of an entire study to the question of why social notables no longer seem to concern themselves with local politics. The evidence is, however, patchy (as we shall see in Chapter 9, the community power studies are particularly suspect in terms of their methodologies), and it appears that the second factor is therefore more important than the first in explaining the lack of academic interest in 'Politics I' at the local level.

This second reason concerns the character of the British local government system and in particular the questions of its autonomy, unity and representativeness. Basically, the argument has been that, in comparison with, say, the United States (where the analysis of community power has been a major academic growth industry for many years), British local government is vertically integrated into the central state apparatus to a much greater extent, it lacks the fragmentary nature of urban government in America, and it is sufficiently representative of all major local interests to avoid the wheeler-dealing of American city politics. None of these three factors is entirely convincing, however.

The question of local government autonomy has already been discussed (see pages 192–4). The view traditionally adopted in British political science has been that increasing regulation by the centre has reduced local autonomy to a minimum. As Blondel and Hall observed some years ago, 'So much emphasis has been placed, particularly in the 1950s, on the fact that objectively local authorities have relatively little influence compared to the central government, that observers have perhaps too easily taken the view (probably sometimes unconsciously) that it was not necessary to consider what distribution there was of the "little" power which was still in local hands' (1967, p. 322). The implication of this assumption has been that, while business or other potentially powerful interests in society may attempt to influence policy at a national level, to do so locally would be a waste of time. As we saw in Chapter 4, however, this assumption can be criticized both empirically and theoretically, for not only is there evidence that, in certain areas of policy at least, local authorities retain considerable autonomy, but there are also grounds for arguing that such autonomy remains necessary if central planning is to take account of regional and local variations. In no way can local authorities therefore be dismissed as the mere tools of central government agencies.

The unity of British local government (which was increased still further following the 1974 reorganization) has been seen as an important factor because it appears to restrict the opportunities for groups such as local businessmen to play a significant brokerage role in local politics. In the United States, where local government is far more fragmented, it is not always entirely clear who is making which decisions, and this has sometimes given rise to some less formal co-ordinative agency (e.g. in the form of party machines or cabals of local businessmen) which allows outside interests to buy themselves a voice in local politics through political donations, bribery or whatever (see Greer 1962). Such a picture of businessmen running a town from behind the scenes appears highly implausible in Britain, however, and one reason for this is that British local government is already formally unified and co-ordinated (although contradictions do still develop, of course, between different levels of local government). It is often pointed out, for example, that just thirty-four authorities, plus a handful of other statutory bodies, accomplish in Greater London what it takes some 1400 different agencies to achieve in metropolitan New York. The implication drawn from this has been that the structural opportunities for external control over local politics are not present in Britain: 'The supremacy of the city council within its own area is a fact of both theory and practice. . . . Council members in England are sure of the fact that they, and only they, are the elected representatives of the people, and therefore they have the right to exclusive control of public policy' (Newton, 1970, pp. 4, 19–20). The alternative implication – that the unity of local government makes it potentially easier for outside interests in Britain to influence local policy-making since they have only to address themselves to a single public authority – has rarely been considered in the literature.

The third factor concerns representativeness, and here the argument has been that local authorities in Britain are usually large enough and sufficiently heterogenous in their membership to provide every major local interest with an effective direct voice in the policy-making process. People do not therefore need to organize politically outside the council when their interests are already being taken into account by those they have elected. This argument leads readily to the conclusion that, 'Politics (and by implicit extension power) are what the political parties do. . . . When you know about formal politics (meaning what the political parties do), you know all there is to know about power in the community' (Bell and Newby, 1971, p. 220). Such an argument is, of course, based upon an acceptance of the representational theory of the state (see pages 150–7), and as such, it suffers from all the inadequacies of that perspective. It is indeed dubious to assume that businessmen, house-owners, council tenants or any other section of the local population are inactive politically because there is no need for them to act.

The ambiguity of much of the empirical research, taken together with the weakness of these theoretical assumptions, led me in 1971 to begin what was originally envisaged as a community power study in the London Borough of Croydon. The work I carried out in Croydon over the following two years provides the basis for the first four chapters in Part 2.

There were a number of reasons for choosing Croydon as the site for the case study, and some of these were undeniably pragmatic. In 1971, for example, I was based at Chelsea College in London and was therefore predisposed to choose a research area within easy reach of the capital. Croydon, situated on the southern boundary of the Greater London region, was therefore always a possible site. Furthermore, I preferred to locate the study in London since London's local government structure had been reorganized back in 1965 while local authorities in other parts of the country were due to be reorganized in 1974. There seemed little to be gained in spending two years analysing political relations in a local authority area which was destined to disappear the moment I finished my work.

There were, however, stronger theoretical reasons for selecting Croydon for this particular research. For a start it was an outer London borough, and this appeared important for two reasons. First, the outer boroughs enjoy more autonomy from the Greater London Council than do the inner city areas (e.g. they are their own education authorities whereas the inner boroughs come under the control of the Inner London Education Authority), and this reflects the fact that, until 1965, they were not part of the London administrative area. Croydon, for example, had been an independent County Borough subject only to the authority of the national government until 1965, and the spirit of civic independence remains strong. The second reason why I wanted to look at an outer borough was that my concern with community power led almost naturally to the selection of a town where both business and middle class interests were likely to figure prominently in local affairs, and it was on this criterion that Croydon was eventually chosen.

Croydon town centre is some ten miles to the south of the City of London. In terms of shopping floor space it is the largest centre in the south of England outside the West End, and the office development which occurred there through the 1960s has established the town as one of the leading insurance and commercial centres in the country. Croydon is also the largest borough in London in terms of its population and was one of only six London boroughs to increase its population through the 1960s. In 1971, the population stood at over one-third of a million and, more significantly, around 50 per cent of these inhabitants were in professional, managerial or white-collar

occupations. The borough therefore provided an excellent opportunity for investigating middle class and business politics at the local
level, while at the same time, it was not 'too middle class' to exclude
a complementary study of the political situation of the working class.

It was these three groups – town centre business enterprises,
suburban middle class owner-occupiers, and working class families
living in privately rented or council accommodation – that provided
the focus for the study, and the key question with which I was
concerned was how they related to the local authority. I was therefore
interested in mapping out different patterns of influence and in
demonstrating the relationship between the interests of a particular
group, the way it acts (or fails to act) politically, and the impact it
achieves on local policy. This core question is taken up in Chapter 5
where I present an analysis of the local authority policy-making
process and demonstrate how certain interests come to be incorporated into this while others are routinely excluded from it. The
discussion in Chapter 5 thus attempts to put some empirical flesh
on the theoretical bones of the argument concerning non-decision-
making, considered in Chapter 1.

The three chapters which follow also attempt to provide empirical
material against which to consider the arguments developed in Part 1.
Chapter 6 contains an account of the political practices of owner-
occupiers in the south of the borough which owes much to the
discussion of housing classes in Chapter 2, and evidence is produced
to support the argument that owner-occupiers (through their residents' associations) not only constitute a highly articulate and effective political group, but also achieve their successes at the expense of
both business and working class interests. Chapter 7, by contrast,
considers the political strategies and effectiveness of the local working
class in the context of the discussion in Chapter 3 of the 'new urban
politics'. Through a discussion of the role of the Labour Party, the
tenants' associations, community associations and 'community
action', the conclusions is drawn that working class interests are
generally excluded from social policy-making and that they lack the
organizational base which is necessary if they are to mobilize
effectively. In Chapter 8, the town centre business interests are considered, and in contrast to most orthodox assumptions, it is shown
that representatives of the large retailing and international companies
are closely involved in local political and quasi-political affairs. This

chapter pays particular attention to the discussion in Chapter 4 of the relationship between capital and the local state and concludes that in Croydon, the relationship is a mutually beneficial one in which the local authority's commitment to private profitability is mediated by an interpersonal 'community of interest and sentiment' which exists between leading politicians and top business leaders in the town.

It should, of course, be noted that the empirical case material reported in these chapters was generated between 1971 and 1973, and it is not only therefore somewhat dated, but it was also collected before some of the key arguments discussed in Part 1 had been developed in British sociology. In reworking this material for publication, therefore, I have addressed myself to certain questions which were not in my mind when the research was originally conducted. This raises the question of how far research conducted in terms of one theoretical orientation can be used to evaluate others; how far, in other words, empirical work is theory- or paradigm-dependent. This is one of the central issues considered in the final chapter.

Chapter 9 does not in any way attempt to provide a conclusion for the book as a whole. Rather, it considers the methodological foundation of the material discussed in Part 2, and in this way attempts to demonstrate the relationship between the two parts of the book. I have already noted that there is too often a hiatus between theoretical and empirical work in contemporary sociology, and by dividing this book into two sections corresponding to these two aspects of the discipline, there is an obvious danger of perpetuating this in the present work. Chapter 9 is an attempt to insure against this by providing a methodological synthesis between two elements, theory and empirical research, which have to be understood in terms of a dialectical relationship with one another. Empirical research, in other words, is dependent upon theory, but it also itself should be expected to contribute to theory. Certainly, in writing the chapters which constitute Part 1, I have been influenced by my own research experiences in Croydon (the discussion of housing classes, for example, was stimulated by my own uneasiness about current Marxist approaches which did not appear consistent with my own findings on the political practices of owner-occupiers in the borough). By the same token, in reworking the case-study material for Part 2, I have inevitably been influenced by new theoretical insights which were not available to me in 1971 (this does not mean that the empirical data have been changed or amended in any way, for, as I argue in Chapter 9, the integrity of the researcher is a crucial criterion of the validity of his work; rather, it means that the same material has been addressed to answer what are sometimes different questions).

The implications of all this as regards the validity and objectivity of the case study material are discussed in Chapter 9, along with a number of other specific problems which arise in urban politics research. Suffice it to say here that, if we accept that it is only through a dialectical progression between theory and empirical research that any headway can be made in resolving the key questions currently facing urban sociology, then it is clear that, far from providing a definitive conclusion, Chapter 9 represents the basis for a new beginning.

5 The local authority

We saw in the last chapter that representational theories of the state see elections as crucial means whereby political elites are obliged to address their policies to popular demands. In order to stay in power, it is argued, political leaders cannot afford to ignore majority preferences on major issues. Applied to the analysis of local government in Britain, this argument appears absurd, for not only do very few people bother to vote in local elections, but those who do generally cast their votes, not according to the records and programmes of the local candidates, but according to their assessment of the record of the national government at the time. Even the most 'optimistic' estimate suggests that a maximum of 25 per cent of the local vote can be explained in terms of local issues and personalities (Green 1972), and this seems something of an overestimate as regards most local elections. Most of us, it seems, know little and care even less about the identity and activities of our representatives in the town hall, and most councillors seem fully aware of this. The result, as Budge and his co-authors suggest, is that, 'Activists, both individually and as a body, are as a general rule freed from the danger of popular sanctions against their actions, since not only is the population ignorant of what they do, but activists are likely to be aware of this popular ignorance' (1972, p. 18). It is hardly surprising, therefore, that local politicians rarely feel the need to follow popular opinion. In Croydon, for example, nearly 70 per cent of all councillors interviewed (and over 80 per cent of leading members such as committee chairmen) described themselves as 'trustees' (Newton 1976), free to make up their own minds on different issues independently of the perceived or anticipated wishes of the majority of the electorate. As one local pressure group leader rather sourly put it, 'They see themselves as the city fathers.'

This awareness of their relative immunity from electoral reprisals may, of course, enable local politicians to take up unpopular causes which would otherwise go unheard or ignored (Newton 1970). They may, for example, pay some regard to the interests of minority underprivileged groups without having to fear too much for the loss of significant electoral support. But by the same token, they may equally feel free to respond readily to the interests of minority privileged groups at the expense of the less fortunate majority. Within the limits of their scope of discretion, therefore, local political leaders can act freely with little concern for democratic accountability, responding not to the anticipated preferences of the majority, but to those demands made directly upon them, ceding to some and rejecting others according to their own political judgements and values.

It follows that any analysis of local policy-making must address itself to three questions. Who are the people who control the process and what are their political values? How much discretion do these people have in determining policy outcomes? And what is the nature of their relationship with political groups outside the local authority? It is these three questions – composition, internal relations, and external relations – which I wish to consider in this chapter.

Social composition

Historically Britain's local government has always been dominated by people drawn from a higher social class than the majority of those they represent. As Prewitt and Eulau observe, 'Even in the most democratic society, the electorate does not choose from among all its members. It chooses from among a pool of eligibles disproportionately drawn from the higher social status groups in society' (1971, p. 293). This is not to suggest that local power has consistently been concentrated in the same hands. But such reshuffling as has taken place, largely as a result of the progressive democratization of local government and the rise of the Labour Party, has generally taken the form of a shift from upper class and big business domination one hundred years ago, to middle class and smaller business domination today, with an increase in some areas in the representation of skilled manual workers.

In Birmingham (Morris and Newton 1970), for example, the

traditional power of big business in the local council has given way to the increasing significance of 'professional-businessmen', and especially 'exchange professionals' such as estate agents and solicitors – men who own their own businesses and who have a substantial interest in the local property market. Similarly in Glossop (Birch 1959), the old economic and social elite which ran the town in the nineteenth century is now virtually insignificant as regards direct representation on the local council. Traditional social and political leaders in these and other towns thus appear to have adopted an increasingly 'cosmopolitan' perspective (Merton 1957b), backing out of local affairs as improvements in communications and transportation over the last century have enabled them to sustain wide-ranging social networks with other members of their class, far beyond the confines of their communities of residence (Pahl 1968). But those who have replaced them in the command posts of Britain's towns and cities, while less socially conspicuous, are nevertheless still by and large a very different breed from most of those who elect them (Sharpe 1962, Maud 1967, vol. 2).

Much the same picture emerges in relation to Croydon where, at least since 1849, the town's governing bodies have invariably been controlled by varying types of businessmen. Before that date, the town had no single or unified system of local administration. Until 1780 it had been managed (to the extent that it was managed at all) by the benevolent hand of the Canterbury archbishopric which maintained a palace and estate in the town, and from then until the mid-nineteenth century the various minimal functions of government were administered by a variety of local trusts, boards and commissions. It was not until 1849 that these functions were brought together under the newly constituted Board of Health. Elected annually on a restricted suffrage, the membership of the Board was from the outset overwhelmingly comprised of local businessmen and upper class benefactors, many of whom had considerable property interests in the town and surrounding area. For thirty-four years, these men used the Board both to provide some basic and much needed public amenities and to consolidate the privileged position which they and their class enjoyed (see Cox 1966). Ably combining altruistic ideals with the profitable pursuit of self-interest, they administered a town in which the disparities between the working class west side and the middle class east continued to grow while business prospered.

In 1883, some of the town's most prominent business and political leaders succeeded, against protests from various small traders in outlying areas, in gaining Croydon's incorporation as a borough, and six years later, following the 1888 Local Government Act, the town was designated one of the new County Boroughs. But although the name and the functions changed, the character of the membership did not, and the faces on the new council appeared little different from those on the old Board of Health. No less than 28 per cent of the members elected to the County Borough council were, on any definition, big businessmen – the owners of the town's largest stores, the biggest companies and so on. Total business representation stood at over 60 per cent, while a further 25 per cent of members merely described themselves as 'gentlemen'. It appears from the records that no manual workers gained election.

Croydon remained a County Borough for the next seventy-six years until the reorganization of London's local government system came into effect in 1965. At this time, Croydon became one of thirty-two London boroughs and lost a number of its responsibilities in the fields of planning, housing and roads to the newly formed Greater London Council. Even before this, the local council had been losing its powers – public transport was taken out of local hands in the 1930s, hospitals were handed over to the NHS after the war, and gas was similarly made the responsibility of the new nationalized regional boards – but the loss of both functions and autonomy under the 1965 reorganization was strongly resented in local political circles, and there is today still a legacy of hostility in Croydon towards the higher tier authority. Although it lost responsibilities, however, the council grew in size as the strongly middle class and staunchly conservative Purley and Coulsdon Urban District was merged with Croydon under the boundary changes at that time.

This merger only served to reinforce the middle class domination of the local authority which had gradually become established since the turn of the century. By 1971, of course, the big businessmen and local gentry who had been so prominent in the late nineteenth century had disappeared from the council altogether. The proportion of small traders had also dipped significantly from 22 per cent of the total membership in 1891 to just 6 per cent in 1971. But this decline of the old upper class and the traditional petty bourgeoisie only reflects the phenomenal increase in the representation of the new middle class and professional businessmen. The working class is still, by and large, left out in the cold. Thus, while the rise of the Labour Party has usually led in other parts of Britain to a substantial increase in manual worker representation in local government, in Croydon it has resulted rather in an increased representation of professional workers. To some extent, this reflects the character of the social composition of the town itself, for unlike northern industrial towns such as Sheffield (Hampton 1970), Wolverhampton (Jones 1969) and Newcastle-under-Lyme (Bealey *et al.* 1965) where up to half of all Labour councillors are drawn from the manual working class, in Croydon the figure is only 14 per cent, and this appears more in line with other southern commercial towns like Brighton (Forrester 1976). Nevertheless, even in Croydon the manual working class accounts for around 50 per cent of the total population, and it is clear that this class is thus considerably under-represented in the council chamber. The Labour councillors may or may not be for the working class, but very few of them are of it, although a considerable proportion appear to have been upwardly mobile in inter-generational terms.

The large increase in the representation of professional workers on the council over the last eighty years is thus accounted for in the main by Labour members, many of whom follow those 'liberal professions' such as teaching, journalism and social work commonly associated with middle class radicalism (see Parkin 1968). Twenty-eight per cent of the Labour group consists of these liberal professionals, the remainder comprising managers (14 per cent), professional businessmen (10 per cent), other professional groups (17 per cent) and skilled manual workers (14 per cent). The composition of the majority Conservative group, on the other hand, falls mainly into the three categories of professional businessmen, most of whom are exchange professionals (29 per cent), company managers and executives (27 per cent), and the traditional professions such as civil servants (24 per cent). This strong business representation in the ranks of the majority group is emphasized even more strongly at the level of the group's leadership, with no less than eight of eleven committee chairmen and five of the seven members of the powerful Policy subcommittee being company executives, professional businessmen or small traders. The dominance of big business in the County Borough council of the 1890s is thus mirrored in the dominance achieved by other sectors of business in the London Borough council of the 1970s.

The membership of the council is not only unrepresentative in terms of occupation, however. On the basis of replies received to a questionnaire survey, I estimate that around 40 per cent of all council members were privately educated and that approximately the same proportion received a state grammar school education. Again there are variations between the party groups with well over half of the Conservative group having attended fee-paying schools compared with around one in eight of Labour members. Furthermore, the sex distribution among council members is grossly distorted against women, males outnumbering females by more than four to one in both groups. There are, in addition, no women on the policy sub-committee, and only one female committee chairperson. This bias against women in top positions cannot be accounted for in terms of differential lengths of council service, for three women have sat on the council for more than twelve years.

Compared with the social composition of the total population, and even with the composition of other local councils which have been studied, the membership of Croydon council thus exhibits some marked peculiarities. The proportion of manual workers is much lower, and the proportion of privately educated members is much higher, than the norm, while the direct representation of business interests in the council (and notably at the higher levels) is very strong. Not that any of this, by itself, means very much, for as Giddens points out,

We are surely not justified in making direct inferences from the social background, or even the educational experience, of elite groups to the way in which they employ whatever power they possess once they attain positions of eminence. Because a man emanates from a specific type of class background, it does not inevitably follow that he will later adopt policies which are designed to promote class interests corresponding to that background [1974, p. xii.]

As we saw in Chapter 1, positional analysis is only the starting point.

Nevertheless, this brief review of the social composition of the local council in Croydon does have two significant implications. The first is that it provides a pointer towards the sorts of beliefs and values which we may expect to find among at least some of the town's political leaders. If there is a tendency for each of us to view the world

Croydon council membership characteristics, 1973

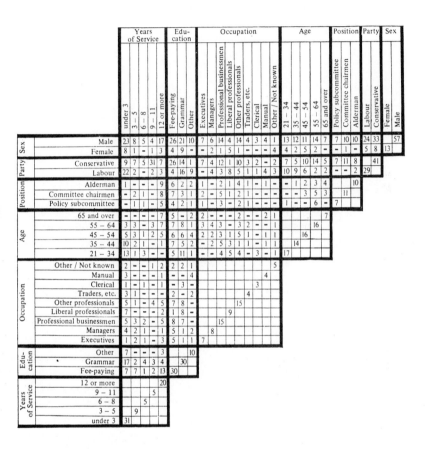

Column groups: **Years of Service** (under 3 / 3–5 / 6–8 / 9–11 / 12 or more) · **Education** (Fee-paying / Grammar / Other) · **Occupation** (Executives / Managers / Professional businessmen / Liberal professionals / Other professionals / Traders, etc. / Clerical / Manual / Other / Not known) · **Age** (21–34 / 35–44 / 45–54 / 55–64 / 65 and over) · **Position** (Policy subcommittee / Committee chairmen / Alderman) · **Party** (Labour / Conservative) · **Sex** (Female / Male)

	under 3	3–5	6–8	9–11	12 or more	Fee-paying	Grammar	Other	Executives	Managers	Professional businessmen	Liberal professionals	Other professionals	Traders, etc.	Clerical	Manual	Other / Not known	21–34	35–44	45–54	55–64	65 and over	Policy subcommittee	Committee chairmen	Alderman	Labour	Conservative	Female	Male
Male	23	8	5	4	17	26	21	10	7	6	14	4	14	4	3	4	1	13	12	11	14	7	7	10	10	24	33		57
Female	8	1	-	1	3	4	9	-	-	2	1	5	1	-	-	-	4	4	2	5	2	-	-	-	1	5	8	13	
Conservative	9	7	5	31	7	26	14	1	-	4	12	1	10	3	2	-	2	7	5	10	14	5	7	11	8		41		
Labour	22	2	-	2	3	4	16	9	-	4	3	8	5	1	1	4	3	10	9	6	2	2	-	-	2	29			
Alderman	1	-	-	-	9	6	2	2	1	-	2	1	4	1	-	1	-	-	1	2	3	4			10				
Committee chairmen	-	2	1	-	8	7	3	1	2	-	5	1	2	1	-	-	-	-	-	3	5	3		11					
Policy subcommittee	-	1	1	-	5	4	2	1	1	-	3	-	2	1	-	-	-	1	-	-	6	-	7						
65 and over	-	-	-	-	7	5	-	2	2	-	-	-	2	-	-	2	1					7							
55 – 64	3	3	-	3	7	7	8	1	3	4	3	-	3	2	-	-	1				16								
45 – 54	5	3	1	2	5	6	6	4	2	2	3	1	5	1	-	1	1			16									
35 – 44	10	2	1	-	1	7	5	2	-	2	5	3	1	1	-	1	1		14										
21 – 34	13	1	3	-	-	5	11	1	-	-	4	5	4	-	3	-	1	17											
Other / Not known	2	-	-	1	2	2	2	1									5												
Manual	3	-	-	-	1	-	-	4								4													
Clerical	1	-	1	-	1	-	3	-							3														
Traders, etc.	3	1	-	-	-	2	-	2						4															
Other professionals	5	1	-	4	5	7	8	-					15																
Liberal professionals	7	-	-	-	2	1	8	-				9																	
Professional businessmen	5	3	2	-	5	8	7	-			15																		
Managers	4	2	1	-	1	5	1	2		8																			
Executives	1	2	1	-	3	5	1	1	7																				
Other	7	-	-	-	3			10																					
Grammar	17	2	4	3	4		30																						
Fee-paying	7	7	1	2	13	30																							
12 or more					20																								
9 – 11				5																									
6 – 8			5																										
3 – 5		9																											
under 3	31																												

Row-group labels (left margin, top to bottom): Sex · Party · Position · Age · Occupation · Education · Years of Service.

Sources: Croydon Council Year Book and questionnaire returns

* Figures for education and age are based solely on questionnaire returns. These were incomplete (only 40 of 70 members replied) but appeared to be representative on all other variables. For the sake of clarity and comparability, therefore, data on age and education have been multiplied by a factor of 7/4 in this table. It is important to note, however, that on these two variables, the figures given only represent estimates based on a 56 per cent response rate.

Where the information was available, figures on occupation have been calculated to include the last full-time occupation of retired respondents, and the husband's occupation of married women not themselves in full-time employment.

in a different way according to where we are standing, then it is clearly significant that so many of the men who fill the top local political positions appear to be standing in much the same position; a businessmen's council is likely to see things through businessmen's eyes. The second implication is that certain groups in the population – notably the middle class in general and the business community in particular – are vastly over-represented in the town hall, and this may mean that their interests are more likely to be taken into account in the course of the decision-making process. Both of these points are explored in more detail in later chapters, but both rest on the assumption that local political leaders can and do have a significant say in local policy-making. We must now consider the validity of this assumption.

The local council: internal relations

The policy-making process in most local authorities in England and Wales has been 'rationalized' in recent years following various central government initiatives, the most significant of which have been the 1972 Baines report and the 1974 reorganization. This has produced two main consequences. First, there has been an increased vertical integration of local, regional and national levels of government. This has resulted in a fragmentation of functions between the levels (e.g. the division between local and structure planning), and in an overall increase in central regulation of local policy-making. Secondly, the internal organization of local authorities themselves has changed. This is not to suggest that before the 1970s local councils were controlled by the elected members while today they are controlled by the officers, for this would be too gross a simplification. Clearly there has been a shift, at least as regards the formal structure of management and policy-making, away from the members, and this is reflected in the development of corporate planning teams (consisting of the heads of all the main council departments) which tend to work closely with small 'inner cabinets' of leading members of the majority groups of the different authorities. But this is only the culmination of a long term trend in local government – in 1967 the Maud report argued that the traditional distinction between making policies and implementing them had long since become blurred – and, more significantly, it is a formal change in organizational structure which may not be directly reflected in organizational practice. The point here is that it has become a sociological cliche that the formal structure of an organization does not necessarily indicate what actually goes on within it, and there is no reason to expect that local authorities constitute an exception to this. Both functionalist (e.g. Blau 1963) and interactionist (e.g. Silverman 1970) approaches to the sociology of formal organizations have stressed the need to examine how members routinely accomplish their 'roles', and it follows that the analysis of the formal organizational framework of local authority decision-making can only be a first step in understanding how policies come to be made.

The formal decision-making procedure in Croydon is broadly similar to that followed by most other local authorities in the country, and it is summarized in the diagram below. It can be seen from this that there are certain strategic positions – notably membership of the Chief Officers' Group and membership of the Policy subcommittee – which would appear to provide the capacity for controlling virtually the entire policy-making process, for the lower-level participants are largely dependent upon them for both the original initiatives and for information about alternative proposals. However, we need to ask whether and how this potential control is exercised in practice. In other words, the formal model outlined in the diagram is little more than a 'script' which may guide to a greater or lesser extent what Gans (1967) has termed the decision-making 'performance'. As one Croydon Chief Officer observed, 'It's extremely difficult to describe the real decision-making practices. You can construct organization charts but these are only the theory and life isn't like that.'

From the perspective of the elected members of the council, the positions of greatest potential power are the seven seats on the Policy subcommittee and, to a lesser extent, the chairmanships of the major service committees such as education, housing and social services (although the chairmen of these committees are usually also members of the Policy subcommittee). All of these key positions, of course, are held by members of the majority party group, which in Croydon means the Conservatives, and they are filled by the leading and generally most senior members of the group. These individuals may nominally be defined as the council's 'political elite'.

Many previous studies of local government in Britain have noted

Local authority decision-making: The formal structure

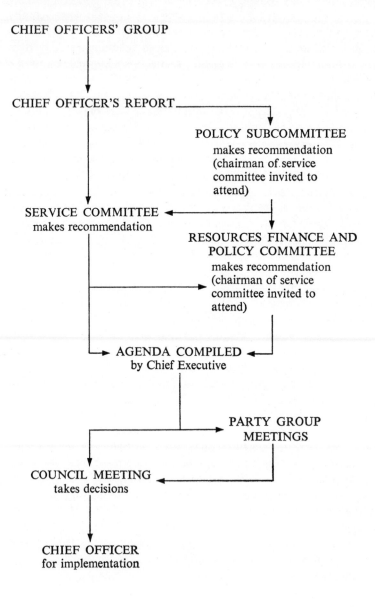

the power which committee chairmen may come to enjoy over their colleagues. For a start, they have a privileged relationship with the appropriate Chief Officer and can draw upon his information and expertise to direct, initiate and curtail committee discussions. As Bealey and his co-authors suggest, 'A strong-willed and capable chairman who is well advised on the technical and legal aspects is likely to get his way' (1965, p. 369). Thus in Croydon, as in many other authorities, committee chairmen meet informally with the relevant officers before every committee meeting in order to discuss the agenda, resolve their strategies, and, as one councillor expressed it, 'to determine what shall be pushed through and what can be left to the committee to decide.' Furthermore, committee chairmen enjoy considerable delegated powers – inevitably since committees meet only eight times in any one year – and in liaison with the Chief Officers, such powers can be used 'on behalf of', yet without the knowledge of, other committee members. Sometimes, the decisions taken under these delegated powers can be reviewed by the committee at a later meeting (e.g. the closure of a children's playground can be reviewed and the decision reversed with little difficulty). At other times, however, the decisions are in practice irreversible (e.g. a land purchase where the decision is contractually binding). As one member put it, 'What's done is done.'

The power of most of the chairmen of the major committees is reinforced by their membership of the Policy subcommittee. This is the only one-party committee of the council – 'The tory caucus with the Town Clerk there' was how one Labour member described it. It is also the first committee to consider any proposal and, as its name suggests, it holds a wide brief to consider the development of council policy over the broad spectrum of the different departments and committees. It considers various proposals before the appropriate service committees meet, and although it can only make 'recommendations' to the other committees (and, through them, to the full council meeting), most councillors agreed with the member who suggested, 'It's a recognized thing that its recommendations are carried out.' This is not particularly surprising, of course, when we remember that its members are the leading figures in the majority group and that they tend also to be the chairmen of the major service committees to whom the recommendations are sent. It is no exaggeration to suggest that the seven men who comprise the Policy sub-committee recommend proposals in one role and then accept them in another.

Even in the unlikely event of a service committee rejecting a Policy subcommittee recommendation, the 'political elite' still has two other strings to its bow. First, its recommendations, together with those of the various service committees, are considered by the Resources Finance and Policy committee, of which Policy is a subcommittee. In other words, all seven members of the Policy subcommittee sit on the very committee which considers the various recommendations which have been made, and its chairman and vice-chairman occupy the same positions on Resources Finance and Policy. Furthermore, this latter committee, which does include a minority of Labour members, always votes on strict party lines, and thus invariably endorses the recommendations of the Conservative group leaders. In short, service committee proposals are unlikely to be accepted where they conflict with those of the Policy subcommittee. Secondly, even where the Policy subcommittee is overruled by the decision taken in a full council meeting, it still retains an effective veto power since it controls the distribution of resources among the various departments of the council. In other words, the Policy subcommittee has the power to decide whether to allocate the necessary finance to a service committee which has resolved on a policy of which it disapproves. In 1972, for example, the council accepted a Health committee proposal for the introduction of a free family planning service in the borough. The Policy subcommittee, however, refused to allocate sufficient additional funds for the scheme to be put into operation, and the decision was therefore not implemented. Little wonder that one Labour councillor said of the Policy subcommittee, 'It lays down the policy of the council and what it says goes. Various attempts to resist it in the past have failed. . . . It's strong because it includes the men who can persuade and dominate their fellows.'

This ability to 'persuade and dominate' is not simply a reflection of the strategic location of the Policy subcommittee in the decision-making process, however, for it also reflects the relationship between the 'political elite' and the rank-and-file of the majority party group. Sherman has argued that, 'In local government today, the group is more powerful and demanding than the party whips in Whitehall' (1973, p. 140), and although this may be something of an exaggeration, there is no doubt that, since the eclipse of the 'independent' councillor (which in Croydon can be dated effectively from the early 1960s although a handful of right-wing independents continued to gain election until the early 1970s), the party caucus has become a central element in the decision-making process. In Croydon, members of both party groups exhibited a marked reluctance to vote against group decisions; only 15 per cent of Labour members reported ever having voted against a group decision, the comparable figure among Conservatives being slightly higher at 20 per cent. Majority group decisions are thus tantamount to council decisions, and the power to control the majority group is thus crucial in determining the ability to control the council.

That the 'political elite' effectively controls the majority group in Croydon is beyond doubt. Conservative group meetings function mainly as a means of disseminating information on decisions which have already been resolved in committee, and as a way of determining voting strategies for forthcoming council meetings. The majority group meeting does not therefore serve as a vehicle for rank and-file involvement in policy-formation, and in this respect, Croydon appears no different from many other authorities (e.g. see Bulpitt 1967). Because it meets after the agenda for the council meeting has been compiled (i.e. after the 'political elite' has made its 'recommendations'), all that usually remains to be done is to ensure that the members formally fall into line behind their leaders. This they invariably do with little trouble. The ideological commitment and political zeal of most Conservative members is relatively low compared with that found in the Labour group – only one quarter of the Conservatives, compared with half of the Labour members, cited 'involvement in decision-making' as their major concern as councillors – and this is reflected in their high level of compliance with the decisions taken by their leaders. As Harris (1971) has pointed out, there is perhaps less excitability and passion on the right of British politics than on the left, and this certainly appeared the case in Croydon where the Conservative rank-and-file was, by and large, fairly content with the passive political role it was called upon to play.

This is not to suggest that there have never been conflicts within the majority group, nor that the rank-and-file members have no control over the leadership. One particularly acrimonious dispute, for example, took place over the leadership's decision to accept the government's call to reorganize secondary education in the borough in the 1960s. This issue is discussed in more detail in Chapter 6, but here we should note that it resulted in the resignation of the chairman of the Education committee following the mobilization of a right-wing faction against him. However, three points need to be made about this. First, the issue was somewhat unique in that most internal dissension within the majority group occurs around questions of personalities or parochial loyalties (mainly northern against southern ward representatives) rather than on a left–right split. Secondly, even in this fairly unique case where tory 'gut-feeling' was strongly opposed to the abolition of the grammar schools, the group leaders were still powerful enough to force the reform through. Indeed, as we shall see in Chapter 6, the 'political elite' twice changed its policy on comprehensive reorganization, yet on both occasions was able to carry with it the support of the great majority of Conservative members. Thirdly, the successful coup against the Education committee chairman was only short-lived, and it resulted in 1974 in an important shift in the relations of power between the leadership and the rank-and-file. Until 1974, the major source of power for the rank-and-file members was their right to elect annually the chairmen of the different committees, but in that year the leader of the group announced that all chairmen would in future be appointed by him (although he was still to be elected by the group). 'It means,' he explained, 'the leader having more political control of the council, and that the load is shared as the leader would wish it to be. It's no good having the chairman of a committee who's opposed to the leader all the time.' Armed with these new powers, the group leader then proceded to reinstate the former Education committee chairman to his old post, and since then the majority group has been reduced to a state of virtual impotence in relation to the leader and his appointees.

Although it is now firmly in control of its own majority group, however, the 'political elite' still depends for its power on its ability to negotiate two other crucial potential limitations posed by the internal organization of the decision-making process. One of these concerns its relationship with the Chief Officers of the council; the other concerns its ability to avoid direct and open confrontation with the Labour group.

The Chief Officers represent the strongest potential limitation on the power of the 'political elite', for not only do they initiate policy discussions (often as a result of central government or internal departmental stimuli, but also sometimes in response to members' own suggestions) and implement them, but they are also involved in the third and more contentious role of actively resolving them. The close relationship between a Chief Officer and a committee chairman, for example, is a two-edged sword, for if the latter uses the expertise of the former, it is also the case that the former can influence the latter through the information he chooses to make available and the way in which he does so. As Heclo (1969) points out, information and expertise constitute crucial power resources in the increasingly complex world of local government. Or as Weber observed, 'The question is always who controls the existing bureaucratic machinery. And such control is possible only in a very limited degree to persons who are not technical specialists' (1947, p. 338).

This point is not lost on the elected members themselves. As one Croydon councillor put it, 'In most things you're in the hands of the officers. They've got the information. Councillors are kept too busy to keep well informed.' This argument was reinforced by a Chief Officer who, citing Parkinson's Law, suggested that committees would sometimes talk for hours about where to locate a bicycle shed, and then accept a proposal involving vast council expenditure in a matter of minutes. Nor is the problem simply that of disparities of technical expertise, for the officers are in practice called upon, not only to 'advise' on policy options, but to make a host of routine decisions about what a policy actually 'means' once it has been decided. In other words, in administering council policies, the officers necessarily enjoy a wide area of discretion in which to draw their own interpretations, and this can substantially affect the impact of any given policy decision. It was for precisely these sorts of reasons, of course, that Pahl came to define 'urban managers' as local authority bureaucrats and to leave the elected members out of his later analyses altogether (see pages 168–9).

There is a danger, however, in overemphasizing the power of the officers in relation to the elected members, and this follows from the failure to distinguish between the majority of the elected members and the small group I have termed the 'political elite'. As Newton concludes from his study of Birmingham council, 'Council members do have some resources to call upon when they confront expert opinion, and these resources are not by any means negligible for some sections of the membership. Most important, perhaps, they are least negligible for the members who generally fill the most important positions ... much of the current literature on officer-member relations overemphasizes the power of the officers and under-emphasizes that of the members' (1976, p. 164). Newton is not alone in this argument; Darke and Walker (1977, p. 33), for example, similarly stress the importance of the relationship between members and officers at the senior levels, Cockburn (1977, p. 31) suggests that the political leadership in Lambeth council has more power than the formal organizational structure would appear to suggest, and Corina (1975) and others have produced similar arguments following studies in other parts of the country.

In Croydon there are strong grounds for suggesting that the relationship of the Chief Officers to the leading members of the majority group is more that of close allies than of daunting superiors. For a start, the 'political elite' can choose its men in its own image, for leading members dominate the Interviews and Appointments committee which selects Chief Officers. More significant than this, however, is the fact that the officers depend upon the leading members as much as the members do upon them; the relationship is symbiotic in that the 'political elite' needs the help, advice and information which only the officers can provide, while the officers in turn are obliged to address themselves to the ideological predispositions of the elite members if their proposals are eventually to be accepted by the council. Even where policies are initiated and formulated by the officers, in other words, they must generally reflect the values and overall objectives of the 'political elite', and in Croydon this is reflected in the lack of any observable tension over the years between bureaucratic advice and majority group preferences. As one business executive observed of his experiences in the town, 'In some boroughs where the councillors are strongly left-wing, you sense when you meet the officers that they're very right-wing. But in Croydon they're all going in the same direction.'

The direction in which they are jointly headed is, needless to say, to the right, and given the long history in Croydon of right-wing domination of the council, first by 'independents' and later by the Conservatives, the compass needle has rarely wavered from this course. Two points arise out of this. First, it may well be that in authorities where a radical Labour group is in control (e.g. the so-called 'red islands' of local government), the bureaucracy does come to impose a strong constraint on the political actions of the members, but this does not appear to be the case in Conservative-controlled authorities like Croydon. This conclusion would seem to support the argument developed in Chapter 4 that constraints on policy-making are less severe when action is directed towards maintaining the status quo rather than fundamentally challenging it. The second point is that, despite professional claims to objectivity and political neutrality on the part of local state bureaucrats, it is clear that where their advice bears upon policy choices, it is and can be no more objective, rational or scientifically based than that of any other group. This point has been made by numerous writers (e.g. Benington and Skelton 1972) and need not be laboured here, except to emphasize the tendency in British local government for conservatism to be represented as in some way politically neutral (see Saunders *et al.* 1978).

Poulantzas (1973) is only one of a number of writers who have identified the dominant political ideology in the western capitalist societies as that which stresses the neutrality of the state. In contrast to pre-capitalist societies where political power is recognized as explicitly class-based and is justified ideologically as the result of 'natural' or 'sacred' principles, Poulantzas suggests that the capitalist state is seen as the representative of the 'general interest', and that its policies are justified ideologically as the result of the application of rational principles: 'What specifically defines the ideologies in question is that they do not aim to be accepted by the dominated classes according to the principle of participation in the sacred: they explicitly declare themselves and are accepted as scientific techniques' (ibid., p. 217). The consequence of this is that any challenge to the state which is premised on the existence of class antagonisms and which attempts to demonstrate the class-bias of state policies comes to be dismissed as 'utopian' in contrast to the scientific rationality of the state itself.

Poulantzas's insights here are directly applicable to the analysis of policy-making in Croydon, for not only is there the strong and pervasive assumption that the policy outcomes agreed by the political elite and the Chief Officers are in some way neutral and objective, but the response to those who challenge this assumption is invariably to define them as 'naive', 'irresponsible' and 'utopian'. It is in this respect that the Labour opposition constitutes an important factor in the policy-making process, for if the impression of rationality is to be sustained, it is necessary for the political elite to maintain a broad political consensus which enables it to represent its actions as 'sensible' and 'reasonable' rather than 'doctrinaire' and sectional.

The Labour leadership in Croydon has long aided them in this, and has been content to follow a policy of moderation and conciliation designed to create and maintain close and informal relations with the political elite. As one Labour leader expressed his philosophy, 'Half a loaf is better than none.' The older, more experienced and generally right-wing Labour leaders have in this way come to enjoy both the respect and the confidence of their Conservative counterparts (reflected in the fact that, while no Labour respondents identified their group leader as an influential man in the council, no less than thirty per cent of Conservatives did). The Labour leaders were quite happy to work with rather than against the political elite – 'I'm quite friendly with the other side. . . . I tend to respect most of the tories. On the whole they're in it to help the people of Croydon. . . . You can get a great deal done by private chats – far more than by shouting your mouth off' – and the elite, in turn, was quite prepared to listen to what the Labour leaders had to offer – 'When X speaks, you listen.' Indeed, the close and informal nature of the relationship between the two was such that the Labour leaders had at times been consulted over a proposal before many Conservative members had got to hear of it. One leading Conservative member, for example, having spent eighteen months in private and secret negotiations to secure the purchase by the council of a local independent school building, then sounded out a leading Labour member to gauge his reactions before he informed members of his own party.

Such close liaison between the two group leaderships brings benefits to both. For the political elite, it has traditionally meant that contentious opposition and public hostility to its policies and to its power have been avoided. By including the Labour leaders in its deliberations (if only somewhat superficially) it has ensured itself a quiescent opposition. For the Labour leaders themselves, of course, the relationship has provided for some degree of involvement in the decision-making process, and with it the possibility of gaining some minor concessions on policy. The relationship has thus been one of mutually satisfying back-scratching.

The entire informal arrangement, of course, is based on the tacit understanding that the Labour leaders can in fact deliver the goods – i.e. that they can control their own rank-and-file. Since 1971, however, this has become increasingly difficult. Until then, the arrangement seems to have worked fairly well. Following each election, new councillors would gradually be introduced to the 'rules of the game', and would learn 'how things were done' and what was expected of them. They were, in other words, socialized into the norms and values of this implicitly understood political subculture (Grant 1971, Dearlove 1973). In this way, the power of the political elite went largely unchallenged and the close informal alliances struck between the two group leaderships – what Budge and his co-authors term 'a system of political stratification' (1972) – were maintained. In 1968, however, Labour's representation on the council was cut to just one councillor and two aldermen, and many of the 'old guard' who lost their seats that year never returned. Thus at the next election in 1971, by which time the political wind had changed dramatically, no fewer than twenty-two of the twenty-nine Labour members returned had no prior local government experience. The consequences were traumatic.

This group of relatively young, inexperienced, and in many cases radical Labour novices brought with it its own ideas of what should be done and how. Its very size imposed too great a strain on the traditional methods of socializing new and over-zealous recruits, and many of its members proved awkwardly irreverent towards the established authority of the group leaders. They objected to being cast as passive lobby-fodder to be bartered in return for compromises in behind-the-scenes 'wheeler-dealing'. They distrusted the informal arrangements worked out by their leader – 'They feel that he hob-nobs in the corridors too much with the other side.' And most of all, they wanted to get involved.

Given their almost total exclusion from what Gans would term the 'actual' decision-making process, the rank-and-file Labour members had only one effective means of attack – publicity generated by full council meetings. Of course, no decision is ever changed at a council meeting – it is the climax of the whole democratic 'performance'. Between 1968 and 1971, when they were faced with an opposition of three, the political elite completed council meetings in record speed, on one occasion approving an eighty-page agenda involving expendi-

ture of £70,000 in just twenty-nine minutes (an achievement aptly
described in the local newspaper as 'democracy on roller-skates').
But the ceremony, ritual, and (most of all) visibility, of council
meetings provided the young Labour radicals with the one opportunity to assert their views and gain an audience for their criticism.
For them, the council meeting, far from being a necessary irrelevance
to be endured, was a ball where the Cinderellas of the decision-
making process could perform in the limelight for a few hours before
returning to the subjugation of the Labour and Conservative ugly
sisters. It was their show and they determined to make full advantage
of it.

In using the full council meetings to voice their views, the Labour
radicals have, since 1971, effectively mounted a challenge to the entire
informal and innovative procedure whereby decision-making is
accomplished. Thus they have consistently attempted to draw attention in public to the disparity which undoubtedly exists between how
decisions are seen to be made, and how they 'know' they are 'really'
made, and thereby to embarrass both sets of party leaders. The
Policy subcommittee and its privileged relationship to the Chief
Officers' Group has frequently been the target of these attacks: 'The
power of the Policy subcommittee is only found in totalitarian
regimes. . . . It gets away with murder'; 'Big issues of how to spend
millions of pounds of ratepayers' money are decided by a small cabal
on the top floor of the council offices over sherry one afternoon';
'Sometimes I wonder why any of us bother to come here. In reality it
is a complete waste of time. Vital decisions have already been made in
a little sanctum'; and so on.

Of course, in one sense these attacks have achieved nothing. The
public critics are still excluded from the private procedures by
which decision-making is accomplished. In the words of a local
newspaper reporter, 'Some amazing horse-dealing goes on, and a lot
of Labour influence takes place behind the scenes. But it's the Labour
moderates rather than the extremists and the idiots who have the
influence and get listened to.' But in a different sense, the radicals
have achieved something – namely, a challenge to the hitherto taken-
for-granted procedures followed by leading members of both party
groups. The usually implicit rules of the game have been wrested
from their context and thrown up for conscious examination and
public scrutiny.

What has previously been accepted as the 'right', 'normal', or even 'obvious' way of doing things has thus been called into question. As one Conservative member lamented, 'The Labour group could have far more influence than they do, if only they went about it *in the right way.*' But it is, of course, paradoxical that when such long-serving members speak of the 'right way' for an opposition to behave, they are in fact referring to behaviour which many outsiders, acquainted only with the formal rules, would possibly see as quite wrong. It is strange, for example, that public and open criticism in the council chamber should be seen by many leading members of both party groups as the wrong way for the opposition to conduct itself, while private wheeler-dealing in the corridors is correspondingly seen as correct and proper.

It is this paradox which has been exploited by the young Labour radicals, and which has presented the political elite with a problem. The elite members recognize that the consistent challenge to their power and the way in which they use it has to be met publicly, for it is articulated publicly. But they also know that they cannot justify their behaviour with reference to the informal and private rules of the game, for these are in many ways the antithesis of the formal rules of democratic government as understood by most outside observers and to which they themselves pay lip-service. It would, after all, be difficult to defend an informal system of private meetings, corridor chats, and backstairs bartering to the satisfaction of those in the public gallery at council meetings. And, of course, no attempt is made to do so. Instead, the political elite has generally responded to public criticism, not with a defence of its own position, but with an attack on the credibility of the critics. This is generally achieved through the authoritative definition of them as 'naive', 'ill-informed', or even 'stupid'. The label itself is of little consequence provided it succeeds in discrediting the critics. Take, for example, the response of one elite member at a council meeting following a radical attack on the power of the Policy subcommittee: 'I'm sorry,' he replied, 'that a young man like Councillor X should talk such rubbish in public. It makes him out to be a bigger fool than everybody knew already.'

It should come as no surprise that in such battles between competing definitions of political reality, the power of the protagonists generally counts for more than the weight of their respective arguments. As

Berger and Luckmann have observed, 'The success of particular conceptual machineries is related to the power possessed by those who operate them. . . . He who has the bigger stick has the better chance of imposing his definitions of reality' (1966, pp. 126–7). In the present case, it is the political elite which holds all the trump cards, not least of which is the crucial support of the local press which has consistently criticized the 'stupidity' of the radicals' attacks (e.g. 'There was a touch of childishness in some of the Labour attacks at Monday's meeting of Croydon council', 'I can't make up my mind whether they are naive, really kept so much in the dark, or hoping to prove their presence to reporters', and so on). The political elite continues to enjoy the power, and the Labour radicals have provided little more than a minor irritation in their enjoyment of it.

In one particular area, however the radicals' refusal to play by the rules of the game has brought about a significant change in the way in which decisions are made. This concerns the relationship between their leaders and the members of the political elite. Thus although the informal consultations and bargaining have continued since 1971, the Labour leaders' manifest failure to provide a docile opposition has weakened the informal system of political stratification. As one senior Conservative put it, 'Up to a point there is a certain amount of consultation between the party leaders. But Z's control over his group is now minimal, with the result that arrangements agreed in good faith between them often come unstuck.' The system of political stratification has therefore been weakened.

But despite this, the political elite remains powerful. It easily controls its own majority party group, it has successfully harnessed the council bureaucracy, and it still enjoys the tacit cooperation of the Labour leadership in maintaining an impression of consensus and rationality in policy-making. The political elite may not be in a position to do as it likes, but as regards its position in the internal organization of the local authority, it can usually get what it wants.

The local council: external relations

We saw that Pahl's later work on urban managerialism led him to identify local managers as mediating between two sets of external political forces – central government on the one hand, and pressures from the local population on the other (see page 169). This argument is useful in that it directs our attention to two distinct aspects of the external environment of the local state. The first concerns the relationship between the local state and higher level authorities, and in Croydon this means principally the Greater London Council and central government. The second concerns the relationship between the local state and different groups in the local population, and in Croydon the principal groups can be crudely classified as the working class in the council estates and in the declining areas in the north of the borough, the middle class in the suburban areas in the east and south, and the town centre business interests.

The three chapters which follow are concerned with tracing the effects of these two sets of forces in the external environment of the local state in Croydon through an analysis of local policy-making in a variety of fields including education, planning, social services, housing and local taxation. The question of the relationship of the local authority to its external environment is thus approached empirically by examining both those cases where local autonomy has been constrained by, say, GLC planning policies or central government fiscal policies, and those where local policies have come to reflect local direct or indirect political pressure. The question to be addressed in the remainder of this chapter, however, is how the internal organization of the local state affects the way in which external pressures come to be exerted upon it.

The starting point for this analysis is Offe's observation that, 'One can only have power over something which according to its own structure *allows power to be exercised upon it* and responds to it' (1974, p. 35). As regards its relation to higher level authorities, of course, the local state is necessarily constituted in such a way that it is largely responsive to pressure from above, for as Hambleton (1978) points out, local authorities enjoy power only in so far as central government is content that they should. This is not to say that local authorities are merely the agents of central government, for as we saw in Chapter 4 they may enjoy a considerable area of discretion, but it is to recognize that they are *subordinate* to central government, with the result that the question of their relative responsiveness is a question of the degree to which they can *resist* pressures from above. The relationship with the local population is, however, entirely different, for here the local council is *superordinate*, with the result that the question of its responsiveness is a question of the degree to which it is *open* to diverse pressures from below. As Offe suggests, this therefore leads to an analysis of the mechanisms whereby particular pressures are selected as being pertinent for political consideration. It is this selectivity which is crucial for determining the relationship between the local state and the local population.

In Chapter 1, I suggested that an important clue to the nature of such selection procedures could be found in the routine interpretive practices of those in positions of power. Referring principally to Dearlove's work in Kensington and Chelsea, I showed how different groups in the local population could be included within or excluded from the local policy-making process according to council members' definitions of their 'respectability', and how these definitions in turn reflected the types of demands which were being made. Those who posed a challenge to the status quo were generally defined as unrespectable and were thus excluded; those whose demands were consistent with the status quo were seen as respectable (or in Poulantzas's terms, rational rather than utopian) and were therefore given a voice in the local political system. Much the same argument has been shown to apply to the relationship between the party groups on Croydon council, with the right-wing Labour leadership being taken into the confidence of the political elite while the left-wing radicals are dismissed as faintly ridiculous. And the same conclusion emerges again when we consider the relationship between the political elite and different groups in the local community.

During interviews with leading council members in Croydon, concern was expressed time and again with the need for local groups to be 'responsible' in their actions and 'moderate' in their demands. According to one informant, for example, 'The opinions of all *responsible* organizations are listened to in matters of particular interest to them', while one of the senior Labour members suggested that, 'Any local organization or pressure group can be influential if they go about it *in the right way.*' Furthermore, it soon became apparent that the 'right way' for a 'responsible' group to behave was similar to the way in which the Labour opposition within the council was expected to behave. Quiet discussions and informal meetings were much preferred to loud demands and highly visible public demonstrations. As one member of the Policy sub-committee explained, 'The most effective means of influencing the council is by backstairs pressure. . . . Demonstrating outside the town hall cuts no ice with me.'

The most obvious problem, of course, is that many groups will not be able to find the 'backstairs'; for them, public protest is virtually the only available channel of political action. Few members of the less privileged strata in society are to be found proposing toasts at civic luncheons, rubbing shoulders with councillors at the Rotary Club, or buying a round of drinks at the nineteenth hole. Indeed, those (such as some of Croydon's tenants' association leaders discussed in Chapter 7) who do manage to achieve access do so only on the terms laid down by those who control the local authority; i.e. they are accepted as 'responsible' only for so long as they keep their demands within the limits of local authority tolerance.

Yet the picture is very different as regards the more privileged groups in the population. For them the doors are wide open and they have no need to demonstrate their views in public. Indeed, when they do act publicly (as in the case of some of the middle class movements discussed in Chapter 6), we may be justified in suspecting that this is with the tacit consent of the local political elite rather than a direct challenge to it. As we shall see in subsequent chapters, representatives of the suburban middle class (to some extent) and of town centre business interests (to a very large extent) enjoy a close and informal relationship with those in positions of power locally, and their interests are in any case frequently taken into account by local policy-making irrespective of whether they actually use these contacts in an attempt to influence the council.

The strategies which may be available to different local groups for pursuing their interests in relation to the local state may therefore be understood to vary along a continuum between conciliatory action (which in most cases will come to be defined as 'responsible') and coercive action (i.e. attempts to force concessions – a strategy which in most cases will come to be defined as 'irresponsible'). These strategies can only be explained with reference to the interests of the different groups in question, and here it is necessary to distinguish those whose interests are broadly consistent with current state policies and those whose interests run counter to them. Thus we can identify four typical sets of relationships between a local authority and different groups in the local population – political partnership and tactical protest in the case of those whose interests are broadly consistent with local policies, competing agreement and non-competing contradiction in the case of those whose interests are not. When political inactivity is also taken into account, two more types result which, following Parkin (1974), can be termed political communion among those with an identity of interests, and political exclusion among those whose interests are incommensurate.

Political strategies and the selectivity of the local state

		Congruence of interests	
		High	*Low*
	Conciliatory	Political partnership	Competing agreement
Political strategy	*Coercive*	Tactical protest	Non-competing contradiction
	Inactivity	Political communion	Political exclusion

Political partnership refers to those situations where a group shares common interests with those in positions of power and adopts conciliatory strategies (e.g. informal negotiations) in an attempt to ensure that particular issues are resolved in a mutually acceptable fashion. It is therefore premised on a broad consensus over general policy questions, the only issue being how best to achieve common objectives. In its most pronounced form, political partnership corresponds to Winkler's concept of corporatism, and as we shall see in Chapter 8, it is perhaps the most characteristic type of relationship between business interests and the local authority in Croydon. Competing agreement (the term is taken from Mathiesen 1974), by contrast, refers to the relationship between a local authority and those groups which do not share its interests but which are nevertheless concerned to limit their actions to those sanctioned by the rules of access. Competing agreement thus refers to what Castells terms 'participatory movements', and in Croydon this type of relationship is most marked in the case of local tenants' associations and community associations (discussed in Chapter 7).

Tactical protest is most likely to occur where those in positions of power locally are constrained to act in a way in which they themselves disagree. As we shall see in Chapter 6, for example, the local authority in Croydon has on a number of occasions been obliged to introduce policies which damage the interests of suburban middle class groups owing to pressure from central government or the GLC. In such circumstances, protests among those affected have been condoned or encouraged in order to strengthen the bargaining power of the local authority against the higher authority. Tactical protest thus refers to the use of coercive strategies in a supportive role, and it differs markedly from non-competing contradiction (again the term is Mathiesen's) which refers to the use of coercive strategies in situations of genuine conflict. In this latter case, groups mobilize against some aspect of local policy by ignoring the rules of access, either because such access is not available to them, or because they anticipate that a participatory strategy would result in failure. Non-competing contradiction thus corresponds to Castells's definition of the protest movement, and examples will be discussed in Chapter 7.

The final two types of relationship refer to those situations where groups do not act at all. Political communion is based on a genuinely authoritative relationship as defined in Chapter 1 – no action is taken because those in power are already acting in the interests of those concerned – and as such, this type of relationship can adequately be explained with reference to representational theories of the state (discussed in Chapter 4). In Croydon, political communion can be identified in the relation between both local business interests and suburban middle class interests and the local authority. Political exclusion, on the other hand, refers to those instances where a potential conflict fails to become manifest. In some cases, this may reflect the impact of ideology – i.e. groups do not act because they fail to recognize any potential conflict – but it would be wrong to suggest, as Cowley and his co-authors seem to do, that the failures of community action can be put down to the inability of lower class groups to overcome 'bourgeois ideology' (1977, p. 13). This is not to deny the relevance of ideology, but it is to suggest, with Offe (1974), that such failures may better be explained through analysis of the way in which certain policies and certain interests are systematically excluded through the internal organization of the local state itself.

There is, therefore, a direct and intimate relationship between the interests of specific groups, the way in which they express, or fail to express, these interests, and the degree to which their interests come to be reflected in the local policy-making process. Clearly the vertical axis in the typology set out above will generally be more salient than the horizontal axis in determining political outcomes – what you want tends to be more important than how you go about getting it – but the rules of selectivity are such that those groups who pose a potential challenge to the status quo are obliged to confront an irresolvable dilemma in terms of their choice of strategy. It is, therefore, only by analysing the mechanisms of selectivity which operate at the level of strategies that it is possible to develop an understanding of the mechanisms of bias which operate at the level of interests. And as Offe points out, such an understanding will, in the final analysis, only become evident by considering those cases where particular groups have come to confront the power of the state. It is to a consideration of these cases that the next three chapters are devoted.

6   The deep south

Croydon is a town of two halves. With a population in 1971 of just over one-third of a million, it is the largest of all London's boroughs. Indeed, at a time when most parts of the capital are rapidly depopulating, Croydon's population has continued to rise, registering an increase of ten thousand through the 1960s. Croydon is, furthermore, among the richest boroughs in London. Its high rateable value (over £64 million in 1973) is in part a reflection of the large-scale commercial development which has taken place in the town in recent years (see Chapter 8), but it also reflects a high level of relative prosperity among many householders in the borough. But to say that Croydon is a growing, thriving, and prosperous town is to overlook the considerable differences which exist between different sections of its population. Foremost among these is the division between the mainly working class residents of the north and west, and the mainly middle class residents of the south and east.

The southern half of the borough, consisting mainly of the old Purley and Coulsdon Urban District, forms part of London's stockbroker belt. Housing here is almost exclusively owner-occupied, and housing densities are low. Property values, on the other hand, are high, and the housing in this area ranges from sobre but somewhat uninspiring rows of suburban semi's to magnificent multi-bedroomed mansions standing aloof and secluded among their private tennis courts and carefully-tended lawns. The pervading atmosphere of southern wards such as Coulsdon, Sanderstead, and Kenley is one of affluence if not opulence, a comfortable prosperity if not an indiscrete privilege.

It takes only a few minutes on the suburban line to London, however, for the scenery to change completely. The areas to the north of the town centre are characterized by rows of late Victorian terraced houses, dull inter-war council estates, and larger houses in once-fashionable areas now intermingled with an array of small workshops and factories. There are few slums, but the dominant atmosphere of most of the northern wards is one of gradual decay and degeneration. The greatest and most visible contrast between north and south concerns space. Housing densities in areas such as Thornton Heath and South Norwood in the north of the borough are generally high, while greenery is for the most part confined behind park railings. The most that the residents of Coulsdon and South Norwood have in common is that they both pay their rates to the same local authority.

This ecological pattern, and the inequalities which it displays, is in large part a reflection of the historical development of the town. The town's expansion began in the mid-nineteenth century, following the establishment of a rail link to London in 1839. The population increased from 5000 in 1801 to 30,000 sixty years later, and during this period, the central focus of the town shifted away from the original settlement (to the west of the present town centre) towards higher ground to the east. Prosperous Victorians were attracted in considerable numbers to the developing east side with its good drainage, fine views, and direct link to the capital. With the break-up of a number of local estates around the turn of the century, further piecemeal development took place around the periphery of the town, and as the population continued to expand through the twentieth century (reaching two hundred thousand by 1921), additional land was opened up for housing development in areas further out. No less than 30,000 new houses were built in the borough in the inter-war years, many of them in newly developing middle class suburbs some three or four miles out of the town centre. The ecological structure of the borough today thus stands as the result of the largely pragmatic and unco-ordinated development over the last hundred years or more.

The question, however, is not so much how the present pattern of residential inequalities and disparities evolved, as how it has been maintained. As Suttles (1972) has pointed out, the stringent application of zoning regulations, density provisions, conservationist policies, and the like may provide a highly significant tool by means of which existing imbalances between the facilities and desirability of different residential areas may consistently be reinforced. It is necessary, then, to consider the extent to which current planning policy in Croydon serves to maintain existing disparities between north and south, and thereby to reflect the interests of property-owners in the more prosperous and advantaged parts of the borough. To this end, I shall first consider the extent to which suburban middle class groups in Croydon have managed successfully to preserve or enhance their relative privileges through political organization and action.

The suburban middle class and the political elite

The first point to note is that the suburban middle class in the southern wards of the borough is generally very efficiently organized. Every ward in the area boasts at least one residents' association, and in most cases, the density of membership of such associations is high – one claimed a 95 per cent paid-up membership of all eligible households. Total memberships in excess of one thousand households are not uncommon. Such associations are, furthermore, often highly bureaucratic. One, for example, was led by a committed and very dedicated chairman at the head of a twelve-man executive committee. Below the committee was a stratum of forty 'road marshals', one for every principal road in the area, whose job it was to collect subscriptions, canvas for new members, and act as intermediaries, relaying information, opinions, and policy suggestions between the committee and the rank-and-file. Below them was an active membership of some 1500 households. This particular association was, in addition, one of eight in the south of the borough affiliated to the Federation of Southern Croydon Residents' Associations, an umbrella group with a collective active membership of 17,000 families.

Clearly, only a small proportion of those who belong to southern residents' groups plays an active part in determining their actions and formulating their policies. Indeed, in some cases it was apparent that, not only were Annual General Meetings to some extent regulated by the careful planning and management of association leaders, but committee meetings too were dominated by a small core of activists. That two or three leaders can effectively control associations with 1000 or more members is by no means indicative of apathy or disinterest among the rank-and-file, however. As we shall see, the suburban middle class has at times exhibited an extraordinary consciousness of its own interests, and has proved itself quite willing to engage in political action when the occasion has called for it.

Rather, the power enjoyed by association leaders reflects their privileged access to local councillors and council officers. In a very real sense, they control their members because they have the capacity to speak for them.

Despite the considerable size of their memberships, the greater part of these associations' political activities occur on an individual and personal level. As Eckstein has noted in his discussion of pressure group politics, 'The most important pressure group activities are not carried on by formally constituted committees, but by spontaneous contact among small numbers of individuals who are in a position to commit those whom they represent' (1960, p. 88). Indeed, we may follow Peter Worsley (1964) in arguing that public pressure group activity may often be interpreted, not in terms of political strength, but of political weakness, for it will usually indicate that less visible channels of influence are either not available, or else have been tried and found wanting. It is significant, then, that the southern residents' associations' leaders have rarely found it necessary to mobilize the numerical support of their organizations in pursuit of political gains.

The significance of face-to-face contacts relative to the mere fact of numerical strength is well illustrated by the case of one very small residents' association based on just two roads, and led by only one man. This association has successfully managed to protect its members' interests (e.g. over proposals for new housing development in the area) due almost entirely to the wide range of personal contacts enjoyed by its leader with a variety of council members and officers. This one man claimed to know on a personal basis a number of chief officers and many elected members: 'Most of the past Mayors have sat in this room and had cups of tea.' Whenever a local issue or complaint has been brought to his notice, he has known exactly who to contact, and following an informal telephone conversation or a personal visit, action by the council has usually been forthcoming.

Many groups include within their memberships local council members, and in such cases this direct voice in the council chamber may prove of considerable value. One association, for example, counted among its membership the chairman of the Planning committee, and this clearly inspired some confidence among the leadership when they became involved in issues (such as housing densities) relating to council policies. Another included an influential member of the Development Control committee who was always concerned to inform the association of any proposals relating to its area, and to give voice to the association's reaction and comments. Direct contacts such as these have proved of greater value than the letters and formal protests of less well-connected groups. As one Conservative member observed, 'A word in the right direction does the job.' Or in the candid words of one association leader, 'You do it by getting in the back door.'

Among the best connected of the middle class organizations in the borough are the local ratepayers' associations. As late as 1960, the council was controlled by 'independent' members (invariably of right-wing persuasion) representing various ratepayers' and residents' associations. Throughout the 1960s, however, the number of independents on the council declined dramatically as the Conservative party began to sponsor its own candidates at local elections, first in Labour-controlled wards, and later in conjunction with Ratepayer associations in wards held by independents. Today, only two associations continue to put up candidates. Nevertheless, the leaders of the town's ratepayers' associations, having often themselves served on the council as independents in the past, are in many cases personally acquainted with both members and officers of the local authority. One consequence of this is that they are able to keep well informed of council plans and proposals. In one case, for example, a Highways Department proposal for the introduction of controlled parking in one area of the borough was first sent to the local ratepayers' association leader for his comments. Such a procedure was, apparently, fairly common: 'This is quite usual. Whenever the council are thinking about issues which affect this area, they always let me know, and ask what I think.'

Clearly, the relationship between the leaders of the various residents' and ratepayers' groups in the town and the local authority is a close and relatively privileged one. Contacts are often informal, frequently friendly, and occur within a context of mutual trust and identification. Most members of the majority group on the council are, after all, themselves members of Croydon's suburban middle class. They recognize the *right* of local residents' leaders to be included in consultations at an early stage of any decision likely to affect the interests of their members: 'They should be listened to, consulted, and involved, when they feel they are threatened by some housing proposal,' said the Conservative deputy leader at a recent council meeting. The relationship, in other words, is that identified in Chapter 5 as 'political partnership'. It is a relationship which enables the leaders of the various residents' organizations to press their demands privately in an atmosphere of cordiality and civility. Put another way, it enables them to play by the rules of the game.

This fundamental and underlying consensus of values and interests between suburban middle class groups and the local political élite enables the former to present their demands as 'non-political' and thus as largely non-contentious. All the residents' and ratepayers' organizations proclaim themselves 'non-political', and stress their disinterest in 'ideological' questions and party political issues. 'I was once accused of having a parish pump mentality,' said the secretary of one ratepayers' association, 'but that's what local government is all about.' In this way, what amount to sectional interests and political demands come to be expressed in terms of 'obvious' solutions and 'the public interest'. The open aspects and extensive areas of 'green belt' land in the south of the borough are thus vigilantly protected from development, not in the interests of those who live there and whose property values remain buoyant, but on behalf of all Croydonians. 'I don't see why they cast covetous eyes at our bit of green belt,' complained one association committee member, discussing residents in the north of the borough, 'they can always come and visit it anytime.' This definition of sectional interests as everybody's interests is generally accepted by a local political elite which shares the values and world views of those who promulgate it.

But of course, if these various middle class organizations are 'non-political', they are in no way apolitical. Their members know full well where their interests lie, and do not hesitate to pursue them with little regard for the consequences for other sections of the population in Croydon. The dire shortage of housing in the borough, for example, is seen, not in terms of a problem to be met by further housing development, but rather in terms of the threat which this poses to the unsullied virginity of the green and pleasant land in which they live. Thus the following was found in the minutes of one southern residents' association: 'We noted that Croydon was officially reported to be short of eleven thousand dwellings; agreed to draw the Federation's attention to the danger that may be applied to the green belt.' They need hardly have worried. Local Conservative councillors were swift to reassure a subsequent meeting of residents that they remained hostile to any idea of housing development encroaching on green belt land.

The contacts they enjoy, and the numerical support they command, thus represent two highly significant political resources in the hands of Association leaders. They have two powerful strings to their bow, and in the unlikely event of the first failing, the second can be brought into use. It is interesting in this regard that no less than 50 per cent of Conservative members who replied to a questionnaire survey indicated the view that residents' associations and similar groups were influential 'in determining or affecting the outcome of issues in which they take an interest' (47 per cent of all council members cited the residents' associations as influential – twice as many as those citing the Chamber of Commerce or the party organizations, which were the next two most frequently mentioned organizations).

With the exception of two special cases discussed later, the contacts and sense of fellow-feeling which residents' leaders enjoy with the political élite usually render any further action unnecessary. Occasionally, however, such contacts prove insufficient, and it is then that the mobilization of numerical support can prove a significant 'second string'.

In 1971, for example, the council announced that a school near the centre of Coulsdon was to be relocated elsewhere to make way for a highly lucrative development of 10,000 square feet of offices, a large supermarket, twenty smaller shops, and a car park. The local residents' association, however, recognized the opportunity to press for the provision of various civic amenities in the development, and in 1972, a deputation from the association met four councillors and the Borough Valuer to discuss the proposals. The deputation was informed that a totally commercial redevelopment of the site was necessary in order to finance the reconstruction of the old school, and that both the GLC and Croydon's Plans subcommittee had already accepted the proposal. The decision was as good as made. Undeterred, the association called a meeting of over 500 local residents, to which the Planning committee chairman and the Deputy Director of Development were both invited. Following this meeting, the Strategic Planning subcommittee (a subcommittee of Resources Finance and Policy) met and resolved to include a civic centre in the redevelopment plan. The regular columnist of the local newspaper was overjoyed: 'I think they will get their centre – Coulsdon needs

one – and I congratulate the residents on their demonstration that
people power works. Coulsdon people know that 1984 is still far off.'
'People power', however, seems rather more effective when the
people concerned are southern residents. As we shall see in Chapter
7, the 'people power' enjoyed by council tenants, homeless families,
and the like is rather less spectacular.

Generally, however, visible demonstrations of strength and support
such as occurred over this issue are unnecessary. Indeed, the active
use of personal and informal contacts is often unnecessary too. As
we shall now see, the high degree of consensus which exists between
the local political elite and southern residents means that the latter
rarely have to act at all.

A green and pleasant land

Undoubtedly the main concerns of the suburban middle class and its
organizations relate to the questions of housing densities, green belt
preservation, and the maintenance of a low rate. In each of these
issues, the suburban middle class has generally found that its interests
are congruent with the policies and preferences of the political elite.

At the Greater London Development Plan Inquiry, in April 1972,
Croydon's Deputy Director of Development found himself in the
unenviable position of having to defend and justify the council's
policies on housing densities and green belt preservation in the south
of the borough against GLC demands that more houses should be
built in Croydon in the future. He estimated that the maximum
number of houses which could be built in the borough in the period to
1981 was just 12,000 – between 6000 and 13,000 short of the number
suggested by the GLC. Explaining why Croydon's estimate fell so
much lower than that of the GLC, he spelt out the council's policy,
and it is worth quoting what he said at some length:

We are in a dilemma. The council quite appreciate the fact that they
have to, and would wish to, help with the overall problem of housing in
London, but they have quite firm policies, some of which are the same as
the GLC's, with regard to green belt and open space and building on
allotments. They have also got policies with regard to densities. They are
very concerned that in fact they maintain the environmental standard of
particularly the outer areas of the borough, where you have under present
thinking fairly low densities. They are prepared to consider applications,

and do so, for increases in these densities; but nothing in the region that we are talking about now, and nothing, I do not think, to bring it appreciably nearer to the eighteen thousand target by 1981 [Evidence to the GLDP Inquiry, Day 227].

Nowhere has the political elite's concern with the interests of the suburban middle class been so clearly and concisely outlined as it was at this inquiry.

The Deputy Director of Development went on to explain this policy in more detail. Housing development in the southern stockbroker belt would not be tolerated, he claimed, at densities in excess of three to five houses to the acre (this, it should be noted, represents one-fifth of the density of development on the new council estate at Fieldway, near New Addington). Building on subdivided plots would not generally be permitted, and he admitted that, where residents in southern wards wished to sell part of their gardens for development, 'It is the council's policy that would stop it.'

This policy has been applied on numerous occasions. Indeed, on the very same day as Croydon's Deputy Director of Development was outlining his council's policy to the inquiry, the local newspaper reported that a proposal to build thirty new houses on a plot at Shirley (a middle class area to the east of the town centre) had been rejected by the council. 'The proposal,' said a council official, 'would result in a cramped and overcrowded layout which would be out of character with existing residential development in the locality.' The developer in question then amended his proposal, and applied for permission to build eleven luxury houses on the site, each selling at around £40,000. This revised application was accepted by the council. 'I condemn this type of luxury building with the present housing shortage,' he told the local press later, 'but it is forced on us by snobby planning committees. . . . I feel absolutely bitter about this waste of land in Croydon.'

There have been countless other similar examples in recent years. In March 1973, for example, at a time when housing developments were under way at densities of fifty people per acre in Upper Norwood, and between seventy and seventy-seven people per acre in Thornton Heath (both, it need hardly be added, in the north of the borough), the council passed an application for a development in Kenley (in the south) at a density of just fifteen persons per acre. Local residents had actually complained that even this density was unacceptable. The Labour group on the council criticized the plan, arguing that such low density development represented a serious under-use of available building land, but their comments fell on deaf ears. As one Conservative member explained, Kenley was an area of 'particular natural beauty', and higher density development would necessitate the destruction of many trees.

Similarly, in June 1972, an application to build ninety-six four-bedroomed houses on a sixteen-acre site at Selsdon met stout resistance from the local residents' association, which claimed that, like Kenley, Selsdon was an area of 'outstanding natural beauty', and that a density of six houses per acre was thus unacceptable. Selsdon's three ward representatives on the council agreed, and the application was subsequently rejected. The developers were told informally that they should re-apply with a new scheme involving lower densities, and a second proposal for sixty detached houses, each with double garages, representing a density of four per acre, was later accepted by the council, much to the disgust of one Labour member who described the incident as evidence of 'rule by residents'. 'One wonders,' said another Labour member of a leading Conservative at the same council meeting, 'whether Alderman Y ever goes north of the Town Hall. The town is divided, and the housing densities reflect the social breakdown and political breakdown of this borough. The council has steadfastly refused modest-price housing in the south of the borough. We are dealing in selfishness here.' But the chairman of the Planning committee argued that Croydon needed larger houses as well as smaller ones, while a Selsdon representative claimed that it would be 'nonsense' to permit any higher density development in his area.

Closely related to the question of housing densities is that of green belt preservation, and here too, the political elite's policies closely reflect the views and interests of the southern residents. Croydon council has consistently refused to countenance any housing development on green belt land, even where the sites in question have been of little aesthetic, recreational, or agricultural value. Southern ward councillors have made regular assurances to their local residents' associations that, in the words of one member, 'People will not be allowed to flood into the area to live.' The residents' associations pledged their support to the council in its stand on this issue prior to the GLDP Inquiry, pressing the council to stand firm against the anticipated critical onslaught from the rest of London. If the council supports the southern residents, then the southern residents also support the council.

Opposition to the council's density and green belt policies with regard to the southern wards has been growing of late. Criticism has come, not only from the GLC, the inner London boroughs, and the council's Labour group, but also from less predictable sources, among them the local newspaper, local development companies (the chairman of a large local development company recently criticized what he called the 'green belt sacred cow'), and even certain members of the Conservative group. One northern ward Conservative member, for example, wrote in his constituency magazine, 'The deep south councillors, while always claiming low densities for their own areas, have never championed the same cause for the northern end of the town. . . . As Tories, we believe in the principle of one nation. It follows then that we must have one Croydon.' Pressure from these various quarters has to some extent weakened the resolve of some southern representatives, and their regular assurances about council policy on densities and green belt have sounded rather less assertive of late. 'I will defend the green belt,' said one member at a meeting of Riddlesdown residents, 'but I have got to be realistic. I am not in favour of development on green belt land, but I do believe that small patches of development will take place.' Indeed, Croydon is seen as one of four future growth areas in the overall planning strategy of the GLC, and it is difficult to see how the escalating demand for housing which this implies can for much longer be resisted in the southern wards. Nevertheless, it is clear that for the moment, the risk of alienating the support of local residents is a risk which most southern representatives remain unprepared to take, and for many, the combined wrath of the rest of London appears less daunting and more acceptable than the prospect of deserting policies to which they are themselves personally committed, and in consequence of facing the antagonism of the residents' associations.

The chief beneficiaries of the council's green belt/density policy in the south have of course been the southern residents. Their exclusivity is assured, the pleasant character of their area is maintained, and (by no means least significant) the value of their properties remains buoyant. There have, on the other hand, been many losers – not least the poor or low income groups in Croydon itself and in more deprived parts of London whose housing need is ignored by a policy which ensures that scarce building land is under-utilized through luxury development. Also significant are the indirect losers – those families living in the huddled north of the borough. The argument of the southern residents' associations, that they are protecting the green belt for the benefit of all people in the borough, begins to look somewhat dubious when it is recognized that the tight restrictions on development in the south effectively increase pressure on densities and open spaces in the north. The result is that an already grossly unbalanced situation is further exaggerated, and the few remaining open spaces in the north become prime development sites. The south's hitherto successful defence of its greenery has thus been achieved only at the considerable expense of the north.

As with its green belt and density policies, so too with its policies on rates and council expenditure, the political elite, consciously or unconsciously, follows the interests of the southern residents. As we shall see later in this chapter, the maintenance of a low rate is the second principal concern of the residents' associations and their members. The interests of the suburban middle class do not generally lie in the increased provision of council services. They, after all, rarely have cause to use the local social and welfare services, nor do they rely on the council for their accommodation, and in many cases, their children attend private schools (and even where they do not, the state schools in the southern wards are generally already adequately equipped, unlike some of the older schools in the north). Increased council expenditure, then, would not greatly benefit Croydon's middle class suburban residents.

On the other hand, the interests of the suburban middle class undoubtedly *do* lie in keeping the rate as low as possible. Quite simply, they are among the principal payers, for they own the most desirable and valuable properties. It is significant, then, that at least until 1974/75 (see pages 266–9), the rate levied by Croydon council was consistently one of the lowest in London. In 1972/73, for example, only seven local authorities out of the thirty-two in the GLC area (excluding the City of London) levied a lower rate than that levied by Croydon. The following year, only four of these authorities bettered Croydon in the 'low rate league'. I shall consider some of the consequences of this later and in Chapter 7, but here we need only note that the inverted Robin Hood role adopted by Croydon council over the years, giving as little as possible to the poor, and leaving the rich to enjoy their prosperity, is entirely congruent with the interests of the southern middle class.

We have seen that the community of interest shared by the political elite and the suburban middle class has generally resulted in the adoption of policies favourable to the latter, and has thus rendered further action on their part unnecessary. There are, however, two situations in which middle class residents may be obliged to engage in more direct forms of political action in order to safeguard their interests. The first is where they come into conflict with other powerful interests within the borough, or where they themselves are divided over a given issue. We have already seen a minor example of this in relation to the development squabble in Coulsdon, and the conflict which arose there between commercial interests and the council on the one hand, and local residents on the other. The second is where the support or sponsorship of the local council is not enough to secure the safeguarding of their interests – i.e. where the final decision on a given issue does not lie with Croydon's decision-makers. I shall first consider the situation where powerful interests within the borough are split, and then in the next section of this chapter go on to analyse a number of cases where outside intervention has necessitated the mobilization of the suburban middle class.

The most obvious and illuminating example in recent years of a division between different (and usually allied) powerful interests in Croydon concerns a bitter conflict which occurred in 1973/74 between the defenders of the suburban middle class interest and the governors and supporters of an organization known as the Whitgift Foundation.

In Chapter 5, I mentioned the historic link which exists between the Canterbury archbishopric and the town of Croydon. A particularly strong facet of this link is that with the name of Archbishop Whitgift who, during his period in the town at the Old Palace, founded a hospital for the poor in 1596 (which still stands today in a central site in the town), and a school for the poor four years later. Today, the Foundation which he established owns not only the hospital (which is now used to accommodate a number of elderly people) and the original school site (which, as we shall see in Chapter 8, now accommodates a large shops and office block complex in the town centre), but also the independent Whitgift School at South Croydon, and the Trinity School of John Whitgift at Shirley, as well as over one hundred acres of parkland at Croham Hurst in the south, the Old Whitgiftians sports grounds in South Croydon, and a number of other sites in the town centre including those of the Central Swimming Baths and of one of the town's largest office blocks. In the early 1970s, a Labour councillor estimated the total assets of the Foundation at around £30 million.

The Foundation is administered by fifteen governors, and until 1974, seven of these were drawn from the membership of the majority Conservative group on Croydon council. Among these seven were some of the most powerful men on the council – the leader and deputy-leader of the council, the chairman of the Education committee (who was also a member of the Policy subcommittee), the chairman of the Plans subcommittee, the chairman of the Development Control committee, and the chairman of the Health committee. Also among the governors of the Foundation were the Bishop of Croydon, two local magistrates, an Old-Whitgiftian, and a number of 'élite' educationalists including the secretary of Kings College and the former headmaster of Westminster School.

By virtue both of the landed wealth which it controls, and the contacts it enjoys with the political elite through densely overlapping memberships, the Whitgift Foundation has traditionally been a potentially powerful institution in the political structure of the town. Certainly the Labour group on the council sees it as such – 36 per cent of Labour respondents cited it as a significant and influential body in the borough. As one Labour member put it at a council meeting in 1973, 'I'm concerned about the relationship between the council and the Foundation. It's not that we have no control over the Foundation, but the control which the Whitgift has over this council chamber.' Similarly, one of his colleagues, referring to the Foundation at the same council meeting, claimed, 'There is in this town a power structure that is undermining the work of this council. The council do not run this town.' The issue which prompted these remarks was the protracted struggle occurring at this time over a Foundation proposal for development on two of its sites in the south of the borough.

In order to understand this issue, it is necessary to realize that the Whitgift Foundation, a registered charity since 1969, stands today as a powerful symbol and supporter of private and selective education. With the introduction of a comprehensive system of secondary education in Croydon, for example, the Foundation had in the late 1960s declared the erstwhile grant-aided Trinity School independent, while the second Whitgift School was already independent. The rejection of the grant was a step which ensured the school's continuing status as a grammar school at a time of growing uncertainty regarding the future of direct grant schools, and it was a step which the Foundation could fairly easily afford to take. In the 1960s, as we shall see in Chapter 8, the site of the old Trinity school had been leased for highly lucrative commercial development, and the annual income of the Foundation had been boosted considerably as a result (£536,000 in 1973, compared with a 1945 figure of just £20,000). This additional income was used primarily to support the two schools (50 per cent of the 1945 income was expended on the schools, compared with 80 per cent today).

Given its strong financial base, and the secure status of its two independent schools, many observers in Croydon were perplexed when, in December 1972, the Foundation announced a proposal to the effect that the forty-year-old buildings of the Whitgift school in South Croydon were to be demolished to make way for development on the site (known as Haling Park), and a new school was to be built on part of the parkland at Croham Hurst. The proposal, which it was estimated would realize a profit of between £5 million and £8 million, was justified by the Foundation on the grounds that the existing school was too small, and the Haling Park site too restricted for the necessary expansion to take place there. This explanation was not readily accepted by others in the town, however. The former chairman of the Foundation, Sir James Marshall, stated publicly, 'I think it's a most stupid scheme. If they have got to make alterations to the school, they have plenty of room to do it, and they have plenty of money to pay for it', while the local newspaper's regular columnist suggested greed as the Foundation's true motive: 'One is left with the impression that the wealthy Foundation want to realize a valuable capital asset. This they have done before with brilliant success with the old Trinity school grounds. To attempt a second coup in the different circumstances of Haling Park smacks of greed.'

In fact, the Foundation appears to have had two principal motives for its Haling Park/Croham Hurst plans. One, certainly, was its desire to improve facilities at the already copiously-endowed Whitgift school. Thus it transpired later that a DES report had pointed out a number of minor faults in the provisions at the school, and this undoubtedly led the governors to consider the possibilities of expansion or reconstruction elsewhere. But in addition, it became clearer as time went by that they also entertained ideas about taking one or two local direct-grant schools under their protective independent wing, thus delivering them from the threat of future state control or insolvency. The prospect of a profit of several million pounds on development of some sort at Haling Park, taken with the possibilities of building a large independent school campus at Croham Hurst which could encompass a new Whitgift school and perhaps another newly independent school as well, was obviously attractive to many of the governors. The Conservative council members sitting on the Foundation were certainly keen to maintain and extend a thriving private education sector in the borough. So too was the Foundation's chairman, himself also a governor of a local direct grant school. And so, for that matter, were the staff and governors of a number of direct grant schools in the town. As the chairman of the governors of one such school coyly put it at the annual speech day in 1973, 'Private independent schools of similar aims and ideals and of comparable qualities, having their establishments in close proximity, should combine their strength and resources against ever-increasing political and other pressures. Nevertheless, from past experience we also know that financial pressures can occur. . . . It is for this reason that we welcome the closest association with the Whitgift Foundation.'

Whether or not the scheme was devised in an attempt to strengthen and extend private education in the borough, it met with intense local hostility. The local press was among the first to comment, arguing that any development at either Haling Park or Croham Hurst 'must surely be resisted'. Croydon simply could not afford to lose more open space or to attract more people into its already over-crowded boundaries. Precisely the same sentiments were voiced by the suburban middle class, particularly worried by virtue of the fact that both proposed developments threatened the greenery of the south of the town. The Croham Hurst Golf Club, upset at the prospect of its greens disappearing under tons of concrete, announced its hostility, enlisted the support of the Golf Development Council and the Sports Council, and mounted a campaign under the poetically dubious but definitively assertive slogan: 'Keep Croydon Green –

Say NO to the Whitgift Scheme.' The Selsdon residents' association swiftly added its support to the campaign, and enlisted the combined opposition of the Federation of Southern Croydon Residents' Associations.

At the outset, the issue was defined by different participants in different ways. Thus it was variously represented as an issue about development in the south, about the future of independent schooling in the borough as a whole, and about the morality and financial wisdom of the Foundation's attempt to make a second fortune out of commercial development of its assets. The fact that the proposals could be assessed and understood in a variety of different ways was significant. It meant, for example, that Labour members found themselves in the dilemma of whether to demand the retention of the status quo, and thus align themselves with the suburban middle class residents in their attempts to retain the open space at Croham Hurst, or whether to support the Foundation and thereby associate themselves with the private education lobby. They attempted to resolve their dilemma by arguing that if the scheme did go ahead, then the land released at Haling Park for development should be used either for a new comprehensive school, or for council housing. Effectively, however, the Labour group played hardly any significant role throughout the issue. They were simply onlookers to a conflict played out almost entirely within the town's middle class interest groups. Furthermore, the conflict between the interests of private education on the one hand, and the interests of southern residents on the other, led to divisions within both the political elite and the Foundation governors. Thus it became clear very early on that the Foundation's decision was far from unanimous, and that leading members of the majority group (who were also Whitgift governors) were hopelessly split. The deputy-leader of the council, for example, stated, 'It seems to me crazy to pull down the school in order to sell the land for some other purpose and build another school', while one of his fellow governors, the chairman of the Development Control committee, announced, 'I am bitterly disappointed from the point of view of the town. It seems to me there is one god at the moment – and that is money. . . . The Whitgift Foundation have done very well out of the town and are obviously going to do a lot better.' Both of these members, it should be noted, represented southern wards. The leader of the council, however (who represented a northern ward), supported the proposals, largely on the educational argument.

Within a few weeks of the Foundation's plans being published, a formidable coalition of opposition had been drawn up against them. Of particular importance here was the local press, not only for its insistent editorial criticism ('Although there was a time when the Foundation could count on the town taking a deferential and obliging attitude toward them, that is not the case today'), but also for its willingness to make pages upon pages available for reports on all the various opponents of the scheme. The *Croydon Advertiser* enjoys what amounts to a local monopoly over the dissemination of news in the town, and its coverage of the Whitgift issue in the early weeks succeeded in creating an impression of almost universal hostility to the scheme. It has, of course, been recognized by many sociologists that 'news' is to a large extent created, rather than reported, and it is clear that much of the opposition was in this sense 'manufactured'. The *Advertiser*'s initial hostility to the Whitgift plan thus proved crucial, for it provided a platform by means of which opponents of the proposals could successfully define the issue as one of development, and represent it as a case of the Foundation against the rest of Croydon.

Perhaps the best example of this occurred in January 1973, when the venerated ex-chairman of the Foundation, Sir James Marshall, again spoke out against the scheme. 'I have offered to help Croham Hurst Golf Club, Croham Valley residents, Haling Park residents, and the Old Boys of the school to oppose this scheme at every step,' he said. 'I think it's a most stupid scheme.' His comments received extraordinary press coverage, making the front page headlines, stimulating two separate articles on inside pages, provoking a sympathetic discussion by the paper's resident columnist, and dominating the editorial. 'If they care at all for public opinion,' proclaimed the editor, implying that Sir James was in some way the personification of such opinion in the borough, 'the Whitgift governors should heed the warning of their former chairman.' In addition to demonstrating that if deference to the Foundation was now dead, deference to Sir James most certainly was not, this extensive press coverage also indicates how local battle lines were being drawn. Nowhere in all those column inches did a favourable word appear for the Foundation, its scheme, or its governors (who by now were effectively cast in the mould of arrogant public enemies).

As opposition grew, so press coverage of it expanded in direct proportion. Other residents' associations entered the fray. The chairman of the Federation of Southern Croydon Residents' Associations announced his federation's intention to 'be part of the fight'. The Member of Parliament for Croydon South, Sir Richard Thompson, wrote an open letter to the chairman of the Foundation, citing widespread public opposition as sufficient reason for a change in heart:

I must tell you candidly that in over twenty years I can hardly recall a proposal which has aroused more misgiving and dismay in Croydon. . . . This great school, of which generations of Croydonians are justly proud, ought to be allowed to remain on its present site . . . the Whitgift Foundation, which occupies a very special place in the estimation of Croydon people, surely ought not to take the lead in a process which must destroy the enjoyment of two vital amenity areas. . . . I hope very much that in the light of all the public reaction to their proposals, the governors may now have second thoughts about pursuing them.

Neither Sir Richard, nor the *Advertiser*, nor any other of the guardians of the public interest and spokesmen for public opinion apparently conceived of the possibility that many Croydonians, especially those in the north of the borough, may possibly have preferred to see a new housing development at Haling Park, and may have been totally disinterested in the fate of the golf links at Croham Hurst.

By March 1973, when the council's Plans subcommittee was eventually convened to consider the proposals, the possibility of a Foundation victory looked even more remote. Following intense pressure from the local press, two more councillors with seats on the Foundation's governing body had publicly announced their opposition to the scheme, among them the chairman of the Plans subcommittee. Both members had previously expressed their support in their roles as governors, but now, in their roles as councillors, they changed not only hats but opinions, and expressed their opposition. 'As councillors,' they explained in a letter to the local newspaper, 'we have to have regard for the known considerable opposition by residents, and intend to vote against it.' This change of heart says something, of course, not only for the persuasiveness of the *Advertiser*, but also for the importance attached by southern ward members to the interests of the suburban middle class. It also meant, as the local paper gleefully noted, that among the Whitgift governors, five now opposed the scheme and two refused to align themselves publicly, while of those governors who also had seats on the council, only one – the leader of the majority group – now openly supported it.

Predictably, the Plans subcommittee engaged in the strategy of which Bachrach and Baratz have written, and failed to make a decision. While the chairman of the committee was a newly converted anti, the vice-chairman (also – incredibly – a Whitgift governor) was uncommitted publicly, but was privately in favour. They called, instead, for further details, and then donned their governors' hats and retreated to consider the situation. For four months, they and their fellow governors, already divided among themselves, were left to ponder the formidable coalition aligned against them in defence of the interests of the suburban middle class – leading members of the majority group, all the southern residents' associations, Sir James Marshall, Sir Richard Thompson, the Whitgift Old Boys, the Sports Council, Croham Hurst Golf Club, and, cementing the coalition together, the *Croydon Advertiser*.

In July, the Foundation made a valiant but by then vain attempt to fight back. In its further submissions to the council, it rested its case on the 1971 DES report on the conditions at the Whitgift school. Four criticisms had apparently been made of the school – namely, that the junior and senior sections should be better segregated, that classrooms were outdated, that sports facilities were indequate, and that there was a lack of handicraft facilities. Although there was no suggestion of DES recognition being withdrawn on these grounds, and although the report was unofficial, the governors felt that improvements would have to be made at a cost of £1 million, and they argued that the Foundation's resources would be stretched if this money had to be met from existing funds and income. This would then result in higher fees and fewer scholarships.

Reading all this, some parents in Croydon may perhaps have wondered why it was that a forty-year-old school, set in beautiful grounds with its own indoor heated swimming pool, needed so much money spent on it so quickly, when a number of state primary schools in the north of the borough were over a hundred years old, desperately short of classrooms and teachers, and graced with dilapidated outdoor lavatories, yet were apparently found quite acceptable by the same government department. Any such thoughts, however, were swiftly anticipated and dealt with by the *Advertiser*. 'The report was clearly a blow to Croydon's prestige independent school,' it explained.

In fact, following the Foundation's public explanation of its cause, the local newspaper began to adopt a rather less antagonistic attitude. The Foundation had promised to landscape any developments at both Haling Park and Croham Hurst, and this, together with its assurance that wooded areas would be preserved, went some way to meeting the southern environmental objection. Furthermore, in demonstrating the need for additional capital to 'maintain standards', and in promising that some of the capital so raised would be used to improve conditions for those old people living at the almshouses in the town centre, the Foundation demonstrated (at least to the *Advertiser*'s satisfaction) that its motives were anything but those of greed. Finally, a suggestion that the Croham Hurst site could be used for two new independent schools struck the paper's editor as eminently sensible. Indeed, he was altogether very impressed: 'We must admit that the detailed plans now put forward by the Whitgift Foundation are more acceptable than the bald announcement made originally that the Whitgift school was to be re-built at Croham Hurst. . . . Now they reveal that they have a case – in many ways a convincing case.'

This Damascus-like conversion came too late to have much effect on the subsequent course of events, however. The suburban middle class batteries had already done irreparable damage to the Foundation's cause. At the next meeting of the Plans subcommittee, both the Haling Park and Croham Hurst applications were unanimously rejected. A Town Hall spokesman, commenting on the three hundred letters of protest (representing around 0.01 per cent of the borough's total population) received by the council, was moved to say, 'In nearly thirty years' local government service, I have never known such opposition.' An unofficial report from GLC planning officers, and an official report from Croydon's Strategic Planning subcommittee, also came out against the scheme, despite the fact that four of the seven members of the latter were also Foundation governors. By the time the full Development Control committee met in September, the result was virtually certain. Development proposals for both sites were rejected, the principal reasons given being the designation of Croham Hurst as green belt, the loss of recreational land, the adverse effect on amenities in the south, and the 'threat' posed by the proposals to the 'natural environment'.

At the full council meeting in October, the Development Control committee's recommendations were accepted by forty-nine votes to three, with six abstentions (four of which were those of Whitgift governors). The Labour group made a belated attempt to criticize the grounds on which the plans had been rejected, and notably the decision that the golf course should be retained. But the deputy-leader of the council claimed, in the words of the newspaper's report of the meeting, 'that although there were plenty of golf courses in Croydon, they had to be looked at in the context of South London as a whole where there was a great deprivation,' while one of his colleagues argued that, 'The land should not be taken for housing which was being provided in new towns. The loss of another golf course would be disastrous.'

Paradoxically, this issue – one of the rare occasions on which the suburban middle class has been obliged to act publicly in response to a challenge to its interests from within the borough – perhaps illustrates better than anything else how the interests of the southern residents are generally anticipated and represented by the political elite, and thus how they come authoritatively to be defined as the 'public interest'. Even where they find themselves in opposition to a proposal which would strengthen private education in the borough (an aim close to the hearts of many Conservative council members), and up against an organization as powerful and well connected as the Whitgift Foundation, their interest in retaining the privileges of open space, green belt, and uncluttered views, prevails. As for the Whitgift Foundation itself, it came out of this issue severely bruised as a result of its attempt to challenge these interests. Shortly after the council's decision, it proposed that the formal link with the council be severed, and the council agreed that, in future, no seats on the Foundation's governing body would be reserved for council nominees. Then in December, the Foundation announced its intention to appeal against the refusal of planning permission, thus effectively removing the issue from local hands. Locally, the Whitgift Foundation had received a bloody nose for perhaps the first time.

The middle class up against it?

Appeal to public inquiries is one example of how decisions affecting Croydon may come to be removed from the context of local decision-making. In this last section of this chapter, I wish to consider the political actions adopted by suburban middle class interests in just this sort of situation. It will be remembered that earlier I suggested that there were two situations in which the southern residents, despite their community of interests shared with the local political elite, may be obliged to engage in open and public political action. The case of a split, such as occurred in the Whitgift issue, was one. The case of the removal of decision-making out of the town altogether was the other.

I wish to consider three examples where this has happened, and to analyse the suburban middle class response in each case. The examples I shall take reflect the range of principal concerns of the southern residents – planning inquiries, the introduction of comprehensive education, and the level of the rate support grant. In all three instances, I wish to argue that, despite frequent appearances to the contrary, the response of the town's middle class can best be interpreted in terms of 'tactical protest' – i.e. public protest whose manifest aims may in some way differ from its latent objectives.

I have already mentioned how, in 1965, Croydon lost its relatively independent County Borough status, to become one of thirty-two London boroughs under the higher-tier Greater London Council. Of course, local autonomy had been progressively eroded long before this. In 1933, for example, control of public transport passed out of local hands to the newly constituted London Passenger Transport Board, while control over electricity and hospitals was lost in 1948 to the National Electricity Board and the National Health Service respectively. Nevertheless, the reduction of functions consequent upon the reorganization of London's government in 1965 was considerable, especially in relation to planning (the GLC assumed control of London's strategic planning, giving it the final say on all development proposals within two hundred yards of any metropolitan road, in addition to, for example, new office development), roads (which assumed particular significance at the time of the proposed Ringway Two controversy in the early 1970s, when a London ringroad was planned to cut through the north of the borough), and housing (a function now shared by the two authorities, much to the consternation of Croydon's political elite which continues stoutly to resist the use of local building land for GLC developments which would inevitably house families from outside Croydon). Not surprisingly, the County Borough council was strongly opposed to the whole idea of merging with the rest of London, and even today, local councillors still express their resentment of what they see as GLC interference in local affairs (especially when the GLC is Labour-controlled). The borough elects only four members to the ninety-six seat GLC, and local councillors are thus understandably worried at the lack of influence which they can exert over decision-making at County Hall.

The GLC, however, is obviously not the only, or even the major, 'outsider' with a significant finger in local affairs. For beyond County Hall lies the Palace of Westminster and the 'faceless men' of Whitehall. The GLC's 'interference' in local affairs is nothing compared with that of the central government. In all three of the cases I wish to discuss here, where decision-making has passed out of local hands and thus apparently beyond the reach of even the suburban middle class, the 'outsider' has been, not the GLC, but central government.

The first example relates to the case of planning inquiries. At public inquiries into planning applications, local residents' groups have often found themselves arguing against large development companies such as Laings or Wates, which are represented by a battery of highly skilled lawyers, and are backed by vast financial resources and a long experience of planning issues. In such cases, they have often attempted to expand their own relatively limited power resources through alliances with other local bodies such as the Chambers of Commerce. The Federation of Southern Croydon Residents' Associations represents just such an attempt to organize readily mobilizable strength in depth. Once a planning issue is 'out in the open', the most that the southern residents can hope for is a highly visible show of numerical support and solidarity.

Often, however, this numerical strength is mobilized *before* the local council has met to consider a particular planning application. Public meetings are called at which local ward representatives are badgered to express their views on the issue in question, and to express their support for the local association's cause. Petitions are organized, and the local council is flooded with letters of protest. Undoubtedly, all this is done in part to 'encourage' any ward representatives who may be wavering under the pressure from northern Conservative members, Labour members, and the rest of London to increase densities and develop less attractive parts of the green belt in southern areas. But in part it can also be seen as tactical protest, for as we have seen, the southern residents and the political elite are generally in accord on such issues. The point is that large-scale and impressive residents' campaigns can be *used* by the political elite as a rationalization for a course of action which it intends to take anyway – i.e. for refusing planning permission. In other words, the local council, despite superficial appearances at the start of such issues, is often the residents' greatest ally against the combined forces of the developers and the Ministry Inspector, and by protesting to the local council, the residents are in fact strengthening this alliance.

Take, for example, the campaign mounted in 1971 by the Riddlesdown Residents' Association in the south of the borough against a Laings' application to develop nearly 900 houses on virtual wasteland on the fringe of the green belt. It was in fact this campaign, described by the *Advertiser* as probably the best residents' association campaign ever mounted in Croydon, which led eventually to the establishment of the southern residents' federation. As soon as the Laings' application was made public, the local association started a constant flow of letters and press releases to the local newspaper, while encouraging no less than 1700 residents to write to the town hall in protest (a scale of postal barrage which makes the 300 or 400 letters received about the Whitgift issue seem insignificant). Raising funds door to door, the association engaged a planning expert to prepare its case, and kept its members informed of developments by launching a special 'Green Belt' newsletter. A large petition was organized and duly dispatched to the town hall, and a highly successful mass meeting of residents was held in protest against any development on green belt land. National and local newspaper correspondents were wined and dined, while two local reporters were taken for a 'drinking session' in the week prior to the inquiry. 'Boy, did we get some publicity!' mused one of the association's leaders afterwards. On the morning of the inquiry, spurred on by a banner headline in the *Advertiser*, hundreds of local residents turned out in support of their leaders. In June 1971, the Minister announced that the Laings' application had been rejected.

From start to finish, this campaign was very efficiently run, and as a 'performance' was extremely well managed. The extent of local hostility to the proposed development was constantly and clearly demonstrated in a number of different ways – letters, petitions, mass meetings, the large attendance at the inquiry – and, perhaps more important, was widely publicized, even in the national press. But for whose benefit? Clearly, although much of the campaign appeared to be directed toward the local council, pressurizing it to reject the planned development, it is in fact better understood as providing the council with further grounds for dismissing the proposal – a step it almost certainly would have taken anyway. Far from being adversaries in the early stages, the council and the residents were allies from the start, each supporting the other against the threat of outside intervention in the green belt question.

The same sort of story emerges out of a consideration of the second example of central government involvement in local affairs – the comprehensive reorganization of secondary education issue. This was in fact seen by many councillors of both party groups as the single most important decision to have been taken in Croydon since the mid 1960s (it was mentioned by over one-third of all members). Certainly it was among the most contentious.

Following the Labour government's Circular 10/65, which called upon all local authorities to prepare and submit proposals for the comprehensive reorganization of secondary education in their areas, the officers in Croydon's Education Department, in consultation with local teachers, began work on preparing such a plan. They were not new to this work – the story of Croydon's secondary education plans began in 1954 when the then Education chief suggested that local grammar school sixth-forms should be amalgamated into a sixth-form college. The ratepayer-controlled council, however, had taken fright at the extent of opposition, and rejected the plan. The idea had again been floated seven years later, but no decision had been taken (see Donnison 1975 for more details). In 1965, however, the initiative came, not from within but from outside, and Circular 10/65 looked to many suspiciously like an offer they could not very easily refuse.

The Education department published its proposals in November

1965. It suggested the abolition of selection examinations at age eleven, except for tests which would still be set to determine which children should take up places at the town's direct grant schools (which were to remain outside the comprehensive system). Existing grammar schools were to become comprehensive schools for fourteen to eighteen-year-olds. Other secondary schools would either 'feed' these schools, taking pupils between the ages of eleven and fourteen, or would take children from eleven to sixteen, at which age transfers could take place to a fourteen to eighteen school for those willing and able to continue their education. The scheme was complicated, and reflected a delicate compromise between the constraints imposed by existing buildings, the desire to retain some variety of secondary schooling and hence the principle of 'parental choice', the reluctance of a Conservative council to abolish selective education, and the demands laid out in Circular 10/65. This was an almost impossible task.

Once the plan had been published, the Minister of Education was said to be satisfied, and local educational pressure groups – the teachers' unions, the Campaign for the Advancement of State Education, the Head Teachers' Association – gave it qualified support. The local newspaper seemed generally in favour, and fully expected the defenders of the grammar schools to accept the scheme with few reservations: 'They can scarcely complain except on points of detail. They have secured almost all they fought for. The grammar schools continue to exist, and with an enhanced standing. . . . It must seem like the fulfilment of Cinderella's dream.' To the defenders of the grammar schools, however, this was certainly not how it seemed. Opposition to the council's proposals developed swiftly among grammar school PTAs and the middle class parents of grammar school children. Foremost among these was a certain Mrs Frost.

Mrs Frost, a Purley housewife, was among the first to write to the local press criticizing the comprehensive plan, and as a result of her letter, many other middle class parents, mainly from the south of the borough, rallied to her flag, and formed what came to be known as the Save Our Schools movement. Pressure from both the grammar schools themselves, and from the SOS campaigners, resulted in the local political elite deferring its decision, and organizing a series of public meetings, the ostensible purpose of which was to inform parents of the plan and gauge their reaction. As the *Advertiser* put it, 'Because of the weight of public opinion – this has really been a town's debate – they have wisely deferred their meeting for a month.' It was at one of these public meetings in Purley that, to many people's surprise and disbelief, the leader of the council announced that the comprehensive plan was to be dropped. 'We have achieved all we fought for,' a jubilant Mrs Frost told the local press, and sure enough, at the subsequent Education committee meeting, the proposals were rejected by nine votes to six.

This amazing volte-face on the part of the majority group leadership was somewhat unique. As we shall see in Chapter 7, the council has rarely allowed itself to be influenced by campaigns of this sort – the angry scenes and public opposition which characterized the string of public meetings held on the issue were qualitatively little different from the sort of behaviour which in other situations has readily been dismissed as 'irresponsible', and thus unworthy of consideration. There have been few other examples in Croydon's recent history where so carefully considered a plan has so readily been discarded by the council leadership. The leader of the council explained this sudden reversal in terms of deference to public opinion. 'It is our duty to do as you would wish,' he told the Purley parents, 'and that is exactly what we have done.' But given the tradition in Croydon of resolute disinterest in public opposition of this sort, such an explanation cannot easily be accepted.

In order fully to understand the council's remarkable 'change of heart' over the comprehensive issue, it is necessary to remember that the plan was only drawn up under pressure from central government, that many local Conservatives on and off the council were fundamentally opposed to the very principle of non-selective education, and that the political elite found itself in the unenviable position of having to defend a policy which it disliked against vociferous attacks from the very people whose views and interests it shared, and on whose electoral support it traditionally relied. In fact, it is apparent that the preferences of the Save Our Schools movement and the council's majority group were congruent from the very outset of this issue. Seen in this way, it is clear that the public (and overwhelmingly middle class) opposition, culminating in Mrs Frost's SOS campaign, was not so much the *cause* of the change in policy as the *rationalization* for it. It may be that in other towns, local politicians were obliged by the weight of public opposition to revise their position on comprehensive reorganization (e.g. see Newton 1976 on the Birmingham experience), but in Croydon it seems more likely that public opposition served to obscure an underlying consensus between council leaders and middle class parents, and was used by the former to jettison a policy which neither they nor the campaigners desired. As the *Times Educational Supplement* observed at the time (21 January 1966), 'The Conservative councillors in Croydon were at best reluctant champions of their own scheme, and like most people, the public opinion they paid heed to was the public opinion of their own side.'

Inevitably, however, although the suburban middle class won this battle – and went on to win several more – it finally lost the war, although it was not until September 1968 that Croydon council finally agreed on a plan for comprehensive reorganization essentially similar to that rejected by them in 1965/66. Given the interest of the central government in bringing about educational reform, the residents' opposition, no matter how well organized and vociferous (and it is worth noting that parents appear to have been far stronger and more effective in Croydon than was the case in many other areas – see, for example, Hampton 1970 and Newton 1976), could hope to do little more than stall official action. Thus, when the members of the Education committee and their bureaucratic advisers were summoned to Whitehall in April 1967 and informed that central government finance for virtually all future planned capital expenditure on schools in the town was to be withheld until such time as a suitable comprehensive plan was submitted, it became clear that the issue was for all intents and purposes resolved. Not even Croydon's articulate and influential middle class could hope to take on the central government and win.

The wrangle over comprehensives illustrates a number of significant points. It provides a vivid demonstration of the strength of the Conservative group leadership for one thing, for like the Grand Old Duke of York, the political elite succeeded in leading its rank and file first in reluctant support of the policy, then against it, and finally in favour once again (although the unfortunate chairman of the Education committee later lost his post as a result – see page 222). The issue also provides a clear illustration of how financial dependency on the central exchequer limits local government autonomy even in the absence of central legislation requiring it to introduce specified policies. But most significantly, this issue shows once again the crucial significance of the content of political demands in relation to the way in which they come to be articulated, and demonstrates that assessment by decision-makers of action as 'responsible' is in large part determined by their opinions of the demands being made. Angry scenes and demonstrations of protest may, as the discussion of the comprehensive education issue reveals, be viewed by them as 'responsible' – as reasonable citizens exercising their democratic rights. Indeed, such behaviour may even be encouraged – the political elite, in organizing and participating in a series of public meetings, facilitated the embryonic middle class campaign. It is only when the demands articulated by a given group are incongruent with the views and interests of the political elite that such behaviour may come to be defined as 'irresponsible'. Political responsibility and political consensus are thus seen as two sides of the same coin.

The third case of tactical protest on the part of the suburban middle class which I wish to examine here occurred after the fieldwork on which this book is based had been completed. Strictly speaking, therefore, I should perhaps not consider it. However, it relates to a highly significant campaign waged in 1974/75 over the rates issue, and it will be remembered that I have argued that the low rate policy is one on which the political elite and the southern residents have traditionally been in complete accord. Given that sociological research of this kind has an unfortunate habit of finding its major conclusions challenged or overturned by the course of future events, I consider it wise to analyse this particular issue in order to see if it represents a possible exception to my 'rule'. I should make it clear, however, that since the rates issue developed after my research was completed in Croydon, the following discussion is based only on local newspaper reports, and is thus inevitably somewhat superficial.

It was in August 1975 that my attention was drawn to the rates issue in Croydon as a result of a news item on BBC Television which indicated that 6000 ratepayers in the borough had been summonsed for non-payment, and that magistrates had given Croydon council permission to enter debtors' homes and remove valuables in lieu of monies owing. Croydon's suburban middle class was apparently up in arms about a mammoth rates increase, and its close relationship with the political elite appeared to have foundered.

The rate fixed for the financial year 1974/75 in Croydon represented a 24 per cent increase over the previous year (compared with a national average increase of 29 per cent). By July 1974, the council was forecasting that, due mainly to inflation, the revenue thus realized would fall £1.5 million short of expected expenditure, and in January 1975 it announced that a supplementary rate was to be levied to balance the local authority's books by the end of the financial year. The supplementary rate was designed to generate an additional income of £3.5 million and was complemented by a further central government grant of £1.5 million. The rate in the pound for domestic payers increased by 3p. A Labour proposal that an increase of nearly 8p in the pound be introduced to allow for necessary additional spending on social services was rejected by the council.

The introduction of the supplementary rate – the first time that Croydon had ever felt it necessary to take such a step – brought only temporary relief, however. In common with all other local authorities, Croydon depends heavily for its revenue, not only on local rates, but also on the government's rate support grant, and this grant has been decreasing in real terms for several years. In 1973/74, for example, Croydon received a grant of £15.7 million, representing 40 per cent of total expenditure. In the following year, the grant of £17.5 million accounted for only 34 per cent of total expenditure, and the grant of £21.8 million fixed by the government for 1975/76 represented only 29 per cent of forecasted spending. The problem, as far as the political elite is concerned, is that Croydon is one of few local authorities in this country with a rateable value per head in excess of £170 (Croydon's average RV in 1975 stood at £194), and is not therefore eligible for part of the rate support grant known as the 'resources grant'. Traditionally, this grant has comprised 12 per cent of the total rate support grant, but in 1975 the government increased it to 25 per cent of the total, thereby effectively decreasing Croydon's RSG. Furthermore, Croydon also receives only a relatively small 'needs grant' (another constituent part of the RSG subsidy) due to its lack of acute social problems.

As April approached, it became clear that the declining real value of the government grant would have to be made up out of local revenue, and that a rates increase of between 60 and 80 per cent would be necessary to accomplish this. In the words of the Director of

Finance, 'It is going to cost us about seventy per cent more in the next financial year to provide exactly the same sort of services we have maintained this year. If we did not put the rates up, we would have to start sacking teachers – that is the alternative.'

The residents' associations responded to this prospect in predictable fashion. They called meetings, which leading council officers and members attended, at which they demanded that the impending increase be cut. They criticized the level of council expenditure, only to be told by the deputy Director of Finance that, 'Croydon is not an extravagant borough.' In fact, in order to keep the increase down, Croydon cut social services (in January it was reported to be short of seven social workers and thirty-five home-helps), stopped decorating the inside of council houses, slashed £400,000 from the education budget, and agreed to reduce its total staff by 5 per cent (although, interestingly, it did not follow most other local authorities in ending its mortgage loans to home-buyers). Time and again at these meetings, the political elite told the residents that the fault was not their's. The GLC had increased its rate levy by 80 per cent, while the real value of the rate support grant had been cut by 10 per cent (at 29 per cent of total expenditure, Croydon's RSG was considerably lower than the average of 55 per cent for the country as a whole). Inflation had done the rest. And, of course, they were absolutely right.

The suburban middle class, however, was unimpressed. Seeing that services had already been cut, the residents' associations claimed that staffing must be too high, although in relation to comparable boroughs such as Kingston, Enfield, and Hounslow, Croydon's staffing ratio per head of population was actually fairly low. Increasingly, the idea of some form of direct action was discussed. In Shirley, two associations threatened to withhold part of the increase, and at Coulsdon, the local residents' association attempted to gain the southern federation's support for a total rate strike, but without success.

In this atmosphere of growing suburban unrest, the Deputy Director of Finance addressed a meeting at Shirley in February and, asked what would happen in the event of a rate strike, told the assembled residents, 'Obviously we can't put you all in prison. But a wholesale refusal to pay is a forbidding prospect, and if we were faced with it, we could only hope central government will see the need for changes.' In an interview with a local reporter after the meeting, he was even more explicit in what he meant. 'There is very great dissatisfaction about high rates,' he said, 'and if very many people adopted a militant attitude and there was agitation, then the government might feel bound to do something.' As a local resident observed, what he seemed to be implying was that, 'If there was sufficient agitation by us, the council could do little, and the government might be forced to do something.' Never has the logic of tactical protest been so clearly outlined and so clearly understood.

Whether or not the deputy director's comments can validly be interpreted as an invitation to action, it is all too clear that the political elite and its chief officers had considerable sympathy with the residents' complaints and anger, and conceived of themselves as very much allied with them against the central government and the GLC. Thus when, in March, an increase in rates (in addition to the supplementary rate levied earlier) of 66 per cent was announced, the leader of the council told the *Advertiser*, 'If this situation arises in a year's time, it will be necessary to destroy services. There will be no way out unless we get outside assistance. It is almost outrageous to ask people to bear this brunt. I apologise to all ratepayers in this town that it should be necessary to ask for such a massive rate increase.... I understand their feelings. But disruption of local government helps nobody.' It was clear by March that, despite the intense local opposition (including the organization of a petition to the House of Commons which gained 18,000 signatures), further government aid would not be forthcoming. It was also clear that the 'disruption' of which the leader of the council spoke was a very real possibility, and that Croydon council could face the unenviable task of dragging its allies off to court.

From March onwards, repeated attempts were made to defuse the situation. The local newspaper, for example, ran a large article under the headline, 'New Rate Seems So HIGH Because It Was So LOW', in which it pointed out, 'Croydon's new rate, although up probably more than anywhere else in the country, is not out of step with others in London. The amount of cash paid by Croydon householders will be far less than many other Londoners. For many years, Croydon ratepayers have enjoyed an exceptionally low levy because of the enormous extra revenue generated annually while the town's commercial centre was growing. The new system of grant allocation, introduced last year specifically to aid poor areas, has hit towns like

Croydon that tried to foster their own prosperity.' Once again, the government was portrayed as the real culprit.

As the months went by, the residents' resolve visibly crumbled. Their case was by no means as strong as many of them had at first imagined – even allowing for the large percentage increase, Croydon's rate was still lower than that of ten other London boroughs – and in the absence of government intervention, the issue came more and more to be defined in terms of the 'relatively deprived' residents against the hapless council. It was a confrontation which few relished. In July, the council sent out 31,000 final rate demands, of which 25,000 were swiftly paid. In August, 6000 summonses were issued, but it is clear that in many of these cases, payment had been withheld out of economic hardship rather than political resolve (e.g. in 1974, 4000 summonses were issued at a time when there was no organized protest on the rates issue). Most of those summonsed paid their debts before the court convened, and although a number of debtors (among them the chairman of the Coulsdon West Residents' Association) maintained that they would continue to withhold payment, the protest effectively petered out.

Far from casting doubt on my previous discussion of the relationship between the southern residents and the political elite, the rates issue confirms my argument. The scale of the protest – at least in the earlier stages when the prospect of bailiffs and jail seemed a long way off – can be accounted for in terms of the relative deprivation (Runciman 1966) experienced by a suburban middle class which had grown accustomed to a very low rate levy, and which for the first time was being asked to pay the equivalent of what thousands of Londoners had been paying for years. But it is clear that the political elite was itself as opposed to the new higher rate as were the southern residents. It did all it realistically could do to reduce services and hence to 'cushion the blow' (while, incidently, further reducing the facilities available to less privileged sections of the population). But its time-tested tactics of slashing services proved inadequate in the face of the reduced rate support grant, the increased GLC levy, and the effects of escalating inflation.

In the early stages, it is clear that the rates protest, like the protests on planning applications and comprehensive education, was an example of tactical protest, apparently directed at the council, while being used by the council to bring pressure on central government.

In its later stages, however, it was a different ball game, and the protest crumbled as central government stood firm. It is worth noting, however, that throughout, not a word was spoken or written about the 'irresponsibility' of those who threatened they would not pay. Instead, they received not brickbats but apologies that they should be asked to bear the increased burden.

The three examples of tactical protest which I have considered are important for three reasons. First, they demonstrate the fundamental alliance which exists over a whole range of political questions between the suburban middle class and the political elite. It is not just that, for most of the time, the former do not have to defend their interests publicly, as they are generally anticipated for them, but that even where they do engage in open political protest, they often do so with the tacit consent of, and in loose alliance with, the local political elite. Tactical protest represents the exception which literally 'proves' the rule.

Secondly, all three examples of tactical protest demonstrate the readiness with which the suburban middle class mobilizes in defence of its residential exclusivity and property values, its children's educational privileges, and the low level of local taxation which it has customarily enjoyed. It has often been said that the middle classes in Britain exhibit a high degree of collective awareness and class consciousness despite the fact that few of them appear to have any explicitly class-based image of their society. The evidence discussed in this chapter strongly reaffirms this argument, for it is something of a paradox that the very people who tend to deny the relevance of class divisions and to support a view of local government as 'non-political' are also those who mobilize most strongly in defence of their economic interests.

Thirdly, it is apparent from the evidence discussed above that those who protest loudest are often those who have least to complain about. As we saw in Chapter 1, Lukes has suggested that the occasional victory by relatively powerless groups may serve to confirm the prevailing image of the political system as democratic and accountable. It is now apparent that we may add to this observation that the occasional defeat (or, more accurately, impression of defeat) sustained by relatively privileged groups may serve much the same function, for when Croydon's middle classes are up in arms, it is all too easy to believe that it is they, rather than the less privileged sections of the population, who are getting a raw deal. In this way, the interests of the have-nots go unnoticed in the clamour of the haves.

This last point serves to reinforce the argument set out in Chapter 2. Because British Marxists have tended to ignore or dismiss as unimportant the real economic divisions between groups such as the suburban middle class and other less fortunate sections of the population, they have too readily fallen into the trap of supporting middle class community action against a local authority on the assumption that they are thereby aiding a popular struggle against a business-dominated local state. Yet we have seen that in Croydon, suburban agitation over the defence of the environment, over the level of local property taxation and so on succeeds only at the expense of primarily working class groups who are obliged to live at higher densities and with fewer social provisions. Nor is this situation unique to Croydon. In Islington, for example, the Barnsbury Association, formed by middle class owner-occupiers, proved very successful in sponsoring a policy of gradual gentrification which led to the displacement of working class tenants. As Cowley and his co-writers observe,

> It is evident that many middle class socialists have completely lost touch with working class aspirations and therefore fail to analyse situations correctly. The Amenity Movement with its blatantly elitist approach to planning can still count on support from middle class socialists because it appears to challenge the brutal planning activities of the large commercial and state developers. This is a mistake because middle class amenity groups are nearly always willing to impose what they regard as disastrous proposals for their own districts on 'soft' working class areas elsewhere [1977, p. 181].

As in Barnsbury, so too in Croydon, the political competence of the middle class is more a cause for concern than for celebration.

7 Participation and protest

Among the shopkeepers, solicitors, estate agents, company directors and other local businessmen who dominate the key positions in the local authority in Croydon, there is a broad consensus as regards the core principles of legislation which does not differ too much from the spirit of Jeremy Bentham's philosophy of utilitarianism developed in the early years of the nineteenth century. At the heart of this consensus lies a primary concern with self-help, individual initiative and private property, expressed in conversation through frequent resort to cliche phrases about the need for people to stand on their own two feet, to pull themselves up by their bootstraps, and to have something they can call their own. While these core values do not preclude compassion for those who cannot help themselves, they have resulted in a traditional concern to avoid any social expenditure beyond a level which is necessary to support those defined as being in need. One leading member of the Conservative group spoke on behalf of most of his colleagues when he explained, 'As a Conservative, I believe in leaving a man to fend for himself unless he really needs help.'

This strong belief that social policies are best when applied sparingly has led to predictable consequences in Croydon over the years. In the 1950s, for example, when the council was controlled by 'independent' right-wing ratepayer groups, day nurseries were closed down, the library service was cut back, and a proposal that school children should clean their own school premises to save on staffing costs was seriously considered, all in an attempt to save money and reduce the rates (see Morris 1957). The picture has remained much the same since. Thus, at the time of the research, social services expenditure in Croydon stood at less than 70 per cent of the London per capita average with the result that council provision of day nurseries, children's services, meals-on-wheels, domestic help for the disabled, temporary accommodation facilities and so on all fell well below the London average. In education, the level of discretionary local authority grants to students in higher education was 70 per cent of that in the rest of London, and Croydon spent less than any other borough on school books, stationery and equipment per head of school population. Despite this, the Policy subcommittee in 1973 vetoed an Education committee proposal to increase expenditure on these latter items. The town's library service was criticized by a confidential D E S report in 1969 as the worst in London, and it singled out for particular cause for concern the libraries in the northern, primarily working class, wards, yet this report was kept secret for no less than four years until a Labour member stumbled upon it and made its contents public in 1973.

The central concern has therefore consistently been to maintain low levels of expenditure, and hence to levy the lowest possible rate (see page 248). Although this has affected all areas of social policy, the area which has perhaps been worst hit has been public housing, for not only does the provision of council housing represent a considerable drain on revenue (mainly because of loan charges), but it represents the very antithesis of the core conservative values of individual self-help and private property ownership. It is one thing to subsidize the 'needy poor', but quite another to spend ratepayers' money on providing low rent housing for large numbers of families who are not considered needy at all. As one Conservative alderman put it, 'A man earning forty pounds a week ought to be able to solve his own housing problem. I tell you, there are more colour televisions on the council estates than on the private housing estates' (£40 per week was approximately the average wage at this time). When we add to this the fact that most council tenants may be expected to vote Labour (if they vote at all), there has clearly been little incentive for the Conservative council to launch any large-scale housing programme.

There is, however, a limit to how far a local authority can ignore its local housing needs, and the demand for council housing in Croydon escalated throughout the late 1960s and early 1970s. By 1973 the 'active' waiting list (an ironic euphemism for a list which has remained virtually stagnant) of families defined by the council's own points system as being in pressing need of accommodation stood at 2500. The total waiting list was around 7000 families, and this did not include several hundred officially recognized homeless families, nor an incalculable number of other families who might have registered had they thought they stood the remotest chance of ever being given a house. Clearly some fresh initiative was needed on the housing question.

In 1970 the Conservative leadership presented its five-year plan for council house development which basically proposed that 300 new homes should be built each year until 1975. These, together with vacancies arising from the death or migration of existing tenants, would provide a total of 4300 vacant units over the period, yet this fell 2500 short of the minimum officially estimated demand of 6800. Furthermore, the council continued to pursue a number of policies which served to exacerbate this shortfall, notable among which were the sale of council houses and the construction of a ringroad around the town centre which displaced hundreds of working class families who had then to be given priority for rehousing. The effect of all this was that by the end of 1973, only two or three out of every one hundred families housed by Croydon council came from the active waiting list.

The five-year housing programme was thus inadequate from the outset, and this inadequacy was later compounded by the fact that the modest target of 300 completions per year was not met until the fourth year of its operation (see the table overleaf). What is immediately clear from an analysis of housing completions in Croydon in the early 1970s is that, while private building has consistently been higher than virtually anywhere else in London, the rate of local authority building has invariably been among the lowest in the GLC area. The lack of council house developments during this period cannot therefore be explained in terms of a shortage of potential development land (since sites have been found by private builders with little trouble), nor (as we have seen) does it reflect any lack of demand. Indeed, the demand continued to grow with the result that the council's temporary accommodation facilities (a service on which Croydon spent just 21 per cent of the London average in 1973) became totally saturated. So desperate did the situation become that, towards the end of my research in the town, council leaders issued a plea to private householders to accommodate a homeless family in the spare room, while reports emerged of Croydon families attempting to register with neighbouring Lambeth for a council house (this at a

Local authority and private house completions in Croydon relative to all London boroughs, 1969–74

Year	Local authority dwellings completed		Private dwellings completed		LA dwellings per private dwelling completed		LA dwellings completed per 1000 population*		Private dwellings completed per 1000 population*		Ranking of Croydon in 32 boroughs for local authority completions	Ranking of Croydon in 32 boroughs for private completions
	All boroughs	Croydon	All boroughs	Croydon	All boroughs	Croydon	All boroughs	Croydon	All boroughs	Croydon		
1969	17,215	288	8198	1364	2.1	0.2	2.2	0.8	1.1	4.2	24	1
1970	22,088	92	8769	1057	2.5	0.1	2.9	0.3	1.2	3.2	31	2
1971	17,936	115	8342	758	2.2	0.2	2.4	0.3	1.1	2.3	31	3
1972	14,771	77	7452	799	2.0	0.1	2.0	0.2	1.0	2.4	28	2
1973	10,948	114	7718	628	1.4	0.2	1.5	0.2	1.1	1.9	26	3
1974	13,859	535	6991	942	2.0	0.6	1.9	1.6	0.9	2.8	12	1

Source: *Local Housing Statistics, England and Wales*, HMSO (1969, 1970, 1971, 1972, 1973, 1974)
* Population figures for each year taken from mid-year estimates.

time when the GLC was calling upon the outer boroughs to help the inner areas with their housing problems!).

Not surprisingly, therefore, housing came to dominate local politics in Croydon at this time, and while the council leadership appeared very concerned about the growing housing shortage, they were nevertheless quick to deny their own responsibility for it. In interviews, press statements and council meetings, they found no shortage of suitable scapegoats. Building contractors were blamed for failing to meet deadlines; building workers 'won't work even when you can get them'; the GLC was accused of using Croydon's land for housing inner London families; local residents were condemned as 'heartless' when they failed to respond to the call to take in a homeless family; the homeless themselves were accused of lacking initiative in looking elsewhere for accommodation; existing council tenants were blamed for staying in scarce local authority housing when they could afford to buy in the private sector; and so on. Some council members suggested that the problem could never be solved because the more houses they provided, the more demand would be stimulated. And despite an impression of earnest endeavour and genuine concern, culminating in a special conference on the housing problem called in 1973, this appears to have been the conclusion drawn by the leadership too.

The conclusion which emerges from this brief review of local authority policies with regard to collective consumption is, therefore, that social expenditure has consistently been restricted in the interests of the maintenance of low rate levels and higher expenditure in other areas (notably on productive infrastructure – see Chapter 8). Often this has been accompanied by statements of concern, as in the housing issue, although at times such statements have been barely credible. Until quite recently, for example, the council imposed a six week time limit on homeless families' use of its temporary accommodation facilities; if they failed to 'solve their own housing problem' during this period, children were then taken into care and the parents separated (see Bailey 1973a). Similarly in 1973, the Social Services committee chairman announced that families would no longer be considered 'homeless' if they rejected the local authority's first offer of accommodation. Such policies throw doubt on the council's protestations of 'compassion' and render ironic Tate's observation that Croydon's treatment of the homelessness problem

'served as a model of how an authority . . . could deal with the problem' (1972, p. 95). What emerges from a consideration of such
policies is that Croydon continues to operate with a tacit distinction
between the 'deserving' and 'undeserving' poor, and that the legacy
of the nineteenth century Poor Law Guardians and the post-war
independent ratepayers has been inherited intact by the political
leaders of the 1970s. It is a legacy from which the working class rarely
benefits.

The participatory response: competing agreement

The question to be addressed in the remainder of this chapter is how
those who have been most adversely affected by this pattern of social
policy have reacted to it. In Chapter 5, we saw that such groups face
the dilemma of whether to risk incorporation by acting within the
system, or to risk isolation by acting outside it. In reality, of course,
this involves not a stark choice between two alternative strategies,
but rather the pursuit of a strategy which is more or less accommodative or more or less coercive. In other words, conciliation and coercion represent polar types on a continuum, and any specific action
is likely to fall at some point between them. In this section, I shall
discuss three types of strategy which may be described as broadly
conciliatory in that all three attempt to establish a mode of participation within the local political system, although as we shall see, they
vary in the degree to which this actually occurs.

The first of these strategies is reliance upon the Labour Party as
the representative voice of the working class. Effectively, this means
reliance on the Labour group on the council, for although the various
ward and constituency party organizations may play a significant
part in drafting election manifestos and selecting candidates for local
elections, their influence over the council group at other times is
minimal. The question, then, is whether the council Labour group
do represent the voice of the working class in the Town Hall, and if
they do, how far they are able to change or modify majority group
policies.

Of particular significance here is the fact that so many Labour
members since 1971 have been drawn from the middle class (see page
213). One consequence of this is that largely homogenous working
class wards such as the massive New Addington council estate come

to be represented, not only by mainly middle class councillors, but also by people who live elsewhere in middle class areas. In the period 1971–4, for example, 30,000 people in New Addington were represented by three Labour councillors, two óf whom did not live on the estate. Two implications follow from this. The first is that the bond between Labour councillors and the wards they represent may be somewhat tenuous, for although many Labour members attempted to cultivate formal links with their constituents (e.g. through regular ward 'surgeries'), what may be termed 'organic' links tend to be relatively weak. As Forester observes,

Because few councillors emerge out of their wards as 'community leaders' . . . this further militates against greater activity and involvement because the elected councillor's reference group is the local political community and not the local community itself. . . . From the elected councillor's point of view, there is no real need to develop the ward association into an effective community institution – provided the vote can be got out at the appropriate time [1976, p. 101].

The principal point of reference for most middle class Labour councillors may therefore be other (mainly middle class) Labour activists rather than the ward – an argument which receives support from Budge *et al.* (1972) and their concept of 'political stratification'.

This leads us to consider the second and more important point which is that middle class Labour councillors may have a very different orientation to local politics than their working class supporters. I noted in Chapter 5 that the cohort of young Labour members elected to the council in 1971 appeared generally more radical, and certainly more aggressive, than their traditional working class colleagues, but what is at issue is the character of this radicalism. In his study based on the Liverpool Constituency Labour Party, for example, Hindess (1971) suggests that the party has effectively been taken over by the middle class and that its dominant political concerns have changed as a result. Citing housing as a specific example, he argues that although middle class activists may still express a concern with housing issues, their orientation is more technocratic than personal. The intimate concerns of the working class activists with concrete questions of local housing provision and policy have thus been eclipsed by the more detached concerns of the middle class socialists with the development of a humane and rational housing programme. The Labour Party, in short, has become divorced from its roots and its explicitly class character has been lost.

Hindess's thesis that the Labour Party has ceased to be the political mouthpiece of the working class has been severely attacked by various writers (not least because of its assumption that the party ever was a genuine working class party), but there appears little disagreement between Hindess and his critics over the fact that middle class activists do appear to have a different orientation to local political issues than working class members. In his study of the Kemptown party in Brighton, for example, Forester (1976) suggests that the former tend to be more 'idealistic' in their concerns while the latter are more 'sectarian', and this appears to bear out Hindess's distinction between the liberal-technocratic middle class and the proletarian parochial working class.

This is a distinction which can also be found in Labour politics in Croydon, and notably in the Labour group on the council. The young Labour radicals elected in 1971 have certainly showed themselves to be as concerned as anybody about the housing issue, and they have consistently sought to demonstrate their allegiance to the cause of the ill-housed and homeless by launching regular and bitter attacks on Croydon's housing policy at council meetings. At the December 1972 meeting, for example, one Labour member dramatically pointed to the Conservative benches and shouted, 'This group of innkeepers in the season of Christmas drive the very children of Croydon into the streets and tell them there is no room.' When the raucous laughter had subsided, one of his colleagues jumped up and shouted angrily at the majority group, 'You should be out of this town, out of this chamber. You have no right to sit here.' The whole performance then came to its climax as the Labour leader, having been passed a note from his back-benches, rose to his feet. 'From this moment on,' he declared, 'the tory council will have to face opposition such as they have never had to face before. I feel that some demonstration is needed in order that those in dire housing need can see and understand who their friends are.' Many of his colleagues were already on their feet and the Labour leader led his group from the council chamber. Only the irate man in the public gallery who had twice been silenced by ushers during the debate and who later explained that he had been waiting for a house for five years seemed churlishly unimpressed by this display of solidarity with his cause.

For the Labour radicals, the housing issue, as with most other issues, is approached from the perspective of socialist principles. They articulate socialist ideology, but they are disdainful of the traditional parochialism of working class politics at the local level. They claim to speak on behalf of, but not at the behest of, the working class, and where socialist principles come into conflict with working class aspirations, it is the former which takes precedence. An obvious example of this occurred in 1971 when Croydon, in common with many other Conservative-controlled authorities, introduced a scheme whereby council houses on selected estates were offered for sale at below their market value to sitting tenants of more than three years residence. Purchases were further facilitated through the offer of local authority mortgage facilities, and although the various tenants' associations in the town were not active in sponsoring this policy, they were broadly in favour of it. The Labour group, however, was not, and a bitter controversy surrounded its passage through the decision-making process.

What was notable about the sales issue was not so much the rancour which ensued between Labour and Conservative councillors as the evident tension which it highlighted between the idealism, universalism and principles of the Labour group and the materialism, parochialism and pragmatism of the representatives of the town's council tenants. Nor was this tension unique to this particular issue for it pervades much of the relationship between the two. One Labour councillor probably spoke for many of his colleagues when he said of the tenants' associations, 'They're not important. They've become individualistic. They don't care about the wider Labour movement and they don't care about other tenants elsewhere.' The two groups are quite simply working in different planes, for although some of the older (and often more working class and more right-wing) members of the council Labour group do maintain close contacts with the tenants' movement and exhibit a marked concern with the specific problems raised by particular tenants, the majority since 1971 have tended to dismiss tenants' groups as relatively insignificant and as having little to contribute to the broader issues of social policy with which they are concerned. Their attitude is illustrated by one councillor who discussed a tenants' meeting he had attended: 'About two hundred people turned up despite the fact that "Coronation Street" was on the telly. But most of the people who spoke concentrated on small individual moans like rotting doors and it wasn't really very successful.'

It would be wrong to suggest, as Hindess perhaps implies, that the 'embourgeoisment' of the Labour Party at the local level has resulted in a dilution of its socialist commitment, for in Croydon the reverse may well be true. But where Hindess is surely correct is in identifying the growing alienation of the working class from the party, and particularly from the party group in the council – the feeling among working class Labour supporters (such as those involved in the tenants' associations) that 'they are somehow losing control of the party, that it doesn't seem like "their party" any more' (1971, pp. 86–7). It follows that while socialist principles may well be championed by the teachers, social workers and others who now represent the Labour Party in the town hall, the party itself does not constitute an effective medium of working class political expression and activity. As Hindess concludes, the working class has thus become increasingly isolated from the formal party political process at the local level.

An alternative channel for working class participation in the local political system is provided by the tenants' movement. In the 1950s, the tenants' associations appeared fairly active and militant, organizing various campaigns and even rent strikes against rent increases, but since then they have become remarkably 'responsible' organizations, and most have built up a close working relationship with the housing department and its senior officers. Some, indeed, have become so 'responsible' as to retreat from any contentious political involvement altogether. One association, for example, conspicuously failed to take any position on either of two major issues affecting its members at the time of the research (the question of where a new school should be built, and the council's refusal to sell houses to tenants on that estate), and instead devoted its entire energies to organizing outings and arranging fêtes (a change in function reminiscent of that undergone by the Neithrop tenants' association in Banbury – see Stacey *et al.* 1975). Others, however, do continue to play a political role, but invariably the scope of their political concerns is restricted to relatively uncontentious issues where compromise between themselves and the local authority is readily possible. On questions such as the provision of a community centre, an increase in the council subsidy for existing facilities, the banning of heavy lorries from residential roads and so on, these associations do achieve a certain degree of success. They enjoy access to both the Housing Manager and the local elected representatives, and they are generally recognized (and recognize themselves) as 'reasonable' people with a right to be heard. As one tenants' leader explained, 'You have to act responsibly. . . . Demonstrations in the High Street aren't our line. The only way you can hope to do anything is through formal consultation.'

The problem, however, is that they enjoy this access and the right to consultation and participation on the council's terms. As Richardson (1977) has pointed out in her study of tenants' participation schemes in three London boroughs, the tenants are not in a position to control decision-making but only to influence it, and the extent to which they achieve this will depend upon 'their own persuasiveness and the willingness of the council representatives to listen to them' (p. 204). By and large, therefore, they achieve their successes only in those areas where the local authority is content that they should, and a wide range of potential issues is thus left off the agenda. Council house rents, for example, were raised in Croydon prior to the enactment of the 1972 Housing Finance Act with scarcely a murmur from the local tenants' associations, and those protests which did subsequently occur took place without their formal participation. Similarly, the level of amenity provisions and the quality of public transport links on isolated estates like New Addington are notoriously poor, yet such issues, it seems, are rarely taken up by the tenants' organizations. And on the broader issues – the dire shortage of low rent housing in the borough, the quality of social services provisions and so on – the tenants' associations have had nothing to say.

It is a familiar, yet nevertheless intuitively valid, argument that organizations like this function as much to control their members as to provide them with a means by which they can organize themselves against the local authority. Sometimes this control function breaks down – as in the case of a protest by young mothers who dumped their children at the council offices in an attempt to force the council to find them an alternative to high rise accommodation – but in general the tenants' associations prove useful to the housing department as channels of information through which council policies can be explained and local grievances can be ascertained. Indeed, one association owes its very existence to the Housing Manager who suggested to a meeting of tenants that they should form an organization to represent them. Similarly, the establishment of an elected council on a neighbouring estate in 1972 was actively aided by the local authority which provided ballot boxes and polling stations as well as giving moral support. But as one Chief Officer recognized in an interview, when the council helps to establish such organizations, 'It ends up by effectively taking them over', and to a large extent this is precisely what has happened. The more 'responsible' the group, the more effectively has the council been able to burden it with consultations and suffocate it with concern. It is not always advisable to play by the rules when the rules are drawn up by one's opponents.

It may be useful to draw a parallel at this point between the situation of Croydon's tenants' associations and Merton's classic work on the sociology of deviant behaviour. Merton (1957a) suggests that deviant behaviour may be explained in terms of a disjuncture between socially defined goals and access to the socially approved means of achieving them, and he distinguishes various modes of adaption to this disjuncture. The 'innovator', for example, pursues the goals by adopting unconventional means (a strategy which I shall discuss in the next section of this chapter); the 'ritualist' loses sight of the goals in his slavish acceptance of conventional means; and the 'retreatist' forsakes both goals and means. Applied to the situation of the tenants' associations, it is possible to identify the retreatist organizations, which have forsaken both their primary objectives and any significant political involvement, and to distinguish them from the ritualist groups which continue to participate in the local political system although their wider goals have been largely abandoned. In both cases they can be seen to have responded to a situation in which their goals (e.g. prevention of rent increases) appear largely unattainable. The organization has therefore adapted accordingly.

Unlike the retreatist groups, who organize splendid fêtes and carnivals but little else, the ritualist groups do achieve something. Community centres do get provided on their estates and subsidies of a few hundred pounds are granted by the local authority towards their running expenses. Action is taken to prevent tenants from parking lorries overnight in narrow estate roads. But these are arguably minor victories (concessions is perhaps a more appropriate term), for while the tenants' associations appear to win, nobody seems to lose; i.e. such victories are in no way redistributive. They are, however, highly charged symbolically, for they aid the legitimation of the political system itself by underlining the prevailing definition of it as pluralistic and accountable. As Lukes (1977a pp. 72–3) points out, political rituals (such as the ritul of tenants' participation) are thus crucial elements in the 'mobilization of bias'; tenants' leaders never raise the fundamental questions of rents, democratic housing management, local housing policy and so on, and for this reason they are able to register the occasional success in their gentlemanly disagreements with the council having long since ceded all the critical territory. The question raised by all this, of course, is whether a different mode of adaption on their part (e.g. 'innovation' in Merton's terms) could prove any more effective. This is a point I shall consider in the next section.

Neither the Labour Party nor the tenants' associations therefore provide the working class in Croydon with an effective means of articulating their demands and grievances. Nor, indeed, do any of the other established institutions of the labour movement – the trades unions are oriented almost exclusively towards industrial issues, while the trades council long ago fell into the hands of the extreme left and has subsequently played only the most peripheral of roles in local politics. An integral part of Hindess's thesis on the decline of working class politics, however, is that as the established Labour organizations decline in significance, new community-based groups may be expected to develop in their place: 'The issues themselves are increasingly raised outside the formal political organizations' (1971, p. 172). This argument is, of course, consistent with the view, considered in Chapter 3, that a new urban politics is developing in Britain – a view which arises out of the growth of new forms of community action over the last ten years or so.

One of the problems faced by the new community organizations is that they lack existing channels of communication with the local authority. Invariably, therefore, their actions must be more public and more visible, and this is likely to strain the indulgence of those they seek to influence. Furthermore, this lack of an institutionalized relationship with the local authority means that they are unlikely to be so well informed about future policy intentions. In other words, not only do such community groups find it more difficult to articulate their views within the formal parameters of the political system, but they are also likely to encounter difficulties in discovering information. This can be a crucial source of weakness for it tends to place these groups in a reactive role, responding to local authority initiatives after these have been formulated and possibly after the time for effective action has passed (see Batley 1972). To take one example from Croydon, a number of working class families discovered in 1965 that their homes lay in the path of a proposed flyover, and with the help of local Labour councillors they organized a campaign against the development. Their protest, however, proved totally ineffective due mainly to the fact that the council had taken its decision several years earlier, and their homes were subsequently demolished. Although the council had fulfilled all its statutory obligations in making its decision public, many of the residents apparently remained in ignorance of it, and this being the case, as one Labour councillor observed at the time, they had 'no opportunity to protest'.

Despite these problems of communication, however, community groups have enjoyed their successes, perhaps the best example of recent years being that of the campaign for a day nursery waged by the Crystal Palace Triangle Association. In common with most other social services provisions in Croydon, the level of nursery facilities in the borough is relatively low; at the time of this campaign, the local authority was spending 40 per cent less per child under five on this service than the average expenditure in London as a whole. Not surprisingly, therefore, the association encountered stout opposition from the council to its demands for a new nursery in Upper Norwood.

What is notable about this campaign is the way in which the organizers successfully maintained a balance between conciliation and coercion. The campaign began, for example, with a demonstration march to the town hall which could easily have been defined by the council and the press as an irresponsible and illegitimate tactic. However, a police request to shorten the march was readily accepted, and the subsequent loss of visible impact was amply compensated by the impression of political sobriety which this helped to create. On reaching the town hall the protesters sat quietly and respectfully through three hours of debate, only to find a Labour proposal for a new day nursery defeated. Undismayed, they again assembled at the town hall the next month. This time their general good humour was pointedly demonstrated, much to the delight of waiting newspaper photographers, by the presentation of a bouquet of flowers and a petition to the new lady mayor by the three-year-old daughter of one of the campaigners. Again, however, their efforts were in vain, for although they were later invited to discuss their grievances with the officers and members concerned, they secured no firm concessions. The association continued to maintain its pressure over the months that followed, during which time it also conducted a house-to-house survey which, it claimed, demonstrated a widespread demand for new nursery facilities in the area. Eventually, after six months, the chairman of the Social Services committee announced that a new day nursery would be built in Upper Norwood.

Three points should be noted about this unusually successful campaign. The first is that the protesters were able and willing to incur considerable costs in terms of time, money and energy over a relatively long period, and this reflects the fact that the campaign was run, organized and supported mainly by middle class residents. As Pickvance (1977b) argues, the capacity to bear such costs is clearly lower among working class groups, and during the period of my research in Croydon I found no comparable campaign in working class areas. The nursery campaign, in other words, was far from typical, and its success rested to a large extent on the control of certain key resources (e.g money, information, social cohesion) which may not ordinarily be available to less privileged groups.

The second point is that the campaign organizers managed to walk the precarious tightrope between exerting pressure on the one hand and remaining within the limits of the rules of the game on the other. Lacking any established private channels of influence, they addressed themselves publicly to the full council meeting, and they mirrored the performance enacted there with their own performance, carefully regulating their members' public behaviour and utilizing various 'props' (petitions, marches, bouquets, surveys) in different scenes with considerable skill. In effect, they mounted a minor street theatre, and at no point did they provide the local authority with the opportunity to define them as anything other than citizens with a legitimate grievance exercising their democratic rights. Furthermore, they also avoided any accusation of sectionalism by creating the impression that 'public opinion' was on their side. They claimed to speak for the silent majority, and they did so 'responsibly'.

It is the third point, however, which is the most important. Although the association's success can in part be related to the resources available to its members and in part to the dramaturgical skills of its leaders, the fact remains that it was a success of little political consequence. The protesters, of course, got their day nursery, but the level of nursery provisions in the borough as a whole was unaffected; indeed, it could be argued that the Crystal Palace Triangle Association succeeded only at the expense of some other less well-organized and less articulate area whose need may well have been greater (cf. Bell and Newby 1976). Like the more active tenants' organizations, therefore, the association was successful only according to its own very specific and highly restricted aims.

It is at this point that we need to refer back to Castells's argument that participatory movements function to reproduce the system of domination rather than to challenge it (see pages 131; that they are, in other words, agencies of social control rather than social change. In this section I have discussed three types of political participation ranging from the traditional reliance on representative government (in this case through the medium of the Labour Party), through involvement in established organizations enjoying institutionalized links with the local authority (illustrated by the tenants' associations), to the newly emergent community groups. In each case the conclusion has been that at best, participation succeeds in securing limited objectives, but that at worst it results merely in the symbolic legitimation of the system without securing any fundamental concessions.

In a recent work, Mathiesen (1974) has suggested that any genuine political alternative necessarily contains two elements; competition and contradiction. The first of these is generally achieved by the sorts of participatory strategies considered above, for these various groups have managed to gain a voice in the political system and thus to compete or articulate with it. The element of contradiction, however, has invariably been absent, for by virtue of their initial decision to pursue their aims within the system, these groups have been obliged to accept at the outset all the premises upon which the established relations of power are founded, including those which point to their own subordination. They have thus confronted the local authority, not as challengers, but as supplicants. Far from representing a challenge to the prevailing pattern of resource allocation, they have strengthened the pattern of distribution by competing for the crumbs while resolutely ignoring the cake. In Mathiesen's terms, they stand in a relation of 'competing agreement' with those in positions of power: 'Competition takes place – about nothing' (ibid., p. 15).

But how far can such conclusions be generalized from a single case study (especially one conducted in a relatively affluent commercial borough)? Perhaps two reservations need to be made. The first is that, even where participation does not lead to any effective shift in the pattern of resource distribution or to any qualitative change in the balance of power relations, it may nevertheless be significant in increasing access to information. As Darke and Walker suggest, 'Even simple dispersal of information cannot be dismissed as a token gesture if it forms part of a wider programme or if it leads to greater public awareness of policy and political influence' (1977, p. 93). Some formal scheme of public participation in planning, for example, had it been operative in the early 1960s, may well at least have alerted the working class families in Croydon whose homes lay in the path of the proposed flyover, and their campaign could have begun at an earlier date (although the question of whether it would have proved any more successful is doubtful). Against this, however, it has to be noted that the accumulated evidence on public participation exercises in Britain nearly all points to the continuing exclusion of the working class (cf. Batley 1972, Dennis 1970, Saunders *et al.* 1978). As Darke and Walker observe, 'If anything, experience is beginning to confirm the prediction that expanding the opportunities for participation in government will allow the already vociferous and politically active to further press their claims unless the authorities allow and compensate by reaching the non-joiners' (1977, p. 91).

This leads us on to the second point which is that, while participation may realize few immediate gains for the working class, it may nevertheless function to combat fatalism and political alienation, and thereby aid the development of collective consciousness (cf. Crouch 1977). In broader terms, it may be argued that an increase in community participation can backfire on a local authority; that having involved people for the first time (albeit peripherally) in policy-making, a local council may find that it has stirred up more than it bargained for. As Cockburn suggests, 'The management gains offered by the community approach at any level of intensity bring with them costs and dangers for the local state' (1977, p. 153), and she illustrates this argument with a discussion of how a couple of neighbourhood councils established by the local authority in Lambeth 'turned the council's own community weapons against it'

(p. 146), much to the chagrin of the majority Labour group. But in cases like this, of course, the participatory mode is itself transcended, for as the contradiction element increases, so the competition element declines. In other words, where participation does produce a challenge to the status quo, it very swiftly ceases to be participatory (indeed, as Cockburn's discussion of the fate of the Home Office Community Development Projects indicates, it may well cease to exist at all).

While participation may carry within it the seeds of a more radical movement, it nevertheless seems to be the case that the social control function is usually paramount. This is accomplished in two principal ways. First, by establishing formal links with a group such as a tenants' association, a local authority can 'educate' its public, inducing trust in decision-makers, the institutions in which they operate and the political culture which they take for granted (see Dennis, 1977). It can, furthermore, explain what is 'possible' and what is not, thereby avoiding any future potentially awkward demands. Secondly, participation provides a local authority with some gauge by which it can monitor the effects of its policies, a 'cybernetic feedback' through which it can secure greater efficiency and avoid future disturbances. This second function does, of course, contradict the first to some extent, for as Offe (1975), Dennis (1977) and others have pointed out, it demands effective rather than token participation, and this may run contrary to the social control function. It is precisely this contradiction which gives rise to the possibility discussed by Cockburn of public participation backfiring on a local council. In Croydon, however, this contradiction has rarely been exploited, and the fate of the various participatory movements discussed in this section strongly confirms the arguments of Castells and Mathiesen that for a fundamental challenge to be mounted, an alternative strategy is called for. The problem, however, is whether an alternative strategy is likely to meet with any greater degree of success.

The protest response: non-competing contradiction

In 1969, as a result of one of its regular economy drives stimulated by the levying of the annual rate, Croydon council introduced drastic cuts of up to 50 per cent in its grants to a variety of local voluntary charitable organizations. The Croydon Guild of Social Service, an umbrella organization representing the organizations affected, immediately sought formal discussions in an attempt to get the grants reinstated, but the subsequent negotiations achieved nothing. The Guild then called a public meeting at which the leaders of groups like the Spastics Society condemned the council's decision and called for a re-examination of the whole issue, but still the local authority stood firm. Even the Vicar of Croydon delivered a sermon at the annual civic service in which he criticized the unfairness of the cuts and took issue with the council's preoccupation with maintaining low rate levels, but he too achieved nothing. Responsible protest had been taken to its limits and had failed.

At the subsequent council meeting where the cuts were formally ratified, an ad hoc collection of left-wing groups, describing themselves collectively as the Radical Action Group, swelled the attendance in the public gallery and began chanting slogans and showering leaflets down onto the heads of the council members assembled below. Police were eventually called and the demonstrators ejected, but further disruptions later in the evening again brought proceedings to a halt, and the police had to be summoned for the second time. Reaction to all this on the part of the council leadership and the local press was as hostile as it was predictable. 'I will not allow our debates to be interfered with,' exclaimed the outraged mayor, while the chairman of the Guild of Social Service was swift to condemn the incident and to disassociate his organization from it. 'We were in no way concerned in this rather unfortunate business,' he assured the local newspaper.

It is not difficult to find other similar incidents. In 1972, for example, at the same time as the day nursery campaigners were parading quietly outside the town hall, protesters inside began shouting, stamping and hurling leaflets in a heated demonstration against council rent increases (as we saw earlier, the tenants' associations took no part in this demonstration). But as in 1969, this protest only succeeded in diverting public attention from the cause to the means used to further it. The editorial in the *Croydon Advertiser* (28 April 1972) spoke for most members of the council when it concluded, 'No one emerged with very much credit from the shambles that was Croydon council meeting on Monday – unless it were the women demonstrating peacefully outside the town hall for day nurseries. Their conduct was reasonably responsible. On the other hand, the rabble that filled the public gallery have nothing to be proud of.'

Similar disruptions, provoking similar reactions, occurred in 1973 when social workers and homeless families protested at a council meeting about the shortage of houses and temporary accommodation, and when teachers and parents complained about the lack of expenditure on education in the borough. Both proved totally ineffective, although both were significant in that they pointed to a developing alliance between state-employed professional service workers and their client populations – as Lewis has recently observed, 'The blatant failure of the state to solve social problems like housing, and the upsurge of the struggle by those affected, produces a tendency among social workers for their involvement to "grow over" into a full-blooded siding with the working class and other oppressed layers in their struggles' (1977, pp. 121–2).

Such protests have not only centred on the town hall, however, for during my research a small-scale squatting movement developed in the town. Empty houses owned by the local authority were occupied by groups of young radicals, mainly as a political gesture rather than as a pragmatic response to the housing shortage, but again they achieved little. In part this was because they had few links with the labour movement or with homeless families themselves, with the result that they searched in vain for several weeks for a genuine homeless family to join them in their squat. But their failure was also related to the fact that, like the council demonstrators, their cause easily became overlooked in the publicity and criticism which their action provoked. Bags of flour bursting over bailiffs' heads make better copy (and are more easily condemned) than the mere repetition of dull demands for a change in housing policy.

Those who disrupt council meetings, squat in empty houses, dump their children on the town hall steps or engage in other 'coercive' strategies thus pose a contradiction to the system while failing to compete within it. While avoiding the problems of incorporation experienced by the tenants' associations, they therefore lay themselves open to strategies of exclusion on the part of the local authority, for their actions are all too easily defined as illegitimate and hence as undeserving of serious attention. As Mathiesen explains, 'The contradiction of this opposition may be disregarded as permanently "outside", and thereby be set aside, because it is beyond doubt that the message does not belong to the established system' (1974, pp. 14–15). Thus we arrive at an appreciation of the central dilemma facing opponents of the status quo: play the game by the rules and become 'defined in' as a minor and accommodating appendage to the system, or attack the system from outside and become 'defined out' as an irritating but inconsequential irrelevance to it.

This dilemma is not in principle irresolvable, but if it is to be overcome, two factors appear essential, neither of which were in evidence in the various spluttering protests which occurred in Croydon. The first of these is genuine and widespread popular support and mobilization. The squatting movement, for example, inevitably took the form of a token gesture rather than a real challenge to the council's housing policies because it failed to reach the victims of these policies. It was therefore not only external to the political system, but also external to those most affected by it, and as such it was from the outset an alien strategy. This argument only serves to underline the point made earlier that effective urban protests must arise out of ongoing struggles and cannot simply be created by radicals on behalf of disadvantaged groups (see page 131). The implication of this is that such protests will invariably be reactive, building upon people's responses to specific policies and decisions. Attempts to initiate protest are always likely to appear utopian if not elitist.

The second necessary factor which was absent in Croydon was political organization. This appears important for at least four reasons: it aids mobilization of the social base, it enables links to be made between different struggles involving different groups, it provides a coherent programme within which the protest can be situated and its goals and direction determined, and it provides a means whereby the protest can articulate with the political system. As Castells says of the movements of the 1960s, so too it may be said of the protests discussed above, 'The problem ... was not their integration into the system and their inadequate spontaneous base, but, on the contrary, their insufficient level of organization and their role as political outsiders. Thus, the results were the absence of any cumulative mass movement, an inability to sustain the advantages obtained in urban services, and political isolation' (1977a, p. 423). The problem, of course, is where this political organization is to be found, and it is here that the growing evidence (in Croydon and elsewhere) of the radicalization of state professional employees may be significant. In other words, it may be suggested that if an organized response is to be forthcoming, its roots may lie in the trades unions representing teachers, social workers and other local authority employees, for these groups are themselves affected by social expenditure cuts (e.g. through reduction of the local authority payroll) while they are at the same time located at the interface of the 'local state' and the client population. The joint protests of teachers and parents, social workers and homeless families, which occurred in Croydon in 1973 may therefore be indicative of a developing trend in local politics, although the evidence for such an assertion is extremely tentative.

One factor in all this which has not been discussed, however, is the problem of ideology. As we saw in Chapter 3, there is a strong argument running through much of the literature on working class protest (or the lack of it) to the effect that the key to the political passivity of disadvantaged groups is not so much the lack of organization as the conditioned acceptance of the dominant value system. In his account of the London squatting movement, for example, Bailey (1973a) suggests that ideological factors prevented the development of a mass movement despite the existence of a strong and committed organization, while Dennis (1970) similarly explains working class apathy in terms of the life-experience of the industrial wage earner which generates a sense of helplessness and hopeless inevitability. Such arguments lead naturally into the suggestion, made by Parkin (1971), that radical political action can only follow from the successful imposition of a radical value system to counter the hegemony of the dominant value system – an argument which has much in common with Gramsci's concern to develop a counter-hegemonic working class ideology. If this is the case, of course, then the prospects for working class radicalism appear bleak indeed, given the current state of the British Labour Party.

This emphasis on ideology as the primary explanation for lower class political passivity has, however, been challenged by a number of writers. Batley (1972), for example, found that while half of the working class families threatened by urban renewal in the Byker ward of Newcastle did not wish to move to another area, they failed to organize any effective protest, not so much because of ideological factors, but more because they were fatalistic about any such protest succeeding and because they lacked any channels for articulating their discontent. The working men's clubs were apolitical while the Labour Party organization was ineffective. Similarly Benington and Skelton (1972) suggest on the basis of their work with the CDP in Coventry that 'a considerable proportion of people felt strong hostility towards the Authorities', and that, 'The "problem" of participation in government is not primarily a problem of the attitudes or behaviour of sections of the public who do not want to participate, but of the structures, processes and values of the governmental system' (p. 10). Such arguments are further supported by Chamberlain (1977) who conducted a study in the London Borough of Barking in which he attempted to discover why some council tenants failed to join a rent strike against the 1972 Housing Finance Act. He found considerable sympathy for those on rent strike from those who had not joined the action, and he discovered little evidence to support Parkin's thesis that radical ideologies do not arise spontaneously among the working class. Rather he concluded that the inaction of those who had failed to join the strike 'arose from a feeling that there was little that they could do that might prove effective in stopping the increase and this was combined with fear that withholding might result in either eviction or blacklisting by the council. Their decision not to take part in the protest was primarily of a pragmatic rather than a moral character' (ibid., p. 171).

In terms of the discussion of non-decision-making (see pages 28–33), therefore, such evidence strongly suggests that the political inactivity of disadvantaged groups is due more to 'negative decision-making' and 'anticipated reactions' than to a 'mobilization of bias'. Put another way, it seems that grievances are often subjectively recognized, but that they fail to 'surface' in the political system because of fatalism (it would not do any good to protest), fear (what would happen to us if we did protest?) and exclusion (how can we protest?). If this is the case, then the problem for radical groups is not so much how to develop a counter-hegemonic ideology, but rather how to develop an organization which can overcome exclusion and a level of political success which can overcome anticipated reactions. In other words, given an effective means of protest, and given an effective demonstration that protest can succeed, the political passivity of disadvantaged groups could be overcome.

What is involved here is the pursuit of a strategy of 'revolutionary reform' (Gorz 1967, Holland 1975). This is a strategy which attempts to walk the tightrope between competing agreement and non-competing contradiction by pushing for reforms within the system while refusing to be constrained by the parameters of possibility laid down by the system. The danger of incorporation will always be present in such a strategy, but its strength is that it provides a basis for popular mobilization around concrete issues and thus avoids the political isolation characteristic of the squatters and others in Croydon. It is a strategy which, in seeking concessions while never being content with what is conceded, can point to real gains as the means of overcoming fatalism and fear, and which at the same time can provide the organization which is so crucial for the mobilization of disadvantaged groups.

There are, however, two obvious problems with such a strategy. The first is that it faces the classic 'Catch-22' paradox of having to secure gains before it can mobilize popular support, while being unable to achieve this without some degree of popular support in the first place. This would appear to limit its potential application to those cases where spontaneous protest is already occurring in response to specific policies such as urban renewal or rent increases (see the discussion of Olives's study of popular protest in Paris, pages 129). The second problem is more daunting, for it is a strategy which can only be pursued through the existing institutions of the Labour movement if it is to avoid political isolation. The problem here is that the Labour movement in Britain itself appears inextricably incorporated into the system – certainly at the local level we have seen that neither the Labour Party nor the tenants' associations appear to be in a position to develop a fundamental challenge, while the trades unions and trades councils show only the slightest interest in issues of collective consumption. If a challenge is to be mounted, it must come through organizations such as these, but the lesson of this chapter would appear only to reinforce the conclusion drawn in Chapter 3 that the likelihood of this happening appears remote.

8 Business interests and local policy

Father Christmas came early to Croydon in 1974. Resplendent in red robe and white wig, he took up residence in Santa's Grotto in the heart of one of the town's leading department stores many weeks before the season of goodwill had begun in most other parts of the country, and there he set about distributing largesse in small parcels to the bewildered children of the town centre shoppers. Although the artificial snow may have appeared to some as rather incongruous in the late autumn sunshine, the sound of sleigh bells in the High Street blended easily with the merry jangling of cash registers, for Croydon's business community is nought if not enterprising, and even the seasons adjust themselves readily to the pursuit of profitability.

Most studies of local government in Britain have concluded that business interests play only a small part in local politics. Shopkeepers, company directors, estate agents and others are, of course, found in significant numbers on most local councils, but this, we are told, is as far as business involvement extends. As Banfield and Wilson assert, 'No businessman would dream of giving leadership to a local council from behind the scenes. If he wanted to take part in local government he would stand for election, and if he won a seat he would regard himself as the representative of a public, not of the business community' (1966, p. 246). Such conclusions have been drawn, not only from studies of small towns (where it may perhaps be argued that there is little reason or incentive for business interests to become involved in the local political system), but also from research in large commercial cities such as Birmingham (Newton 1976) where the economic significance of commerce and retailing is as great, if not greater, as it is in Croydon, and where local policy-making in planning, roads and so on may be expected to have an important impact on the profitability of the private sector. From this it would seem that in Croydon too, we should expect to find that local businessmen confine their initiative to economic affairs while keeping their political involvement to a minimum. As one informant told me early in my research in the town, 'These big firms are too big to piss around with local politics.'

We have seen that nearly half of the membership of Croydon council are businessmen (see page 213). Furthermore, business interests dominate the council's strategic positions, occupying eight out of eleven committee chairmanships and five of the seven seats on the Policy subcommittee. The leader of the council owns a couple of shops in the north of the borough, the deputy-leader is in partnership with another leading Conservative member in a solicitor's practice in the south, and their senior colleagues in the majority group include another solicitor, a chartered surveyor, an estate agent/company director and two other company directors. Not only are businessmen as a whole well represented in the council, therefore, but those with property interests (e.g. developers and exchange professionals) are particularly prominent. Conspicuous by their absence, however, are the senior and middle management of the various international companies with their British head offices in the town. The businessmen on the council are thus mainly members of the local bourgeoisie.

Invariably, with so many local businessmen with direct or indirect property interests occupying key positions in the council, there have been cases in Croydon where leading members have found themselves involved in development issues in both their private and official capacities. In 1973, for example, a local building company applied to the council for permission to develop fourteen houses in the south of the borough. The solicitors acting for the company were both prominent councillors, the company's agent was another leading member of the majority group, and yet another Conservative member was involved in the issue by virtue of his agreement to sell part of his land for the development. All scrupulously declared their interests. In the same year, when the Strategic Planning subcommittee met to consider the Whitgift Foundation proposals for development at Haling Park (see pages 249–58), no less than four of the seven committee members turned out to be governors of the Foundation. Such cases are by no means rare (the chairman of the Plans subcommittee, for example, regularly declared an interest with regard to his position as managing director of a company supplying materials to the building industry), and although, as the local newspaper observed, 'An unfortunate impression may be given in such circumstances', it is nevertheless clear that no businessman gains an unfair or illegitimate advantage through his membership of the local authority. The fact that so many council members are businessmen, in other words, cannot of itself be taken as indicative of Banfield and Wilson's 'leadership from behind the scenes'. As we shall see, business interests are influential in local politics in Croydon, but this influence has nothing to do with the pursuit of self-interest by individual council members. Indeed, those sections of the business community which appear to gain most from local policy-making are precisely those which are not represented directly in the council chamber.

The town centre redevelopment

Croydon's economy today is dominated by the commercial sector. The town centre is littered with more than fifty office blocks, and the Victorian town hall which imperiously dominated the skyline in the 1950s is today almost totally eclipsed by the glittering blocks of twenty or more storeys which surround it. As Rennison observes, 'Standing on the roof of one of the many tower blocks, the visitor might well imagine that he is in the City of London such is the proliferation of great buildings defining great wealth' (*Financial Times*, 8 February 1973). Or as the mayor put it (rather less subtly) when he officially opened the new Nestlé's block in 1965, 'They could be excused for believing they own Croydon.'

The story of the transformation of the town centre began after the last war when, in accordance with the 1947 Town and Country Planning Act, Croydon council (they a County Borough) prepared a plan for post-war reconstruction. The plan eventually submitted to the Minister of Housing and Local Government was an ambitious document calling for the enlargement of the central business district, the establishment of five comprehensive redevelopment areas, and the construction of a number of new roads around the town centre. The plan proved too ambitious for the government, however, and the proposals finally accepted in 1954 constituted a much diluted version of the original proposals. The council leadership was undeterred. In the following year the Finance committee, under the chairmanship

of Sir James Marshall (who was also leader of the council) recommended that the local authority purchase a two-acre site near the
town centre to facilitate a road widening scheme. According to Sir
James, the most expeditious way of achieving this was through sponsoring a special bill in Parliament, and this was agreed. Perhaps the
most important clause of what was to become the 1956 Croydon
Corporation Act was that which authorized the local authority 'to
develop either themselves or by selling or leasing to others land bought
under the bill and not required for street works requirements.' In
other words, the council was empowered to buy up land in the town
centre without having to face public inquiries, and then to release
parcels of this land for private development. This Act represented the
key which was to open the floodgates of commercial redevelopment
in the years that followed, for like the Community Land Act of
twenty years later, it enabled the local authority to adopt a brokerage
role, clearing and preparing prime development sites for private
developers to step in. As Lamarche says of Quebec, so it may also be
said of Croydon, 'It is as if the role of the city was to clear and plough
its own land in order for others to sow and harvest the best fruit'
(1976, p. 104).

The harvest was not long in coming. Armed with its new powers,
the council purchased the two acres it needed for the road scheme, to
which it added a further two acres already in municipal ownership.
The road was then widened, and the remaining land was leased to the
Norwich Union Insurance Company for development. Following
discussions with the council, Norwich Union agreed to include in its
initial plans for a shopping development additional proposals for two
hundred thousand square feet of office space. By 1959, Croydon's
first three new office blocks, diminutive by today's standards, had
been completed on the site. But from such small acorns, large oak
trees grow. The Norwich Union development proved a commercial
success, and other developers were not slow in recognizing the town's
potential. Croydon was within ten miles of the centre of London and
rail links with the City were excellent. Office rents in the town at this
time were between one-third and one-half of those in central London,
local wage rates were somewhat lower, local property taxes were
considerably lower and the council was willing to provide productive
infrastructure to support any new commercial development. Furthermore, it was government policy at this time to encourage firms in

central London to relocate in the suburbs and the new towns. In every sense, therefore, Croydon was ripe for redevelopment.

Croydon council was, however, somewhat taken aback by the extent of the demand for offices in the town centre. Hastily, forty-five acres in the north-east of the town centre were designated for redevelopment, and when this had been allocated, further sites were found elsewhere. Having engendered the office boom, Sir James and his colleagues sat back and watched with some amazement as their infant swiftly grew to elephantine proportions. The role of the local authority was from now on limited to the collection of an expanding rateable revenue (which increased by around 20 per cent as a result of the office developments), the provision of supportive infrastructure, and the consideration of an escalating number of planning applications. No comprehensive redevelopment plan was ever produced, the only concession to planning orthodoxy being the appointment of an architects panel which considered applications on a piecemeal basis but which had no powers for directing the overall pattern of development (see Lovejoy 1971). The result was all too predictable: 'The main office area is a mixture of unrelated designs and some blocks, particularly on the edges of the central area, are badly out of scale with their surroundings. There is little relief to the eye from the harshness of many of the buildings; routine commercial architecture has, in the main, been the order of the day' (Walker 1970, p. 59). Not that the developers, or indeed the council, were too much concerned with aesthetics. Profit levels on the one hand and rateable revenue on the other appear to have been the main considerations (Marriott 1967), and on these criteria, the redevelopment was wholly successful.

By the end of the 1960s there were five million square feet of offices in the town centre in addition to a further one and a half million in outlying areas of the borough. Many large national and international companies had moved into the town, including a host of insurance companies, and office rents had risen steeply from as low as 50p per square foot in the late 1950s to around £5 per square foot just ten years later. Not surprisingly, developers enjoyed a bonanza. Two local businessmen, for example, concluded a deal with the Church Commissioners (major landowners in the town) to develop an area of small shops into 400,000 square feet of offices and 200,000 square feet of shopping precinct. The latter proved less successful than was

hoped (due mainly to competition from the more favourably located
Whitgift Centre completed a few years later), but this did not prevent
them from selling their holding in 1972 to the British Land Company
for a reported £10 million. Even more profitable, however, was the
Whitgift Centre with 537,000 square feet of offices and 460,000
square feet of shops arranged on two levels on a twelve-acre site in the
centre of the town. This project proved a personal success for Sir
James Marshall who was at this time not only chairman of the council's planning committee, but also chairman of the Whitgift Foundation. In his latter role, Sir James sold the lease of the site (which had
previously been the home of the Trinity grammar school) to Ravenseft Properties in 1965 for an annual rental of £200,000, plus a share
in the profits, plus a £1 million lump sum which was used to build a
new school three miles out of the town. The entire project was a great
commercial success for both Ravenseft and the Foundation. Every
shop was let before construction had been completed, many of the
town's established stores built access into the centre, and the council
obliged by developing a large multi-storey car park to service it.

The council, in fact, did much during these years to ensure the
commercial viability of the mushrooming shops and offices. Some of
its accomplishments, such as the development of a new Technical
College campus in the late 1950s or even the construction of the
Fairfield Halls entertainment complex in the early 1960s, could be
described as aiding the reproduction of labour power. Certainly, as
we shall see, the college has attracted the interest of a number of
the larger companies as a training ground for future employees,
while the Fairfield Halls figure prominently in brochures advertising
the attractions of the town for professional and managerial workers.
But having said this, the council's prime role has been to provide the
infrastructure necessary for the new developments; those facilities
which are a prerequisite for sustained profitability but the provision
of which is not itself commercially viable. Of particular importance
here has been the council's ringroad and car park development
scheme.

The ringroad was an ambitious, costly and socially disruptive
development, planned in six stages (one of which included the four-
lane centrally heated flyover that dispersed the working class
families discussed in Chapter 7), which was designed to circumvent
the town centre and to afford easy access to it for private cars and

commercial deliveries. Integral to the plan was the concomitant development of a series of ten multi-storey car parks inside the ring to service the shops and offices contained within it. The cost of the ringroad ran into millions of pounds and hundreds of working class houses demolished, while the development of the car parks alone was budgeted to take up 5 per cent of annual expenditure for years ahead. Given Croydon council's commitment to a low rate policy, the ringroad and car parks have been two of the very few areas of council spending which have not been subject to cuts in the annual attempts to pare down total expenditure. In the spring of 1973, for example, the council agreed to reduce committee estimates in health education and social services while at the same time authorizing the allocation of a further £500,000 to the construction of the sixth car park in the series. Attacked by some Labour members, the council leadership made clear its commitment to policies explicitly designed to aid private profitability in the town centre. As one Conservative member explained, 'We must not strangle the town, particularly around the Whitgift Centre, because people want to park there.' Or as one of his colleagues said of the car parks, 'They are needed for the Whitgift Centre shops and surrounding area.'

The baldness of these statements is indicative of the inability of the council leadership to distinguish between business interests and the public interest. For them, the two are synonymous, yet it is clear that their policies have only benefited the town centre enterprises at the expense of many other groups in the local population. As Simmie says of urban road schemes like the ringroad, 'In the first place, they tend to destroy more poor homes than rich ones, while at the same time employing funds which, among other things, means the foregoing of other opportunities such as the building of more local authority housing. After they are built, they do not serve the poor unless they possess private transport. . . . Expenditure from public funds on urban motorways is therefore progressive in the benefits it generates, and regressive in the incidence of costs' (1974, p. 146). There is little doubt, therefore, as to who has reaped the benefits and who has paid the costs of the council's support of the redevelopment since the late 1950s.

What is interesting, however, is that the working class – those who lost their homes, saw the waiting list increase and bore the brunt of the successive cuts in social expenditure – were not the only ones to be disadvantaged by the town centre redevelopment. Local industry, for a start, has periodically expressed its disquiet at the growing imbalance between the commercial and industrial sectors, and has complained particularly about the impact this has had on the supply of labour. Croydon has traditionally been a centre for light engineering, and companies like Philips, Trojans, Mullards and AGI employ thousands of skilled workers, but both Croydon and the GLC are united in a policy of discouraging industrial expansion in the borough. Of the 250 acres zoned for industrial use, 20 per cent is being used for non-industrial purposes, but any land that falls vacant in these zoned areas is reserved for the relocation of non-conforming users from other parts of the borough and for local industry displaced by council development schemes. What all this amounts to is that local industry is effectively prevented from expanding due to shortage of both labour and land, and many companies have in consequence either closed down or moved out. Things came to a head in 1967 when Philips, which employs some 3000 workers on a thirty-acre factory site, announced that it was considering relocating elsewhere due to the council's policy of attracting commerce at the expense of industry; a threat which was later withdrawn but which was clearly indicative of the growing concern of industrial capital with the pattern of local authority policies.

Perhaps more significant than the concern expressed by local industry, however, has been the resentment caused by the town centre redevelopment among small entrepreneurs in outlying areas of the borough. There is in Croydon a significant economic and political division in the business community between the centre and the periphery, the big multi-nationals and retailers on the one hand, and the small shopkeepers in the outer areas on the other. To some extent, this is expressed in the separation between the Croydon Chamber of Commerce, which offers its members a wide range of commercial and export services, and the seven smaller Chambers of Trade which are composed almost entirely of small shopkeepers, and it is instructive to note that all seven rejected a Chamber of Commerce proposal for amalgamation in 1973/74 despite the obvious advantages of amalgamation in terms of political muscle. The evident tension which exists between these two groups reflects two main factors: the loss of trade experienced by the petty bourgeoisie as custom has increasingly been attracted to the town centre, and the neglect of the outlying areas by the local authority as it has concentrated its resources on developing infrastructural support for the town centre enterprises.

The first factor is illustrated by the fate of traders in the Crown Hill area which lies immediately to the west of the town centre. Traders in this area have undoubtedly been adversely affected by the development of the Croydon and Whitgift shopping precincts, and the council's ringroad scheme threatened them with virtual extinction by further reinforcing their isolation from the main shopping thoroughfare and by diverting the main traffic routes (including bus routes) away from their shops and directly into the centre. This latter threat to their livelihood was later mediated to some extent by the addition of a sliproad to the original ringroad plan, but this concession has been of only limited comfort given the intense competition which the area now experiences from the large stores just a few hundred yards away up the hill.

Such loss of trade has been exacerbated in some of the shopping areas further out of the centre by local authority neglect and sub-sequent planning blight. A classic example is the area known as the Crystal Palace Triangle in Upper Norwood; a relatively prosperous part of south London until the war, but an area which has ex-perienced urban decay and commercial decline ever since. Part of the reason for the continuing decline has been that the area falls on the boundaries of three London boroughs (Croydon, Bromley and Lambeth), and this has led to a planning stalemate, with Croydon and Lambeth in particular disputing the route of a new road and thus delaying any redevelopment. But in addition to this, there are strong grounds for arguing that Croydon council has been reluctant to encourage redevelopment in Upper Norwood until such time as the town centre development has been completed. Certainly, many traders in the area are convinced that the Triangle could have been redeveloped successfully many years ago had it not been for Croy-don's stubbornness; the chairman of the Upper Norwood Chamber of Trade was quoted in the *Croydon Advertiser* (12 December 1973) as saying, 'Croydon has always been fed up with Upper Norwood. They are only interested in the prosperity of the town centre', and these sentiments were echoed by the leader of a local amenity society who told me, 'We've long been convinced that the reason Croydon delayed the redevelopment of the Triangle was so that there would be no competition to their new town centre. If the Triangle had been developed fifteen years ago, Norwood people wouldn't have gone all the way to Croydon to shop.'

Whether or not such arguments are accepted, the fact remains that they are believed by many small shopkeepers who have thus come to associate Croydon council with the interests of the big town centre companies, and who feel themselves left out in the cold. The situation is thus analogous to that identified by Lojkine (1977) in his study of redevelopment in Lyon and Rennes (see pages 163–5), for he too documented an increasing alienation of the petty bourgeoisie from the municipal authorities they have traditionally supported. Lojkine's suggestion that this may result in the radicalization of the small shopkeepers is not, however, borne out by my own impressions, and it is important to remember that antagonism towards 'monopoly capital' is by no means exclusive to the left.

The most obvious and interesting question raised by the examples of how the town centre development has affected the interests of the small shopkeepers is why it is that a local authority dominated by *local* businessmen pursued such a policy in the first place. As we saw earlier, the big companies which have benefited most are not generally speaking, represented in the council chamber at all. An obvious but misleading response to this question would be to argue that local political leaders have either been the pawns of the big companies or have been the agents through which the logic of capitalist development has expressed itself. Such arguments must surely be rejected given that the local authority was itself largely responsible for sponsoring the redevelopment in the first place through the 1956 Act of Parliament (i.e. it took an active rather than a reactive role), and that its leading members have remained firmly committed to it ever since (e.g. when the new leader of the council took over from Sir James Marshall in 1965, he announced his intention 'to make Croydon the greatest commercial centre outside central London'). Although the scale and speed of the redevelopment surprised everybody, it was nevertheless the result of a deliberate and purposive policy adopted by a council which was dominated by small and medium sized business interests.

A number of factors have probably contributed to the council's firm commitment to commercial development in the town centre.

One concerns the values of those in positions of power, for leading politicians see the redevelopment as the expression both of their belief in free enterprise and of their intense civic pride; they regularly draw comparisons between Croydon and Manhattan, and the analogy is evaluated entirely positively. A second factor has, of course, been the desire to expand the local tax base and thus to maintain a low rate levy. But in addition to factors such as these, it is impossible to explain why the redevelopment took place without taking into account the pivotal role played by Sir James Marshall.

In arguing thus, I am not suggesting that the redevelopment could not have taken place without Sir James, for the material conditions for the office boom were clearly in evidence in the 1950s: he, like other men, made his own history, but he did not do so under conditions of his own choosing. I am arguing, however, that until 1965, Sir James reigned supreme in Croydon, a political Gulliver in the Lilliputian land of local government, and that the way in which the redevelopment was accomplished was directly attributable to him. As Marriott observes,

> This practical approach to the replanning of Croydon reflects the driving force of one man, Sir James Marshall. . . . Although an elected representative rather than an official, this hard-headed autocrat was in a sense comparable to an American-style town boss. What Marshall said, went. Extremely commercially minded and an orthodox Conservative, he was, as it were, the managing director of Croydon. He got things done quickly – and they worked. When I talked to him about the transformation of Croydon, he remarked wryly that 'the best committee is a committee of one'. A property developer who had operated in Croydon recalled that, 'One didn't get anywhere if Sir James disapproved of one' [1967, pp. 185–6].

Entering the council in 1928, he was identified just four years later by the (now defunct) *Croydon Times* as one of Croydon's 'men of mark': 'Economy is his watchword.' He became an alderman in 1936 (and was therefore never again subject to popular election), a magistrate in 1937, and chairman of the Whitgift Foundation in 1944. He was leader of the council throughout the early years of the redevelopment, and as chairman of the Finance committee, it was he who masterminded the Croydon Corporation Act. Later, as chairman of both the Planning committee and the Whitgift Foundation, he was directly involved in many of the schemes which followed including, of course, the development of the Whitgift

Centre. His multiplicity of roles gave him a finger in every significant pie of the period, and he commanded (and, as his intervention in the Haling Park issue in 1973 demonstrated, still commands) great respect and not a little deference in the town. Undeniably, he left his personal imprint on the town, and although the conditions were ripe for commercial exploitation, Sir James provided the spark which ignited the mixture.

Even after Sir James's departure, however, the local authority remained committed to further office development, even though this has increasingly brought it into conflict with the national government and, more particularly, the GLC. The famous 'Brown ban' on office development in 1964 had little impact in Croydon since most proposed developments at the time were either in progress or had been contracted, but the later restrictions imposed by the Office Development Permit scheme (under which any project of over 10,000 square feet had to gain government approval) did begin to limit the council's aspirations. These restrictions were then further tightened in the early 1970s by the GLC. At the 1972 Greater London Development Plan inquiry, the GLC sought to limit the allocation of additional office space in the borough to 1,000,000 square feet over a five-year period, two-thirds of this being already accounted for by the proposed redevelopment of the East Croydon station site. Croydon, on the other hand, demanded a minimum allocation of over 50 per cent more than the GLC maximum, and the town's deputy director of development thus found himself in the unenviable position of having to argue this case while at the same time refusing to countenance any change in council policy on housing densities:

Q: You want to make the position worse as far as I can see.

A: I suppose you could say that as far as housing is concerned. If we had more office floor space than we have in Croydon, I suppose it would add greater pressure for housing.

Q: I would have thought you would be saying to us that insofar as the GLC has a policy for the redistribution of employment, the allocations in outer London boroughs should be such that Croydon takes a lesser proportionate share rather than a greater.

A: I am in a little bit of difficulty here, sir. . . . [GLDP Inquiry, 1972, day 227]

By 1974, the GLC announced that no further office development was to be allowed in Croydon, even where a government permit had been granted.

Croydon council has, however, continued to fight vigorously against GLC restrictions on behalf of private developers. In 1974, for example, a local building company purchased one of the few remaining undeveloped sites in the town centre and submitted a plan to demolish the church and church hall which then stood on the site and replace them with a relatively modest seven storey office block. Croydon accepted the plan but the GLC rejected it, arguing instead that the site should be used for some form of housing development. Spokesmen for both the company and the council jointly condemned this 'interference' from County Hall. As one executive in the company told me, 'Croydon was happy to have the office development but the GLC wants a block of flats. It's a political thing. There's no love lost between Croydon and the GLC.'

Croydon council has thus consistently allied itself with developers and with the interests of those companies which occupy the offices they build. They have done so at the cost of alienating many sections of the local petty bourgeoisie, locally-based industrial capital and higher governmental authorities. In part this policy reflects specific historical factors, the desire to increase rateable revenue and a firmly-rooted belief in the virtues of a free enterprise system. But it also reflects the nature of the relationship which has come to be established between the local authority and large commercial capital. It is with a consideration of this relationship that the remainder of this chapter is concerned.

A community of interest and sentiment

We have already seen that, although Croydon council is to a large extent run by businessmen, the town centre business interests – the large retailers and the various national and multi-national companies – are not generally represented in its membership. This does not mean that they are politically inactive, however, for what is immediately apparent when one begins to analyse the membership of a wide variety of boards, committees and quasi-political organizations in the town is that, far from being 'too big to piss around with local politics', the senior management levels of these companies are intimately engaged in the administrative and political life of the town. As a Chamber of Commerce official explained when discussing two of the largest companies, 'The managing director of X and the chairman of Y both take an active interest in Croydon. It's amazing how many different committees they're involved in and how much they know about local affairs. . . . They'll even know if the mayor's secretary has resigned! I don't know where they find the time.' Indeed, he suggested (and this was confirmed in subsequent interviews) that in both cases it was explicit company policy to encourage middle and senior management to become personally involved in the town: 'If a man wants promotion, he will involve himself in the community as much as in his job.'

This high level of participation in local affairs takes on a particular significance when we recognize that, in virtually every case, the organizations in which town centre businessmen become involved are those in which local authority members and officers are also to be found. The list of such bodies is extensive, and it includes the Chamber of Commerce, the Technical College board of governors, the council's Youth Employment subcommittee (which includes coopted members from business, the trades unions and the teaching profession), hospital management committees, the local magistrates bench, the National Savings committee and the governing committee of the National Savings Bank, the Rotary Club and other social, professional and sporting clubs, the Whitgift Foundation governing body and the managing committees of other less prominent local charities, the Bishop of Croydon's Industrial Chaplaincy, and so on. In all of these cases, to a greater or lesser extent, representatives of town centre businesses regularly rub shoulders with some of the most politically powerful individuals in the borough.

Consider, for example, the Chamber of Commerce, to which most of the big companies belong and in which many play an active and official part. The Chamber of course, offers a number of commercial benefits and services to its members, and these are likely to be of interest to some of the larger companies, although most already have their own expertise in the fields of taxation, marketing, exports and so on. The Chamber of Commerce is also the principal organized voice of business in the politics of the town, although here again, as we shall see, most of the big companies enjoy direct relationships with the local authority and are therefore unlikely to need the Chamber to represent them. This leaves the Chamber's 'social' function, and it is arguably this – i.e. the opportunity which it offers for social intercourse with both business and political leaders in the town – which represents its main attraction to the large town centre enterprises.

Included in the membership of Croydon Chamber of Commerce are a number of local councillors with business interests in the town, and notably the chairman of the Highways committee (a local estate agent and director of a property company) and the chairman of the Plans subcommittee (managing director and chairman of a large builders' merchants and director of a property development company). As one local shopkeeper and former chairman of the Chamber put it, 'You get to know local councillors of both parties through the Chamber.' While it would be misleading as well as melodramatic to describe the Chamber in Croydon as a 'front organization' (cf. Minnis 1967), it is therefore apparent that, for the larger companies, it may function more as a means of establishing and maintaining contacts with other business and political leaders than as a servicing organization or a local pressure group. Thus the informant quoted above told me, 'The large multi-national companies based in the town rarely do more than hold an annual reception for Chamber members. Mind you, they spend a lot on it. And they only do that much if they can be sure that the mayor, most of the councillors, and the chief officers are going to attend. They do it to get to know the most important people in the borough. . . . They justify the expense in terms of establishing contacts and goodwill.'

This is not, of course, how the companies themselves explain their involvement, for most of those I visited claimed that their participation in the Chamber and in other organizations stemmed from a recognition of corporate responsibility and personal obligation towards the town. 'It would be morally wrong for me not to be involved in it,' explained one department store chairman about his company's membership of the Chamber. 'Businessmen are good workers and good organizers, and many of them have got a social conscience,' said another who was himself engaged in a host of local bodies. The big multi-nationals, too, point to corporate philanthropy as the reason for their involvement, one company in particular stressing its obligation to become immersed in local activities on account of its situation as an important local employer.

Even when these companies become involved in explicitly commercial transactions, the assertion of altruism is commonly found. In 1972, for example, the Philips pension fund 'saved' one of Croydon's independent schools which had run into financial difficulties and which was to be bought out by the local authority. At the last minute, the pension fund matched the council's offer for the land and buildings and leased the site back to the school as a long-term investment. The *Croydon Advertiser,* however, saw this more as a moral than a commercial transaction: 'They are a local firm, and I understand that the fund feels it should help where it can on educational and moral grounds' (8 December 1972). Yet as a Labour councillor later observed, 'If Philips wanted to be charitable they could have given the money to the school.'

Business claims of philanthropy should not, however, be dismissed as mere subterfuge, for such claims are genuinely made. What is apparent, though, is that altruistic motives may result in the advancement of company interests. Two cases in point concern big business involvement in the Technical College and the Rotary Club.

In addition to their participation on the college board of governors, where they sit side by side with the leader of the council and some of his senior colleagues, high-level management in some of the largest companies in the town also provide direct financial support for the Technical College. They sponsor training courses (e.g. one food-processing company finances courses in catering), they finance systems of awards (e.g. the same company pays for top pupils to visit some of its overseas factories), and they make occasional gifts of equipment (IBM, for example, donated a computer). For all of this corporate concern, the college authorities are undoubtedly very grateful, but unsolicited aid rarely comes without implicit conditions. As one company executive mused, 'I suppose we do have considerable influence in the tech college, but really it's the old problem of academic freedom versus demand by business. We sometimes have head-on clashes over this, but we usually get our own way by threatening to boycott the courses we support.' Philanthropy, it seems, breeds dependence, and in the case of the Technical College, it is clear that the pay-off for the companies is that some of the expense of training skilled labour-power is being met directly by state subsidy (cf. O'Connor 1972 and his discussion of social investment in human capital).

Corporate involvement in the Rotary Club similarly shares the twin functions of altruism and self-interest. The Rotary movement is both charitable and social; it exists to promote worthy causes and to facilitate social intercourse. Unlike some other businessmen's clubs such as the Lions or Round Table, however, Rotary tends to place less emphasis on physical involvement in charitable work, and more on financial support of good causes, and its social function is very significant for most members. Regular lunches enable the seventy or eighty members to meet together in an atmosphere of cordiality, and among these are a number of local political figures. As the *Croydon Advertiser* noted on the occasion of the club's fiftieth birthday celebrations (2 June 1972): 'Croydon club has become a meeting place of many of the prominent businessmen in the town. It is not surprising that in a borough where businessmen play an important part in council work, there has been quite a sprinkling of councillors, aldermen and even mayors in the ranks of its members.' The *Advertiser* was in a good position to discuss such matters, for the managing director of the newspaper had at that time been an active Rotarian for many years (as well as a former magistrate).

The picture which clearly emerges from an analysis of the involvement of town centre business interests in bodies like the Chamber of Commerce, the Technical College, the Rotary Club, the magistrates bench and the variety of other organizations outlined above is that there exists in Croydon a relatively dense and cohesive network of business and political activists, interacting regularly and relatively informally in a variety of institutional contexts. Indeed, many businessmen themselves recognize this. The manager of one large company, for example, explained that when he first came to Croydon, he had expected to find an impersonal and anonymous way of life, but that he had been pleasantly surprised: 'The same people keep cropping up in different situations with different hats on. It's just like a village really. Always the same people involved in any activity – the people who run the place if you like.' Similarly a department store executive observed that, 'When you become involved in Croydon to any extent, you come up against the same people in any number of different situations.'

What is also apparent is that this relatively small core of organizational leaders is self-selecting, self-perpetuating and exclusive. With few exceptions, the bodies to which they belong recruit through invitation only: Rotarians are chosen by existing members, the business representatives on the Youth Employment subcommittee are selected by the Chamber of Commerce, magistrates are appointed by the Lord Chancellor on the recommendation of a local selection committee of three J P's, and so on. Vacancies in these and other institutions are thus filled by approaching individuals drawn from a narrowly defined group of eligibles, each of whom generally know each other and consider each other eminently suitable for any positions of responsibility which may need filling. One department store chief, for example, claimed with some justification that if he so desired, he could sit on virtually every committee in the town given the regularity with which he was approached. Similarly, the chairman of one of the council's committees described it as part of his job to get to know a range of 'suitable' people so that the 'right man' could be found to fill the 'right position' whenever necessary.

Not surprisingly, perhaps, some of the Labour councillors with whom I spoke saw this exclusive network of business and political leaders in terms of a 'clique' or even a 'conspiracy'. One, for example, identified what he termed a 'circuit' comprising members of Rotary, the Whitgift Foundation and the Chamber of Commerce, while others pointed to the magistrates bench as the centre of influence in the town. As one observed, 'The real establishment is the local bench. They see each other regularly. They're all chosen because they are reliable. Many of them are councillors so they know each other pretty well anyway. That's the real establishment of Croydon – the bench.' In their study of Rochdale, Bartlett and Walker conclude that, 'The bench appears part of a mysterious old boy network' (1973, p. 139), and the same appears to be the case in Croydon. Certainly, the faces seen dispensing justice in the courts often appear almost indistinguishable from those found controlling private education through the Whitgift Foundation, lunching at the Rotary Club, or governing the policies of the Technical College.

Having said this, however, it would be fatuous to describe this network in terms of a conspiracy. It is, rather, what Kadushin (1968) terms a 'social circle' with no clearly defined goals, no formal rules of interaction, and no explicit criteria of membership. Croydon's businessmen and political leaders meet regularly, but such meetings cannot be interpreted as deliberate attempts to direct and manipulate local policy-making. In this sense, Banfield and Wilson were correct when they claimed that no businessman would dream of giving leadership to a local council from behind the scenes. There is no business conspiracy to run Croydon, and the image of smoke-filled rooms which is found in so much of the American literature on local politics has no equivalent here.

Yet despite this, participation in this social circle is highly valued by the top executives of the big companies, and some have gone to quite extraordinary lengths to establish and maintain personal contacts with leading local politicians. One company, for example, moved into the town in the mid 1960s and promptly distributed 130 food hampers to local council members, Members of Parliament, and other prominent social, economic and political leaders. A representative of the company explained in an interview, 'Obviously there's a fine distinction between respectable involvement and dirty tactics.... We did it to let these various people know we'd arrived in the town.... Most of them thought it was a splendid gesture.' One of the recipients, however, was a local Labour MP who considered it far from splendid and who questioned the company's motives. The company representative, however, was unrepentant: 'It's ridiculous to think that men in public office can be bribed by a few packets of tea.'

Besides raising the interesting question, which I have considered elsewhere (Chibnall and Saunders 1977), of where public relations exercises end and corrupt practices begin, this incident also leads us to ask why the company felt it necessary to make such gifts in the first place. Clearly, in common-sense terms, the company representative was justified in denying corrupt motives in that the size of the gifts was relatively small and they were made quite openly. Equally, philanthropic motives can presumably be discounted since the addresses on the hampers were those of 'local influentials' (the respondent's own description) rather than the more obvious worthy causes. We are led to the conclusion, therefore, that the whole exercise was oriented towards the establishment of contacts with those who run the town. Taken on its own, of course, the gift of a hamper is unlikely to achieve much in this direction, but a public relations exercise like this must be considered in the wider context of big firm's local political strategies.

The same company, for example, prior to its relocation in Croydon, had invited the mayor, the town clerk/chief executive and leading members of the council to a dinner in London, and this gesture was reciprocated by the local authority once the company had moved into the town, top executives being invited to a civic dinner at the town hall. The initial cordiality established by these two gastronomic exercises was then reinforced by the gift of the food hampers, and has since been maintained and developed, not only through mutual involvement in various committees, clubs and organizations, but also through a series of golf matches between company teams, council teams and magistrates teams, arranged in order to 'get to know these various people on a different basis'. The company has also made gifts of silverware to the Corporation. As a Labour 'moderate' put it, 'There is a happy relationship between the council and big business. . . . X have given pieces of silver to the council on various occasions to mark their appreciation of the friendly spirit.' Nor is this the only company to have made such gifts, for a development company with extensive past and present commercial commitments in the town has also donated silverware in appreciation of the 'easy working relationship' it has enjoyed with the local authority.

But why should these big firms bother? What is it that leads them to devote considerable time and money to establishing close relationships with local political leaders? Part of the answer would appear to lie in their desire for predictability, for as Weber recognized, rational entrepreneurship depends increasingly on calculability in economic management. In these terms, business expenditure of time and money can be understood as analogous to an insurance premium, an investment in 'goodwill' which may or may not need to be drawn upon in the course of future unpredictable eventualities. Where the norms of bureaucratic administration stress universalism and formality, those of personal friendship stress particularism and informality, and in this sense, the various public relations exercises and the involvement in local affairs can be understood as attempts to foster what may be termed 'institutionalized friendship', with all the implications that has for the quality of relationships between big business and the local authority. In short, personal face-to-face relations introduce an element of particularism into an otherwise bureaucratic situation, and thus render future policy-making more amenable to prediction. As one company manager explained, 'You don't ask for a bloody great factory belching out smoke in the middle of the High Street, but as long as your demands are sensible, they are invariably met.' Such confidence is a reflection of the nature of the relationship which has been established with those in positions of political power. Corporate investment in goodwill can thus be explained, not in terms of the pursuit of any definitive short-term objectives, but rather as the nurturing of a favourable political climate for the future.

This conclusion was reinforced time and again in interviews with the leaders of big business in the town. The manager of one company, for example, explained that, as a major ratepayer, his firm expected the local authority to pay attention to its demands and grievances, and that, 'When there's something we're concerned about, we begin to think how long it has been since the mayor last came to lunch.' An executive in another large company observed, 'We don't have any men on the council as yet, but we have good contacts with councillors and officers. There's always someone in higher management who knows the appropriate man on the council whenever a problem occurs.' And the chairman of one of the town centre department stores, when asked about his relationship with the local council, replied, 'I wouldn't say that they contact us for advice, but they do let us know what they're planning to do.'

Most of these business leaders could point to one or two cases where their personal contacts had proved directly valuable. One cited his company's application for planning permission for an extension to one of its buildings. Another described how he had acted over the siting of a bus stop near his store, while a third similarly reported that he had succeeded in having parking meters outside his store replaced by a bus stop. Yet another had entered into close discussions with the council to establish a direct access from one of the new multi-storey car parks into his store. Such issues may appear somewhat trivial, but their commercial significance can be considerable. When shoppers alight from a bus directly outside the open doors of one department store, or emerge from a car park into the heart of another, the volume of trade may be expected to expand accordingly. Certainly, Croydon is not the only town in which businessmen attach importance to securing a favourable location for facilities such as bus stops (see Regan and Morris 1969).

Other companies have benefited from explicitly commercial transactions with the local authority. In 1974, for example, a large local development company which had traditionally enjoyed a good relationship with the council approached the town hall with a proposal which it claimed would benefit both of them. The firm owned a large area of land in the east of the borough where it had for some years been developing a large private housing estate, but the slump in the housing market at that time had reduced turnover and was threatening the company with acute liquidity problems. In order to overcome these, while at the same time ensuring for itself a higher level of future predictability in a notoriously volatile market, the company offered to build over 150 houses on the estate and to offer them for sale at a fixed price to families nominated by Croydon council from its housing waiting list. This, it was claimed, would help the council reduce its waiting list (always assuming that sufficient families could be found who could afford to take up the offer), while in return, the council was asked to agree to purchase any of the houses which remained unsold. Croydon accepted the deal.

It has often been noted that the public sector provides a convenient safety net for developers in times of slump, for local authority housing contracts enable them to ride out a depression in the industry and to return to the more lucrative private sector when the market recovers. This deal with Croydon was, however, even better than most from the company's point of view, for it enabled it to continue developing its own houses on its own estate with a guaranteed market (and hence a guaranteed return on capital). As a company representative explained, 'We're giving Croydon a fixed selling price and they give us the guarantee that they'll buy from us if we can't sell them. So Croydon's getting people housed, and we have the benefit of being able to put millions of pounds into another section on the estate knowing that we won't be stuck with unsold property.' What this amounted to was that Croydon undertook to orchestrate demand for a local company facing a crisis of under-consumption and over-production. As a Labour councillor observed, the agreement was 'a business deal to bale out a private developer facing short-term problems'.

This example provides a clear illustration of the partnership which exists between Croydon council and the big companies. There is an easy working relationship between them which is made all the easier by the pervasive personal contacts which exist between them. As one businessman put it, 'Certainly there are a lot of people here who have close contacts with Croydon. . . . I know Croydon as one of the most efficient local authorities we deal with. You don't get the bureaucracy and delays of planning that you get in other boroughs.' This is not to suggest, of course, that business leaders are constantly utilizing their contacts with a view to influencing council policy, since for much of the time they have no need to. They can invite the mayor to lunch, but rarely feel they have to. They know whom they can contact at the town hall should the need arise, but the need rarely does. As Hacker says of America, so too it may be said of Croydon: 'There is a community of interest and sentiment among the elite, and this renders any thought of a "conspiracy" both invalid and irrelevant' (1965, p. 141).

Policy-making and corporate representation

Two features of big business involvement in local politics in Croydon need to be emphasized. The first is its personal and informal character; it is not so much the companies themselves that become involved as specific leading members of these companies, and such influence as occurs thus takes place on a personal rather than a corporate level. The second is that the influence of big business has rarely been in evidence in questions of policy-formulation, for the consistent support of town centre enterprises by the local authority (e.g. through its continuing support for further office development and its provision of productive infrastructure) has taken place with little prompting from interests outside the town hall. Where the influence of the large retailing and commercial interests has been felt, therefore, is not in the broad issues of policy, but in the specific and detailed questions of implementation. To take just one example, the council is committed to building car parks to service the town centre shops and offices, and what therefore concerns the big companies is where these car parks are to be provided and whether they are to be located in the most advantageous locations for their own commercial prosperity. It is on questions such as these that influence has been exerted and personal contacts utilized, for on the broader issues there has been a fundamental consensus.

In recent years, however, there have been some signs that this essentially personal mode of influence over policy implementation is coming to be complemented by the development of a more formal mode of involvement in the policy-making process itself. At the centre of this tendency towards corporate representation in local politics stands the Croydon Chamber of Commerce.

In 1965, the Chamber of Commerce launched a public campaign aimed at achieving closer consultative links with the local authority on a regular and formal basis. More specifically, it suggested that a Joint Advisory Committee be established with the role of bringing together council and business representatives to consider plans and proposals at an early stage of their formulation. The justification for this was that those who paid the piper should at least have a say in calling the tune: 'This Chamber membership pays more than one-third of the rates and it should be consulted when the council spends our money. . . . It is a peculiarity of our rating system that the group of people who pay the highest rates in a town such as ours have possibly the least to say in how they are expended.' The council, however, appeared unimpressed by this argument at that time. Both the town clerk and the two party group leaders rejected the Chamber's proposal, and the mayor explained that, 'The Chamber are wrong in their contention that they should be consulted before any action is taken, because we are elected to govern the town. You cannot possibly say that every time a problem arises, the Chamber has first to approve our action.'

Privately, however, the relationship between the council and the Chamber did begin to change. The first public indication of this came in 1968 when the local newspaper reported that the Chamber's arguments for closer consultation 'now appear to have been accepted, privately at least, by key council members'. Indeed, it later transpired that, although the advisory committee had never been formally established, various local business leaders had since 1966 been invited to regular lunches at the town hall, and it seems that by the end of the decade, the Chamber had achieved *de facto* most of what it had demanded five years earlier. In December 1972, for example, the *Croydon Advertiser* reported that, 'In recent years, the liaison between the Chamber and Croydon council has increased in value until now the two are constantly in touch', and a few months later the Chamber's vice-chairman felt confident enough to proclaim in public that his organization was, 'The most powerful organized body in this town in either the political, business or social fields.'

Such claims were echoed in interviews with both businessmen and politicians. A Chamber official, for example, told me, 'We enjoy a good relationship with the borough council which has been cemented over the years. Individuals on both sides change, but there's a tradition of close co-operation and friendly liaison. . . . I've been here three and a half years, and I can't say that we've come unstuck once in all that time. . . . The council usually agrees with our suggestions and amends its policies accordingly.' Chamber officers have regular meetings with council officers and committee chairmen, and the Chamber itself is now recognized by many councillors as playing an integral part in the policy-making process. As one put it, 'The council needs the Chamber to take part in policy, therefore the Chamber don't need to be a pressure group. . . . They are entitled to very close contact with committees – that's the chairman's job.' Similarly, another observed, 'The council wants to keep well in with the Chamber of Commerce. We do this by regular social and semi-social meetings with them, and by inviting them to the town hall to discuss specific issues.' Even the mayor referred in a speech to the relationship between the Chamber and the council as 'a partnership which surely has to grow'.

Such statements are interesting in the light of the earlier discussion of corporatism (see pages 169–73), for it would appear that the Chamber of Commerce has become increasingly integrated into a quasi-official position within the system of local policy-making; if it 'does not need to be a pressure group', then this is because it now operates in the corporate rather than the pluralist sector. The fruits of its new-found 'partnership' with the local authority are not hard to find. The Chamber played an important part, for example, in achieving the Crown Hill/Church Street sliproad when traders in that area found themselves threatened with isolation from the town centre as a result of the council's ringroad plans, and it also secured a commitment from the local authority to renew leases on shops in that area for a minimum period of three years at a time in order to reduce the likelihood of planning blight and consequent commercial stagnation. It has also utilized its privileged relationship with the local authority to secure a relaxation of six-day trading restrictions in the borough, to resist the commercial threat of a proposed hyper-market, to change various parking restrictions in out-of-town shopping centres, and so on. But perhaps its biggest potential break-through during the period of the research was the council's agreement to include the Chamber in the planning of the proposed large-scale redevelopment of West Croydon. Provisional plans for this were only drawn up by the local authority following discussions with Chamber of Commerce representatives, and these plans were then again submitted to the Chamber for further comments and suggestions. Given GLC and government restrictions on future office development in the borough, of course, the West Croydon proposals were inevitably long-term, but a Chamber official assured me that, 'The Chamber will be consulted at every stage right the way through to completion.' Its participation in this scheme is thus a significant indication of the new political role of the Chamber. As the *Croydon Advertiser* noted in 1972, 'The massive redevelopment at West Croydon will be one of the first major projects in the town to have included the Chamber of Commerce officials in its planning at such an early stage.'

What is notable about the Chamber's participation in local policy-making is that most of the issues in which it has become involved appear to reflect the interests and concerns, not of the big town centre companies, but of the smaller shopkeepers and traders who have often suffered in recent years from the council's commitment to the large retailing and commercial enterprises. Indeed, as I noted earlier, these larger companies do not seem to look to the Chamber to represent their interests since they can usually do this quite adequately themselves. The result has been that the Chamber has come to represent the voice of the petty bourgeoisie in the town. The development of close formal consultative links between it and the local authority thus raises two possibilities.

The first is that this new partnership represents little more than a mode of legitimation for the continuing political hegemony of large commercial interests. According to this argument, the representation achieved by the Chamber of Commerce amounts to little more than tokenism, and the concessions which it has secured on behalf of small shopkeepers have been of precious little consequence. The primary role of the Chamber thus appears symbolic, for not only does it create the impression that small businessmen have a voice in local politics, but it also maintains the illusion that there is a single business interest in the town. In other words, by drawing its membership from all sections of local enterprise – large and small, commercial and industrial – and by claiming to speak for all of them, it can be argued that the Chamber portrays an image of unity when in fact the large commercial firms have consistently gained at the expense of other sectors and in any case enjoy a relationship with those in positions of power which these other sectors cannot hope to emulate. If this argument is accepted, then the claims made by town centre business-men that their membership of the Chamber is seen by them as a 'moral responsibility' take on a new significance. In other words, their professed obligation to become involved in the Chamber may be understood as a tacit recognition on their part of the need to display support for and solidarity with an organization which obscures the fundamental cleavage between themselves and other 'fractions of capital'. In this sense, the Chamber can be seen as aiding the local authority in maintaining the unity of local capital under the hegemony of the large commercial enterprises.

The second possibility, however, is that the partnership between the council and the Chamber of Commerce is now providing petty bourgeois interests with a collective and corporate means of represen-tation as a counter-balance or complement to the influence achieved by the big companies through membership of the 'social circle'. This argument would suggest that, although they were left out in the cold during the redevelopment years and had, therefore, to press their demands and grievances as best they could in competition with other groups in the pluralist sector, small businessmen have subsequently increasingly achieved a degree of functional representation through the incorporation of the Chamber within the policy-making process. It could then further be argued that the local authority has been willing to expose itself to the influence of these small business in-terests, partly because of the need to stem the growing political alienation of its traditional petty bourgeois support base, and partly because by the late 1960s, when the Chamber first made its break-through, the town centre redevelopment had virtually been completed and the large companies had become firmly established (i.e. the council's primary objective had been realized, and it could therefore turn its attention to the possibly incompatible demands of other groups). According to this argument, therefore, big business can be seen to have achieved some degree of direct involvement in local politics on an individual level, while small business achieved this some years later on a collective level.

This second line of argument appears the more compelling, if only because the gains achieved by the Chamber on behalf of small business, taken together with its potential impact on the future planning of West Croydon, can hardly be dismissed as 'token'. Furthermore, although the support of the Chamber by the large companies may in part reflect their concern to maintain a political unity of capital in the town, it is clear that such unity is by no means entirely spurious. Although they have their differences over some areas of policy, all sections of business do share many other interests in common (e.g. an interest in maintaining low levels of local property taxation), and in these cases, the Chamber can genuinely claim to speak on behalf of the business community as a whole. It does therefore seem that, although they have achieved it in rather different ways, both large and small business interests now occupy a privileged position within the local political system.

Underlying this is the local authority's active commitment to the values and principles of private enterprise. The relationship between business and the council is one of partnership, not manipulation, and this reflects the fundamental agreement between the two over policy priorities. Far from being the passive tool of business interests, the local authority has operated autonomously of outside political pressures, but in doing so it has not acted in isolation from them. In other words, it has sought to integrate business interests into the local political system, either informally (through the 'social circle') or formally (through consultation), with the result that these interests have provided a continuing source of guidance and direction for its own policy initiatives. As Parsons (1967b) has argued, influence derives from mutual trust and understanding, and this is in turn grounded in a sense of shared objectives and common purpose. These conditions exist in Croydon in the relationship between business and political leaders. In their clubs, committees and boards, as well as in their more formal consultative meetings, the various representatives of Croydon's business community interact regularly with political leaders who generally believe what they believe, think what they think, and want what they want. No pressure group, no matter how well-organized or how well-connected, enjoys a relationship like this, for in such a fertile context, opinions, suggestions and modes of thought pass almost imperceptably, like osmosis, from businessmen to politicians, and from politicians to businessmen. In the relationship between the town's political and business leaders, political partnership has reached its highest and most sublimated form.

9 The sociology of urban politics research

Any empirical work in the social sciences must expect to encounter a number of common problems. Basically, these fall into two broad categories; problems internal to the research enterprise, including the questions of objectivity, value-commitment, reliability and validity which all reflect the epistemological question of the relationship between the researcher, his theory and the subjects of his study; and problems which may be considered external to the research, foremost among which are the difficulties which arise out of the social and political context in which the study is situated. Given that the central objective of this book has been to consider various theoretical issues raised by recent work in urban sociology in the light of case study material, this final chapter is devoted to a discussion of the particular problems which confront empirical research in this field. Through a discussion of methodology, therefore, this chapter attempts to show how the empirical material considered in Part 2 of the book relates to the theoretical discussion in Part 1. While it in no way attempts to provide a conclusion or summary of the arguments developed in the previous eight chapters, it does attempt to set out a framework by means of which these arguments can be evaluated and assessed.

Urban politics research encounters the familiar problems of any empirical work in a particularly acute form. As regards 'external' problems, for example, the context in which it takes place is one in which the subjects of the study are likely to prove particularly inaccessible. As Schmid (1969) has recognized, the study of power relations is inevitably organized against the vertical lines of political domination which it attempts to analyse, and it must therefore overcome hurdles not often faced in studies of lower status and less privileged groups in society. Access to society's underdogs generally proves relatively simple, partly because it involves the sociologist in intrusions upon people who are less prestigious and powerful than himself, and partly because it is often supported by powerful institutions in the world of government or big business (see Jenkins 1971, Nicolaus 1972). It need not follow from this that the sociologist engaged in such work is, in Nicolaus's graphic description, an 'Uncle Tom' for the ruling class, although it has to be noted that where his work leads him to question the sacred orthodoxies of his sponsors, he may find that it is swiftly terminated (the fate of the government-sponsored Community Development Projects provides one recent example of what is not an uncommon experience in the social sciences). The point is, then, that while all social research takes place within a context of relations of domination and authority, the constraints which this imposes only become immediately visible when an attempt is made to study the dominant groups themselves, for their privacy cannot easily be violated, their secrecy cannot simply be penetrated, and their support is unlikely to be forthcoming. It is somewhat simpler to infiltrate a working men's club than it is to gain entry to the Masonic Lodge, and the difficulties of conducting participant-observation on the factory floor are likely to pale into insignificance when the sociologist moves into the boardroom.

Such problems of access are exacerbated by two further difficulties. One is that the various organs of government in Britain exhibit an extraordinarily clandestine character and their secrets are safeguarded by a host of socio-legal devices, ranging from the Official Secrets Act to a viciously restrictive libel law, the like of which have been deemed 'unconstitutional' in a more open society such as the United States. It is surely significant, for example, that following her newspaper's successful exposure of the Watergate scandal in America, the publisher of the *Washington Post* expressed doubts as to whether such a scandal could ever have been revealed in Britain, given the severity of the libel laws. The second point follows on from this, for it is also apparent that in Britain there exist entrenched informal norms of political exclusivity which pervade what Walter Bagehot and many commentators since have identified as a 'deferential' political culture. It may well be the case, as Berger (1966, p. 51) suggests, that the logic of his discipline leads the sociologist 'to debunk the social systems he is studying', but in Britain, this may well be mediated by an equally strong reluctance to break traditional political taboos. As Banfield observes,

The case study method requires that the investigator go behind the scenes to discover what 'really' happens. In the United States this is easy: there is a widespread feeling (witness the affair at the Pentagon papers) that it is outrageous for a public body to have any secrets. In Britain by contrast, the general opinion, certainly the opinion of persons in office, is that what goes on behind the scenes is not at all the business of 'outsiders'. It would be surprising if British political scientists did not share this attitude to some degree, at least to the extent of feeling embarrassed to ask questions that will be viewed as invasions of official privacy [1972, p. 164].

In addition to such 'external' problems, however, urban politics research also encounters some daunting problems internal to itself. The problem of values, for example, is likely to arise in particularly acute form when the subject matter of research is itself political. The question of the relationship between theoretical concepts and empirical observation also becomes a central issue, especially when concepts of 'objective interests' and 'structural constraint' figure so fundamentally in the theoretical literature but pose such formidable difficulties in their empirical application. But in addition to all this, urban politics research must, at the very outset, confront a problem which rarely occurs in most conventional sociological studies, for before it can begin to analyse what the powerful do, it must first identify who the powerful are. Most survey research, of course, is based on the identification of a theoretical population (e.g. 'affluent workers', 'working class under-achievers', 'prison recidivists' or whatever), and then proceeds to construct a sampling frame which corresponds to this population (e.g. car workers, eleven-plus failures, prisoners serving a second sentence, and so on), and this process is never without its problems. Research in urban politics, however, has often come unstuck at this first hurdle (hence the long and protracted community power debate in the United States), for the identification of a theoretical population has inevitably been based upon a prior commitment to a particular theory of power, and as we saw in Chapter 1, such theories appear essentially contestable. Indeed, it is a central paradox of such research that its aim has often been to demonstrate who has power in a particular community, yet the decision as to where to look has been determined by an initial judgement of where power lies. It is to a consideration of this first and critical problem of identification that I now turn.

The problem of identification

I noted in the introduction to Part 2 that in Britain, the assumption has usually been made that the contours of political power at the local level correspond to the formal institutions of local government; that power resides in the town hall (with the officers, the members or both) and nowhere else. This assumption has guided, and has subsequently been supported by, the two studies conducted in this country that have explicitly addressed themselves to the question of community power. The first of these was part of a cross-national comparative study carried out by Miller (1970) in the city of Bristol in the mid 1950s, while the second was a study of the neighbouring city of Bath conducted some ten years later by Green (1967).

In his Bristol study, Miller followed the method outlined by Hunter (1953) in his pioneering analysis of the community power structure in Atlanta, and set out to trace the distribution of power in the city by discovering those who were reputed to be in some way influential. The use of this reputational method rests, as its critics have rightly pointed out, on the assumption that power may not be readily observable (i.e. that powerful groups or individuals may be operating behind the scenes), and thus on the argument that reputed influence provides the best available indicator of underlying patterns of domination in a community. This assumption led Miller to compile an initial list of names of people considered by various informants to be powerful, and he then asked a 'panel of judges' to assess and rank these names in order of their influence in the city. In this way he discovered a group whom he designated 'top influentials', over one-third of whom were local businessmen. The members of this group were then asked to rank each other, and Miller identified those who were most frequently mentioned at this stage of the procedure as 'key influentials'. Twenty-five per cent of these were local businessmen, while less than half were members of the local authority. Despite these findings, however, Miller concluded that, 'The council is the major arena of community decision. . . . Community organizations play important roles in debating the issues, but these are definitely secondary or supplementary activities. The community value system condemns any pressure tactics on the council as "bad taste" ' (1970, p. 42).

This conclusion is hardly surprising, of course, but what has provoked comment and criticism is Miller's identification as 'key influentials' a number of individuals who were neither officers nor members of the city council. Newton (1969), for example, while citing with approval Miller's argument that decision-making is located within the formal apparatus of local government, nevertheless then takes issue with the method used in the Bristol study, arguing that the reputational technique led to the discovery of 'influentials' who were clearly not influential in local political affairs (the Vice-Chancellor of the university was one example). Such criticism of the reputational method is by no means novel, for a common argument developed during the American community power debate was that it involves a tortuous, indirect and fundamentally invalid technique, oriented towards the analysis of epiphenomena (i.e. reputations for power or 'second-hand opinions') while ignoring the phenomenon itself (i.e. the exercise of power in observable decision-making situations). However, Miller did not rest his case on reputational data alone, for he went on to demonstrate a positive correlation between reputed influence and a variety of other more direct indicators of local political involvement, the only exception being that top and key influentials were 'under-reported' in local press coverage (an exception which Miller explained with reference to the norms of discretion among powerful groups in British society). While the study was undeniably weak on methodological grounds, therefore, it did nevertheless generate some interesting case material, for even if we reject the identification of a local 'power elite' due to the inadequacies of the reputational method, it is still remarkable that businessmen and others outside the local authority were so frequently believed to be powerful by Miller's informants.

This last point raises the question of what sort of data we should expect from the use of the reputational approach. As observable indicators of unobservable power relations, reputations for power leave a lot to be desired, for it is impossible to establish their reliability. Some studies, for example, have attempted to demonstrate the validity of the reputational method as a technique for identifying powerful groups and individuals by showing that its results are generally consistent with those achieved through more direct observational methods (e.g. Blankenship 1964). Other studies, however, have suggested that the results achieved by this method are essentially incompatible with those generated by alternative techniques (e.g. Freeman *et al.* 1963). Yet this argument appears of little value. As Rose points out,

> If a reputational analysis yields a power structure similar to that revealed by the positional approach or, for that matter, any more direct approach, its critics denounce its claim to expert inside knowledge, for if it appears that power is not exercised covertly, there is thus no need to employ an indirect method of study. If, however, a reputational analysis yields a power structure different from anything determined by more direct methods, its critics claim there is no basis for validation [1967, p. 266].

Clearly, the discovery of 'influentials' by the reputational method will only be accepted as valid by those who already believe that power is exercised behind the scenes, although even here there is likely to be a problem of ascertaining whether there are other influentials operating behind those whom the method identifies (the so-called 'malady of infinite regression').

As a means of determining where power lies, the reputational approach is useless. As one means of generating an initial sampling frame, however, it may have its applications, for as we saw in Chapter 1, reputed influence can itself be a significant political resource. In other words, people may defer to those whom they believe to be powerful (hence the concept of anticipated reactions), and this provides good grounds for retaining a reputational approach in any study. In Croydon, for example, nearly half of all council members cited the southern residents' associations as being influential, and this not only served to direct my attention towards these organizations, but it also indicated one possible reason for the council's concern with housing densities and green belt preservation in the south of the borough. Used in this way, of course, the traditional reputational technique undergoes a number of transformations, not least of which is the abandonment of the panel of judges used to rank lists of reputed influentials, for if reputations constitute symbolic power resources rather than objective indicators of the distribution of power, then such a panel becomes redundant. Reputations are 'real' for those who define them as such. It should also be added that, to the extent that relations of domination become routinized, any reputational approach will be of only limited value in generating evidence on the symbolic basis of power, given its reliance on a well-developed political consciousness among informants. Not surprisingly, therefore, this approach played only a very marginal part in the Croydon case study.

The second community power study conducted in Britain used a very different technique of identification, for Green began his research in Bath by selecting for interview only council members and officers – a procedure he termed the 'prior identification method': 'The problem of identification in the present study was a difficult one. The only solution seemed to be to attempt a definition of the most likely decision-makers – in other words, to use empirical and theoretical considerations to narrow down the focus of attention before the data were collected' (1967, p. 8). This essentially positional approach was thus based on the assumption that we already 'know' where power lies; Green merely applied his common-sense knowledge about British local government, and hoped that if his initial assumptions were misplaced or too restrictive that this would be rectified later in the research through reputational analysis and the study of specific instances of local decision-making.

Given his domain assumptions, however, later 'anomalies' thrown up during the research were all too easily explained away. Reputational questions put to all council members, for example, resulted in around half of his informants citing the Chamber of Commerce and the Preservation Trust as being influential organizations in the city, yet Green dismissed these findings, arguing in particular that the claims by Labour members that the Chamber played a significant role in local politics merely reflected their ideological predispositions and prejudices. Similarly, when he asked councillors to name influential individuals, other than council members, only five names were mentioned more than once (three of these being ex-council members), and Green took this as confirming what he already 'knew'; namely, that the local authority constituted the locus of political power, and that virtually nobody outside the town hall played a part of any significance in the local decision-making process. Yet this finding could equally have been explained in terms of the reluctance or inability of council members to name influential people outside the council. Councillors are not always the most reliable informants, for as Blondel and Hall point out, 'In some sectors of local political life at least, councillors are not only themselves somewhat unconcerned about power, but not particularly anxious to know where power lies' (1967, p. 334). Indeed, Green's own data would appear to confirm this, for he notes that, although council officers exerted a considerable degree of influence over the policy-making process, the members were often reluctant to admit this in interviews. How much more reluctant, then, were they likely to be when it came to naming as influential individuals with no formal status within the local authority whatsoever?

The major check on the prior identification method, however, consisted not of reputational analysis but of a study of post-war decision-making in the city. This took two forms; first, an analysis of seventeen post-war issues as reported in the local press, and second-ly, an in-depth case study of one contemporary issue concerning the proposed development of a new university. Of the seventeen issues, he found that the council had prevailed against outside opposition on all but four occasions, and he explained these excep-tions, not in terms of 'the supposed manouvrerings of small groups behind the scenes', but as local authority deference to 'public opinion' (1967, p. 125). Similarly, the university issue also pointed to the supremacy of the council in the local political system. Again, therefore, his initial assumptions were apparently supported by his later evidence.

The analysis of the seventeen issues, however, was clearly suspect, for it was totally reliant upon the way in which the local newspaper had reported them at the time. The dangers here are obvious, for news is created and not simply 'reported', and local press reports, taken as the sole source of data on these issues, are almost certainly, highly unreliable, partial and incomplete accounts (e.g. see the discussion by Murphy, 1976, of the relationship between the pro-vincial press and local government). Indeed, Green's own first-hand account of the university development issue indicated that local press coverage often failed to mention even the names, still less the activi-ties, of some of the key people involved, and this only confirms Miller's argument that in Britain, the powerful rarely seek publicity.

The inadequacies of the reputational approach and of the analysis of the seventeen issues thus leaves the reliability of the prior identi-fication method resting upon the one case study of decision-making which Green himself accomplished, yet even here there is a problem. The university development issue, we are told, was probably the biggest and most contentious political issue to have occurred in

Bath since the war, and while Green's account may therefore provide interesting and useful case material on an example of 'rancorous conflict' (Gamson 1966), it can clearly tell us little about the routines of ruling in the city. As the various critics of issue analysis have frequently argued, a case like this cannot provide any evidence of how power relations ordinarily operate (hence the development of the concept of non-decision-making, discussed in Chapter 1). Quite simply, if any groups or individuals were disposed to exercise influence quietly and covertly in Bath, the last issue they would have chosen to get involved in was one as public and contentious as this. To conclude, therefore, it can be argued that if business or any other interests in the city were in any way politically active, it seems highly unlikely that Green's informants would have told him so, or that the local press would have reported it, or that the university development issue would have revealed it. The basic assumption enshrined in the prior identification method was thus never seriously exposed to any challenge by the later work which was built upon it.

Having said this, it is necessary to make two more general points about the problem of identification. The first is that, in any study of urban politics, some prior decisions will have to be made about the initial criteria which are to govern where the researcher is to begin looking. Green's prior identification method was inadequate, not because it grounded the research in an initial positional framework, but because the range of positions covered was too narrow to allow subsequent techniques of identification (reputational and issue analysis) to broaden its scope. The second point is that any initial positional analysis will necessarily reflect theoretical considerations; Green's concentration on council members and officers, for example, clearly reveals a prior commitment to some form of 'representational' theory (see pages 150–7). This is inevitable, for there can be no atheoretical method, no neutral research instrument by means of which the 'real' distribution of power can in some way be directly revealed. These two points carry considerable implications for research practice in the field of urban politics, and it is worth considering them in more detail.

The criticism which can be made of Green's initial positional framework was that it was arbitrarily limited to those who held formally defined positions of authority in the local political system. The purpose of this first step, it should be remembered, is not to identify those who are powerful, but those who enjoy positions of potential power or influence by virtue of their privileged access to strategic political resources. Clearly, council members and officers must therefore be included in this initial sweep, but so too must those outside the town hall who control local material resources, who enjoy strong numerical support, who occupy strategic locations in social-political networks, who have expert knowledge or are in a position to control the distribution of information, and so on, for all of these resources provide a capacity for power, and it is the task of positional analysis to document their distribution.

This, of course, represents a formidable task, and it seems that any population eventually identified will be incomplete for at least two reasons. First, it is not possible at an early stage in any research accurately to assess the distribution of key resources, nor to include all those with significant access to them. However, in the initial stages at least, range appears more important than completeness; Green's analysis, after all, was complete in that it included all those whom he believed were occupying powerful positions in the city, but its range was highly limited. Secondly, incompleteness will reflect the fact that certain types of strategic resources (e.g. privileged contacts through membership of important social networks) will not be open to observation and evaluation at the start of any research. It follows from this that positional analysis must be supplemented throughout every stage of the study by information collected through interviews, documentary analysis, observation and so on. In the Croydon study, for example, an initial positional sample was drawn up which comprised twenty organizational leaders, ranging from the chairmen or secretaries of local residents' and tenants' groups to a senior officer of the Chamber of Commerce, six business leaders, three from the town's three largest department stores and three from the largest international companies based in the town centre, five prominent council members, six chief officers, and a representative from the local newspaper. Of the thirty-eight names on this list, twenty-five were eventually interviewed. However, as a result of these interviews and of information gathered from local newspaper reports, local authority documents, observation at various meetings of the council and other local organizations, discussions with a number of local activists, and a short postal questionnaire distributed to all council members, a further twelve individuals were later contacted and interviewed, including eight more council members and four more businessmen, this bringing the total number of formal interviews conducted to thirty-seven. Clearly this eventual sample was in no sense 'complete', but it was relatively comprehensive in its range in that it included representatives of most of the sections of the local population which arguably had access to key political resources.

What all this amounts to is that the problem of identification was resolved in the Croydon study through the initial use of a broadly conceived positional framework supplemented by both reputational and issue analysis, and in this way, the sample was allowed to 'snow-ball' (Bonjean 1963), thus providing some safeguard against the premature exclusion of potentially powerful groups and individuals. It is important to note, however, that these three techniques were used only to develop a basis for the research, and not to provide any authoritative findings. Each of these techniques may prove useful as methods of preliminary identification, but as methods of analysis they are inadequate. Nor can these inadequacies be overcome (as Freeman *et al.* 1963, Presthus 1964, and others have suggested) by using them as complementary methods, for it is surely facile to argue that a combination of a reputational approach which discovers elites which may not exist with issue analysis, which may fail to discover those which do, can generate satisfactory results. Each of these approaches is embedded within a distinct paradigm, and it makes little sense to suggest, as Abu-Laban (1965) proposes, that they constitute neutral instruments of discovery which only generate 'biased' results when they are manipulated by 'biased' investigators. Rather, as Walton has demonstrated, each is intimately related to a particular theory of power (i.e. instrumentalist and pluralist) which is associated with specific social science disciplines (i.e. sociology and political science): 'The disciplinary background of the investigator tends to determine the method of investigation he will adopt, which in turn tends to determine the image of the power structure that results from the investigation' (1966, p. 688).

It follows from this that the crucial question concerns, not so much the choice of research technique, but more the relationship between theory and empirical work. It is simply misguided to assume (as many contributors to the American community power debate appeared to assume) that the 'true' nature of power relations is there to be discovered if only the right blend of research techniques can be found, for the search for evidence, the identification of evidence, and the conclusions drawn on the basis of the evidence all necessarily reflect the prior role of theory in guiding research and interpreting its findings. The importance of Walton's work is that it serves to high-light the fact that no research technique is ever neutral and that any empirical analysis embodies certain core theoretical presuppositions. The question, therefore, is not which method is most appropriate, but which perspective is most relevant. The community power debate was not a debate about method (although this was how it was gen-erally represented), but was rather a fundamental theoretical dispute about the nature of political power and the foundations of social order. And as we saw in Chapter 1, at the heart of this dispute lay the key epistemological issue about the scientific basis of knowledge.

Theory and methodology

The findings of the Croydon case study discussed in Chapters 5 to 8 were achieved from a variety of sources, but foremost among these was the series of interviews conducted with those who had been identified as potentially powerful through the positional analysis. These interviews were unstructured, for a formal questionnaire had been tried at the 'pilot' stage but was abandoned as being too cum-bersome and obstructive; it was not entirely clear what questions I should be asking, and it had soon become apparent that a string of prearranged and perhaps somewhat banal questions was eliciting little more than a string of prearranged and certainly banal answers. Furthermore, the biggest attraction offered by structured question-naire research – quantification – was not applicable in this case, partly because of the small size of the interview sample, partly because simple quantifiable data had already been gathered through the use of a postal questionnaire sent to all council members, and partly because there was little else which could meaningfully be quantified.

Power, I soon realized, was inherently immeasurable in statistical terms. It is one thing to tabulate councillors' ages and classify their occupations, but quite another to attach numerical indicators to variations in power relationships. Despite the various attempts to represent such relationships in terms of a mathematical language (e.g. Coleman 1973, Danzger 1964, Emerson 1962, Harsanyi 1962), it is clear that power is inherently unquantifiable, partly because it is not a unilinear phenomenon, and partly because it is not an individual attribute. The problem of unilinearity is that power may vary according to its scope (the number of different situations in which it is exercised), its frequency (how often it is exercised in any one situation), its domain (the number of people subject to it), its strength (how far their actions can be affected), its accuracy (how far its effect corresponds to the original objective), its range (how many different options it opens up), and its opportunity cost (what has to be foregone in order to secure a successful outcome). Even if (implausibly) all these dimensions could be integrated into a single index, however, the result would still be meaningless since power is a quality of social relationships rather than an attribute of individuals. Consider, for example, the attempt by Laumann and Pappi (1973) to calculate individuals' 'influence status' by multiplying their 'influence rank' (the number of times they are cited as influential by others) by the number of decisions in which they have been involved. Not only does this procedure fall foul of the fallacy of assuming complementarity between reputational and issue analysis, but it provides no theoretical or logical justification for multiplying the results of these two techniques together (even in terms of the formal rules of mathematics this appears invalid since the numerical values of the two variables are not equivalent), and it violates the very concept of power by assuming that it is an individual attribute which can be decontextualized from the social relationships in which it is embedded. As Cicourel has warned, 'Viewing variables as quantitative because available data are expressed in numerical form or because it is considered more "scientific" does not provide a solution to the problems of measurement, but avoids them in favour of measurement by fiat' (1964, p. 33).

In the absence of quantifiable data, much of the evidence discussed in the previous chapters may be termed qualitative if not impressionistic. It is evidence which has been brought together from a variety of sources to support a particular line of argument, and the way in which it has been interpreted has depended to a large extent on the prior acceptance of certain key theoretical and epistemological premises, many of which (e.g. the commitment to a concept of objective interests or the rejection of the positivist postulate of phenomenalism) can in the last instance only be defended with reference to a specific and personal evaluative position. It appears, in other words, that the findings discussed in these chapters do not so much provide a 'test' of the theoretical positions established in Part 1 as an application of them. How much faith, then, can be placed in empirical research of this nature?

The first question to be considered here concerns the role of personal values in such research, and this raises two distinct points. The first is that it is now something of a cliché in empirical sociology to recognize that values in large part determine the direction of research; there is little dispute today with Weber's assertion that personal values determine the selection of subject matter and that 'cultural (i.e. evaluative) interests give purely empirical scientific work its direction' (1949, p. 22). The second point, however, is that many writers have gone beyond this in arguing that the very apprehension of social reality is itself inherently evaluative, and that there is therefore no distinction between fact and value. Gouldner (1973a), for example, suggests that the myth of value-freedom, which developed in western sociology on the basis of Weber's work, has constituted an ideology through which social scientists have been able to justify the suspension of any critical judgement on their society. Value-freedom, in other words, has provided a respectable label for conservatism. Similarly, Becker (1967) has identified a 'hierarchy of credibility' in society by means of which research which challenges dominant groups' conceptions of the world comes to be seen as biased, whereas that which implicitly adopts their perspective is accepted as impartial. For Becker, all research is necessarily partial and politically charged since it is always conducted from a specific social-political viewpoint. It is therefore incumbent upon the sociologist to declare whose side he is on.

In a reply to Becker's paper, however, Gouldner (1973b) takes issue with this conclusion, and dismisses as naive and complacent the view that, by openly declaring his values, the sociologist can provide an adequate criterion by means of which the objectivity of his work can be assessed: 'A bland confession of partisanship merely betrays smugness and naivete. It is smug because it assumes that the values we have are good enough; it is naive because it assumes that we know the values we have' (ibid., p. 54). He also criticizes Becker's call for an unsentimental commitment to the perspective of society's underdogs, arguing first that this results, not in a truly critical sociology, but in attacks on the middle range functionaries of the ruling class (a point which Pahl finds particularly compelling in his reformulation of the urban managerialist thesis discussed on pages 166-9), and secondly, that Becker is here perpetuating a new myth of a sentiment-free sociology. For Gouldner, the supposition that objectivity can be achieved through rational rather than emotional partisanship is entirely spurious, for he believes that it is precisely the heart rather than the head which should dictate whose side we take. From this perspective, sociology should be on the side of those who suffer from social injustices, and it follows that the task of sociological work lies in aiding the liberation of oppressed groups: 'Granted, all standpoints are partisan; and granted, no one escapes a partisan standpoint. But aren't some forms of partisanship more liberating than others?' (ibid., p. 56). As we shall see, Gouldner here comes close to the perspective associated with critical theory which attempts to resolve the problems of values and objectivity in terms of the liberatory potential of critical social theory.

In assessing arguments such as these, it is necessary to distinguish between value-freedom and objectivity. Nobody today, it seems, is prepared to argue for a value-free social science. Indeed, it is at least doubtful whether Weber himself ever intended to suggest that value-freedom, in the sense of a non-committed, non-partisan and non-political approach to the study of social life, was either possible or desirable. Dawe, for example, has drawn attention to Weber's argument that all accounts of reality are not only guided by values, but are necessarily one-sided:

Weber is arguing for the centrality of value to social science, not merely as a 'principle of selection of subject matter', but as the *sine qua non* of all meaningful knowledge of social reality. Without the attribution of value, knowledge of all social phenomena is inconceivable . . . our concepts, our propositions, our theories and our view of methodology all derive their meaning from the attribution of value [1971, p. 42].

Furthermore, even those who are today sometimes identified as positivists do not subscribe to the classic positivist principle of the separation of the scientific and the moral realms. Popper, for example, argues that any call for individual scientists to be cleansed of their values and their passions in their pursuit of knowledge is both naive and abhorrent: 'We cannot rob the scientist of his partisanship without also robbing him of his humanity, and we cannot suppress or destroy his value judgements without destroying him as a human being and a scientist' (1976, p. 97).

This consensus over the inherently evaluative nature of social science research raises obvious problems concerning its objectivity, for it is clearly necessary to stipulate the criteria according to which work may be deemed objective, even though it has been conducted from a one-sided viewpoint. The problem, in other words, is how we are to distinguish social science from personal opinion, versions of the 'truth' from varieties of dogma.

For Gouldner, the answer is that objectivity is guaranteed only by the moral character of the researcher. This involves first, a commitment to humanitarian values rather than to the specific interests of any particular group or faction (irrespective of whether they are underdogs), and secondly, an impeccable integrity such that the researcher does not turn a blind eye to those phenomena he encounters which run counter to those values. He concludes, 'Objectivity consists in the capacity to know and to use – to seek out, or at least to accept it when it is otherwise provided – information inimical to our own desires and values, and to overcome our own fear of such information' (1973b, p. 59). The similarity between this and Popper's norm of falsification (which basically holds that science consists of the attempt to refute rather than confirm the theories it develops) is evident, the essential difference being (as we shall see) that while Gouldner places his faith in individual integrity, Popper prefers to rely on the critical spirit of the scientific community.

Faith in individual integrity does not appear to constitute a very satisfactory foundation for an objective social science. It is somewhat disturbing, for example, especially in the light of Gouldner's earlier comments on the complacency of many sociologists, to learn that 'the reports of fieldworkers in general and community sociologists in particular have to be accepted at their face value. Their reliability has to be judged in terms of the respect for, and confidence in, the author's integrity, the inner consistency of his work, and the extent to which it agrees with one's own preconceptions' (Bell and Newby 1971, p. 75). Yet this view shows signs of entering into sociological orthodoxy. Fairbrother, for example, rejects the Popperian norm of insistent criticism, and asserts instead that, 'The acceptance of a research report should be in terms of trust rather than doubt as at present' (1977, p. 359). He argues that there are no formal rules of procedure which can guarantee validity and reliability, and that provided the researcher gives a reflexive account of his research experience (including an account of the relationship between himself and the subjects on whom his report is based), his findings should be accepted on trust. He concludes, 'The research worker must be trusted to produce a report that is just in its empirical reference and honest to the moral concerns of the research worker. There can be no other basis for respecting the integrity of the research worker or for accepting the research report' (ibid., p. 367). It is but a short step from here to an acceptance of Feyerabend's anarchistic epistemology in which science takes its place as one among a number of competing belief systems, and in which no methodological prescriptions, other than respect for human life, can be allowed to interfere with the pursuit of knowledge (Feyerabend 1975). From such a perspective, any claim to objectivity becomes vacuous.

Clearly, more is needed than mere indulgence for the personal whims and assumed integrity of research workers, and what is essentially at issue here is the role of criticism. Popper's work is central to this, for he finds the guarantee of objectivity in the freedom of criticism which pertains in the scientific community. Thus, although individual researchers necessarily work within an evaluative frame of reference, the critical reception which their work receives among their contemporaries is sufficient to distil the scientific findings from the value-based assumptions. Against this, however, are those theorists such as Adorno (1976) who see the vital role of criticism in terms not of debate within a community of scholars, but of the necessity of adopting a critical stance towards the society in which the researcher is working. From this latter perspective, social science is doomed to become an instrument of repression unless it makes an explicit commitment to the goal of human liberation, and objectivity (to the extent that the term has any meaning at all) thus involves the critical transcendence of the systematically distorted discourse through which the society customarily comes to be known and experienced.

Both of these perspectives have their problems. Popper's advocacy of criticism in science has been the subject of intense debate, and Kuhn (1970a) in particular has suggested that, far from working in an open and critical community, most researchers are ordinarily constrained by the boundaries of a particular paradigm whose basic beliefs are shared in common with their colleagues. Normal scientific activity thus engages criticism only within the context of a particular set of core assumptions. This argument has significant implications for the social sciences, for although there is clearly no single paradigm in sociology (Friedrichs 1970), it may be argued that there are a number of largely incommensurable paradigms (e.g. positivist, realist and conventionalist approaches), each with its own set of ontological assumptions and its own criteria of adequacy. What is acceptable scientific practice to one school may prove unacceptable to another (e.g. consider the arguments over non-decision-making, discussed in Chapter 1, or the divergent perspectives on the state and political power, reviewed in Chapter 4). Objectivity, therefore, cannot be established through an appeal to any single and universally recognized set of scientific values, and sociological research in consequence is usually addressed to one of a range of competing and often imperialistic schools of thought between which there may be little consensus. Popper is therefore correct in identifying mutual criticism as inherent in the social sciences, the problem being that more often than not, this involves the disciples of different paradigms talking past each other rather than a community of scholars assessing each other's work on the basis of agreed criteria as to what constitutes valid knowledge.

Critical theory also encounters problems, however. It is not simply that critical theory is committed to certain core assumptions (e.g. the view that advanced capitalist societies are repressive) which others may dispute, although this clearly is the case (e.g. Adorno describes the basic divide between himself and Popper as being over the latter's view that 'we live in the best world which ever existed' – Adorno, 1976, p. 120). In addition to this, there are problems with the criteria of adequacy which this perspective itself has developed. Thus it will be recalled that critical theory rests upon its commitment to human liberation; by revealing the nature of repression, it aims to provide individuals with the capacity for transcending it. It follows that the validity of any work must depend, in part at least, on its acceptance by those who experience repression. As Fay argues,

The claims of such a theory can only be validated partially in terms of the responses that the social actors themselves have to the theory. This is to say that whether it indeed offers a way out of an untenable situation (and is therefore a true theory) is partially determined by whether those for whom it is written recognize it as a way out and act on its principles. It is an internal – and decisive – criticism of any critical theory if it is rejected by the people to whom it is addressed [1975, pp. 109–10].

The implications of this for power research were spelled out in the discussion of Habermas's concept of real interests (see pages 37–9). There we saw that, from the perspective of critical theory, individuals must remain the arbiters of their own interests, although they can only accomplish this in a situation of free and undistorted communication. This is, perhaps, a laudable argument, but it gets us nowhere given that such a situation does not exist in contemporary capitalist societies. Habermas himself recognizes this, and suggests that the interests which individuals would identify have therefore to be hypothetically imagined; a 'solution' broadly similar to that proposed by Lukes, and one which suffers from the same weaknesses. What is basically at issue here is the question of whether popular assent can constitute the ultimate criterion of validity. While Popper pins his faith in the reactions of the scientific community, critical theorists pin theirs on the reactions of the community as a whole.

The argument that validity rests ultimately on whether the subjects of study accept or reject the argument is a position found, not only in critical theory, but also in ethnomethodology. Fay's conclusion, for example, appears broadly consistent with that reached by Phillipson from an ethnomethodological perspective: 'Validity is to be established by ensuring continuity and compatibility between the sociologist's interpretations and members' commonsense interpretations. The sociologist's models have to be faithful to the ways in which members themselves decide adequacy in everyday terms' (1972, p. 151). Where these two approaches differ, of course, is that critical theory suggests that subjects must come to address themselves to the account they are offered, while ethnomethodology is concerned rather that the sociologist tailor his account to reflect his subjects' existing world views. One is thus inherently radical while the other is inherently conservative. Neither, however, appears adequate from our present perspective, for throughout this book I have argued that it is possible to develop an objective (though one-sided) account of local political relations which can stand independently of the assessments made of it by the actors involved. This appears an important principle in research such as this; when Vidich and Bensman (1958) published their study of political life in 'Springdale', for example, it provoked a popular furore, but it would be crass to suggest that this necessitates the rejection of their work as invalid. Criteria of adequacy are necessary, but they cannot be grounded in the community of subjects.

Having said this, it is necessary to add immediately that this argument does not imply an ontologically privileged status for any particular theory. The position associated with Athusserian epistemology, that reality can be distinguished from the world of phenomenal appearances, that theory enjoys an absolute autonomy from the determinacy of the mode of production, and that historical materialism thus represents the scientific mode of analysis while all other social theories are situated at the level of ideological practice, cannot be sustained. As Walton and Gamble observe, 'We might well ask, "Why is Althusser's science not itself an ideology?" ... Althusser's attempt at avoiding relativism is a pseudo-solution, because his idea of science gives us no clear criteria for choosing between theories at the conceptual level' (1972, p. 125).

Relativism, it seems, is to some extent unavoidable, but this need not imply an acceptance of Feyerabend's dictum that in science, 'anything goes'. Recent work by Ford (1975) is useful here. She identifies four conceptions of 'truth' in social science, the first of which concerns the basic beliefs which underlie any theory and which guide any research practice. This, of course, is a 'truth' which cannot be tested, which is not contingent upon observation, and which is not open to logical discourse. It is rather the 'truth' of the metatheoretical judgements upon which all social science is based, judgements 'in which we believe because we believe' (ibid., p. 88). Because these judgements cannot themselves be judged, they cannot be rejected from the standpoint of any alternative set of basic beliefs. Ultimately, therefore, we accept or reject any sociological account according to our own personal evaluations of the ontological assumptions embedded within it, and it follows from this, as Bell and Newby (1977) have argued, that tolerance of epistemological pluralism must be safeguarded as a central value in the social sciences.

It does not follow, however, that any sociological account is as valid as any other, for there are other criteria of validity or 'truth' which Ford identifies. One of these is reminiscent of Gouldner's criterion of integrity and his argument that the sociologist is on trust to report inconvenient findings which do not accord with his personal beliefs and values. 'In this context,' writes Ford, 'a "false" judgement is simply one which has been uttered with the deliberate intent to deceive or mislead' (1975, p. 84). Another concerns logical consistency; where an account is found to be internally inconsistent, it may be rejected as invalid. This corresponds to the criterion of adequacy advanced by Laclau (1975) in his review of the debate between Miliband and Poulantzas, although his view that this is the only criterion by means of which competing accounts can be assessed appears too restrictive. Ford's final conception of 'truth' concerns testability; that any argument should be open to empirical disconfirmation. This, as we have already seen, is problematic for two reasons. First, empirical observation is itself to some extent paradigm-dependent; where we look and what we 'see' reflects our prior judgement concerning how social reality is constituted. This, however, does not rule out the principle of testability as it is applied within rather than to specific paradigms. The second problem is that some paradigms are explicitly anti-empiricist; the argument that substance differs from its phenomenal form, for example, effectively excludes the possibility of empirical testing. I shall return to this latter point in a moment.

The principle of testability may be achieved through implicit or explicit prediction. Of course, as Ryan (1970) argues, sociological generalizations are rarely of a form which can sustain any elaborate prediction, and where predictions are made, they are highly contingent upon a wide range of empirical conditions. Notwithstanding this, however, explicit predictions can sometimes be found in the literature (cf. Winkler 1977 on the development of corporatism), while much research contains implicit predictions or hypotheses which are amenable to empirical investigation. To take just one example from the Croydon study, a key argument in Chapter 6 was that local authority policies on housing densities and property taxation reflected the interests and the influence of southern owner-occupiers. Shortly after completing the research, however, I was obliged to reconsider this argument when it came to my attention that Croydon had levied the highest rate increase in the country in 1975, and that this had resulted in a 'residents' revolt' in the south of the borough. On closer examination, as I show in Chapter 6, the rate rise was found to reflect GLC and government policies rather than any shift in the political balance locally, and the subsequent protests among owner-occupiers could better be explained as examples of 'tactical protest' than as a direct and serious challenge to the local authority itself. The point of this example is that it demonstrates the importance of counterfactual conditions in any argument. In other words, for any sociological explanation to be considered valid, there must be in principle some means of specifying the conditions which would be considered sufficient to force, if not the abandonment, then at least the critical re-examination of the argument (see Lakatos, 1970, on 'sophisticated falsification' as a criterion of scientific knowledge).

It is precisely this condition which is lacking in those approaches that deny the role of empirical observation in determining the validity of a theoretical account. The obvious example here concerns the various 'structuralist' theories of the state (see pages 180-9), for although these can be criticized on the grounds of logical inconsistency (e.g. through the Hindess/Hirst critique of the concept of relative autonomy), they are effectively immune from empirical challenge since they claim retrospectively to be able to explain both reformist and repressive state policies in terms of a single and untestable principle of economic determinacy in the last instance. Against this, I would follow Ford in arguing that testability, together with internal consistency and individual integrity, must remain a fundamental principle of social science research, and the Croydon case study stands or falls on the application of these three criteria.

The political context

In recent years, British sociology has been characterized by considerable soul-searching and internal criticism concerning questions of epistemology. This rekindled interest in the philosophical foundations of the discipline has been all to the good, but there is a danger that methodological debate may come to focus exclusively on the internal problems of the research enterprise and thus to overlook the sociological context in which it occurs. In the previous sections, for example, I have considered the problems of determining who should be studied and how, but such questions tend to take for granted the dubious assumption that the sociologist exercises free choice in such matters. In the case of research in the area of power relations in society, this is clearly not so, for the problem of identification raises the question of free access to the subjects of study, while the problem of values and objectivity leads us to consider whether the researcher is in a position to report what he finds, irrespective of its 'scientific' validity.

The problem of access has already been touched upon at the start of this chapter. There we saw that gaining access to powerful interests in society can present many more problems than are likely to be encountered in studies of lower class groups, and that the norm of official privacy in Britain is such as to severely hamper the study of governmental institutions. The consequence of this is that the range of research techniques which may effectively be available in studies of political power is considerably curtailed. It is one thing to decide upon the best method for analysing the actions of the powerful, but it is quite another to implement it.

In this situation, the least problematic research techniques are those 'unobtrusive measures' (Webb *et al.* 1966) which generate data without any personal engagement in the situation on the part of the researcher. Foremost among these are documentary sources such as council year books, biographies, directories of company and government information, *Who's Who* and so on, as well as newspaper reports and other media sources. Yet sources of information like these, although important to any research project, are of only limited use. They are, for a start, the 'concrete' manifestations of a prior process of social construction in which 'facts' have been created within a common-sense framework of interpretation. The significance of this became clear in the earlier discussion of Green's study of Bath, for his reliance on newspaper reports as accounts of 'what happened' in the seventeen issues he selected for analysis was seen to constitute a severe weakness in the research. Furthermore, official reports may, as Hindess (1973) suggests, arrange data according to a system of classification which is based upon objectives and theoretical assumptions which the researcher does not share. And in addition to all this, there is the problem that documentary sources may simply not say very much. Certainly they are unlikely to provide information on some of the more interesting and pertinent questions to which the research is addressed.

Clearly, documentary sources must be supplemented by other modes of research. In the Croydon study, for example, we have seen that the major research instrument consisted of a series of unstructured interviews with those identified as potentially powerful by means of positional analysis. But interviews too are problematic, partly because they involve the researcher and his informant in a process of negotiating reality which may result in a loss of reliability, and partly because interviewees are in a position in which they need only tell the researcher what they want him or her to hear. There are ways in which this can be overcome to some degree (e.g. through in-depth discussions in which both parties gradually drop their guard, or by aggressive questioning of apparent inconsistencies in informants' accounts), but these can only go some way towards reducing the relatively formalistic impression which is likely to emerge from most interviews. Indeed, when we consider the sorts of research techniques which are most likely to be available in studies of power relations, it soon becomes apparent that they are all characterized by the ability of powerful interests to keep the researcher at arm's length. Documentary sources, interviews, questionnaires, observation (where this is possible – e.g. at council meetings) – all these will tend to produce a fairly formal picture even though the aim of such research is precisely to transcend the formal façade of local politics.

The one technique which appears to offer the best chance for overcoming this difficulty is itself probably the most awkward to use in the analysis of political power, and this is participant-observation. In his review of the literature on urban managerialism, Norman (1975) has argued that, if we are to determine who is responsible for policy-making in local government and how the routines of ruling come to be maintained, then studies from the inside are necessary. This may be achieved covertly (e.g. by gaining election as a councillor or by gaining employment in the town hall) or overtly (e.g. by being accepted as an observer by a local council), but in both cases there are likely to be problems. The covert observer must not only beware the obvious ethical problems entailed in his role, but will inevitably achieve only a partial picture of what is going on around him. The newly elected councillor, for example, is unlikely to be privy to the private discussions of the party leaders, still less to the inner workings of the council bureaucracy. The overt observer, on the other hand, is constantly at the mercy of his sponsors, and given the clandestine character of government in Britain is unlikely to be afforded the sort of freedom which Wolfinger apparently enjoyed in New Haven during his study with Dahl. Thus, one British sociologist who is currently engaged in overt participant-observation in a County

Planning Department writes, 'The probability of uneven access remains unresolved – participant-observers can never guarantee to be "where the action is" (especially in studying decision-making, which may be covert, behind-the-scenes, let alone accounting for non-decisions) nor can they be entirely sure of access to all or even a majority of relevant actors' (Flynn, 1977, pp. 12–13).

Participant-observation is thus limited in its scope in this type of research, especially when the concern is with 'community power' rather than local authority decision-making *per se*, for it would clearly be necessary to gain access, not only to the town hall, but also to various community groups, the Chamber of Commerce, the boardrooms of major companies, and even to such secretive organizations as the Freemasons (in Brighton, for example, two recent council committee meetings were postponed because they clashed with Masonic Lodge meetings, yet data on the membership and activities of the Freemasons are notoriously difficult to discover). It may be possible, of course, to engage in participant-observation through activity in relatively open community movements such as squatting campaigns (e.g. Bailey 1973a), but this is likely to create further problems since it will involve an open and explicit political commitment on the part of the researcher to one particular group, and this is likely to prejudice any possibility of achieving comparable access to other groups (e.g. see Bell, 1977b, on the problem of over-identification with the local Labour Party in the Banbury re-study), especially where the group concerned is defined as 'irresponsible' by those in positions of power. Although participant-observation is not entirely ruled out in the study of urban politics, it is nevertheless the case that all the usual problems associated with it are likely to be magnified and exacerbated, and it may well be that the expenditure of time and energy which it requires is barely justified by the results it is likely to generate.

Problems of access are therefore considerable, but even these difficulties may pale into insignificance beside the problems which the researcher in this field may encounter when he comes to write his findings. Of particular significance here is the issue of legal restriction and censorship.

The problem posed for research by the British libel laws is one which has received scant attention from sociologists, yet the long debates over methodology and epistemology within the discipline count for little if, in the final result, research findings are suppressed by outside political–legal agencies. Anxious deliberations about the objectivity of sociological accounts appear literally academic in a situation in which a writ can successfully be served, not even on the grounds of misrepresentation of the 'truth', but merely on the criterion of intentional defamation. As Bell and Newby observe, ' "Truth" ... is not a concept which carries any weight in the current libel lexicon; if published truth is littered with an intent to defame it becomes libellous' (1977, p. 170). The problem here is obvious, for the logic of his discipline should lead the sociologist to question current orthodoxies, to raise as problematic that which is customarily taken for granted, and to look at familiar situations from unfamiliar angles. Following this logic in the study of the powerful may well prove a recipe for legal disaster.

One of the few attempts in the sociological literature to grapple with the question of the libel laws has been provided by Bell and Newby who encountered problems in their attempt to compile a collection of articles in which sociologists could re-examine the research in which they had been engaged. Under the threat of legal action, one article had eventually to be withdrawn from the book altogether while two more had to be amended to include replies from the various offended parties. In their epilogue to the book, Bell and Newby sound a warning which is highly relevant to our present concerns:

> If British sociologists are to direct more research effort towards the powerful, they should be more aware of what they are letting themselves in for; we have seen in recent years that the writ is now a standard weapon used to suppress knowledge ... the shape of the sociological product is not just an issue of epistemology, nor even, in Becker's sense, the product of collective action; it is also moulded by the risk of a writ [ibid., p. 171].

Part of the reason why this problem has so conspicuously been ignored by British sociology is that most research has not encountered it: businessmen, politicians and even academics may sue for libel, but this is not ordinarily the prerogative of those less fortunate groups who most often find themselves subject to sociological inquiry. Another reason, however, is that it is virtually impossible to write sensibly about the libel law without citing contemporary examples of what may be considered libellous, yet such a course of action would merely itself invite a court action. I myself, for example, have suffered the frustration of seeing a manuscript (not, of course, the present one) jettisoned by a publisher following advice by legal counsel, and although it would be instructive to outline the reasons for that decision, it is clearly not possible to do so. It may, however, be noted that the phenomenon of anticipated reactions operates in this sort of research, just as it does in the political relations which the research purports to study, for as Bell and Newby argue, the possibility of legal action is likely to mould the way in which sociological work is accomplished, irrespective of whether such action ever comes to be taken.

An appreciation of the external constraints which operate in this field of research thus reveals the central paradox of the sociological study of urban politics; that the researcher, like any other 'outsider', faces a dilemma as regards his relationship to the local political system. If he conducts his research 'responsibly', he is likely to produce a formal account which fails to achieve the original objectives of the project, while if he conducts it 'irresponsibly', he may succeed in producing a more worthwhile sociological account but incur the opposition of powerful local interests in the process. The dilemma which confronts the political activist thus also confronts the sociologist, and among all the problems associated with the study of urban politics, this may well be the most enduring of all.

References

ABU-LABAN, B. (1965). 'The reputational approach in the study of community power: a critical evaluation'. *Pacific Sociological Review*, vol. 8, pp. 35–42

ADORNO, T. (1976). 'On the logic of the social sciences'. In T. Adorno, *The positivist dispute in German sociology*. Heinemann

ALT, J. (1971). 'Some social and political correlates of County Borough expenditures'. *British Journal of Political Science*, vol. 1, pp. 49–62

ALTHUSSER, L. (1969). *For Marx*. Allen Lane

AMBROSE, P. (1976). 'The land market and the housing system'. *Urban and Regional Studies Working Papers*, no. 3. University of Sussex

AMBROSE, P. (1977). *The British land use non-planning system*. Paper given at the inaugural meeting of the Conference of Socialist Planners, London

AMBROSE, P. and COLENUTT, B. (1975). *The property machine*. Penguin

ANDERSON, P. (1965). 'Origins of the present crisis'. In P. Anderson and R. Blackburn, *Towards socialism*. Fontana

BACHRACH, P. and BARATZ, M. (1970). *Power and poverty*. Oxford University Press

BAILEY, R. (1973a). *The squatters*. Penguin

BAILEY, R. (1973b). 'Housing: alienation and beyond'. In I. Taylor and L. Taylor, *Politics and deviance*. Penguin

BALL, M. (1976). 'Owner-occupation', in Political Economy of Housing Workshop, *Housing and class in Britain*, Conference of Socialist Economists, London

BALL, M. (1978). 'British housing policy and the house building industry'. *Capital and Class*, no. 4, pp. 78–99

BANFIELD, E. (1972). 'Urban renewal and the planners'. *Policy and Politics*, vol. 1, pp. 163–9

BANFIELD, E. and WILSON, J. (1966). *City politics*. Harvard University Press

BARAN, P. and SWEEZY, P. (1966). *Monopoly capital*. Monthly Review Press, New York

BARRY, B. (1976). 'The public interest'. In A. Quinton, *Political philosophy*. Oxford University Press

BARTLETT, D. and WALKER, J. (1973). 'Inner circle'. *New Society*, vol. 24, p. 139

BATLEY, R. (1972). 'An explanation of non-participation in planning'. *Policy and Politics*, vol. 1, pp. 95–114

BEALEY, F., BLONDEL, J. and MCCANN, W. (1965). *Constituency politics: a study of Newcastle-Under-Lyme*. Faber

BECKER, H. (1967). 'Whose side are we on?' *Social Problems*, vol. 14, pp. 239–47

BELL, C. (1977a). 'On housing classes'. *Australian and New Zealand Journal of Sociology*, vol. 13, pp. 36–40

BELL, C. (1977b). 'Reflections on the Banbury re-study'. In C. Bell and H. Newby, *Doing sociological research*. Allen & Unwin

BELL, C. and NEWBY, H. (1971). *Community studies*. Allen & Unwin

BELL, C. and NEWBY, H. (1976). 'Community, communion, class and community action'. In D. Herbert and R. Johnson, *Social areas in cities*. Wiley

BELL, C. and NEWBY, H. (1977). *Doing sociological research*. Allen & Unwin

BENINGTON, J. and SKELTON, P. (1972). *Public participation in decision-making by governments*. Paper given at the annual meeting of the Institute of Municipal Treasurers and Accountants, Portsmouth

BENTHAM, J. (1894). *The theory of legislation*. Kegan Paul

BERGER, P. (1966). *Invitation to sociology*. Penguin

BERGER, P. and LUCKMANN, T. (1966). *The social construction of reality*. Penguin

BIERSTEDT, R. (1950). 'An analysis of social power'. *American Sociological Review*, vol. 15, pp. 730–8

BIRCH, A. (1959). *Small town politics*. Oxford University Press

BIRCH, A. (1964). *Representative and responsible government*. Allen & Unwin

BLANKENSHIP, L. (1964).' Community power and decision-making: a comparative evaluation of measurement techniques'. *Social Forces*, vol. 43, pp. 207–16

BLAU, P. (1963). *The dynamics of bureaucracy*. University of Chicago Press

BLONDEL, J. and HALL, R. (1967). 'Conflict, decision-making and the perceptions of local councillors'. *Political Studies*, vol. 15, pp. 322–50

BOADEN, N. (1971). *Urban policy-making*. Cambridge University Press

BODDY, M. (1976). 'Building societies and owner-occupation'. In Political Economy of Housing Workshop, *Housing and class in Britain*, Conference of Socialist Economists, London

BOGGS, C. (1976). *Gramsci's Marxism*, Pluto Press

BONJEAN, C. (1963). 'Community leadership: a case study and conceptual refinement'. *American Journal of Sociology*, vol. 68, pp. 672–81

BORJA, J. (1977). 'Urban movements in Spain'. In M. Harloe, *Captive cities*. Wiley

BRADSHAW, A. (1976). 'A critique of Steven Lukes, "Power: a radical view" '. *Sociology*, vol. 10, pp. 121–7

BUDGE, I., BRAND, J., MARGOLIS, M. and SMITH, A. (1972). *Political stratification and democracy*. Macmillan

BULPITT, J. (1967). *Party politics in English local government*. Longmans

BURNS, T. (1972). Review of Silverman, 'The theory of organizations'. *Contemporary Sociology*, vol. 1, pp. 308–11

CARCHEDI, G. (1975). 'On the economic identification of the new middle class'. *Economy and Society*, vol. 4, pp. 1–86

CASTELLS, M. (1975). 'Advanced capitalism, collective consumption and urban contradictions'. In L. Lindberg, R. Alford, C. Crouch and C. Offe, *Stress and contradiction in modern capitalism*. Lexington Books

CASTELLS, M. (1976). 'Theoretical propositions for an experimental study of urban social movements'. In C. Pickvance, *Urban sociology: critical essays*. Tavistock

CASTELLS, M. (1977a). *The urban question*. Edward Arnold

CASTELLS, M. (1977b). 'Towards a political urban sociology'. In M. Harloe, *Captive cities*. Wiley

CAWSON, A. (1978). Pluralism, corporatism and the role of the state'. *Government and Opposition*, vol. 13, pp. 178–98

CHAMBERLAIN, C. (1977). 'Attitudes towards direct political action in

Britain'. In C. Crouch, *British political sociology yearbook*, vol. 3: *Participation in politics*. Croom Helm

CHIBNALL, S. and SAUNDERS, P. (1977). 'Worlds apart: notes on the social reality of corruption'. *British Journal of Sociology*, vol. 28, pp. 138–54

CICOUREL, A. (1964). *Method and measurement in sociology*. Free Press, Glencoe

CLARK, G. (1972). 'The lesson of Acklam Road'. In E. Butterworth and D. Weir, *Social problems of modern Britain*. Fontana

CLARKE, J., CONNELL, I. and MCDONOUGH, R. (1977). 'Misrecognizing ideology: ideology in political power and social classes'. In *On Ideology*. Hutchinson

CLARKE, S. and GINSBURG, N. (1975). 'The political economy of housing'. In Political Economy of Housing Workshop, *Political economy and the housing question*. Conference of Socialist Economists, London

CLEGG, S. (1975). *Power, rule and domination*. Routledge & Kegan Paul

CLEMENTS, R. (1969). *Local notables and the city council*. Macmillan

COCKBURN, C. (1977). *The local state*. Pluto Press

COLEMAN, J. (1973). 'Loss of power'. *American Sociological Review*, vol. 38, pp. 1–17

COLLISON, P. (1963). *The Cutteslowe walls*. Faber

COMMUNITY DEVELOPMENT PROJECT (1976a). *Profits against houses.* CDP Information and Intelligence Unit, London

COMMUNITY DEVELOPMENT PROJECT (1976b). *Whatever happened to council housing?* CDP Information and Intelligence Unit, London

CONNOLLY, W. (1972). 'On interests in politics'. *Politics and Society*, vol. 2, pp. 459–77

CORINA, L. (1975). 'Local government decision-making'. *Papers in Community Studies*, no. 2, University of York

CORRIGAN, P. (1977). 'The welfare state as an arena of class struggle'. *Marxism Today*, vol. 21, pp. 87–93

CORRIGAN, P. and GINSBURG, N. (1975). 'Tenants' struggle and class struggle'. In Political Economy of Housing Workshop, *Political economy and the housing question*. Conference of Socialist Economists, London

COUPER, M. and BRINDLEY, T. (1975). 'Housing classes and housing values'. *Sociological Review*, vol. 23, pp. 563–76

COWLEY, J., KAYE, A., MAYO, M. and THOMPSON, M. (1977). *Community or class struggle?* Stage 1, London

COX, R. (1966). *Urban development of Croydon, 1870–1940.* Unpublished M A thesis. University of Leicester

COX, W. HARVEY (1976). *Cities: the public dimension.* Penguin

CRENSON, M. (1971). *The un-politics of air pollution.* Johns Hopkins Press, Baltimore, Md.

CREWE, I. (1974). 'Introduction: studying elites in Britain'. In I. Crewe, *British political sociology yearbook*, vol. 1: *Élites in western democracy.* Croom Helm

CROUCH, C. (1977). 'Introduction: The place of participation in the study of politics'. In C. Crouch, *British political sociology year book*, vol. 3: *Participation in politics.* Croom Helm

CULLINGWORTH, J. (1972). *Problems of an urban society*, vol. 2: *The social content of planning.* Allen & Unwin

DAHL, R. (1956). *A preface to democratic theory.* University of Chicago Press

DAHL, R. (1961). *Who governs?* Yale University Press

DAHL, R. (1963). *Modern political analysis.* Prentice-Hall, Englewood Cliffs, N.J.

DAMER, S. (1974). 'Wine Alley: the sociology of a dreadful enclosure'. *Sociological Review*, vol. 22, pp. 221–48

DANZGER, M. (1964). 'Community power structure: problems and continuities'. *American Sociological Review*, vol. 29, pp. 707–17

DARKE, R. and WALKER, R. (1977). *Local government and the public.* Leonard Hill

DAVIES, B. (1968). *Social needs and resources in local services*, Michael Joseph

DAVIES, J. (1972), *The evangelistic bureaucrat.* Tavistock

DAVIES, J. and TAYLOR, J. (1970). 'Race, community and no conflict'. *New Society*, vol. 9, pp. 67–9

DAWE, A. (1971). 'The relevance of values'. In A. Sahay, *Max Weber and modern sociology.* Routledge & Kegan Paul

DEARLOVE, J. (1973). *The politics of policy in local government.* Cambridge University Press

DENNIS, N. (1970). *People and planning.* Faber

DENNIS, N. (1977). 'In dispraise of political trust'. In W. Sewell and J. Coppock, *Public participation in planning.* Wiley

DICKENS, P. (1977). *Social change, housing and the state*. Paper given at the Centre for Environmental Studies urban sociology conference, University of York

DONNISON, D. (1975). *Social policy and administration revisited*. Allen & Unwin

DUNHAM, A. (1972). 'Property, city planning and liberty'. In M. Stewart, *The city: problems of planning*. Penguin

DURKHEIM, E. (1962). *The division of labour in society*. Collier-Macmillan

ECKSTEIN, H. (1960). *Pressure group politics*, Allen & Unwin

EMERSON, R. (1962), 'Power dependence relations', *American Sociological Review*, vol. 27, pp. 31–41

ENGELS, F. (1969a). 'The housing question'. In K. Marx and F. Engels, *Selected works*, vol. 2, Progress publishers, Moscow

ENGELS, F. (1969b). Introduction to K. Marx, 'The civil war in France'. In *Selected works*, vol. 2. Progress Publishers, Moscow

ENGELS, F. (1970). 'Origins of the family, private property and the state'. In K. Marx and F. Engels, *Selected works*, vol. 3. Progress Publishers, Moscow

ESPING-ANDERSEN, G., FRIEDLAND, R. and WRIGHT, E. (1976). 'Modes of class struggle and the capitalist state'. *Kapitalistate*, no. 4/5, pp. 186–220

FAIRBROTHER, P. (1977). 'Experience and trust in sociological work'. *Sociology*, vol. 11, pp. 359–68

FAY, B. (1975). *Social theory and political practice*. Allen & Unwin

FERRES, P. (1977). 'Improving communications for local political issues'. In R. Darke and R. Walker, *Local government and the public*. Leonard Hill

FEYERABEND, P. (1975). *Against method*. New Left Books

FLETCHER, C. (1976). 'The relevance of domestic property to sociological understanding'. *Sociology*, vol. 10, pp. 451–68

FLYNN, R. (1977). *Urban managers in local government planning: project methodology*. Paper given at the SSRC workshop on qualitative data, University of Warwick

FLYNN, R. (1978). 'Planning and the state'. *Urban and Regional Studies Unit working paper*, University of Kent

FORD, JANET (1975). 'The role of the building society manager in the urban stratification system'. *Urban Studies*, vol. 12, pp. 295–302

FORD, JULIENNE (1975). *Paradigms and fairy tales*, vol. 1. Routledge & Kegan Paul

FORESTER, T. (1976). *The Labour Party and the working class*. Heinemann

FRASER, D. (1973). *The evolution of the British welfare state*. Macmillan

FREEMAN, L., FARACO, T., BLOOMBERG, W. and SUNSHINE, M. (1963). 'Locating leaders in local communities: a comparison of some alternative approaches'. *American Sociological Review*, vol. 28, pp. 791–8

FRIEDRICHS, R. (1970). *A sociology of sociology*, Collier-Macmillan, Toronto

GAMBLE, A. and WALTON, P. (1976). *Capitalism in crisis*. Macmillan

GAMSON, W. (1966). 'Rancorous conflict in community politics'. *American Sociological Review*, vol. 31, pp. 71–81

GAMST-NEILSEN, K. (1974). *Resistance from below – against exploitation of housing conditions*. Unpublished paper, University of Copenhagen

GANS, H. (1967). *The Levittowners*, Pantheon

GANS, H. (1968). 'Urbanism and suburbanism as ways of life'. In R. Pahl, *Readings in urban sociology*. Pergamon

GERTH, H. and MILLS, C. W. (1948). *From Max Weber*. Routledge & Kegan Paul

GIDDENS, A. (1968). 'Power in the recent writings of Talcott Parsons'. *Sociology*, vol. 2, pp. 257–72

GIDDENS, A. (1971). *Capitalism and modern social theory*. Cambridge University Press

GIDDENS, A. (1974). Preface to P. Stanworth and A. Giddens, *Élites and power in British society*. Cambridge University Press

GIDDENS, A. (1976). *New rules of sociological method*. Hutchinson

GILBERT, B. (1970). *British social policy, 1914–39*. Batsford

GLASS, R. (1968). 'Urban sociology in Great Britain'. In R. Pahl, *Readings in urban sociology*. Pergamon

GOFFMAN, E. (1961). *Asylums*. Doubleday Anchor Books, New York

GOLD, D., LO, C. and WRIGHT, E. (1976). 'Recent developments in Marxist theories of the capitalist state'. *Monthly Review*, vol. 27, pp. 37–51

GOODE, W. (1972). 'The place of force in human society'. *American Sociological Review*, vol. 37, pp. 507–19

GORZ, A. (1967). *Strategy for labor*. Beacon Press, Boston

GOULDNER, A. (1970). *The coming crisis of Western sociology*. Heinemann

GOULDNER, A. (1973a). 'Anti-minotaur: the myth of a value-free sociology'. In A. Gouldner, *For sociology*. Penguin

GOULDNER, A. (1973b). 'The sociologist as partisan'. In A. Gouldner, *For sociology*. Penguin

GRANT, W. (1971). 'Local councils, conflict and rules of the game'. *British Journal of Political Science*, vol. 1, pp. 253–5

GRAY, F. (1976). 'The management of local authority housing'. In Political Economy of Housing Workshop, *Housing and class in Britain*. Conference of Socialist Economists, London

GRAY, J. (1975). *On the contestability of social and political concepts.* Unpublished paper, Department of Government, University of Essex

GREEN, B. (1967). *Community decision-making in Georgian City.* Unpublished PhD thesis, University of Bath

GREEN, G. (1972). 'National, city and ward components of local voting'. *Policy and Politics*, vol. 1, pp. 45–54

GREER, S. (1962). *Governing the metropolis*. Wiley, New York

HABERMAS, J. (1976). *Legitimation crisis*. Heinemann

HACKER, A. (1965). 'Power to do what?' In I. Horwitz, *The new sociology*. Oxford University Press

HADDON, R. (1970). 'A minority in a welfare state society'. *New Atlantis*, vol. 2, pp. 80–133

HAIN, P. (1976). 'The future of community politics'. In P. Hain, *Community politics*. John Calder

HALL, P. (1972). 'A symbolic-interactionist analysis of politics'. *Sociological Inquiry*, vol. 42, pp. 35–75

HAMBLETON, R. (1978). *Policy planning and local government.* Hutchinson

HAMPTON, W. (1970). *Democracy and community: a study of politics in Sheffield.* Oxford University Press

HARLOE, M. (1977). Introduction to M. Harloe. *Captive cities.* Wiley

HARRIS, N. (1971). *Beliefs in society.* Penguin

HARSANYI, J. (1962). 'Measurement of social power, opportunity costs and the theory of two-person bargaining games'. *Behavioural Science*, vol. 7, pp. 67–80

HARVEY, D. (1973). *Social justice and the city*. Edward Arnold

HARVEY, D. (1977). 'Government policies, financial institutions and neighbourhood change in United States cities'. In M. Harloe, *Captive cities*. Wiley

HECLO, H. (1969). 'The councillor's job'. *Public Administration*, vol. 47, pp. 185–202

HEYBEBRAND, W. (1972). Review of T. Parsons, 'The system of modern society'. *Contemporary Sociology*, vol. 1, pp. 387–95

HILL, R. (1977). 'Two divergent theories of the state'. *International Journal of Urban and Regional Research*, vol. 1, pp. 37–44

HINDESS, B. (1971). *The decline of working class politics*. Paladin

HINDESS, B. (1973). *The use of official statistics in sociology*, Macmillan

HINDESS, B. (1978). 'Class and politics in Marxist theory'. In G. Littlejohn, B. Smart, J. Wakeford and N. Yuval-Davis, *Power and the state*. Croom Helm

HIRSCH, J. (1978). 'The state apparatus and social reproduction: elements of a theory of the bourgeois state'. In J. Holloway and S. Picciotto, *State and capital*. Edward Arnold

HIRST, P. (1977). 'Economic classes and politics'. In A. Hunt, *Class and class structure*. Lawrence & Wishart

HOLLAND, S. (1975). *The socialist challenge*. Quartet Books

HOLLOWAY, J. and PICCIOTTO, S. (1978). 'Introduction: towards a materialist theory of the state'. In J. Holloway and S. Picciotto, *State and capital*. Edward Arnold

HORKHEIMER, M. and ADORNO, T. (1973). *Aspects of sociology*. Heinemann

HUNT, A. (1977). 'Theory and politics in the identification of the working class'. In A. Hunt, *Class and class structure*. Lawrence & Wishart

HUNTER, F. (1953). *Community power structure*. University of North Carolina Press

JENKINS, R. (1971). *The production of knowledge at the Institute of Race Relations*. Independent Labour Party

JESSOP, B. (1978). 'Capitalism and democracy: the best possible political shell?' In G. Littlejohn, B. Smart, J. Wakeford, and N. Yuval-Davis, *Power and the state*. Croom Helm

JONES, G. (1969). *Borough politics*. Macmillan

KADUSHIN, C. (1968). 'Power, influence and social circles'. *American Sociological Review*, vol. 33, pp. 685–99

KAYE, A., MAYO, M. and THOMPSON, M. (1977). 'Inner London's housing crisis'. In J. Cowley, A. Kaye, M. Mayo, and M. Thompson, *Community or class struggle?* Stage 1, London

KEAT, R. and URRY, J. (1975). *Social theory as science*. Routledge & Kegan Paul

KUHN, T. (1970a). *The structure of scientific revolutions*, 2nd ed., University of Chicago Press

KUHN, T. (1970b). 'Reflections on my critics'. In I. Lakatos and A. Musgrave, *Criticism and the growth of knowledge*. Cambridge University Press

LACLAU, E. (1975). 'The specificity of the political'. *Economy and Society*, vol. 5, pp. 87–111

LAKATOS, I. (1970). 'Falsification and the methodology of scientific research programmes'. In I. Lakatos and A. Musgrave, *Criticism and the growth of knowledge*. Cambridge University Press

LAMARCHE, F. (1976). 'Property development and the economic foundations of the urban question'. In C. Pickvance, *Urban sociology: critical essays*. Tavistock

LAMBERT, J. and FILKIN, C. (1971). 'Race relations research'. *Race*, vol. 12, pp. 329–35

LASKI, H. (1935). *The state in theory and practice*. Allen & Unwin

LAUMANN, E. and PAPPI, F. (1969). 'New directions in the study of community elites'. *American Sociological Review*, vol. 38, pp. 212–30

LEHMAN, E. (1969). 'Toward a macro-sociology of power'. *American Sociological Review*, vol. 34, pp. 453–65

LENIN, V. I. (1960). 'The state and revolution'. In K. Marx, F. Engels and V. I. Lenin, *The essential left*. Unwin

LEWIS, J. (1977). 'British capitalism, the welfare state and the first radicalization of state employees'. In J. Cowley, A. Kaye, M. Mayo, and M. Thompson, *Community or class struggle?* Stage 1, London

LICHFIELD, N. and CHAPMAN, H. (1968). 'Cost-benefit analysis and road proposals for a shopping centre'. *Journal of Transport Economics and Policy*, vol. 2, pp. 280–320

LOJKINE, J. (1976). 'Contribution to a Marxist theory of capitalist urbanization'. In C. Pickvance, *Urban sociology: critical essays*. Tavistock

LOJKINE, J. (1977). 'Big firm's strategies, urban policy and urban social movements'. In M. Harloe, *Captive cities*. Wiley

LONG, N. (1958). 'The local community as an ecology of games'. *American Journal of Sociology*, vol. 64, pp. 251–61

LOVEJOY, D. (1971). 'Croydon's road to chaos'. *Architect*, December

LUKES, S. (1974). *Power: a radical view*. Macmillan

LUKES, S. (1976). 'Reply to Bradshaw'. *Sociology*, vol. 10, pp. 129–32

LUKES, S. (1977a). 'Political ritual and social integration'. In S. Lukes, *Essays in social theory*. Macmillan

LUKES, S. (1977b). 'Relativism: cognitive and moral'. In *ibid.*

LUKES, S. (1977c). 'Power and structure'. In *ibid.*

LUKES, S. (1977d). 'The new democracy'. In *ibid.*

LYND, R. and LYND, H. (1937). *Middletown in transition*. Harcourt Brace, New York

MACPHERSON, C. (1973). *Democratic theory: essays in retrieval*. Clarendon Press

MACPHERSON, C. (1977). *The life and times of liberal democracy*. Oxford University Press

MANN, M. (1973). *Consciousness and action in the western working class*. Macmillan

MARCH, J. (1966). 'The power of power'. In D. Easton, *Varieties of political theory*. Prentice-Hall, Englewood Cliffs, N.J.

MARCUSE, H. (1964). *One-dimensional man*. Routledge & Kegan Paul

MARRIOTT, O. (1967). *The property boom*. Hamish Hamilton

MARTIN, R. (1971). 'The concept of power: a critical defence'. *British Journal of Sociology*, vol. 22, pp. 240–56

MARX, K. (1964). *The economic and philosophic manuscripts of 1844*. International Publishers, New York

MARX, K. (1969a). 'Wages, prices and profit'. In K. Marx and F. Engels, *Selected works*, vol. 2. Progress Publishers, Moscow

MARX, K. (1969b). 'The civil war in France'. In K. Marx and F. Engels, *Selected works*, vol. 2. Progress Publishers, Moscow

MARX, K. (1973). *Grundrisse: foundations of the critique of political economy*. Penguin

MARX, K. (1976). *Capital*. vol. 1. Penguin

MARX, K. and ENGELS, F. (1969). 'Manifesto of the Communist Party'. In K. Marx and F. Engels, *Selected works*, vol. 1. Progress Publishers, Moscow

MARX, K. and ENGELS, F. (1974). *The German ideology*. Lawrence & Wishart

MATHIESEN, T. (1974). *The politics of abolition*. Martin Robertson

MAUD, J. (1967). *The management of local government*, vol. 2. HMSO

MENNELL, S. (1974). *Sociological theory: uses and utilities*. Nelson, Sunbury

MERELMAN, R. (1968). 'On the neo-elitist critique of community power'. *American Political Science Review*, vol. 62, pp. 451–60

MERRETT, S. (1976). 'Gentrification'. In Political Economy of Housing Workshop, *Housing and class in Britain*. Conference of Socialist Economists, London

MERTON, R. (1957a). 'Social structure and anomie'. In R. Merton, *Social theory and social structure*. Free Press, Glencoe

MERTON, R. (1957b). 'Patterns of influence: local and cosmopolitan influentials'. In *ibid.*

MILIBAND, R. (1965). 'Marx and the state'. In R. Miliband and J. Saville, *Socialist Register*. Merlin Press

MILIBAND, R. (1969). *The state in capitalist society*. Weidenfeld & Nicolson

MILIBAND, R. (1972). *Parliamentary socialism*, 2nd ed. Merlin Press

MILIBAND, R. (1977). *Marxism and politics*. Oxford University Press

MILLER, D. (1970). *International community power structures*. Indiana University Press

MILLS, C. W. (1956). *The power elite*. Oxford University Press

MILLS, C. W. (1959). *The sociological imagination*. Oxford University Press

MINGIONE, E. (1977). 'Sociological approach to regional and urban development'. *Comparative Urban Research*, vol. 4, pp. 21–38

MINNIS, J. (1967). *The care and feeding of power structures revisited*. Southern Conference Educational Fund Organizers' Library, Kentucky

MOORE, R. (1977). 'Becoming a sociologist in Sparkbrook'. In C. Bell and H. Newby, *Doing sociological research*. Allen & Unwin

MOORHOUSE, B., WILSON, M. and CHAMBERLAIN, C. (1972). 'Rent strikes: direct action and the working class'. In R. Miliband and J. Saville, *The Socialist register*. Merlin Press

MORRIS, D. and NEWTON, K. (1970). 'Profile of a local political elite: businessmen as community decision-makers in Birmingham, 1838–1966'. *New Atlantis*, vol. 1, pp. 111–23

MORRIS, T. (1957). *The criminal area: a study in social ecology*. Routledge & Kegan Paul

MURPHY, D. (1976). *The silent watchdog*. Constable

MUSIL, J. (1968). 'The development of Prague's ecological structure'. In R. Pahl, *Readings in urban sociology*. Pergamon

MUTCH, W. (1977). 'The expansion of Turnhouse, Edinburgh airport'. In W. Sewell and J. Coppock, *Public participation in planning*. Wiley

NEWBY, H., BELL, C., ROSE, D. and SAUNDERS, P. (1978). *Property, Paternalism and Power*. Hutchinson

NEWTON, K. (1969). 'A critique of the pluralist model'. *Acta Sociologica*, vol. 12, pp. 208–18

NEWTON, K. (1970). *Community decision-makers and community decision-making in England and the United States*. Paper given at World Congress of Sociology, Bulgaria

NEWTON, K. (1975). 'Community politics and decision-making: the American experience and its lessons'. In K. Young, *Essays on the study of urban politics*. Macmillan

NEWTON, K. (1976). *Second city politics*. Oxford University Press

NICOLAUS, M. (1972). 'The professional organization of sociology: a view from below'. In R. Blackburn, *Ideology in social science*. Fontana

NORMAN, P. (1975). 'Managerialism: a review of recent work'. In *Proceedings of the conference on urban change and conflict*, Centre for Environmental Studies, London

O'CONNOR, J. (1973). *The fiscal crisis of the state*. St Martin's Press, New York

OFFE, C. (1972). 'Advanced capitalism and the welfare state'. *Politics and society*, vol. 2, pp. 479–88

OFFE, C. (1974). 'Structural problems of the capitalist state'. In K. Beyme, *German political studies*, vol. 1, Sage

OFFE, C. (1975). 'The theory of the capitalist state and the problem of policy-formation'. In L. Lindberg, R. Alford, C. Crouch and C. Offe, *Stress and contradiction in modern capitalism*. Lexington Books

OFFE, C. (1976). 'Political authority and class structures'. In P. Connerton, *Critical sociology*. Penguin

OLIVES, J. (1976). 'The struggle against urban renewal in the "Cité d'Aliarte" (Paris)'. In C. Pickvance, *Urban sociology: critical essays*. Tavistock

PAHL, R. (1968). 'The rural-urban continuum'. In R. Pahl, *Readings in urban sociology*. Pergamon

PAHL, R. (1970). *Patterns of urban life*. Longman

PAHL, R. (1975). *Whose city?* 2nd ed. Penguin

PAHL, R. (1977a). 'Collective consumption and the state in capitalist and state socialist societies'. In R. Scase, *Industrial society: class, cleavage and control*. Tavistock

PAHL, R. (1977b). 'Stratification, the relation between states and urban and regional development.' *International Journal of Urban and Regional Research*, vol. 1, pp. 6–17

PAHL, R. (1977c). 'Managers, technical experts and the state'. In M. Harloe, *Captive cities*. Wiley

PARKIN, F. (1968). *Middle class radicals*. Manchester University Press

PARKIN, F. (1971). *Class, inequality and political order*. MacGibbon & Kee

PARKIN, F. (1974). 'Strategies of social closure in class formation'. In F. Parkin, *The social analysis of class structure*. Tavistock

PARRY, G. (1969). *Political elites*, Allen & Unwin

PARRY, G., and MORRISS, P. (1974). 'When is a decision not a decision?' In I. Crewe, *British political sociology year book*, vol. 1: *Elites in western democracy*. Croom Helm

PARSONS, T. (1966). 'The political aspect of social structure and process'. In D. Easton, *Varieties of political theory*. Prentice-Hall, Englewood Cliffs, N.J.

PARSONS, T. (1967a). 'On the concept of political power'. In T. Parsons, *Sociological theory and modern society*, Free Press, Glencoe

PARSONS, T. (1967b). 'On the concept of influence'. In ibid.

PHILLIPS, D. (1973). *Abandoning method*. Jossey-Bass

PHILLIPSON, M. (1972). 'Theory, method and conceptualization'. In P. Filmer, M. Phillipson, D. Silverman and D. Walsh, *New directions in sociological theory*. Macmillan

PICKVANCE, C. (1976). 'On the study of urban social movements'. In C. Pickvance, *Urban sociology: critical essays*. Tavistock

PICKVANCE, C. (1977a). 'Marxist approaches to the study of urban politics.' *International Journal of Urban and Regional Research*, vol. 1, pp. 218–55

PICKVANCE, C. (1977b). 'From social base to social force: some analytical issues in the study of urban protest'. In M. Harloe, *Captive cities*. Wiley

PICKVANCE, C. (1978). Review of M. Castells, 'The urban question'. *Sociological Review*, vol. 26, pp. 173–6

PLAMENATZ, J. (1958). *The English utilitarians*, 2nd ed. Blackwell

POLSBY, N. (1959). 'Three problems in the analysis of community power'. *American Sociological Review*, vol. 24, pp. 796–803

POPPER, K. (1976). 'The logic of the social sciences'. In T. Adorno, *The positivist dispute in German sociology*. Heinemann

POSNER, C. (1970). *Reflections on the revolution in France, 1968*. Penguin

POULANTZAS, N. (1969). 'The problem of the capitalist state'. *New Left Review*, no. 58, pp. 67–78

POULANTZAS, N. (1973). *Political power and social classes*. New Left Books

POULANTZAS, N. (1975). *Classes in contemporary capitalism*. New Left Books

POULANTZAS, N. (1976). 'The capitalist state: a reply to Miliband and Laclau'. *New Left Review*, no. 95, pp. 63–83

PRESTHUS, R. (1964). *Men at the top*. Oxford University Press

PREWITT, K., and EULAU, H. (1971). 'Social bias in leadership selection, political recruitment and electoral context'. *Journal of Politics*, vol. 33, pp. 293–315

REGAN, D. and MORRIS, A. (1969). 'Local government corruption and public confidence'. *Public Law* (no vol. no.), pp. 132–52

RENNER, K. (1949). *The institutions of private law and their social functions*. Routledge & Kegan Paul

REPO, M. (1977). 'Organizing the poor – against the working class'. In J. Cowley, A. Kaye, M. Mayo, and M. Thompson, *Community or class struggle?* Stage 1, London

REX, J. (1968). 'The sociology of a zone of transition'. In R. Pahl, *Readings in urban sociology.* Pergamon

REX, J. (1971). 'The concept of housing class and the sociology of race relations'. *Race*, vol. 12, pp. 293–301

REX, J. (1977). 'Sociological theory and the city'. *Australian and New Zealand Journal of Sociology*, vol. 13, pp. 218–23

REX, J. and MOORE, R. (1967). *Race, community and conflict.* Oxford University Press

RICCI, D. (1971). *Community power and democratic theory.* Random House, New York

RICHARDSON, A. (1977). 'Tenant participation in council house management'. In R. Darke and R. Walker, *Local government and the public.* Leonard Hill

RISING FREE (n.d.). *Take over the city.* Rising Free, London

ROBSON, B. (1975). *Urban social areas.* Oxford University Press

ROSE, A. (1967). *The power structure.* Oxford University Press

ROSE, DAMARIS (1978). *Social reproduction and the growth of working class home-ownership, 1850–1930.* Unpublished paper, University of Sussex

ROSE, DAVID, SAUNDERS, P., NEWBY, H. and BELL, C. (1976). 'Ideologies of property: a case study'. *Sociological Review*, vol. 24, pp. 699–730

ROWEIS, S. (1975). 'Urban planning in early and late capitalist societies'. *Papers on Planning and Design*, no. 7. University of Toronto, Department of Urban and Regional Planning

RUNCIMAN, W. (1966). *Relative deprivation and social justice.* Routledge & Kegan Paul

RUNCIMAN, W. (1970). 'False consciousness'. In W. Runciman, *Sociology in its place and other essays.* Cambridge University Press

RUSSELL, B. (1940). *Power: a new social analysis.* Basic Books

RYAN, A. (1970). *The philosophy of the social sciences.* Macmillan

SAUNDERS, P., NEWBY, H., BELL, C. and ROSE, D. (1970). 'Rural community and rural community power'. In H. Newby, *International perspectives in rural sociology.* Wiley

SAVILLE, J. (1973). 'The ideology of Labourism'. In R. Benewick, *Knowledge and beliefs in politics*. Allen & Unwin

SCHAAR, H. (1970). 'Legitimacy in the modern state'. In P. Green and S. Levinson, *Power and community: dissenting essays in political science*. Random House, New York

SCHIFFERES, S. (1976). 'Council tenants and housing policy in the 1930s'. In Political Economy of Housing Workshop, *Housing and class in Britain*. Conference of Socialist Economists, London

SCHMID, H. (1969). 'Science and the control of social systems'. In L. Dencik, *Scientific research and politics*. Studentletteratur, Lund

SCHUMPETER, J. (1954). *Capitalism, socialism and democracy*. Allen & Unwin

SHARPE, L. (1962). 'Elected representatives in local government'. *British Journal of Sociology*, vol. 13, pp. 189–209

SHAW, M. (1974). 'The theory of the state and politics: a central paradox of Marxism'. *Economy and Society*, vol. 3, pp. 429–50

SHERMAN, A. (1975). 'Fabian re-think local government – forward from elitism'. *Local Government Review*, vol. 137

SILBURN, R. (1975). 'The potential and limitations of community action'. In C. Lambert and D. Weir, *Cities in modern Britain*. Fontana

SILVERMAN, D. (1970). *The theory of organizations*. Heinemann

SIMMIE, J. (1974). *Citizens in conflict*. Hutchinson

STACEY, M., BATSTONE, E., BELL, C. and MURCOTT, A. (1975). *Power, persistence and change*. Routledge & Kegan Paul

SUTTLES, G. (1972). *The social construction of communities*. University of Chicago Press

SZELENYI, I. (1977). *Class analysis and beyond: further dilemmas for the new urban sociology*. Unpublished paper. School of Social Sciences, University of South Australia, Flinders

TABB, W. (1972). 'Alternative futures and distributional planning'. *Journal of the American Institute of Planners*, vol. 38, pp. 25–32

TATE, B. (1976). 'Personal health and welfare services', in G. Rhodes, *The new government of London: the first five years*. Weidenfeld & Nicolson

TOWNSEND, P. (1976). 'How the rich stay rich'. *New Statesman*, vol. 92, pp. 441–2

VAN DOORN, J. (1962). 'Sociology and the problem of power'. *Sociologica Neerlandica*, vol. 1, pp. 2–51

VEBLEN, T. (1964). *Absentee ownership and business enterprise in recent times*. Sentry Press, New York

VIDICH, A. and BENSMAN, J. (1958). *Small town in mass society*. Princeton University Press

WALKER, P. (1973). 'Croydon: boom town of the sixties'. In J. Gent, *Croydon: the story of a hundred years*. Croydon Natural History and Scientific Society

WALL, G. (1966). 'The concept of interest in politics'. *Politics and Society*, vol. 5, pp. 487–510

WALTON, J. (1966). 'Discipline, method and community power: a note on the sociology of knowledge'. *American Sociological Review*, vol. 31, pp. 684–9

WALTON, P. and GAMBLE, A. (1972). *From alienation to surplus value.* Sheed & Ward

WEBB, E., CAMPBELL, D., SCHWARTZ, R. and SECHREST, L. (1966). *Unobtrusive measures*. Rand McNally, Chicago

WEBER, M. (1947). *The theory of social and economic organization.* Macmillan, New York

WEBER, M. (1949). *The methodology of the social sciences.* Free Press, New York

WESTERGAARD, J. (1977). 'Class inequality and corporatism'. In A. Hunt, *Class and class structure*. Lawrence & Wishart

WESTERGAARD, J. and RESLER, H. (1975). *Class in a capitalist society.* Heinemann

WILLIAMS, O. (1975). 'Urban politics as political ecology'. In K. Young, *Essays on the study of urban politics*. Macmillan

WILLIAMS, R. (1977). *Marxism and literature.* Oxford University Press

WINCH, P. (1958). *The idea of a social science.* Routledge & Kegan Paul

WINKLER, J. (1976). 'Corporatism'. *European Journal of Sociology*, vol. 17, pp. 100–36

WINKLER, J. (1977). 'The corporate economy: theory and administration'. In R. Scase, *Industrial society: class, cleavage and control,* Allen & Unwin

WOLFF, K. (1964). *The sociology of Georg Simmel*. Free Press, Glencoe

WOLFINGER, R. (1960). 'Reputation and reality in the study of community power'. *American Sociological Review*, vol. 25, pp. 636–44

WOLFINGER, R. (1962). 'Plea for a decent burial'. *American Sociological Review*, vol. 27, pp. 841–7

WOLFINGER, R. (1971). 'Non-decisions and the study of local politics'. *American Political Science Review*, vol. 65, pp. 1063–80

WORSLEY, P. (1964). 'The distribution of power in industrial society'. In P. Halmos, *Sociological Review*, monograph no. 8: *The development of industrial societies*

WRONG, D. (1968). 'Some problems in defining social power'. *American Journal of Sociology*, vol. 73, pp. 673–81

YAFFE, D. (1973). 'The crisis of profitability'. *New Left Review*, no. 80, pp. 45–62

YOUNG, T. (1976). 'The industrial connection'. In P. Hain, *Community politics*. John Calder

ZIMMERMAN, D. (1973). 'The practicalities of rule use'. In G. Salaman and K. Thompson, *People in organizations*. Longman

Index of subjects

action approach, 58, 138–9, 162–3, 167, 186–7
authority, 27, 28, 34, 235

Banbury, 282, 349
Barking, 295
Bath, 72, 328, 331–3, 347
Birmingham, 68, 74, 139, 202, 210–11, 223, 265, 297
Brighton, 213, 280, 349
Bristol, 63, 202, 328–9
Bromley, 305
bureaucracy, 166, 169, 172, 176, 316; and local government decision-making, 171, 192, 201, 216, 219, 222–6, 230, 332
business interests: in local government, 211–16, 298, 306; relationship with local government, 234, 309–24, 328–9

Camden, 191, 196
Chamber of Commerce, 243, 260, 304–5, 310–11, 314, 320–4, 331, 334
Chicago school of human ecology, 13, 137, 139, 191
Church Commissioners, 301

citizenship, 142
class: acquisition classes, 67–8; alliances, 112–13, 118, 126, 164, 178–9; consciousness, 118–19, 133, 271, 289, 294–6; housing classes, 18, 67–76, 93–8; Marxist conceptions, 66, 73, 76–7, 79, 98–9; political leadership and class background, 210–16; and politics, 151–2, 154, 161–2, 166, 175, 180–8, 279–80; property classes, 67–8, 90; Weberian conceptions, 66–8, 73–4, 75; working class incorporation, 283–4, 290, 296; *see also* ideology; necessary non-correspondence; state
Clay Cross, 193
coercion, 26, 145, 148, 151, 153
coercive political strategy, 63, 233–5, 278, 292–3
collective consumption, 17, 106–9, 112–14, 116–17, 121–6, 142, 143, 144–5, 147, 171, 178–9, 277
communications, in local government, 62

Index of names